TRUE BLUE

FOCUS PUBLISHING
PTY LTD

A Focus Publishing Book Project

Focus Publishing Pty Ltd
ABN 55 003 600 360
PO Box 518 Edgecliff NSW 2027
Australia
Telephone 61 2 9327 4777
Fax 61 2 9362 3753
Email focus@focus.com.au
Website www.focus.com.au

Chairman: Steven Rich
Publisher: Jaqui Lane
Associate Publisher: Jenny Walkden
Associate Publisher: Gillian Fitzgerald
Project Director: William E Munt
Production Manager: Timothy Ho
Client Services: Sophie Beaumont

Managing Editor for Ford Australia: John M. Wright
Editor: Rosalind Wright
Art Director: Neville Wilkinson
Design Concept: Andrew McLagan
Cover Concept: Deidre Stein
Finished Artist: Sarah Cory

Tuckey, William P. [1936 –]
True Blue: 75 Years of Ford in Australia

Bibliography
Includes index
ISBN 1 875359 72 9

1. Ford Motor Company of Australia – History.
2. Ford automobile – History. I. Title.

TRUE
BLUE

75 Years of Ford
in Australia

Bill Tuckey

Contents

ROLL OF **HONOUR**

The Ford Company of Australia gives special thanks to the following companies and organisations, without whom *True Blue: 75 Years of Ford in Australia* would be a lesser publication. As Ford Australia's preferred suppliers, each of these organisations has played a unique role in helping Ford Australia achieve its 75th anniversary.

Gold Participants

Automotive Division – Toll Logistics

Denso International Australia Pty Ltd

Finemores Pty Ltd

Flexiglass Challenge Industries

J Walter Thompson Australia Pty Ltd

"K" Line (Australia) Pty Limited

Pacific Dunlop Limited

Plexicor Australia

Tenneco Automotive

Wallenius Wilhelmsen

Silver Participants

Air International Group

Arrowcrest Group Pty Ltd

Astor Base Metals Pty Ltd

Autoliv Australia Pty Ltd

BHP Coated Steel – Australia

Bridgestone TG Australia Pty Ltd

Britax Rainsfords Pty Ltd

BTR Automotive Drivetrain Systems

Hook Plastics

Mobil Oil Australia Pty Ltd

Orbseal Australia

Qantas Airways Limited

RJ Pound Services Pty Ltd

Robert Bosch (Australia) Pty Ltd

Silcraft Pty Ltd

Sumitomo Australia Ltd/Sumitomo Wiring Systems Ltd

Tokyo Boeki (Australia) Pty Ltd

Venture Industries Pty Ltd

Bronze Participants

Australian Arrow Pty Ltd

Automotive Components Limited

Bostik (Australia) Pty Ltd

Castrol Australia Pty Limited

CHEP Australia/Cleanaway

CMI Limited

Coughlin Logistics

Delphi Automotive Systems Australia Ltd

Dowsett Engineering & Materials Handling Pty Ltd

EGR

FMS Audio Sdn Bhd

Hella Australia Pty Ltd

Johnson Controls Australia Pty Ltd

Kirwan Group Services

Mark IV Automotive Pty Limited

Menzies Group of Companies

Meritor LVS Australia Pty Ltd

Mett Diecasting Pty Ltd

Milne Dunkley Customs & Forwarding

NYK Line (Australia) Pty Ltd

Parker Hannifin (Australia) Pty Limited

PBR International Ltd

PricewaterhouseCoopers

Sodexho

Textron Fastening Systems Pty Ltd

TI Group Automotive Systems

Tripac International Pty Ltd

Wayne Richardson Sales/Gaska Tape Australia

Foreword

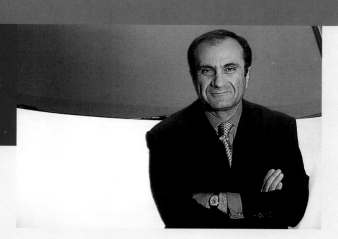

I am very proud to write the foreword to *True Blue: 75 Years of Ford in Australia*. Although I cannot claim to have been around for all those years, I have certainly spent many of them with Ford Australia plugged in close to my heart.

I can also say that I am a real old-fashioned petrolhead and there are few cars which bring on the passion as intensely as the classic Australian Fords. The Phase III GTHO is surely the greatest Aussie automotive icon ever. Can you imagine what a thrill it was for me to come to work for Ford during that period of history, as a young Lebanese Australian with high octane fuel running through his veins?

Ford has been a major participant in Australia's industrial revolution. The Model T put us on wheels. The V8 broke the back of our great rural distances. And Falcon is the second longest continuously running model name in the automotive world (behind Fairlane).

In 75 years there have been dramatic changes in our entire culture, most of them for the better. When I was a schoolkid in the Melbourne suburb of Northcote in the 1950s, I quickly became accustomed to eating my pide bread sandwiches and taboulleh away from the gaze of my peers, most of whom were of Anglo–Celtic stock. Although the first great wave of postwar immigration had occurred in the late 1940s (the Nasser family being part of it), we were a huge distance away from becoming the mature multicultural society we are today.

Being Australian in the 21st century does not mean being isolated and insular but, rather, part of an increasingly interconnected world. But this globalisation does not entail any loss of national identity. Take the Falcon, for example: it combines the best of Ford's international technology. I'm proud of my involvement with Ford Australia and I am a firm believer that the Ford Falcon must continue to be immediately recognisable as (a) a Ford and (b) a Falcon.

There is no more Australian car than the Falcon, no other car which is designed from the ground up in this country. And so it is that Ford Australia is able to respond directly to the needs of our customers with vehicles that satisfy their demands, cars that call Australia home. Every Falcon carries in its DNA the glory days of the GTHOs racing at Mount Panorama. Every Falcon draws on 40 years of history.

And with 75 years of history in this country the Ford Motor Company's roots are deeper into the Aussie soil than any other carmaker's.

But of course the greatest asset of Ford Australia is not its fine product range, but the people whose dedication and sheer hard work inform every element of our business. My congratulations to every one of them on this impressive milestone – 75 years!

Jacques Nasser

Jacques Nasser
CEO and President, Ford Motor Company

Prologue

One far-sighted business decision taken in 1924 by the Ford Motor Company sealed the Industrial Revolution for Australia on July 1, 1925. In 1914 Ford's Model T had been the top selling car in this market but the company's share had begun to slip and so came about the big business decision for the Ford Motor Company, the father of mass production, to set up shop in Australia. On that opening day of the 1925–26 business year, poised to drive into a new industrial future, the first locally produced Model T emerged on its spindly wheels from the Ford factory in Gheringhap Street, Geelong, Victoria.

This factory was rather a makeshift affair but the converted Dalgety's woolshed was itself an appropriate metaphor for immense change: not only would the local production of motor cars speed Australia's industrial development, it would also bring new efficiency to primary industry. Since the very early years of the 20th century, the Model T had been bringing newfound mobility both in the cities and the bush. This process would gather new momentum as we began to build our own cars.

In Australia as it already had in the United States, the Model T was changing the possibilities of life. Before the advent of 'Tin Lizzie' very few people ever travelled further than about 20 miles from their birthplace.

It was Hubert C. French, an executive of the Ford Motor Company of Canada, whose vision underwrote Ford's future in Australia. In April 1924, as French compiled a long report to his boss, Wallace R. Campbell, recommending that the company open a factory in Australia, it is most improbable that thoughts of July 2000 (and Ford's 75th anniversary of marriage to Australia) entered his mind. Few of us think about the symmetry of long distance anniversaries at the start of an adventure and this big-framed, diligent Canadian was focused on a more immediate future.

French believed the remedy for sagging sales was local assembly. He realised, too, that the establishment of such

Below: the founding father, Henry Ford I, about 1920, at the peak of his fame and power and the biggest auto maker in the world. Right: the grille on the 1933 model of the third of the three cars that made him famous, the V8; the first two were the Model T and Model A.

an operation would enable the company to take better advantage of government legislation, which already imposed huge tariff penalties on fully imported cars.

Hubert French's meticulously elaborated advice was duly accepted and it has become a happy coincidence that the Ford Motor Company of Australia produced its first Model T on July 1, 1925.

Others joined it in the wintry sunlight and soon a line of

FORD'S HISTORY IS EMBEDDED IN OUR WAY

cars was parked down Gheringhap Street within 100 metres of Corio Bay with its deep water harbour (a key criterion favouring Geelong over other venues in the selection process). Geelong was already Australia's fourth largest city in 1925 but its future prosperity would become entwined with Ford's; today Geelong and Ford go together like the horse and carriage which the immortal Model T superseded. One recalls a line of the great American poet Robert Lowell:

the Pierce Arrow clears its throat in a horse stall.

('Grandparents')

The horse had bolted, banished by the motor car with a life of its own and a mechanical throat to clear ...

By 1925 the horse stalls of Australia were home to a rapidly increasing number of motor cars, a high percentage of them Model T Fords. It came as no surprise when an international panel of judges chose the vehicle which put our world on wheels to be the Car of the 20th Century: how could the T not have won?

In the 75 years of history which have accrued since that first Geelong-built Ford idled out of the Gheringhap Street factory, the Ford Motor Company of Australia has played a major role in our industrial, social, and cultural history; the Ford blue oval is patterned into our national patina.

The next defining point in this process occurred in June 1960, when the first locally manufactured Ford Falcon was driven off the assembly line at Broadmeadows. The even number of that year (40 before 2000) was another fortuitous quirk.

It's a new century, the new millennium. To adapt the words of William Clay (Bill) Ford Jnr, if the 20th century automotive industrial revolution belongs to Ford for giving the world personal mobility (and its major secondary industry), then so will the 21st. Ford plans to become the automotive manufacturer which – shall we say 'who', because this is a most people-driven organisation? – will deliver that mobility with no social/environmental trade-offs: a kind industrialism, a force towards a better world.

Ford, driven by Bill Ford and president Jac Nasser (the former president of Ford Australia, now managing the Ford world) is already becoming a leading player in 21st century communications technology, what we may call tertiary industry. Ford's Internet sites set the standard for the automotive industry. And which other automotive company will provide every single employee with a personal computer?

Glenn Seton's V8Supercar showcases the AU Falcon's purposeful line and the Ford brand in a most powerful way.

LIFE: THINK V8, THINK FORD; THINK UTE, THINK FORD

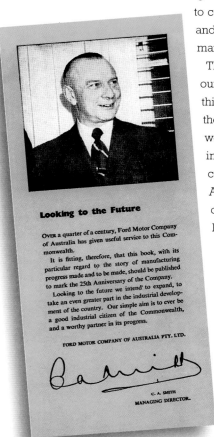

Looking to the Future

OVER a quarter of a century, Ford Motor Company of Australia has given useful service to this Commonwealth.

It is fitting, therefore, that this book, with its particular regard to the story of manufacturing progress made and to be made, should be published to mark the 25th Anniversary of the Company.

Looking to the future we intend' to expand, to take an even greater part in the industrial development of the country. Our simple aim is to ever be a good industrial citizen of the Commonwealth, and a worthy partner in its progress.

FORD MOTOR COMPANY OF AUSTRALIA PTY. LTD.

C. A. SMITH
MANAGING DIRECTOR.

But the future of the planet itself is an even higher priority, which is where 'no social trade-offs' applies.

Early last century Henry Ford is reported to have said buyers could choose any colour provided it was black. But the metaphorical colour for Fords of the 21st century will be green, whatever the hue of their paintwork.

The purpose of this book is to celebrate 75 years of the Ford Motor Company of Australia. Serendipity smiles brightly because there could be no better year in which to celebrate two birthdays: 75 years of Ford in Australia and 40 years of the Ford Falcon as a locally, proudly manufactured Australian car.

This history is not only long, but deeply embedded in our way of life. Just a couple of examples: think 'V8', think Ford; think 'ute', think Ford and the creation of the coupe utility by one Lewis Bandt in 1933–34 – a world first. The single word 'Customline' conjures images of the big, fast Fords of the 1950s, V8s of course, and offering trademark Ford value for money. After Customline came Fairlane and after Fairlane came LTD, all of these key words in the liturgy of the Ford Motor Company in Australia.

Long before the creation of the local operation in 1925, Fords had brought improved mobility to Australians. The V8-powered Fords seemed further to shrink the distances between farflung Australian centres in the 1930s. (It's important to remember in this country of V8SuperCar racing, where the love affair with the V8 engine – its thundering heartbeat, its ineluctable rhythm – has been and remains passionate, that it was Ford which introduced this concept to the mass market. A March 1934 Australian advertisement for the Ford V8, priced from £275, pointed out that 'no other car under £1000 offers this quality feature', namely a V8 engine.)

So from the unpretentious but remarkably effective and inexpensive Model T through much of the first quarter of the century to the 'thrill and luxury of V8 performance' from 1932, it was the Ford Motor Company which raised Australians' standard of automobility. Ford invited this country into a love affair with the V8 engine, the dating of which goes back very much further than the first Falcon

GT and further even than those flashy Customlines. For many Australians the long drive out of the Depression took place behind the wheel of a Ford V8, some sweet '34 sedan or '36 Roadster, or that new tough kid on the block, the coupe utility, all of them capable of unravelling distance at a rate of 65 miles per hour: the reassuring and unmistakable exhaust note of the Ford V8 popular music sounded across the vastnesses of Australia.

Through three-quarters of a helter-skelter century (more change by most measures in 100 years than in the previous thousand), good fortune did not always irradiate Ford Australia (although in 1982 the company finally toppled GM-H from its long reign as market leader, the Falcon strongly backed by the new small car champion, Laser). Neither has the Falcon always soared successfully. A Pollyanna perspective has not been perennially present or, in the toughest times, possible – even through the proverbial rose-coloured lenses.

Ford has had to react not just to market forces, but to ever changing government legislation, the vagaries of the national economy and the complexity of international events. It has always been a matter not just of considering the present but the short and medium-term future as well, which requires great insight and sometimes a high degree of risk. Priorities inevitably compete but in the end it is the needs of the customer that must always come first.

Through good times and bad strong threads of continuity have been woven into the history of the Ford Motor Company in Australia. This is nowhere more clearly illustrated than in the case of the Ford Falcon, introduced here in September 1960. After a difficult beginning, the Falcon became Australia's best selling passenger car more often than not from 1975 until this time of writing, and has been consistent in providing Australian motorists with a special blend of ruggedness, spaciousness, value for money, style and excellent driving characteristics. The Falcon has long been the Great Australian Road Car, the Legend.

It is a matter of special pride to Ford that 'Falcon' is the second longest-running automotive model name in the world. Commodore dates back a mere 22 years, or three of what have now been six generations of Falcon. The Mitsubishi Magna was launched in 1985, the locally manufactured Toyota Camry two years later.

And what is the oldest extant model name in the automotive world? Fairlane. The first Fairlane, taking its name from Henry Ford's Dearborn mansion, Fair Lane, was introduced in 1955 and on August 20, 1959 a Fairlane had the honour of being the first car to emerge from Broadmeadows. In 1967 a uniquely Australian Fairlane, based on the Falcon, was introduced and this has been the best selling vehicle in the market sector it inaugurated for nearly 90 per cent of the years since that conspicuous debut.

'Branding' is a vogue term nowadays, but it has long been a Ford Motor Company speciality. Few symbols of any kind are as widely and fondly recognised as the Blue Oval.

Neither 'Falcon' nor 'Fairlane' still exists in the US but they have been bywords of the Australian automotive industry since 1960 and 1959 respectively.

It's a story too little told but, by 1972, the Falcon was every bit as Australian in its design as the Holden Kingswood and, from the 1978 launch of the Opel-derived Commodore, very much more so. Today, the Falcon and its siblings are the only cars designed and manufactured in Australia, starting literally from a clean sheet of paper. As a direct consequence the Falcon is unique to Australia and better suited to the harsh and varied demands of this continent than any other – truly the Great Australian Road Car.

Both Falcon and Fairlane have long called Australia home, the harsh lessons of this continent etched into their DNA. But, equally, the global research and development knowledge of Ford also informs every aspect of their design: the best of Australia, the best of the world.

There are only five places in the world which can design and build a car from the proverbial clean sheet

of paper – North America, Western Europe, Japan, Korea and Australia. Ford Australia stands monument to the determination that Australia will always be one of this elite.

And now, as the 75th anniversary of Ford's wedding to Australia arrives, it's time not only to celebrate but also, in the process, to put three-quarters of a century of automotive and social history into perspective.

Fifty years ago, then managing director Charles A. Smith wrote in celebration of 25 years of Ford Australia: 'Looking to the future we intend to expand, to take an even greater part in the industrial development of the country'.

Smith's 1950 hope has been surpassed. Ford is immensely proud of its contribution to this history, its participation in Australia's maturing into one of the world's great manufacturing nations.

John M. Wright

Charlie Sherson, in 1999 the oldest living original Ford Australia employee, with a Model T and the 1997 GT Falcon outside the Ford Discovery Centre, Geelong. Left: Ford Australia proudly sponsors the Geelong Cats. How many Fords have driven down the road to Kardinia Park?

CHAPTER 1

The **Maple Leaf** Connection

The first Ford car to land in Australia, a two-cylinder Model A in 1904, was shipped by a New York agent called Robert Lockwood, who also had the export business for Daisy air rifles. From then on Fords were imported – first privately and later directly from Ford Canada – by a motley crew of distributors, agents, dealers and privateers. The Canadian subsidiary was the source partly because it was building right-hand drive cars for the UK market, but also because as a member of the British Empire its products were blessed with 'most favoured nation' tariffs.

The first Australian car assembly plant was baptised on July 1, 1925. On that day a spidery Model T Ford inched its way off a primitive production line in an ex-Dalgety wool store in Geelong, the bustling port south west of Melbourne which was destined to become the Motown of Australia and was already our fourth largest city.

The history of Ford in Australia, and thus that of Geelong, is woven deeply into the tapestry of Australian lives. It begins at the turn of the century, covering the building of the first assembly plants in the 1920s, the invention of the world's first coupe utility in the 1930s, and the conversion of the Ford factories to war production. Then there was the little-known (and narrowly lost) battle with General Motors (GM) for the government contract to manufacture the first indigenous Aussie car, the lessons learned from having to sell badly made British vehicles and, from 1960, finding out the hard way how to design and build cars for this difficult country.

It was always Hard Yakka, to use those words that only an Australian can hope to understand. GM had bought its way into the local car industry in 1931 by taking over a near-bankrupt Holden's Motor Body Builders, of which it was then the major client. Six years earlier Ford had committed itself to the much more challenging route of investing in local employment in both assembly and component supply, an early indicator of the way Ford Australia thinks about its employees and an insight into

why the name Ford generates such loyalty.

However, let us begin at the beginning. Automotive historian Pedr Davis, in his book *Wheels Across Australia*, says the first imported car to reach Australia was probably an American Hertel in 1897, a marque which quickly vanished without making the slightest impact on the world. Davis also suggests that while there is still argument about who built Australia's first car, it was possibly one H. Knight-Eaton, who demonstrated a petrol-powered tricycle in Sydney's George Street in April 1896.

The oldest locally built vehicle still running is the gargantuan steam car built by John and David Shearer, agricultural implement makers of Mannum, in South Australia, which first ran in 1896 and now resides in the

IN 1914 A MODEL T W

Top: Model Ts lined up outside the old Dalgety's wool store in Gheringhap Street, Geelong. Right: Henry and son Edsel Ford in front of the Pressed Steel Building being built in the Rouge complex at Dearborn, Michigan, in October 1938. Opposite: a 1915 Model T touring car.

superb Birdwood Mill Museum in the Barossa Valley.

The Hertel did, however, open the floodgates to imported cars from all over the world: the famous 1901 curved-dash Oldsmobile, Benz, de Dion, Argyll, Panhard et Levassor, Darracq, Metallurgique, Bianchi, Crossley, Peugeot, Locomobile, Talbot, Beeston, Gladiator, Fiat, Renault and others.

At the start of World War I (WW1) in 1914 there were more than 100 different makes on the market – most of them imported, but some with local bodies tacked onto imported chassis – and a handful locally designed and built, such as the Tarrant and the Australis. There were about 38,000 vehicles on the roads. By 1920 this would explode to almost 76,000, about half of them Model T Fords.

Ford Australia really began in August 1909, when a Canadian named Robert C. Durance left the British-founded Australian Dunlop Rubber Company to become Ford Canada's sole local representative. Dunlop had sponsored the first-ever motorsport event in Australia, run at Melbourne's Aspendale horse racetrack on March 12, 1904, organised by Dunlop executive Harry James, a co-founder of what became the Royal Automobile Club of Victoria (RACV).

It was won by Colonel Harley Tarrant, born in the Victorian goldmining town of Clunes in 1860, a mining surveyor who laid out the rich silver district around Silverton outside Broken Hill, now a ghost town and the site of many feature film shoots, including *Mad Max II*.

THE FIRST CAR TO CIRCUMNAVIGATE AUSTRALIA

ask him to recommend the wealthiest businessman in the district, walk into the office of that hapless individual and tell him the bank manager personally wanted him to take on the Ford business. Durance later wrote: 'In every case the man would be greatly flattered, and in not a single case did I fail to sign these people up'.

Seldom did they ever make a better business decision. Between 1909 and the opening of the Geelong plant in 1925 Australians bought more than 140,000 Model T Fords (it was also a bonus for Dunlop, because tyre sales soared accordingly and the only other Australian tyre maker was

Tarrant started making 2-horsepower kerosene engines for the rural and mining industries and with two partners moved into importing Scottish Argylls and French de Dions. Tarrant began building his own cars and in 1905 in an Argyll he won the large car class of that first city-to-city race, the Sydney–Melbourne Dunlop Reliability Motor Contest, with prize money of 100 guineas (£105). In September that year, with his firm's latest twin-cylinder 8-hp Tarrant, the dashing driver (he of the flowing Colonel Custer moustache who would gain his colonelcy in WW1), won the second Dunlop interstate race.

It was run from Melbourne to Sydney over the appallingly rough bush tracks and river crossings of the day, but when there was no clear winner in Sydney the 19 left of the 28 starters were sent up to Medlow Bath in the Blue Mountains and back. With still no result, six survivors had to race back to Melbourne – a total distance of 1276 miles (2053 kilometres).

It was Durance's Dunlop association with Tarrant which led him to name Tarrant Motors – then importing de Dion, Benz, Fiat and Sunbeam cars and Commer and Thornycroft trucks – as Ford's first Victorian distributor. Tarrant Motors also owned the Melbourne Motor Body works, fabricating bodies to fit onto imported chassis, and was the first to put an Australian-bodied Ford into the market. Durance was one hell of a salesman, but he wasn't too picky about to whom he handed the franchise.

Setting out to create a national network, he would drive his Model T into town, go straight to a local bank manager,

Barnet Glass, which Dunlop had bought in 1905).

At first the spindly-looking car appeared too fragile for Australia's punishing conditions. About half the weight of imported American and European cars, it had only two forward gears instead of their three or four. But it cost about half as much, was phenomenally reliable and, when it did break, it could be fixed by a country blacksmith or farrier.

An eccentric adventurer called Francis Birtles – a sort of Hans Tholstrup of the 1900s – made 88 trips around and across Australia by horse, bicycle and car, covering an estimated 800,000 km. In 1914 a Model T became the first car to circumnavigate the continent, driven by Birtles; his passengers were Frank Hurley, a soon-to-be-

Opposite: a surviving example of Ford's Quadricycle, before a statue of the founder.
Above left: even today Model Ts can be seen meeting the challenges of Australian roads.
Above: Henry Ford driving an immense Ford Model K in New York City, in 1906. The six-cylinder car sold poorly and was soon dropped from Ford's US range.

Right: a beautifully restored Model A, the second car to bear the name. Below right: Model A convertible cabriolet from 1930. Opposite: Ford's early assembly lines in the US produced half the nation's cars with only one sixth of the automotive workforce.

Tarrant: Victoria's first dealer

While early Fords were privately imported, Tarrant's of Melbourne was the first official outlet to land a Ford here. It arrived in 1906, a four-cylinder, 15 horsepower Model N, bought by one William Moffatt for £191.

Tarrant's was the first firm in Australia to build an aircraft engine, a 90 horsepower air-cooled Renault design used during WW1.

Colonel Harley Tarrant was taxed by the Army with organising the first Australian Motor Transport Corps, which sailed overseas in 1915, and had three companies working in France by 1918.

Three who started work as garage mechanics with Tarrant's later became famous as 'The Three Harrys': Hawker, Busteed and Kauper. Harry Hawker became test pilot of the original British Sopwith Aircraft Company and was the first pilot to try to fly the Atlantic, but crashed. Harry Kauper was Hawker's aircraft mechanic and Harry Busteed – who once landed a plane in a Melbourne suburban street – also became a pilot.

Also on the staff of Tarrant's from its inception was a brilliant English coachbuilder called James Flood, who left to found his own firm in 1907. His son James became Australia's greatest automotive historian/publisher.

After WW1 Tarrant's changed its name to Autocar Industries and its associated body-building business to Melbourne Motor Body Works. In 1939 the three partners in what was then one of the largest vehicle distributors in Australia sold out and retired. Over almost 40 years of existence the company had held agencies for around 50 different marques.

Tarrant's sold its huge Melbourne Motor Body Works to Ruskin Motor Bodies Limited, which was bought by Austin Motor Company in 1945 and formed the basis for the startup of BMC (later Leyland) in Australia.

famous photographer, and a dog, Wowser.

In *Wheels Across Australia* Davis reports Birtles used the same Model T to cross Australia three times, including one trip through Birdsville via Innamincka and Sturt's Stony Desert. He was given to singing as he drove; one song had a single chorus and 219 verses, little of which was printable.

In the run-up to WW1 the Federal Government sought to encourage the mewling infant motor industry, so the tariff on imported cars kept rising, from 2.5 per cent in 1902 to 35 per cent in 1914, when locally bodied chassis accounted for about 40 per cent of the total market. In 1917, with wartime shipping increasingly scarce, the government banned all auto imports for more than a year. After that it legislated to guarantee the local body builders two thirds of the new car market by requiring importers to bring in two bare chassis for every fully assembled one.

The playing field was tilted even more in 1920, when the quota system was replaced by a doubling of tariffs on imported bodies and lower tariffs for chassis brought in unassembled. It was the sort of protective industry barrier Australia maintained until the 1980s, and it caused some interesting moments.

In *Aussie Cars*, Tony Davis says a Melbourne firm, E. W. Brown Motors, tried in 1917 to circumvent the rules by selling the Palm, built from Model T components imported from North America, modified for right-hand drive and given local mudguards, hubcaps and a

different grille. Ford stopped them with a court action claiming patent infringement.

Ford distributors in each State were assembling the Model T, with a choice of five body styles from two-seater to six-seater but just one engine, a 2.9 litre, 22.5 horsepower four-cylinder. Some light truck chassis were also shipped, local body builders adapting them into vans, tray tops, buses – even ambulances. There were some modifications, such as a larger radiator to handle Australia's hot summers, but in *The History of Ford in Australia* Norm Darwin debunks the story that you could have a Model T 'in any colour you like as long as it's black'.

According to Darwin, Henry Ford switched to a fast-drying paint called Black Japan Varnish because of bottlenecks in his Rouge, Michigan, paint shop. Ford

Canada didn't have the same capacity problem, so Australia got some Ts in dark blue.

By 1914 the Model T was the top selling car in Australia, with 1142 registrations that year (second was the de Dion with 285 although, as Darwin says, in those days not all vehicles were registered). Because of the war, shipping freight rates went up and so did vehicle retail prices, but because of the war nobody was buying vehicles anyway, and by 1915 there were 5000 unsold Fords at grass.

In a replica of the template that applies today, the distributors and dealers offered to reduce their profit margins in return for a Ford rebate. It was a revolutionary idea, but it cleared all the stock in eight months.

After the war, however, with a drought of skilled labour because of the dreadful toll of the killing fields of Europe, there was a shortage of cars and many were of ordinary quality. The distributors hadn't invested any money in their networks and their production systems of marrying chassis to imported bodies were as primitive as before the war. They had not been following Henry Ford's 'bible'

Artist Norman Rockwell was inspired to record the way Ford cars changed America's rural way of life.

on the ethics, conduct, look and financial operations of a Ford dealership.

Some dealers even started ordering fully built cars direct from Ford Canada, and there were growing complaints of poor body quality, delivery delays, component shortages and overpricing of cars and replacement parts.

By 1923 Ford Canada had watched its market share fall far enough. It decided that two senior executives – the tall, beefy Hubert C. French, destined to become Ford Australia's first managing director, and one Mel Brooks – should take ship at once to see just what games these descendants of convicts were playing. They arrived in November and set out on an extraordinary trek of evaluation of all Ford distributors and dealers, by car, rail and ship.

The result is a fascinating document, kept in Ford Australia's archives in a fat black folder with 'H. C. French' gold-blocked on the cover. His remarkable typed reports are the basis of Chapter Three, 'Hubert's Excellent Adventure'.

French was convinced Ford should start its own

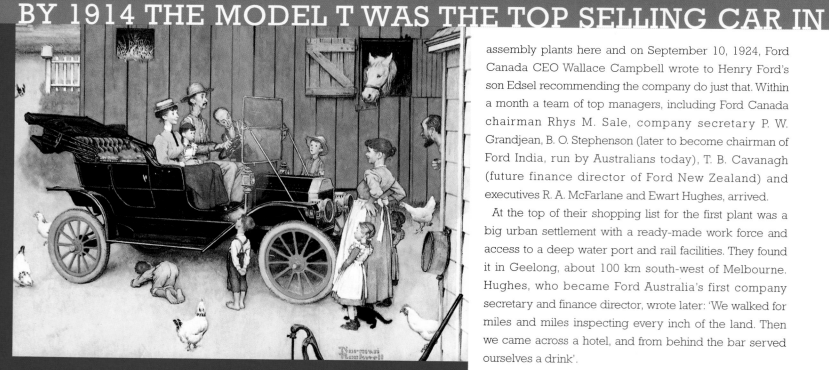

BY 1914 THE MODEL T WAS THE TOP SELLING CAR IN

assembly plants here and on September 10, 1924, Ford Canada CEO Wallace Campbell wrote to Henry Ford's son Edsel recommending the company do just that. Within a month a team of top managers, including Ford Canada chairman Rhys M. Sale, company secretary P. W. Grandjean, B. O. Stephenson (later to become chairman of Ford India, run by Australians today), T. B. Cavanagh (future finance director of Ford New Zealand) and executives R. A. McFarlane and Ewart Hughes, arrived.

At the top of their shopping list for the first plant was a big urban settlement with a ready-made work force and access to a deep water port and rail facilities. They found it in Geelong, about 100 km south-west of Melbourne. Hughes, who became Ford Australia's first company secretary and finance director, wrote later: 'We walked for miles and miles inspecting every inch of the land. Then we came across a hotel, and from behind the bar served ourselves a drink'.

Then, as if to dispel the image of boozed executives stumbling around making momentous decisions in a beery haze: 'But the fact there was a hotel on the site did not influence our decision, for the site had the greater advantages of being closer to our market, and to material supplies, in the State with the lowest taxation rates, close to main roads and railways and with a deep water harbour frontage'.

That pub was the Corio Shire Hotel, operated by a man called Young on an area of 40 hectares (100 acres) owned by the Geelong Harbour Trust, and bordered by the Melbourne road to the north and with the Melbourne–Geelong rail line crossing the property at the south-west corner.

Ford decided to keep the only building on the site, a disused wool store, as the shell to start the factory. (The hotel would continue to trade for several years after the plant opened but had to shut its doors after the Victorian Prohibition League wrote endless letters to Ford Australia and its lawyers, the *coup de grace* one to Henry Ford, a

12-metre long production line in another wool store rented from Dalgety in Gheringhap Street (opposite where the excellent Ford Discovery Centre opened for business 74 years later) on the edge of the town centre, just three months after the company was formed, due mainly to the expertise of about 20 Canadian engineers and manufacturing people sent out to take the plant on stream.

USTRALIA

teetotaller and non-smoker.)

Three other assembly plants would open in 1925. In Sydney Ford bought a disused meatworks near the Homebush abattoirs, in Hobart an old Cascade brewery, and in Fremantle a farmers' cooperative warehouse. The Brisbane site, on the edge of the airport at Eagle Farm, was purpose-built and opened in 1926, with a smaller site in Adelaide.

Ford Australia was formed with a working capital of £1.5 million, a wholly owned subsidiary of Ford Motor Company of Canada Limited. It invited tenders for two extra single-storey buildings flanking the wool store. Geelong was euphoric. The new factory would create 500 new jobs for the area, its role to build bodies on chassis shipped from Canada as well as body kits – in what the industry calls CKD or Completely Knocked Down form – for the other plants.

Amazingly, the first Model T came off the end of a crude

An even more fantastic achievement was the manufacture of 6541 cars in the remaining six months of that first year. It was a hugely successful debut for the car which really should have become famous as 'Australia's Own'.

Bibliography
Paul Bird, Cecil Clutton, and Anthony Harding, *The Vintage Car Guide,* Doubleday, 1959.
Geoffrey Blainey, *Jumping Over The Wheel,* Allen & Unwin, 1993.
Norm Darwin, *The History of Ford in Australia,* Eddie Ford Publications Pty Ltd, 1986.
Pedr Davis, *Wheels Across Australia,* Marque Publishing Company, 1987.
Tony Davis, *Aussie Cars,* Marque Publishing Company, 1987.
Bill Tuckey, editor, *Australian Motoring Year No.3,* BFT Publishing Group, 1985.
Bill Tuckey, *The Book of Australian Motor Racing,* Murray Publishers, 1965.

CHAPTER 2

Henry Ford's **Legacies**

To understand Henry Ford it is best to visit an astonishing place called the Henry Ford Museum and Greenfield Village, sitting cheek by jowl with the small test track across the road from the Ford Motor Company's global headquarters in Dearborn, a somewhat down-at-heel suburb of Detroit, Michigan.

Ford created this place at the behest of his close friend, genius inventor Thomas A. Edison, but it is no longer a Ford property, being run by an independent trust and funded by grants and admission charges. It is an enormous building on 102 hectares, the whole place a theatre of 300 years of American life, family, history and technology.

Just as William Randolph Hearst combed the world for rare and wondrous things for his bizarre San Simeon palace on the hill above Highway One in California, so did Ford's people search the planet for artefacts which reflected the development of what would become the most powerful country in the world. Yes, it is a Norman Rockwell painting come to life, but it is no less fascinating for that.

On September 27, 1928, Thomas Edison laid the foundation stone, adding his footprints and name in wet concrete at the front of a red-brick building that replicates three of America's most famous: Independence Hall, Congress Hall and the Old City Hall of Philadelphia.

Like Gettysburg in Pennsylvania, the site of the swaying, surging, tragic 1863 three-day battle which turned the tide for the North in the American Civil War, and Arlington Cemetery across the Potomac from Washington, this place has escaped the excesses of American commercial exploitation which have Disneyfied even the homelands of the Amish people.

As you walk through the displays of, say, kitchens of every 50 years from the 18th century on, or the progress from the world's first television set, you time-travel the transformation of America from a primitive rural and agricultural society.

It is at once a tribute to American ingenuity and creativity and a monument to its inherent capacity for violence. Not 10 metres away from the first 'coming or going' 1947 Studebaker, the first Chevrolet Corvette and Ford Mustang is the Lincoln Continental convertible in which John F. Kennedy was assassinated and the Ford Theatre chair in which Abraham Lincoln sat when he was killed by John Wilkes Booth.

There are some wondrous and rare cars there, but it is not a car museum. There is a chrome-plated 1946 roadside diner complete with jukeboxes in each booth, a 1950s drive-in theatre running movies of the era, a Holiday Inn motel room from the 1960s, Admiral Byrd's Ford Tri-Motor aircraft which took him over the South Pole, a gigantic Pennsylvania steam locomotive on its own tracks, an original Massey–Harris combine harvester and

Two glimpses of the Henry Ford Museum in Dearborn: the first Chevrolet Corvette from 1953. The initial run of 319 was all hand-assembled. Below: an early McDonald's store. Page 10: one of the first Model Ts to leave Geelong's new plant in 1926.

the caravan Charles Lindbergh and his family used for holidays, with a diary of where they had been and what they had seen carved into the woodwork.

There are displays of generations of glass, ceramics, crystal, jewellery, pewter, watches, stoves, washing machines, furniture, irons, office machines, printers, cameras, phonographs, telephones, metalworking and lighting. I have been there three times and not seen it all.

And outside in Greenfield Village you find the houses Henry Ford transported here to honour famous men. There is Menlo Park Street with Edison's laboratories, alongside Sarah Jordan's boarding house, where he lived. There is Harvey Firestone's (working) farm; the Ohio home and bicycle shop of the Wright brothers' family; Noah

Webster's house where he worked on the famous dictionary; botanist Luther Burbank's house and experimental garden. There are original 19th century taverns and general stores, and then the Scotch Settlement school where Henry Ford got his early education and – of course – the house where he was born.

History has tended to mythologise the founder as a natural engineering genius who rose above his hard-scrabble farm roots to revolutionise the way cars were designed and built in the early years of Detroit-to-be-Motown. In fact, Ford appears to have been doggedly single-minded, careless at times of other people's feelings, hard-nosed in some aspects of industrial relations and not always willing to delegate. There can be no questioning, however, the vision which saw him create the gigantic Michigan plant, a dark satanic mill called the Rouge, in which Ford cars were literally created from raw iron ore, loaded from Ford mines into Ford ships, and rubber and timber from Ford plantations.

In his superb book *Ford – The Men and The Machine* British author Robert Lacey says the Ford family arrived in Dearborn from Ireland in 1832, lured by empty cheap land once peopled by Indians and still thick with deer, turkey and wolves. Henry was born on July 30, 1863, a few hours after dawn.

The white timber house has two parlours, a dining room and kitchen, with two bedrooms upstairs. It is the house of well-founded farmer William Ford and his wife Mary who, while refugees from the Irish potato famine, had been helped to establish themselves by Ford relatives already in America. By the time Henry was born William Ford owned 120 acres (48.5 hectares) of land and was a prominent Masonic citizen, Justice of the Peace and Protestant church warden.

Henry Ford's schooling started in a one-room school, but Lacey says the tales about his childhood ability in mechanical things, particularly fixing watches, are mainly rewriting history into myth, just as Henry liked to recall his poor farming background. However, he steadfastly maintained many years later that seeing a steam engine driving towards his father's horse and buggy one day when he was 13 was his Damascene conversion.

At 16 he became an apprentice in the James Flower &

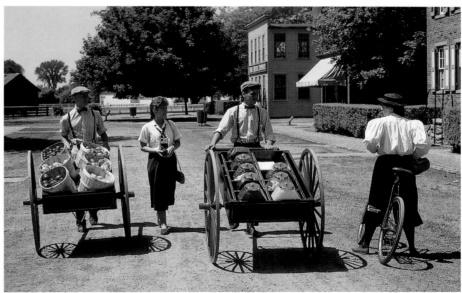

Brothers Machine Shop in Detroit, a place well regarded for its training and workmanship, which also produced one David Dunbar Buick. But he stayed there only a matter of months before moving to the Detroit Dry Dock Company, where he came under the influence of a brilliant engineer called Frank Kirby.

His next job was as a travelling demonstrator and repairman for Westinghouse engines and machines but the turning point probably came when he got a job as a

Top: the home of Orville and Wilbur Wright, re-erected in the Henry Ford Museum and Greenfield Village.
Above: staff in period costumes appear in the streets of the vast Greenfield Village.

FORD WORKED (IN COMPANY TIME) ON DEVELOPING

The founder possibly pondered the differences between his (second) Quadricycle and the 10 millionth Model T behind him. More than 15 million would eventually roll out of Highland Park. Opposite: Henry Ford's share certificate, declaring that he owned 255 shares in the Ford Motor Company, incorporated on 16 June, 1903. Capital was $150,000, shares were valued at $100 each. Below: Ford's Discovery Centre in Geelong.

mechanic-engineer with the Edison Illuminating Company.

Every man and his dog were building cars and engines at that time, and Ford worked (in the company's time) on developing his own little internal combustion engine. He became chief engineer and by 1896, working with two friends in a backyard shed, had created a four-cylinder engine fitted to a wooden wagon. This segued into the famous two-cylinder Quadricycle, and in 1898 he had built a horseless carriage more recognisable as a car, with brass lamps, running boards and mudguards. In 1899 a William Murphy formed the Detroit Automobile Company with Henry Ford as 'mechanical superintendent'. It had some very important Detroit millionaires as shareholders

and on January 12, 1900, the company unveiled Detroit's first car, a black delivery wagon. But after little more than a year the company went broke.

At 37 Henry Ford was a failure. Undaunted, he built a race car; it won handsomely on its first outing and financial backers came from everywhere – five of them from the failed Detroit Automobile Company, including Murphy. They staked $US60,000 to form, on November 30, 1901, the Henry Ford Company: 'Builders Of High-Grade Automobiles And Tourist Cars', said the letterhead. However, Ford couldn't give up his old habit of working on his race car in the company's time and didn't make much progress with the new people's car he was supposed to design. So within six months Murphy and his partners paid him out and renamed the firm the Cadillac Automobile Company, which eventually became the flagship of General Motors. Henry Ford had struck out again.

But there were plenty of jobs and financial backers in a city with 23 car makers and 132 component suppliers. In partnership with a cycling champion called Tom Cooper, Ford built two cars to race. They were The Arrow and 999, the latter the biggest and most powerful car in the country. The 999 was a beast to drive, and they had to enlist another cyclist, Barney Oldfield. He drove the car to its first race win, but within six months Ford had had another falling-out with his partner and in October 1902 he sold the 999 to Cooper and left.

Henry Ford had already secretly signed a partnership agreement with an Alex Malcomson to build a new car. He

brought with him a design for a new two-cylinder engine – this would form the basis of what was known as the Model A. Ford & Malcomson became the Ford Motor Company, its logo a blue-and-white oval in a script similar to Ford's own handwriting, cut on a child's printing set.

Ford Motor Company didn't actually build the first Model As, instead assembling them from wooden bodies, leather upholstery, transmissions, wheels and the rest bought from outside suppliers. Mostly the cars were put together by the Dodge brothers and hauled to Ford for final finishing. By March 1904 Ford had sold 658 cars and Henry had bought his first dress suit. By the start of 1905 the company was in big new headquarters and building 25 vehicles a day, two updated versions of the Model A and an all-new Model B four-cylinder.

Then in May 1906 came a falling-out with Malcomson, but this time it wasn't Henry who was shown the door. After a complicated share-distribution deal Henry Ford ended up with complete control of his company, and to this day the family still has the major say over the world's second biggest corporation – the largest with its founder's name over the door.

By 1907 Ford knew exactly where he was going, and his goal, as he put it in that year, was to 'build a motor car for

IS OWN INTERNAL COMBUSTION ENGINE

the great multitude'. It would be simple, light, cheap and tough. It wasn't the Model T, but the Model N. And while it presaged mass production, Henry Ford didn't invent that process system, as popular history would have it.

Singer sewing machines, Colt small arms and McCormick agricultural equipment were already coming down production lines, according to Robert Lacey's book. The real secret of the Model T was that instead of casting each engine cylinder separately and then bolting them together, all four would be cast in one piece. As well, the transmission was a 'planetary' design which used fabric belts, not unlike the continuously variable transmission developed by the Dutch firm DAF in the 1960s and now increasingly appearing in small cars.

Henry Ford turned 45 three months before the Model T was unveiled in early October 1908. It was his real strengths – his imagination and restlessness as a tinkerer and inventor – that made the car so innovative and so cheap. His ability to get down to the basics, to discard unnecessary complexities, to simplify decisions, brought out all those brilliant, unrealised creations from the long-neglected and frustrated attic of his remarkable mind.

The Model T quickly built up a six-months' waiting list. The farmers of America loved it – and in Australia it was quickly christened the 'Squatter's Joy' – not least because you could jack up a corner and remove a wheel to run a power takeoff to a circular saw or other machinery. It had a flexible chassis where others were rigid and shook occupants to the teeth fillings. During US Prohibition the bootleggers found to their delight it could carry at speed but without breakage 90 one-gallon jars of liquor for a total load worth $US3600 – vast money in those days.

Ford was operating on a kind of production line, but it wasn't continuous. Teams would build up components at a station, and the package – say, an engine – would be pulled along to the next zone, where another team would take up the next assembly task.

Ford wanted to build the world's biggest and best factory, and the company bought a 57-acre (23-hectare) former horse racetrack at a site called Highland Park on the edge of Detroit. Production doubled and redoubled, to nearly 79,000 a year by 1912. All parts were now machined in a jig, instead of being hand-crafted, so they fitted exactly and were interchangeable, thus making for speed and quality.

This was a far more significant development than the moving production line for which Henry Ford became famous. Evolving as it did from the bicycle and carriage trades, the vehicle manufacturing process was based on skilled tradesmen making most parts individually, sometimes even blacksmithing them. When an owner's car stopped out in the boonies with a broken part, he literally had to find someone (and it was often the town smith) to fabricate a replacement, because few bits were dimensionally identical.

The new accuracy of fit was additionally important because it allowed companies to ship chassis and components to, for instance, Australia, where they could be mated to local bodies built to blueprints and drawings sent ahead of the bits and pieces.

The Ford company was constantly looking for new technology to give components greater accuracy. By 1913 it had hit on the system – still much in place today – of bringing the items for assembly to the workers at each station on a continually moving line. Conveyors moved everything. No worker had to move, lift or truck anything. By 1914, at the start of WW1, Highland Park was producing nearly 150,000 cars a year with the same workforce of around 6900 as it had had in 1912. This was

Opposite: views of the Rouge, above, the basic oxygen furnace and below, Ford's fleet of five vessels delivered six million tons of iron ore, coal and limestone from various ports in the Great Lakes to the plant annually in the 1960s. Above: Henry Ford bought out partner Alex Malcomson in 1906; thereafter he had complete control of his company.

real productivity. Thus was born the system that changed the automotive world.

Some people who knew Henry Ford well have said there was a Ford you liked and a Ford you couldn't understand. His industrial relations were a good example. As Highland Park reached its thundering peak, he was paying the going rate for a 10-hour day for the line workers. Then in 1913 his management introduced a major reform aimed at reducing labour turnover – a wage increase of around

America. To supplement Highland Park he bought land in 1915 at the junction of the Rouge and Detroit rivers, in pursuit of his dream of owning all the raw materials that went into producing a motor vehicle. The Rouge plant started by building warships, called Eagles. The company was selling more than a million Model Ts a year from 1921 on. According to Robert Lacey, Ford began to feel that the Model T was all the world would ever need, so he began to diversify into buying a railway, building aircraft,

IN AUSTRALIA THE MOI

13 per cent, followed three months later by another big increase coupled to an eight-hour day, but cleverly woven into it were conditions about profit-sharing based on length of service, marital status and age.

Detroit was in recession, but the new conditions actually increased labour turnover because the workers didn't like the moving assembly line. They saw it as a slave system, subjugating skilled tradesmen to inflexible timing ('Fordism' was the pejorative term coined during this era) and, when the unions started to get tough, Ford employed an army of vicious security thugs to break up the protests and gatherings.

By the early 1920s Henry Ford was the richest man in

inventing the supermarket and designing a new kind of hospital. He even bought a newspaper, the *Dearborn Independent*, which he tried, but failed, to turn into a national paper.

He spent summers in the Adirondack Mountains with naturalist John Burroughs, inventor Thomas Edison, and tyre-maker Harvey Firestone, a flotilla of six vehicles with chauffeurs and attendants, a Model T-based kitchen, and a dining tent which seated 20.

Henry's son Edsel became president of the Ford Motor Company on December 31, 1918, at the age of 25, with a shareholding of about 40 per cent. The dynasty had begun. Edsel was a car buff with his garages stocked with performance cars, just as Edsel II's home would be years down the track. Father and son were enormously close, although Henry did not know how to hand over the full reins of power.

Right: the Shearer Steam Car, Australia's oldest surviving motor car, was built at Mannum, South Australia, in 1896.
Opposite: Ford dealers at a 1960s function admire a Quadricycle Mark 2; the sign on the wall compares the dimensions of Falcon and Cortina with the much earlier design. The original Quadricycle had as its 'horn' an ordinary doorbell.

By 1919 Ford dominated the world's motor industry, but Henry still scorned the self-starter that Charles F. Kettering had invented for Cadillac seven years earlier. Every third car bought in the US was a Model T, so why worry? Ford refused to follow the 1920s move into credit purchasing, or to emulate General Motors by changing styling every year.

However, what he did do during this period was expand the empire by building almost identical factories (whether necessary or not, every roof designed to withstand 10 feet of snow!) in Europe, South Africa and, of course, Australia.

Ford's German operation also turned 75 in 2000.

But despite Henry Ford's excellent vision of a global car company's needs, he gradually lost much of his business acumen. Model T sales started falling from 1923, despite the addition of hundreds of new dealership outlets, and he refused to listen to engineers who pleaded for a new model with an engine of at least six cylinders. Finally, on May 26, 1927, as the 15-millionth Model T came off the line, Edsel and Henry together announced that the Tin Lizzie would soon be replaced by an all-new car, the second Model A.

Few people in the world would have realised at the time that a long, long way away, in Australia, the blue and white oval had already entered a new era.

Bibliography

Robert Lacey, *Ford – The Men and The Machine*, Pan Books, 1986.

L T WAS QUICKLY CHRISTENED THE 'SQUATTER'S JOY'

For Australian Desk - Sales Dept.   COPY

Report by Mr. L.W. Brooke, of Trip from Sydney to Melbourne

Leaving Sydney on Monday morning Novr. 26th, en route to Melbourne we were accompanied by Mr. Ryrie, one of the sales staff of Davies & Davies. The first town we came through was Liverpool, which is included in the territory worked by the dealer in the next town, viz: Campbelltown. In my estimation this town is large enough to support a dealer, being 22 miles from Sydney, and 14 miles from Campbelltown. From there we went on to Campbelltown and called on J. Bryne & Co. who have recently been appointed dealers for this vicinity. Mr. Bryne has a small partner who is a mechanic and looks after the service. Their premises are very small and contain practically no more garage equipment, their whole area only £6 cars in operation, £6 of which is for cars - Fords. They carry a per£1 stock for parts and accessories itory with £30/-/-, and with to transient motorists. Mr. Bryne seemed rather a bright sort of a chap, and with constructive help by distributors, we believe here a dealer here is very promising throughout. Lack of knowledge in systematic selling and giving service. The dealer here is moving into new premises shortly, where he will have a great deal more room. From the appearance of the big service after a new front is put on it should make good premises for this territory, - being the labor stations in Sydney. The prices of this schedule are very high, £8/10/- charge on a motor overhaul, less reboring and rebabbiting.

From there to the next stop, Camden, which is 8 miles, we travelled, and found the dealer J.J. Shaw, who has been established for a number of years. Mr. Shaw has premises on the main street of Camden, which are covered with various signs, such as Mobiloil, with only one Ford sign, in front of the building. The painter is only visible from the street directly whereas it should have been £15/0/-/- as the Ford cars is approximately £60/-/-, and a very small there are 4 other carriages in the territory. These equipment was in use, and a very small there are 4 other carriages at a 15 per cent discount, but the major portion of the Ford service work, although there are few. He claimed to be getting 75 per cent garages buy some of the parts from him at a 15 per cent discount. He had no mechanic is purchased direct from Davies & Davies, at the same discount.

The next stop was Bowral Engineering Works at Bowral, where Mr. Harding is in charge and who represents us in that district. This man is an Englishman, and feels quite proud and satisfied with the work that he has done in the last four months, having sold 3 cars and 4 trucks, and expects to sell 20 in the current year. Has a population of 5000 families, and 150 Ford cars in operation - carries a stock of Ford parts amounting to £400/-/-, and really seems to be giving good service in his community. In fact he pays too much personal attention to the mechanical side of the work. The District Organiser will have to change his ideas, showing him where it would be more profitable to spend his time selling, and others to do the mechanical side. Here again he should be given help by securing more money to put in his business. Believe this man is the makings of a good dealer, but is handicapped financially. While his present premises are very small, he has just started construction of a new building in which he will make adequate room for this territory. Australia seems now to evident that in the selection of dealers for this territory, that the distributors for New South Wales are picking mechanics instead of business men, where a man knowing anything about a be in the stage that Canada was a few years ago, and is so proud of the position he holds in the motor car is considered a genius.

CHAPTER 3

Hubert's Excellent Adventure

Sir Laurence Hartnett is enshrined as the 'father of the Holden' in Australia, but he was no longer a General Motors employee when the car was born in 1948. However, there can be no doubt that Hubert C. French was the parent of Ford in Australia, sent out by Ford Canada in 1923 to find out why, while the rest of the world couldn't get enough of the Model T, sales in Australia were sliding.

Now we know, thanks to the long and carefully kept letters French sent to headquarters in Ontario from November 12, 1923. They are history solidified in amber; priceless documents, a measured (albeit from a North American perspective) analysis of a country's topography, economic situation, social habits, politics and culture.

French was devastating in his evaluation, ruthless in his comments. He visited every distributor from Townsville to Hobart to Perth, travelling by car, ship and train, and his reports led directly to the founding of Ford Australia. Few would contemplate such an exhaustive review, even if commissioned today!

Rafferty ruled the Australian vehicle market after those first two Model As were sold, one to Sydney engineer F. H. Gordon (who in 1919 produced a local six-cylinder car called the Australian Six) and the other to retail store entrepreneur Mark Foy. This was followed by the Model N, and in 1906 the dealer called Tarrant's in Maryborough, Queensland, sold a car to the town clerk. This earned them a Ford agency and, as we turned the corner of the century, a place in history as the longest-running Ford dealership in Australia.

The second oldest is Trevan Car Sales, appointed in 1910 in Lismore, northern NSW, and expanding to the nearby towns of Ballina, Casino, Murwillumbah and Mullumbimby – at its peak the group would sell more than 2000 Model Ts in a year.

The first contact French and his cohort, a senior engineer from the Windsor (Ontario) plant called Mel Brooks, made was with NSW distributors/assemblers

Arthur and Lewis Davies, then trading as Davies & Fehon in Hunter Street, Sydney.

It began badly, starting with the hotel accommodation, which French described as 'the worst in the place'. The Davies brothers gave them a cold welcome in their office.

'They were certainly not pleased with our visit and, I believe, were not clever enough to conceal it', French wrote. 'They informed me that their territory was well represented by district organisers who visited each dealer about once a month. The dealers on whom I have called all stated that they have not seen a representative of Davies & Fehon more frequently than twice a year, and

Opposite: Ford Australia's founder and first managing director Hubert C. French – 'The General'. He retired in 1950 after 25 years in the chair, to live in Barwon Heads, near Geelong. Below: a restored Model T outside Trevans Ford dealership in Lismore, NSW, the second oldest in Australia.

one very important dealership, which I visited, with a very large population, had only been visited twice in 10 years.'

French and Brooks found that with a few exceptions the entire Australian network – remember, this was for the world's top-selling car – was a shambles. And French did not spare his tongue. Take this report on the dealer at Windsor, 30 kilometres west of Sydney. 'We found the dealer working on a bench in his shop amongst discarded petrol cans, refuse and dirt. His premises would offend any self-respecting animal as housing. His stock room was in a state of chaos and it goes without saying that his sales have been extremely small in comparison with his opportunities.

'This man has no conception of his responsibilities as a

Ford dealer, knows nothing of salesmanship or merchandising and I sincerely question if he is even a fourth-rate mechanic. He states that he is selling two cars per week and I take it that this means that people are coming in and buying two cars per week.'

But French was impressed with Richard Trevan in Lismore, finding him well organised. He gave French his first insight into the way distributors were lining their pockets at the expense of the dealers. Dealers had been appointed on the basis of having to pay cash for their first new Model T and agreeing to order another six during the next 12 months. They were paid a commission on sales of only 10 per cent and Trevan told French he couldn't afford to employ a salesman on that basis.

As well, Davies & Fehon had refined the art of agreeing to a price reduction with Ford Canada, then shipping all the existing prepaid stock to the dealers, who had to sell at the new price. French also found distributors were competing with dealers on retail sales and undercutting them on workshop and parts pricing.

The two Canadians had a typical introduction to Queensland. They arrived on a Sunday, November 11, during a heatwave, and booked into the then-best hotel in Brisbane, Lennons. (For the second time in his letters to head office French noted they had been booked into two small single rooms but, thinking frugally, were able to change this to one larger twin room.)

They found their Queensland distributor, Charles Whatmore, was 'down the bay in his motor yacht and would not return to Brisbane until some time Monday'. Like many North Americans even now, French had little understanding of Australia's size, and was disappointed he couldn't get all 230 Queensland dealers into Brisbane for a conference over the next two days.

It turned out that Sydney's Davies & Fehon owned 51 per cent of Whatmore's business and anyway there was virtually no contact with any dealer 100 kilometres beyond Brisbane. His report reads, in part: 'Whatmore has made a lot of money and is considered wealthy … Native cunning combined with shrewdness has been responsible for his success. Of course he is a puppet who jumps every time Lew Davies pulls the strings'.

But French was no back-of-an-envelope analyst. In a

'TO ATTEMPT TO EDUCATE C

Assembly plants in each State were among Hubert French's recommendations to Ford Canada. From top left, clockwise, plants in Brisbane, Sydney, Adelaide and Fremantle were all vital to the company's growth. Henry Ford insisted that all factories were to be built with access to water, but that didn't always happen. Opposite: the Geelong plant in 1938.

package sent on December 6 he enclosed samples of Queensland Motors advertising, a list of Ford dealers, Queensland sales by model since 1920, analyses of sales, cost sheets for cartage, bank exchange details, customs entry figures, a map of the city of Brisbane and suburbs, a guide and tariff schedule for Queensland Railways and coastal shipping, a railways timetable, and a list of rival cars with prices he saw in Brisbane. The list included a car called the Renown, which used a Ford chassis, shipped by a man called Brown from New York

without Ford Canada's knowledge, converted to right-hand drive and equipped with copy Rolls–Royce radiators, mudguards, tops, and disc wheels to replace the spoked Model T wheels. (It was too close in price to the Model T Deluxe and failed in the market.)

Not far out from Sydney on the way to Melbourne they stayed overnight in what French described as 'a splendid little inn that was built in 1834' – the Surveyor-General Hotel in Berrima as we know it today, the oldest continually licensed hotel on the Australian mainland.

He was becoming impressed by some dealers and beginning to understand what historian Geoffrey Blainey later described as 'the tyranny of distance'. But there were exceptions. The Wagga dealer, H. T. Smith, a racehorse owner and big bettor, sold Oakland, Vauxhall and Renault and told French he wouldn't sell more than 50 Fords a year because people in his territory were so prosperous they would buy bigger and more expensive cars.

When they met the Geelong dealer, by the name of Margetts, in the future home of Ford, they found: 'This dealer states that he will sell in 1923, 53 cars and trucks,

and I am perfectly convinced that this figure should have been nearer 250. Margetts is young and ambitious, needs more finances in his business, and is eager and anxious for our help out of his difficulties. From all that I can gather, little or nothing has been done to rectify this very deplorable situation'.

Brooks' task was to analyse the parts and service side of the Ford business, so French handled the politics. When they got to Melbourne they found the Davies brothers had acquired some kind of controlling influence over what had been the Tarrant business, although Tarrant was now gone

PRESENT DISTRIBUTORS IS HOPELESS AND USELESS'

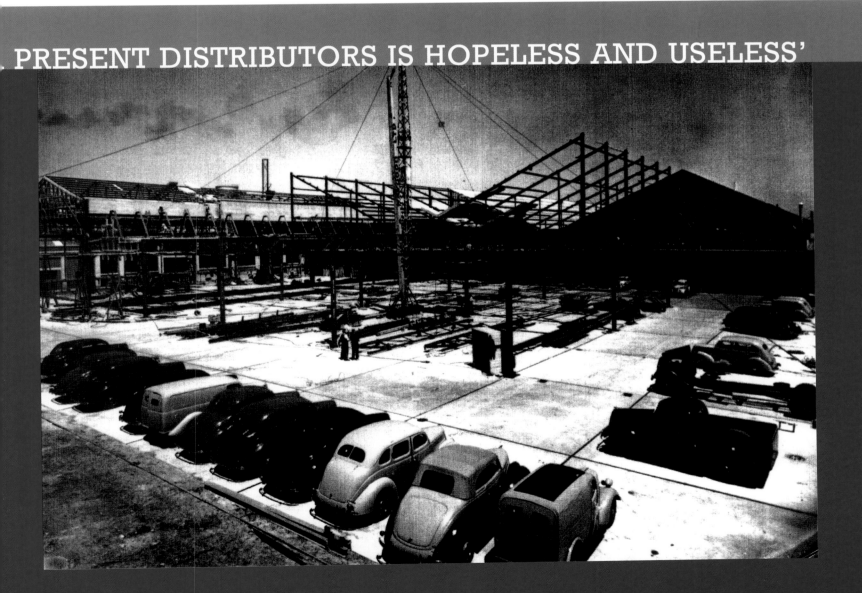

Hubert French was an honoured guest at Broadmeadows when the first XK Falcons were going down the line in 1960, 10 years after his retirement. His 25 years in the chair at Ford Australia remains a record unlikely to be surpassed.

and the company's franchises included Oakland, Fiat, Sunbeam, Rover, Durant, Rugby, Star, Wolseley and Ford. It was actually assembling bodies built by Holden's Motor Body Builders in Adelaide and trucked to Melbourne onto imported Ford chassis.

After dissecting the Tarrant operation, French wrote to Canada on December 14: 'Since my arrival in Australia the word Distributor has come to mean nothing more nor less than a bunch of easy-living, luxury-loving and opulent Directors, whose only thought is to squeeze more profits out of the business without a vestige of a thought of the future welfare of the Ford Motor Company. A band of vultures who will stoop to anything to satisfy their greedy hunger for profits'.

But French wasn't single-minded. He looked at the factory of match manufacturer Bryant & May in Church Street, Richmond, Victoria (beautifully restored by the Hamilton family in the 1980s as headquarters for its Porsche business), and the non-union factory of agricultural equipment maker H. V. McKay, employing

2500 people, and the similar shop of Massey–Harris. He talked to Sir George Knibbs, then director of research and industry for the Federal Government, and to the Tariff Board about future import duty protection. French saw clearly the grip the labour unions had by then on Australian industry, that the government-run railroads were inefficient and education levels lower than could be desired, but was confident of the country's sound economic condition and vast natural resources.

He fell for the Tasmanian picture postcard trick, the State replanted by English settlers to remind them of home, and wrote this extraordinary report to head office: 'Tasmania is rich in possibilities, has no labour disturbances, and is peopled by folk who live a peaceful life without much thought or knowledge of poverty. All these conditions would lead me to believe that Tasmania would be the logical spot for the location of any manufacturing plant who [sic] had in mind supplying the Australian market...'.

South Australia, with more cars per head than any other State, and 46 dealers, was fertile ground for French and

Brooks to examine tractor sales, selling systems, salesmen's wages and commissions, service follow-up, prospecting, parts and accessory sales, upholstery options and so on.

Western Australia was in the hands of Graves & Dwyer, but a year earlier Graves had been declared bankrupt and insane while Dwyer was middle-aged and in poor health; the business was effectively run by a general manager called Harris. Of 7280 cars then registered in WA, nearly 37 per cent were Fords.

This made up French's mind. In another report to Canada he wrote that Ford should eliminate all State distributors, except Nettlefolds in Tasmania, which would mean vastly increased profits for the company because it would be keeping the distributor's margin of £25 per car, plus the sale of parts. He forecast sales of 30,000 cars in the first full year – the 1923 figure was 17,803 cars and trucks – through five or six State branches.

'To attempt to educate our present Distributors is both hopeless and useless, and both Brooks and myself are devoting our entire time and effort to the Dealer Organisation, in order that we may have them thoroughly in hand when the right time comes.'

He called a national convention of all State distributors in Sydney in early February 1924. They all promised to make a greater sales effort, but French was merciless. Except in remote areas dealers would have to drop all other franchises and handle Ford exclusively. He told them GM Canada was about to launch a major attack with Chevrolet and that GM had just signed a contract with Holden's Motor Body Builders to build all GM bodies in Australia.

The meeting turned nasty, French referring to the fact that the distributors had consistently refused to give the factory financial statements and had been profiteering on spare parts. The Davies brothers stormed out, only to come back the next day and apologise.

As a kind of foreword to his final report, French wrote 20 single-spaced typed pages on Australia. It contained good and bad, fact and fiction. He estimated there were about 106,000 vehicles on Australian roads, about one-third of them Fords. Fords were seen as cheap and nasty, but reliable; there was still no sedan model, Australian

bodies were of indifferent quality and the transmission was increasingly perceived as old-fashioned. Other American, English and European cars were believed to be superior. He criticised the roads: 'There are not five miles of plain concrete pavement in the whole of Australia … The best class of city road is the wood block … All the main thoroughfares of Melbourne and Sydney are wood-blocked.

'The worst kind of road, which is altogether too common, is that formed and originally metalled with crushed bluestone, but in the course of time the bluestone has been worn away in places, leaving large pot holes.' And he criticised the idiocy of having three different railway gauges.

Neither did he like the political system, describing over-government as Australia's 'greatest disease', with 13 houses of parliament, six Governors and one Governor-General for just six million people.

He also said the country north from Lake Eyre to Darwin (where he hadn't been) would one day support a large population, and added disparaging remarks about Australia's indigenous people.

His final report to Wallace Campbell in Canada recommended replacing all distributors with a body-building and assembly plant in each State, along with State sales branches. He spoke highly of Australians' intelligence, willingness to work and learn, and enthusiasm for sports – less highly of the poor education system, 'excessive class distinction' and perceived fondness for gambling.

And so it goes. Dearborn agreed, and the suits set sail to discover Geelong. But the Model T was withering on the vine worldwide, and an ageing and stubborn Henry Ford was refusing to replace it. This, and the change from State distributors to sales branches, was about to ravage Australian Ford sales.

Bibliography

Norm Darwin, *The History of Ford in Australia,* Eddie Ford Publications Pty Ltd, 1986.

Bill Tuckey, editor, *Australian Motoring Year No.3,* BFT Publishing Group, 1985.

The Hubert C. French letters, Ford Australia archives.

Count down

Model T yearly output globally went from 168,220 in 1913 to 308,213 in 1915, reaching its first million-year in 1922. It peaked at 2,055,309 in 1923, but dropped to 2,024,254 the next year and continued to decline. At the same time, the cheap Chevrolet being produced by General Motors had increased sales by more than 200 per cent, and by 1926 Ford's market share in the US had dropped from 57 per cent in that peak 1923 to 34 per cent and falling.

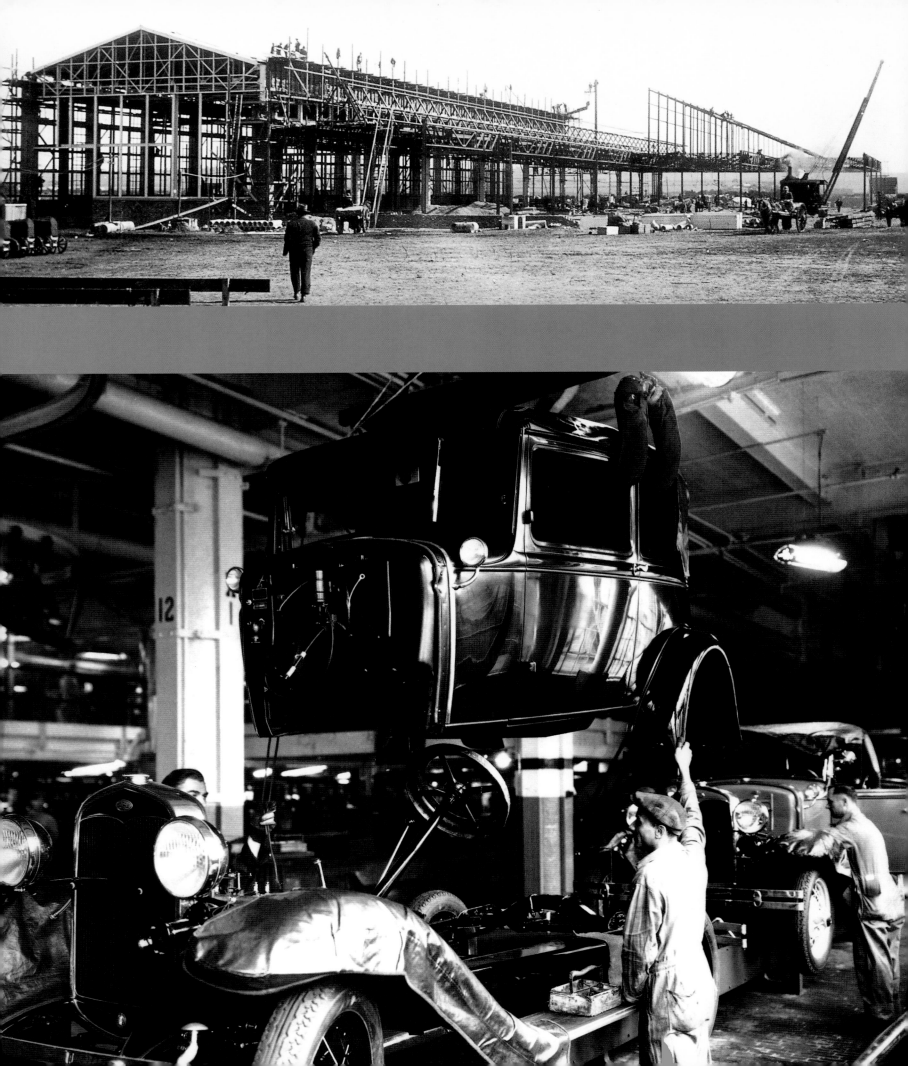

CHAPTER 4

Geelong And The **Roller-Coaster**

Hubert French's excellent adventure ended in July 1924 when he and Mel Brooks took ship for Canada, using the trip to complete the final report French had started in April. They had left behind a clutch of distraught distributors faced not only with the loss of their dealer profit margins both in vehicles and spare parts, but those from the assembly contracts and other franchises Ford would force them to drop if it established its own Australian operation.

But they hadn't given up. In August the six State distributors, united in diversity, sent Sydney dealer Arthur Davies as a representative to Canada to meet with Wallace R. Campbell, who had taken over as vice-president Ford Canada (in US terms, the CEO) in 1922 when only 40 (he would retire in 1946, having overseen the growth of Ford Australia).

According to Ford historian Norm Darwin, Davies said Campbell waited for him to arrive before making the final decision. Davies came with an alternative: the distributors would put in £5 million to fund a joint company to build new assembly facilities and an improved distribution structure, with Ford agreeing to a five-year contract for the franchise. Campbell rejected the idea on the basis that it was against Ford policy.

Davies pulled his other rabbit out of the hat: what about Ford and the distributors in a 50:50 joint venture for the same amount, but with no franchise guarantee? Campbell gave this the flick as well, saying Henry Ford was against any outside shareholding.

Davies didn't know it, but he had been torpedoed by events from almost 10 years before. On December 30, 1918, Henry Ford had resigned as president of the Ford Motor Company and gone to California, ostensibly on holidays. His son Edsel succeeded the next day and his main task was to buy out the company's shareholders on the most favourable terms.

His father had been playing ducks and drakes with the main stockholders for some years. In July 1913 the

Industrial premises in Gheringhap Street, Geelong. Corio Flour Mill in the centre with Dalgety's wool store on the right, where Fords were assembled while the Geelong plant was being built. Opposite: the Geelong Advertiser of March 31, 1925, trumpeted the great news. 'Decision received with pleasure by whole community', read the fifth bannerline. The extensive story described it as 'perhaps the most important statement that has ever been issued in regard to industrial undertakings in Geelong'.

brothers John and Horace Dodge had resigned from the board and given Ford one year's notice that they would stop supplying machined parts to the company. They kept their shares and were relying on the huge dividends from the increasingly profitable Ford Motor Company to fund a car-making business of their own – their 1914 return alone was $US1.22 million, a staggering sum in those days. As well, treasurer and vice-president James Couzens had resigned in October 1915, but retained his 11 per cent stake in the company and a seat on the board.

The company's accumulated profits in August 1916

totalled almost $US60 million, despite Henry having got rid of $10 million with his famous $5 a day minimum wage payment to his workers, and in 1914 another $11 million by refunding $US50 to every buyer of a Model T. He also kept reducing the price of the Model T, from the original $US825 in 1908 to $440 in 1914 and eventually to just $260.

He was quick to point out that while it cost the company money it attracted large numbers of new buyers and indeed, by 1915 Ford was the biggest car maker in the world and had nearly 45 per cent of the total US market.

Every dollar going out was money the shareholders wouldn't get, but Henry pointed out that as he held 58.5 per cent of shares he was damaging himself as well.

When he announced in late 1916 that the company would distribute no more dividends, investing its cash in expansion instead (mainly into the huge new plant down on the Rouge River), the Dodge Brothers sued him for almost $US40 million.

After nearly two years of hearings and appeals the Michigan State Superior Court decided against Ford, ordering the company to pay the shareholders some $US19.3 million – a fortune then. Of course, Henry would get 58.5 per cent of that, so he couldn't be too unhappy.

Then, after covert negotiations masterminded by Edsel, Ford bought the remaining 41.5 per cent from six shareholders for a massive $US105,820,894. This in effect valued the company at something like $US250 million (a few years later a still-unknown financial group tried to buy it from Henry Ford for a reported $US1 billion).

Edsel, then the 25-year-old president, got 42 per cent, while Henry kept 55 per cent and his wife Clara 3 per cent. A year later, in May 1920, Edsel stood with his father, holding the hand of his two-year-old son Henry Ford II, as they opened the awesome Rouge plant.

So it was Edsel who in September 1924 received Wallace Campbell's Ford Canada assessment of the Australian situation. French had done his homework well. Campbell's analysis pivoted on the high import duties then applying to completely built up (CBU) and disassembled (CKD – completely knocked down) vehicles shipped into Australia, and on the fact that three different railway gauges and inferior coastal shipping made assembly plants in all States except Tasmania essential. He also highlighted the profits that would flow to Ford from eliminating the distributor margins on both cars and parts, while reducing the prices of cars and increasing dealer profit.

He estimated production of 30,000 cars a year and outlined three different ways of financing the $3.5 million he calculated a new plant would cost. He offered the choice of floating 49 per cent of a new company on the Australian stock exchanges, a first mortgage bond issue in Australia, or 'a direct advance from a source friendly to

the company, repayable from accumulated profits'.

Campbell had been forwarding copies of French's interim reports to Edsel as a matter of course, so it was no surprise that the reaction was almost instant. Just three weeks after Campbell sent his analysis the Ford company secretary wrote that Ford Canada would be extended a line of credit of $US3 million, secured by three series of notes each of $1 million per year, to be repaid at interest of 4 per cent, the whole transaction in gold coin.

Everything happened on July 1, 1925. A Fordson tractor turned the first soil on the new site, the six distributors got their marching orders, and the first Model Ts started wobbling off the temporary production line the Canadians had jigged together in the former Dalgety's wool store the company had rented on Gheringhap Street.

To keep things simple, the first (and only) model was a four-door fabric-top tourer costing £185; the coupe, two-door and four-door sedan and truck and van models would follow later. The bodies were sourced from a South Australian builder, because Ford's own body plant would not be ready until 1928.

Things didn't begin well for Ford's new Australian managing director. Hubert French, a big man at 110 kilograms and standing almost 190 centimetres, was called 'The General'

by his troops but his background was law and engineering. When younger he built speedboats and had twice gone bankrupt through gambling on horse races.

He was only 43 when he took on the Australian job and

Right: the Geelong plant in 1936; Corio Bay can be seen at top right. Below: Ford kept its original promise to give preference to Geelong residents, something that caused bitterness when the Broadmeadows plant was announced in the 1960s.

GOOD JOBS FOR MEN

AVAILABLE NOW
WITH

FORD
GEELONG

OVERTIME BEING WORKED

SEE OUR EMPLOYMENT OFFICER, MR. FROST
THIS MORNING — SATURDAY

EMPLOYMENT OFFICE IN MELBOURNE ROAD WILL BE
OPEN FROM 8.30 A.M.

If unable to call to-day we are open each weekday from 7.30 a.m.

For Telephone enquiries ring 70211, Extension 304

FORD MOTOR COMPANY OF AUSTRALIA LTD.
MELBOURNE ROAD, NORLANE

at 68 he retired to continue living at Barwon Heads, 20 kilometres from Geelong, a quiet seaside village now famous as the setting of the ABC television show *SeaChange*.

He found the roseate blush of producing nearly 6500 cars in the first six months didn't last: in 1926 Ford sold 13,322 Model Ts and in 1927 just 10,141. Rivals

sold in December of that year.

Rouge started turning out the A on November 1, 1927; it made its American debut on December 2 to what amounted to national hysteria – Ford had to hire Madison Square Garden for a week to take the crowds that had begun queuing outside the main New York dealership at 3:00 am. Australia would see the new Ford on May 15, 1928,

BUSES RAN OUT FROM THE CBD CARRYIN

had more modern, better styled and more comfortable cars. The trend was similar in other countries: Henry had clung to his icon for far too long.

Finally, he capitulated to his son's desperate urgings. On May 26, 1927, he and Edsel drove the 15-millionth Model T – now in the Ford Museum in Detroit – off the line at Highland Park. Five days later all Ford plants shut down to re-tool for the Model A. England stopped building the T on August 19, and Ireland on December 31, while Geelong kept producing them alongside the new Model A until late in 1928, the last Model T being

when it was unveiled in all capital cities at the same time.

But back to the first Australian Model T. While the Canadian manufacturing experts were the core of Geelong's operation, Ford had also head-hunted staff from its former distributors. Scott Inglis (father of Sir Brian Inglis, future Ford Australia managing director and the first Australian appointed to that role) left the SA distributorship of the Duncan family to become Ford's sales director.

Grace Morris, 23, moved from Victorian distributor Tarrant's in 1925 to become secretary to Ford's State

PEOPLE TO MARVEL AT THE FIRST PRODUCTION LINE

manager, living in a former 'coffee palace' in Geelong and working in a temporary office above the gas company showrooms in Ryrie Street. In 1995, then 93 years old, Mrs Grace Tuck, as she became, told Ford historian Adrian Ryan: 'It was a big move in those days for any young woman to leave home. We worked every Saturday morning and if we worked (overtime) at night we got two shillings. That was tea money'. She saw the foundations laid for the new plant and remembers how buses would run out from the Geelong CBD carrying people to marvel at the first production line in Australia.

Charlie Sherson, in 1999 the oldest original Ford Australia employee, was still clear in much of his memory when Adrian Ryan interviewed him in February 1995. He started with Ford on May 5, 1925, in the old wool store, answering a newspaper advertisement for trimmers and body workers. He joined a number of other former Tarrant's tradesmen.

'I hopped on the train and came down to meet Herbie West, he was the main man in charge of the Dalgety place. He said: Can you start right away? But I only had the clothes I was standing up in and had to find

accommodation and in those days you had to supply tools so I had to come home and get my tools.'

He started the next morning in the trim shop, trimming and upholstering the already built and painted bodies before they were mated to the assembled imported chassis.

Sherson remembers that when they moved operations to the new plant there were only four walls and no roof. 'They made sheds out of the boxes that brought the parts from America and we were working in these sheds. After Christmas our building was just about finished and laid out American-style, which surprised us because it was so different.'

The Model A launch caused a sensation in Australia, especially in Geelong and Melbourne, particularly as details of the American models had been 'selectively leaked' over the previous two months. Some 7000 workers and Geelong residents got a sneak preview at the plant and a reported 100,000 saw it there and at the Melbourne Town Hall over the next four days.

In Launceston the company's Tasmanian State manager parked a car in the main street and dropped lighted matches into the petrol filler pipe to demonstrate the non-flammable tank. Police asked him to cease and desist.

The A came as a full range of tourer, roadster, coupe, two-door (Tudor), four-door sedan (Fordor), 1.5-tonne truck and what today we would call a cab-chassis.

The car was an immediate hit around the world, even though it didn't have a six-cylinder engine. What it did have was a strong and reliable transmission, pneumatic tyres, hydraulic dampers and a tough and torquey four-cylinder heart. In the first four years of production 29,424 rolled out of Geelong.

Factories in other States gradually came on stream with the Model A, the last one being the new Fremantle plant in March 1930, assembling chassis, bodies and parts for the A and the AA truck, shipped from Corio Bay, Geelong. After WW2 it changed to assembling Fordson tractors and acting as a car distribution centre, one of its main jobs fixing damage to cars sent from Geelong by train. Ford archivist

Adrian Ryan says this often included filling bullet holes left by outback shooters using the passing train for target practice.

Charlie Sherson remembers the plant workers were working 8.75 hours a day, bundying-in at 7:30 am. The bodies went through the paint shop first, then onto his trim line, then to the assembly line to be mated to the chassis, a system that persisted from Model T right through Model A. Sherson says the workers never saw any of the top management people on the shop floor, unlike today.

In 1926 he was foreman of a three-man team that went to Hobart to set up the first small Model T assembly line in the old Cascade Brewery plant Ford had acquired, complete with huge water wheel on one side. He was also seconded later to Homebush in Sydney's west to help set up the new factory.

A contemporary of Sherson's, Ted Frost, who worked with Ford Geelong from 1926 to 1969, told Adrian Ryan in 1995: 'H. C. French was very much loved. He was so much of a gentleman'. He described the director of

manufacturer, C. C. ('Slim') Westman, one of the original Canadians, as 'tough on the exterior but underneath he had a soft streak'. Frost's earliest shifts were dedicated to hand-beating the Model T doors, before the press machines came into action.

He remembers helping to hand-build around 100 bodies made of lacquered oilcloth over a wooden frame. 'They didn't sell all that well …'

With Model A the best market penetration Ford got was around 20 per cent in 1928, while GM products secured 32 per cent. But as the Great Depression started to bite, line workers were put onto piece rates. Even the new 1930 models, with steel bodies (but still with timber frames) from Ford's own stamping plant and more overall length and interior room, couldn't challenge the economy.

The Model A was significantly more expensive than the T (it cost more to make); in *Ford – The Men and The Machine* Robert Lacey estimates the model changeover cost Ford around $250 million, whereas in 1929 GM had launched an all-new six-cylinder Chevrolet with only six weeks of plant shut-down. By 1930 Ford in the US had

Rare AR

Norm Darwin claims the first Model A assembled and sold in Australia was known as the AR and is quite rare in North America. This was because some US States banned them as the braking system didn't have a separate parking brake – Ford had to fit new backing plates, hubs and wheel caps and move the handbrake from beside the driver to next to the gear lever. He says that from the chassis numbers it would seem Ford US had 'dumped' the unusable parts on Ford Canada for use in its export markets.

The Ford Organisation in Australia

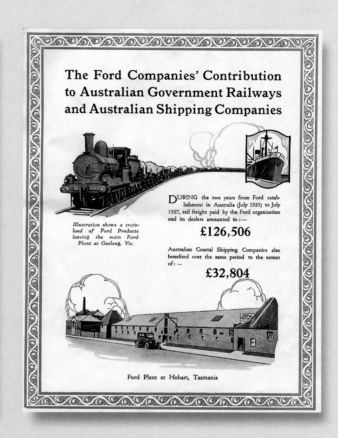

The Ford Companies' Contribution to Australian Government Railways and Australian Shipping Companies

Illustration shows a trainload of Ford Products leaving the main Ford Plant at Geelong, Vic.

DURING the two years from Ford establishment in Australia (July 1925) to July 1927, rail freight paid by the Ford organisation and its dealers amounted to :—

£126,506

Australian Coastal Shipping Companies also benefited over the same period to the extent of :—

£32,804

Ford Plant at Hobart, Tasmania

How the Ford Companies of Australia spent £3,163,733 in two years (July 1925 to July 1927) in the Commonwealth

Spent for £1,784,000. Production Materials~Building Construction~ Steamship Freights~Supplies~Insurance~ Advertising~Other Services

GOVERNMENT TREASURY
CUSTOMS DUTY
GOVERNMENT TAXES
RAIL FREIGHTS
RATES & TAXES TO LOCAL AUTHORITIES
£799,163

WAGES £580,570
FORD WORKS PAYMASTER

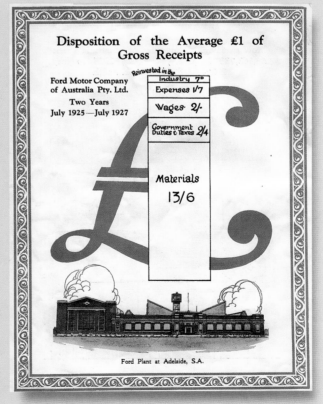

Disposition of the Average £1 of Gross Receipts

Ford Motor Company of Australia Pty. Ltd.
Two Years
July 1925—July 1927

Reinvested in the Industry 7°
Expenses 1/7
Wages 2/-
Government Duties & Taxes 2/4
Materials 13/6

Ford Plant at Adelaide, S.A.

After two years of operation Ford Australia indulged in a little corporate boasting. This booklet, highly stylised in the fashion of the time, made the point about the company's contribution to the Australian economy.

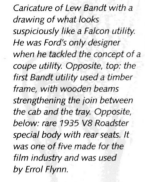

Caricature of Lew Bandt with a drawing of what looks suspiciously like a Falcon utility. He was Ford's only designer when he tackled the concept of a coupe utility. Opposite, top: the first Bandt utility used a timber frame, with wooden beams strengthening the join between the cab and the tray. Opposite, below: rare 1935 V8 Roadster special body with rear seats. It was one of five made for the film industry and was used by Errol Flynn.

surrendered the number one sales spot to GM and Chevrolet. It has never regained it.

Henry's reaction to the Chevrolet six was to switch to a V8. The world was familiar with V8 engines – Darracq had a 200-horsepower V8 racing back in 1906 and V8s in various production models from 1920 to 1930, but Cadillac in 1915 came out with the first V8 to be made in significant numbers and at a reasonable price. It was a 5.2 litre side-valve fixed-head unit capable of 2300 rpm – dizzying stuff for the time – and was so advanced it carried Cadillac through to 1929, when it was replaced by a 5.6 litre version, plus a V12. But the Ford engine had to be simple and able to be built on a line, where previous engines had been largely hand-built.

Henry Ford personally supervised the development, rejecting a reported 30 different prototypes, all based on a single casting – deemed impossible with the technology of the time. He authorised massive investment in new foundry, casting and machining facilities at the Rouge.

The result was another car for the masses, but this time one with real potential and youth appeal. The side-valve V8 was the progenitor of an entire motorsport industry as well as the hot rod movement; it even got publicity as the favourite getaway car of John Dillinger and Clyde Barrow (of Bonnie and Clyde fame).

This time there was hardly any shut-down between models. At the Rouge, the last of 4,813,617 Model As built there came off the line on February 28, 1932. Nine days later the first Ford V8 rolled out, ensconced in a wide range of body styles dominated by a distinctive, handsome grille.

The V8 quickly went into production at Geelong, and the hanky was whipped off on August 25, 1932. There were five body styles plus the option of the four-cylinder engine, followed a couple of months later by commercial versions.

Only 748 were sold before year's end, but that accounted for nearly 25 per cent of a Depression market, and 8931 would be built in 1935.

The 1935 versions would be the first to get an all-steel body (albeit still with a fabric roof insert at first) and demanded substantial new investment in body facilities at the Geelong and Eagle Farm (Brisbane) plants. It would also be the first car out of the completely new factory on the Homebush (Sydney) site which had taken 10 years to build since Ford Canada first acquired the land.

Meanwhile, Ford Australia had dipped a toe in British Empire waters. Norm Darwin in *The History of Ford in Australia* says production of an all-new British Ford small car, the 8 horsepower Y-Type, started in August 1932; the first Geelong-assembled cars didn't reach market until July 1933.

Geelong was actually building bodies for imported chassis and engines for this and the 10 horsepower C-Type that followed in 1935. They're significant mainly because they were the ancestors of the Ford Anglia and Prefect, which reached Australia in 1939 but had their greatest success after WW2.

But perhaps the most famous of Ford Australia's contributions to global motor industry folklore began in 1933, when a letter from a Gippsland farmer's wife to managing director Hubert French effectively created what today is America's biggest-selling motor vehicle – the pickup (and in 1999 a Ford at that), as it has been for years.

The letter has not survived, but it is known that in part she wrote: 'Why don't you build people like us a vehicle to go to church in on Sunday, and which can carry our pigs to market on Monday?'. There had been Model T and A utilities available, but all needed custom bodies on a separate cab-chassis – which even came in two wheelbases with the V8.

French handballed the letter to Westman. He called in one Lewis T. Bandt, then 22 and Ford's only designer. Born in Geelong, Bandt started in 1924 as an apprentice with Ford distributor and bodybuilder Duncan & Fraser in Adelaide, then in 1927 moved to the Tarrant-owned Melbourne Body Works. In 1928 he joined Ford Australia as a draftsman. Bandt told the story many times afterwards.

'Slim Westman came to me one day and said he wanted the front end of a V8 sedan combined with a utility tray. He'd remembered the old buckboard-type bodies on Model Ts and felt there should be some way of modifying present models to create a new vehicle for which there would be a ready demand.

'Westman quite rightly reckoned that if we cut down a car and put a tray on the back the whole thing would tear in half once there was a load in the back. I told him that I would design it with a frame that came from the very back pillar, through to the central pillars, near the doors. I would arrange for another pillar to further strengthen that weak point where the cabin and the tray joined. I said: Boss, them pigs are going to have a luxury ride around the city of Geelong.'

He sketched the ute on a 10-metre blackboard, giving it a 1200-pound (545-kilogram) payload on a wheelbase of 9 feet 4 inches (2845 millimetres). Westman ordered two prototypes built and asked for, and got, £10,000 for the tooling.

'Tom Carrie [Ford's first pattern maker] made a sample body', Bandt said. Sales manager Tom Lamb loved it.

'Heck, give me a hundred and I'll sell them tomorrow', he said. The utility – which Bandt christened 'coupe utility' – went straight into production in 1934, the first major job in the expanded Geelong tool shop and body press shop. Contrary to legend, it wasn't an all-steel body, although it

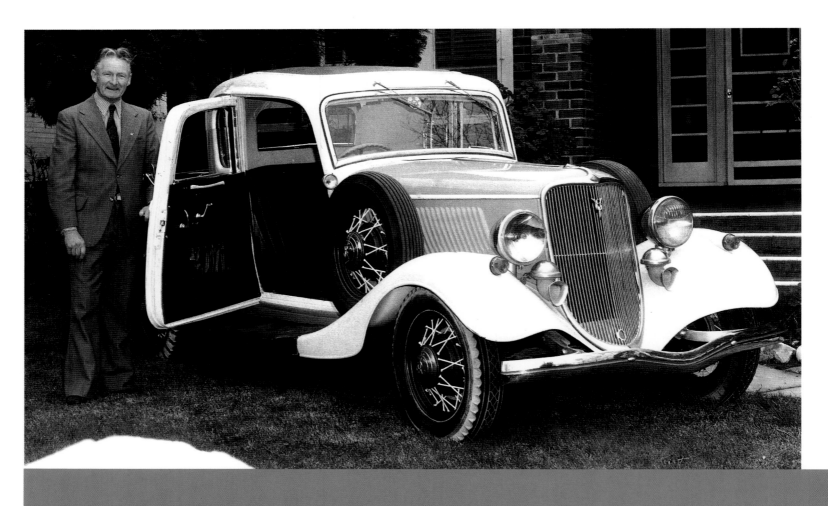

'BOSS, THEM PIGS AI

Lew Bandt in his later years with the 1934 ute he restored and drove regularly. Tragically, he was killed in it in a head-on crash. Repaired and restored by Ford, it is now on permanent loan to the Discovery Centre. Opposite, top left: Ford's top selling vehicle in the US, the F150 SuperCrew pickup. Top right: the unique Cortina five-door coupe Bandt created for his wife. Below: a Ford factory football team, proudly sporting the V (of V8) on the front of their jerseys.

did depart from American practice in incorporating the pickup bed with the cabin and the wheel arches inside the tray, but it still used a timber frame in the main body. The first scale drawing was in January 1933, Bandt recalled, and it took nine months to make the tooling.

The first utes came off the line in 1934 and two were sent to Canada. 'In 1935 I was sent to Canada and the US', Bandt said. He met Henry Ford and saw the giant Rouge plant. 'Mr Ford called in his men who took one look at it and said: What's that?. Mr Ford replied: It's a kangaroo chaser, and told them he was about to build a model there.'

The Bandt coupe utility was the foundation stone of what today is the world's biggest-selling motor vehicle, the pickup truck, or utility.

By the early 1960s Bandt was Ford Australia's

superintendent of automotive engineering, a title which later evolved into chief engineer. He designed the Zephyr and Falcon station wagons and utes, built for the 1962 Miss Australia quest – Ford was a long-time sponsor – six convertible Falcons with retractable hardtops (based on XL Falcon utes, they never went into production) and played a role in virtually every Australian Ford until he retired in 1976.

After retiring he found a 1934 coupe utility and faithfully restored it; an accomplished artist, he painted the ute with murals depicting Australian scenes and animals. In 1987 Lew Bandt was driving it back to Geelong after filming an ABC documentary when he was killed in a head-on crash with a gravel truck.

Adrian Ryan arranged with the Bandt family to have the ute repaired and restored by the Early Ford V8 Car Club of Australia, with help from companies such as Dunlop and Wattyl. Ford keeps it in trust for the family as a perpetual memorial to Lew Bandt. And naturally, Bandt's own original full-scale blueprint drawings of the 1934 coupe-utility are among the most cherished artefacts in the company's archives, now located in the Ford Discovery Centre across the road from the site of the original Ford buildings in Gheringhap Street.

Bibliography

Norm Darwin, *The History of Ford in Australia,*
Eddie Ford Publications Pty Ltd, 1986.
Robert Lacey, *Ford – The Men and The Machine,*
Pan Books, 1986.
Bill Tuckey, editor, *Australian Motoring Year No.3,*
BFT Publishing Group, 1985.

GOING TO HAVE A LUXURY RIDE AROUND THE CITY'

CHAPTER 5

Clouds On The Horizon

The Great Depression brought the motor industry to its knees. After the Wall Street crash in October 1929 the Federal government devalued the Australian dollar by 25 per cent, which immediately increased the cost of imports, while hurting Australia's major earners – wool, wheat, beef and minerals. But huge job losses – nearly 30 per cent of Australians were unemployed by 1932 – and a heart-rending drought saw vehicle sales plummet, Ford's from 14,089 in 1929 to 2476 in 1932.

Distributors and dealers were selling vehicles for less than cost, just to keep up cash flow. Holden's Motor Body Builders was badly hit in August 1929, when General Motors started reducing its orders and the company began to collapse.

In February 1930, the Holden board accepted GM's terms for a complete takeover for the price of £1,111,600; General Motors–Holden's Limited (GM–H) was formed in 1931. In *Wheels Across Australia*, Pedr Davis says the industry persuaded Canberra to reduce the wholesale sales tax on new cars. But when the Federal government tried to offset the resulting loss of revenue by extending sales tax to used cars, the NSW Chamber of Automotive Industries took them to the High Court, which in December 1934 found against the government.

Ford even had to resort in 1933 to paid advertising to counter what the print ads called 'many unfounded rumours and the circulation of mischievous propaganda' suggesting it was going to stop importing the V8 engine from Ford Canada. It said 'most emphatically' that Ford Australia would continue building cars with V8 engines and that 78 per cent of its content represented Australian materials and labour – an interesting claim, since the engines and transmissions were shipped out from Canada fully built.

There were signs of an industry recovery in 1933, when 20,654 cars and trucks were registered, but it would take until 1936 for the company to get back to the volumes of

Advertising followed the American influence, typically showing the car much bigger than it actually was. This is a 1937–38 Club Coupe. Below left: advertisement announcing 'advance showings' of the Model A range in Melbourne Town Hall. Opposite: one of the prettiest pre-war Fords – a nicely restored Australian Phaeton of 1933.

THE HEARING ATTRACTED FOUR PROP

1929. The answer then – and the formula still applies generally in the business – was to lift productivity, produce more with fewer workers and reduce operating costs.

Trim shop foreman Charlie Sherson remembered: 'The pressure was enormous. Every month they would come to me and say: "We want more production". They used to time the lavatory visits … never allowed to talk … never allowed to lift your head … I'd hate to see those days come back'.

It took the Vehicle Builders' Union almost 10 years to get an agreement with Ford to enrol men on the shop floor. Sherson says it was because the union – annual membership cost apprentices sixpence, tradesmen one shilling – was of no use. Before he joined Ford, he was laid off from Tarrant's Melbourne Motor Body Works on the then-accepted basis that jobs had to be found for servicemen demobbed after the Great War. Sherson says he tried for months to get the union to find him a job. He finally raged at the union secretary: 'You can stick your union'.

When the same secretary came down to Geelong to recruit members and found Sherson on the shop floor he asked him to help out. Sherson told him where to go.

On Monday July 2, 1934 John Ballimore joined Ford Geelong in the pay division. In a 1988 interview he recalled that as assistant paymaster part of his job was to make up the payroll and fortnightly pay packets for around 1200 employees.

'I'd go to the addressograph and stamp out the 1200 pay envelopes; we'd draft them up with the names on and someone would count the money out. There would be three checkers who would put it in the envelopes. Then at lunchtime we'd pay out from little cages which were portable and were scattered around the factory.'

The basic wage was one-and-fourpence an hour for a 48-hour week, higher than the award rate at the time. There was no overtime; if they worked back in the evenings they would get a meal voucher for a one shilling meal at the pub across the road. There would be no paid overtime until WW2 began.

The company was on an hourly hiring basis in those days; a man would be brought on for one hour's work. Ballimore recalled: 'We were known as the pay division, and whenever we walked out of the factory we'd see the poor fellows hiding behind crates and so on, thinking we'd come to pay them off. It was a very, very sad time. They were very thankful to get even an hour's work.

'We had a cypress hedge that ran the full length of the frontage and palm trees each side and perhaps 200 men would line up along that cypress hedge every morning on the footpath. The employment officer was a chap called Bill Jamieson, and Bill would go out in the mornings and he would walk along and pick out perhaps half a dozen and the other 194 would ride their bikes away.

'The chief means of getting to work in those days was, of course, the bicycle. The road was just second-rate, in fact in the early days it was a limestone road and was only

changed because when wet the limestone was very dangerous for cyclists.'

But according to Ballimore, there was a strong *esprit de corps*. The factory football team played in guernseys with a big 'V8' on them. 'I can't recall where they put the numbers', he said in 1988.

In 1935 Ford changed its model codes. It advertised the new Model 48 as having an all-steel body, but in fact there was still a fair bit of timber in the car and the roof retained its fabric centre. The huge Canadian-built Hamilton press needed to punch out the required panels for the turrets would come into play only for the 1937 models, using an

ALS FOR LOCAL MANUFACTURE OF COMPLETE CARS

Australian-designed-and-made die which took 39,000 man-hours to produce.

Henry Ford had never quibbled at spending money on production facilities and in those first 10 years from 1925 Ford Australia spent the astronomical (for those days) sum of $US272 million on plant, building, wages and Australian

By 1936 advertising material was picturing the utility as what we would call today a 'recreational vehicle'. This was the 'wellside' ute. Opposite: in November 1939, only a few months after its home market debut, the new small Anglia was added to the Prefect range and to replace the Y model 8 hp tourer. Ford was building the small British cars in Geelong from imported chassis and drivetrains, including coupe and soft-top utilities.

component suppliers. And the component suppliers had followed Ford to Geelong, as they still do when new auto plants are established on greenfield sites around the world, and the zero-inventory 'just-in-time' systems – which the world copied from the Japanese in the late 1980s – demand parts factories cheek-by-jowl with the assembly plants.

When J. H. Scullin became Prime Minister in October 1929, he introduced five new tariff schedules within eight months, most aimed at protecting local industry. The one which most favoured the local assemblers was a 50 per cent duty on all imported vehicles and chassis.

And there were plenty of local component makers to protect. A 1929–30 Tariff Board inquiry into springs identified no fewer than 45 spring makers.

Familiar names that started business in Australia during

the 1930s included National Springs, Robert Bosch, Repco, Smith Sons & Rees (KLG spark plugs), Henderson's, Olympic Tyre & Rubber Company and RVB. A Richmond (Victoria) company called Tilbury & Lewis, in January 1934, released the first Australian car radio produced commercially, sold under the name Pyrox, followed late that year by Radio Corporation's Air Chief – and this at a time when the British government was discussing banning car radios on the grounds they were a dangerous distraction for the driver.

Henderson's Melbourne-based Federal Spring Works made springs for Ford and trucked them to the wharf by horse and cart for loading on the SS *Edina,* bound for the wharf in Corio Bay on the edge of Ford's property.

Pilkington Brothers (Australia) Pty Ltd added a Geelong plant to the one it already had at Kilkenny in Adelaide (which supplied glass to GM–H) so it could meet Ford's needs.

Between April 1930 and November 1933 there were 12 Tariff Board inquiries into local components. On January 6, 1932 the Scullin government was voted out in favour of the Joseph Lyons-led conservatives, and immediately Australia had import licensing, soon followed by an import duty on pressed metal panels. In 1936 that government sent to the Tariff Board the most significant reference in the history of the Australian motor industry.

As Walter Uhlenbruch quotes in his paper *Australian Motor Vehicles and Parts,* written for the Committee for Economic Development of Australia (CEDA) in 1986, the board was asked to consider 'the question of the best means of giving effect to the government's policy of establishing in Australia the manufacturing of engines and chassis of motor vehicles with consideration to the general national and economic aspect'.

The hearing attracted, among others, four proposals for local manufacture of complete cars. They came from someone identified only as W. R. White, the Australian Ball Bearing Company, Australian-Made Motor Cars And Aeroplanes Limited and from one anonymous proposer. A four-cylinder model proposal from the Ball Bearing Company was espoused by its director Bob Chamberlain, a racing driver famous (with his brother) for building the revolutionary and lovely Chamberlain Special race car.

While the Ford V8 was shrinking Australia's vast rural distances and powering utes to take the pigs to market, smaller cars were well represented in Ford Australia's model lineup.

The New FORD 8 h.p. "The ANGLIA"

THE BRILLIANT, NEW "ANGLIA" 8 HORSE-POWER

The Tourer

Plenty of room for four people in this precision-built, English-styled model . . . plenty of economy, too, in its 45 to 50 m.p.g. performance. Note how the hood folds flush with body, enhancing the smooth, racy lines.

Spacious luggage compartment concealed behind rear seat, which is hinged at bottom for ease of access. Spare wheel and tyre in lock-up compartment at rear of car.

Wide choice of attractive body colours and genuine leather upholstery

ALUMINUM CYLINDER HEADS
Better engine performance with regular fuels. New aluminum pistons reduce oil consumption. Chrome-nickel alloy valves help maintain engine efficiency.

MORE FLEXIBLE SPRINGS
Improved riding comfort. Spring leaves of new design for quieter and easier action. They are the transverse double cantilever type for greater steadiness and safety.

"CLEAR VISION" VENTILATION
A simplified built-in design. Nothing to obstruct vision. Provides draft-free ventilation at all speeds. Windshield opens.

ALL STEEL BODY
Strongest, safest body construction. Does not deteriorate with age. Improved safety glass throughout in all De Luxe closed cars.

VALVE SEAT INSERTS
High tungsten chrome alloy exhaust valve seat inserts. Corrosion-proof and unusually wear-resistant at high temperatures. Longer life.

STRONG RIGID FRAME
Double-drop, double-channel. Two members forming X-brace are continued full length of side rails.

GREATER GAS ECONOMY
New dual carburetor, and dual intake manifold, give better operating efficiency. More miles per gallon. More power. Easier cold-weather starting.

NEW FORD V-8 DE LUXE TUDOR SEDAN—*An outstanding value at a low price. Two wide doors, with 38-inch entrance. Interior especially attractive with new tufted upholstery, new garnish moulding and new cove headlining. New comfortable, individual bucket seats in front compartment. Driver's seat is adjustable. There is also a New Ford V-8 Standard Tudor Sedan at slightly lower cost.*

IN 1934 THERE WERE 38,393 REGISTRATIONS – FORD

Brochure for 1933–34 model. Shown here is a Tudor (Ford-speak for two doors – not a reference to the British monarchy).

Pedr Davis says in *Wheels Across Australia* the directors of the Australian-Made Motor Cars company – Edward Davies, Charles Butler and Member of Parliament D. J. Malone – claimed they would build a factory near St Marys, west of Sydney which, among other things, would build a six-cylinder car called the Flying Kangaroo.

Ford Australia told the board it was opposed to local chassis manufacturing and GM–H opted for a step-by-step program. It all vanished into history, and other

entrepreneurs, including aviator Charles Kingsford Smith with his Southern Cross car, and other makes Hamard, Buckingham and Auscar, all failed during the 1930s.

The board handed down its report on September 6, 1937. Its four main conclusions can be summarised as:

1. It would be unwise 'at present' to encourage or enforce the manufacture of a complete motor vehicle;

2. Some chassis parts could be made locally without great additional cost;

3. The board considered the present retail prices of cars were far too high and any local manufacturing should not have the effect of increasing them;

4. The board had been unable to agree on the best way of giving effect to the government's policy.

In short, it had tossed the lot into the too-hard basket.

The real problem was that there was not enough local volume to amortise the cost of setting up factories to produce expensive components such as transmissions, engines and electrical wiring. GM–H, in 1935, had moved some way to easing the burden when it changed its parts-buying policy from requiring local parts to be 10 per cent cheaper than imported components to vice versa.

Ford Australia's archives reveal that in 1934 Australia bought only 27,254 cars and 11,139 commercial vehicles for a total of 38,393 registrations – Ford was back at number one with 7959 units.

But because the Lyons government's new import licensing arrangements discriminated against the US in favour of Great Britain, imports of UK and European cars went up from 22 per cent of the total market in 1935 to 45 per cent in 1939.

Importation of a vehicle chassis from anywhere other than Britain required the written consent of the Minister for Trade, and all British original parts (except assembled chassis) were given total exemption from import duty. The trade-off was a bounty paid to

S BACK AT NUMBER 1

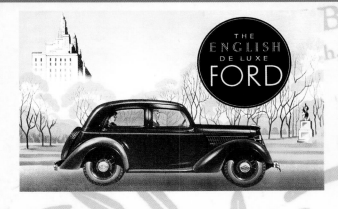

manufacturers who set up local production of chassis or components with a minimum of 50 per cent local shareholding. J. D. Beruldsen, in *Beneath The Bonnet* (his comprehensive history of the development of the Australian components industry), says that in 1945 and 1946 National Radiators was being paid a bounty of 10 shillings for every radiator produced.

Meanwhile, Ford was charging along, racking up increased sales every year from 1936 to 1939. Its 1936

Above: the locally assembled Ford V8 was dramatically cheaper than any car of comparable performance. Henry Ford had not invented the V8 but he certainly brought V8 motoring into the 'low-price field'.

47

models, coded 68, did away with laced wire wheels for the first time. In 1935–36 Ford opened extensions to the Geelong plant – mainly to accommodate the new press and the Keller profiling machines – and the Sydney plant, allowing assembly of the British small cars, tractors and commercial vehicles.

The fully imported Lincoln Zephyr arrived in 1936, complete with V12 engine, a precursor to the company's future focus on large luxury cars. Geelong was now starting to design unique Australian body styles, such as the 1938 two-door coupe, the V8 four-door sedan and a panel van on the coupe utility platform. And demonstrating that car makers sponsoring golfers and golf tournaments is nothing new, American players Gene Sarazen and Helen Hicks were supplied with Ford V8 sedans for a 1936 Australian tour.

Jack Trevan, one of the two sons of Richard Trevan, who in 1910 established in Lismore what has become the second longest-running Ford dealership in Australia, recalls that his father drove the acclaimed pair around for their visit to the northern rivers of NSW and Brisbane, and was given a set of Sarazen's clubs as a gesture. 'Sadly, I don't know where they are now', he said late in 1999.

However, in October 1937, managing director Hubert French poured a large bucket of cold water over proceedings. Apparently disturbed by the Federal government's flim-flamming over the future of the industry, he chopped the budget for the planned expansion of Geelong – new buildings and equipment – from £500,000 to £150,000.

But the company kept expanding the model range, churning out forward-cab truck chassis, forward-control buses and coaches, even semi-trailer prime movers. Bodybuilders created all kinds of variations on the V8 chassis, including petrol tankers, PMG mail vans, tippers, and Ford imported 'woody' station wagons.

The Australian passenger car market peaked at 56,016 in 1938, falling to 51,353 registrations in 1939 as war clouds darkened the sky over Europe. Chevrolet had held the top spot narrowly over Ford from 1934 on, but Ford beat GM–H in 1939. Total Ford sales in that grim year were 13,497, of which 9409 were V8s (6498 cars and 2911 trucks).

In 1939 Ford was selling the 91 series of models: sedans, coupe convertibles, light and heavy trucks all sourced from Canada and assembled; and the

The 10 hp British models were replaced by a name that became famous – the Prefect. Ford Australia started assembling them in 1939 and the range soon comprised four passenger and three commercial variants. After the war the company picked up where it had left off, with just a minor change to the grille. Opposite: V8 trucks formed the basis of much wartime production; there were many models, like this tipper and dropside from 1939–1940.

AUSTRALIA'S MOST POPULAR HEAVY-DUTY TRUCKS . . . . . NEWLY

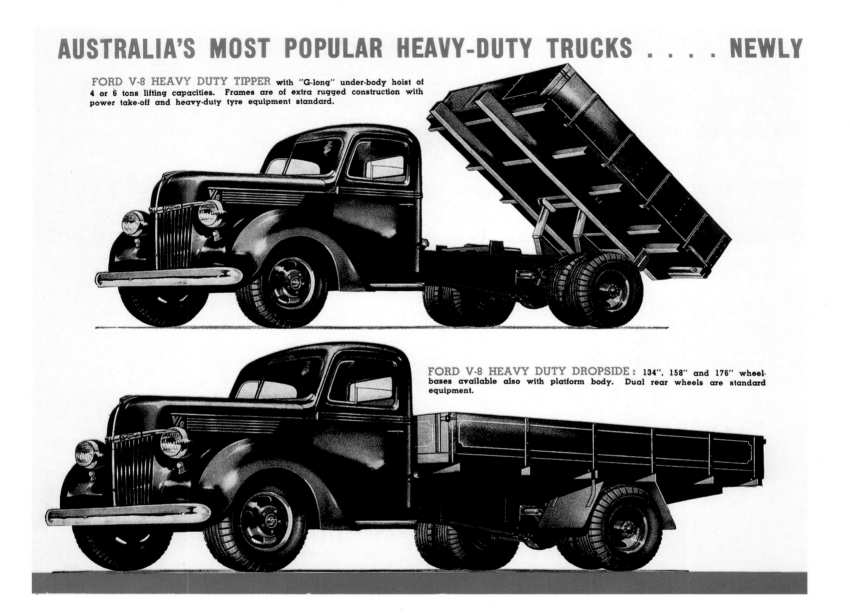

FORD V-8 HEAVY DUTY TIPPER with "G-long" under-body hoist of 4 or 6 tons lifting capacities. Frames are of extra rugged construction with power take-off and heavy-duty tyre equipment standard.

FORD V-8 HEAVY DUTY DROPSIDE: 134", 158" and 176" wheel-bases available also with platform body. Dual rear wheels are standard equipment.

8 horsepower Anglia and 8 horsepower Prefect, with bodies fabricated in Ford's Geelong plant and the chassis and drivetrain imported. The North American Ford luxury line, Mercury, was imported for the first time in 1939, which also saw the introduction of the hydraulic brakes most rivals had had for three years. The company's official records show total 1939 vehicle production of 13,497 – its highest level since 1925. The numbers for 1942 were 13,462, declining to 9314 in 1943, the majority of which were trucks for the war effort.

Bibliography

J. D. Beruldsen, *Beneath The Bonnet,*
Longman Cheshire, 1989.

Pedr Davis, *Wheels Across Australia,*
Marque Publishing, 1987.

Geoff Easdown, *A History of the Ford Motor Company in Australia,* Golden Press, 1987.

The Geelong Advertiser, generally.

Walter J. Uhlenbruch, *Australian Motor Vehicles and Parts* Committee For Economic Development Of Australia, 1986.

John Wright, *Heart of the Lion,*
Allen & Unwin, 1998.

CHAPTER 6

Henry Goes To War

About 110 kilometres south of Darwin on the Stuart Highway you will come to a small place called Adelaide River. Part way through the town take a left turn at the sign that says 'Adelaide River War Cemetery'. Drive about a kilometre up that road and turn in through the gates and you will feel a sense of awe.

For here, buried side by side, across a manicured brilliant green lawn shawled by the blazing purples and reds of poinsettias, flame trees and jacarandas, are the 10 who died in the Post Office during Darwin's first air raid on February 19, 1942: the postmaster – Hurtle Bald, his wife Alice and their daughter Iris; four telephonists – Emily Young, Freda Stasinowsky, Eileen Mullen and her sister Jean, and other Postmaster-General's Department employees – Archibald Halls, Arthur Wellington and Walter Rowlings. Their catafalque is a simple blonde brick wall, remembering the innocent.

The great journalist Douglas Lockwood, who was the Melbourne *Herald Sun*'s Darwin correspondent for years, wrote the only definitive books on the Darwin raids. The truth was totally censored by the Federal government at the time.

In *The Front Door*, Lockwood says 243 people were killed and more than 300 wounded in two raids on that first day, by 242 carrier-borne and land-based aircraft, under the command of the same Japanese high-rankers, Masuo Fuchida and Chuicho Nagumo, who had led the Pearl Harbor attack – and with more planes than hit Pearl Harbor.

They sank eight ships in Darwin's harbour, including the US destroyer *Peary*. Among those killed was Wing-Commander Archibald Tindal, after whom today's RAAF base near Katherine in the Northern Territory is named. The Darwin RAAF station commander, Wing-Commander Sturt Griffith, after the war became motoring editor of the *Sydney Morning Herald*.

Darwin was bombed 59 more times, up to 12 November

1943; few Australians aged less than 50 today would know that. Those raids were the nation's first taste of war at home, and they immediately accelerated the process of putting the country and its entire industrial structure on a full wartime footing. Until then the war had been a long way away, even though we had sent the Sixth Division, 2nd AIF to the Middle East and young RAAF pilots to Canada and the UK, and the citizenry had been feeling some pain.

At the end of 1939, four months after the war erupted, there were 600,302 passenger cars registered in Australia. At first there was no petrol rationing – after all, didn't Great Britain own 28 per cent of the world's tanker

AT FIRST THERE WAS NO PETI

Above: wartime Ford V8 trucks came in both two-wheel and four-wheel drive and two wheelbases, using the tough unstoppable side-valve flathead V8. Right: Ford also produced forward-control V8 trucks as artillery haulers and general purpose vehicles, like this wireless van, designed around an American 3 tonne chassis with Marmon–Herrington 4WD systems. GM–H built similar vehicles on Chevrolet basics; all were given the nickname 'blitz buggies'. Opposite, top: the Adelaide River War Cemetery in the Northern Territory, with its memorial to the Darwin Post Office staff killed in the first Japanese air raid. Opposite: based on the 1940 model, a standard military staff car and 15 cwt coupe utility in a Melbourne street parade. Page 50, top: Ford Eagle class submarine chaser. Below: ships were built in Geelong and launched straight into Corio Bay.

storage, and didn't Britannia rule the waves? Instead the Federal government decided to limit fuel usage by increasing prices, thus inventing a technique (along with taking over income tax powers from the States as a 'temporary wartime action') that would metamorphose into a useful revenue-raising Budget tool for generations.

About the only thing increasing the petrol price did was encourage hoarding. In her history of the first 25 years of the National Roads and Motorists Association (NRMA), *On The Road*, Rosemary Broomham says there were reports that some country people had stashed enough petrol to last three years, the most outrageous cache a hoard of

L RATIONING – DIDN'T BRITANNIA RULE THE WAVES?

8800 gallons (about 40,000 litres) in 44-gallon (200-litre) drums. Service station trading hours were limited voluntarily, new pump installations were banned and home delivery carriers of bread, meat, milk and ice were abused for increasing their prices accordingly.

But by September 1940 Britain didn't want to know about sending tankers on the long sea routes to Australia, and on October 1 Canberra set a ration for private car owners of four to 10 gallons (18 to 45 litres) a week according to horsepower, the matrix an average of 2000 miles (3220 km) travelled per year (today the Australian annual national average is around 16,000 km). The screams of protest from motoring associations like the NRMA forced this to be doubled to 4000 miles (6440 km); commercial users were allowed up to 15,000 miles (24,000 km).

Ford Australia didn't really need to be told that the new unpleasantness in Europe wouldn't sell too many vehicles in Australia. In 1940 it was still selling Canada-sourced and locally assembled sedans – including the new Mercury – and commercials, as well as Anglia/Prefect models from the UK using imported components like engines and transmissions, but local bodies.

The Canadian kits continued through 1941 and into 1942, but ended abruptly after December 7, 1941 and Pearl Harbor.

Ford's five Australian plants – Geelong, Homebush, Eagle Farm, Adelaide and Fremantle – were automatically swung over to war production, as were GM–H's and those of component suppliers such as Smiths Sons & Rees, A. G. Healing and Cable Makers (Aust) Pty Ltd.

The managing director of GM–H, Laurence Hartnett, was named director of ordnance production and later knighted for his work.

The range of weaponry, munitions and *matériel* produced by the two car makers was truly awesome. GM–H was manufacturing aircraft, torpedo and marine diesel engines, tank guns, howitzers, major airframe assemblies for six types of aircraft, refrigerators and coolrooms, 200 different types of vehicle bodies and eight types of small marine vessels.

Adelaide body builder T. J. Richards was turning out wings for Wirraway, Beaufort and Mosquito aircraft, James Hardie brake drum linings for Spitfires, and Duly &

Hansford bomb switches, bolts and nuts.

To Ford fell the heavy metal. It did, of course, produce a huge range of engines and military vehicles, but was more importantly given the task of building armoured cars (based on Ford V8 truck chassis), Bren gun carriers (what today we call APCs, armoured personnel carriers), marine mines, long-range aircraft fuel tanks, marine gearboxes, machine tools and wheels.

After two years the US Air Force asked Ford to expand its facilities to be able to recondition first the nine-cylinder Wright Cyclone aircraft engines and then the Pratt &

Whitney engines for the legendary B19 Flying Fortresses. A Ford plant in the outer Brisbane suburb of Rocklea was, at its peak, rebuilding eight engines a day with a workforce of 1100.

But it was more complex than bald history can explain. In *Beneath The Bonnet*, J. D. Beruldsen says building Gypsy Major aircraft engines demanded GM–H's engineers to make 41,500 mathematical conversions (before calculators, remember) from metric to imperial measurements so they could do drawings for the 720 components.

By early 1942 Ford managing director Hubert French decided things were getting serious. He ordered

Opposite, top: Fords were no stranger to war service, as here in action in 1914–1918. Photo courtesy the Australian War Memorial.
Above: to Ford came the heavy metal; the company's war effort produced a huge range of engines and military vehicles.

£100,000 worth of machine shop and plant modernisation and extension to boost production. Under strict Ford rules an investment of this size had first to be approved by Ford Canada. But the big Canadian, 'The General', waved that away, growling: 'The buildings and machinery are vital to Australia's war effort and there's no time for red tape. I'll deal with Canada when the war is over'. Canada wasn't told until 1946.

Ford Australia's biggest war effort, however, was in designing and building landing craft, barges, cargo ships, lighters, tenders, work boats, tugs, pontoons and floating docks. It became the largest shipbuilding plant in the country. The biggest were built on huge rigs outside the factory and then slid into Corio Bay, while landing craft were built in Lismore in northern NSW and dropped into the Richmond River to go to sea via the mouth at Ballina.

The Eagle Farm (Brisbane) plant produced the most maritime designs, moving the landing craft onto wooden bogeys and then onto transporters which hauled them almost a kilometre to the Brisbane River.

The company never ceased to amaze its American colleagues with the lateral thinking and quick work of its staff – an Australian characteristic very much alive today, a defining element of the local automotive industry, and an

'THERE'S NO TIME FOR RED TAPE – I'LL DEAL WITH FO

Left: shipbuilding at Geelong. They were powered by the ubiquitous V8, modified for marine use. Below: there was great public interest in the wartime output. Below left: Ford Australia was the only manufacturer of mines in the southern hemisphere. Centre left: Lockheed P38 Lightning fighter carrying Ford-built drop tanks.

D CANADA AFTER THE WAR'

inheritance of the very earliest days of convict settlement, when newcomers to a harsh continent had to learn to improvise, to think on their feet or die.

Within five weeks of the Geelong design staff's production of working drawings to US specification of a 44-foot (13.4-metre) landing craft to carry troops and vehicles, the first one, the ALC15 (ALC stood for Australian landing craft), was trialling in Corio Bay with 25

room and wheelhouse; it was built in Geelong and sailed to New Guinea and New Britain.

The first action Ford landing craft saw was late in 1942 at Buna, Gona and Sanananda on the northern coast of Papua New Guinea, in some of the most horrible fighting of the whole Pacific war, including Iwo Jima and Guadalcanal.

Here the famous 39th Battalion – the 'Ragged Bloody Heroes' – the 2/14th AIF and other elements, who had, along with other Australian units at Milne Bay become the first to stop the Japanese southern movement by fighting them all the way along the Kokoda Trail, pushed back the Japanese metre by bloody metre and drove them into the sea.

After the war Hubert French liked to tell the story of the long-range fuel tanks.

'It was August 1943 and the Allied campaign on the Huon Peninsula, New Guinea was in progress. A potential threat to the campaign was the Japanese air base at Wewak that lay outside the normal effective range of our fighter planes.

'Early in the month a Thunderbolt fighter landed in the field outside our Geelong plant. Our assignment was to design and build auxiliary petrol tanks to give extra range. I well remember how the designers worked around the clock until a pilot model tank had been produced and successfully tested.'

commandos and a 15-tonne tank aboard.

Then there was the ALC40 with a rated payload of 40 tonnes (although legend has it that one such, named Queer Alec, carried 98 tonnes for 1000 sea miles, including 300 miles of open sea, for 36 hours non-stop). The largest landing craft Ford built was the ALC120, a 65-foot (20-metre) monster, with a load rating of 120 tonnes, five Mercury V8 engines, eight berths, a galley, mess

The US Army Air Corps looked at the prototype and on the spot ordered 100 to be built in 10 days; there were no working drawings, no tooling, just that prototype. French said the plant worked 12-hour shifts, built the 100 tanks by hand and threw in 15 more for good measure. 'Some days later I received the following telegram: Thanks for delivering the goods, listen in to the news tonight.'

It was signed by General George C. Kenney,

Left: armoured car manufacture, Geelong. Opposite: towards the end of the war women comprised 40 per cent of Ford's workforce, trained to do arduous and technical production tasks. Many stayed on afterwards.

FORD'S BIGGEST EFFORT WAS IN DESIGNING AND BU

commander of air services in the South West Pacific area. The news was that the Port Moresby-based Thunderbolts had destroyed 200 Japanese planes on the ground at Wewak, as they sat there feeling safe outside Allied air range. Historian Norm Darwin records that Ford went on to produce 65,442 droppable wing tanks and belly tanks, not just for the P47 Thunderbolt but also for the P39 Airacobra, P40 Kittyhawk, P38 Lightning, Spitfire and Mosquito.

Lew Bandt, the father of the utility, was one who worked on the fuel tanks project. Another memory concerned heavy-duty truck wheels. Ford built thousands of V8-powered two-wheel and four-wheel drive trucks, including the famous forward-control model commonly called 'Blitz'. Initially the wheels were imported from

Below: Ford-powered and built landing barges in action. Opposite below: engine reconditioning at Rocklea, Qld. Right: life was still relatively normal in 1940, although this was the last new passenger model produced pre-war.

Style Book of the *1940* **Ford Cars**

DING LANDING CRAFT

Britain, but when this stopped Slim Westman found a blacksmith and had him make some dies, so Ford could start stamping out its own. Somehow after the war Ford Canada got to hear about this and cabled Westman: 'We doubt whether it could be done, and even if it could, it would be no good'. Westman didn't bother telling them Ford Australia had stamped out many thousands right through the war.

By 1944 there were 5275 men and women working in the Ford plants, almost 4000 more than before the war. The main problems were lack of machine tools and other precision equipment, because none could be imported, and the shortage of skilled labour, even though some categories were classified as essential to the war effort and thus not conscripted.

So Ford, like many other industries, threw out the call to women. Near the end of the war 40 per cent of Ford Australia's workforce was female, women with no previous factory skills who had learned to weld, use lathes, the lot (they were paid only two-thirds of the male rate, to begin with).

Jessie Pitman was 92 when she was interviewed by Ford archivist Adrian Ryan in 1995. As a 40-year-old widow she was the first woman to be employed in Ford's industrial relations office, in 1941. She remembered that initially women could work only from 8 am to 4 pm, but as pressure grew they were moved onto night shifts.

Slim Westman told her the women would all be laid off after the war, but many stayed on – Jessie until she reached pension age. She said Westman had a tough

*Opposite: Marmon–Herrington trucks awaiting delivery. Below: vessels of many kinds were produced. The biggest craft was a 20-metre mammoth with five Mercury V8 engines.
Right: plenty of room for three across the rear seat then, as now, in the mainstream Fords.*

exterior but was very soft-hearted.

'He'd come out there in his pyjamas sometimes on the night shift, you know.'

The Canadian Westman developed a passion for Australian football. 'He used to play football out on the green opposite Ford's ... the air raid shelters were over there', she recalled. His superiors eventually forbade him to join in but he would stand at the window of her office watching the others play and took a great interest in the Geelong club. (This was an era long before corporate sponsorship but now it is almost impossible to imagine the Geelong team colours – blue and white – without the matching Ford oval in close proximity; Ford Australia's long running sponsorship of the Geelong Cats is a fine metaphor for the bond between the company and the city.)

In 1941 French hatched a bold plan for Ford to manufacture its own trucks instead of using the imported Canadian chassis and V8 engines. In *A History of the Ford Motor Company in Australia*, Geoff Easdown says his plan involved spending more than £3 million to set it up, including plant and machine tools from the US. But Australia's foreign exchange reserves in those days were held in the Bank of London's sterling pool, and Britain would not release the necessary US dollars.

French had planned at least two wheelbases, four-wheel drive, and the use of the International Harvester foundry to produce engine blocks and other castings for the V8, with remaining components to be sourced from local

parts makers. French wrote: 'We propose the army trucks produced under this arrangement shall be sold to the government at a price that is calculated upon the basis of cost, plus 4 per cent'.

His only condition was that Ford be given an option to buy any or all of the plant and equipment within six months of the war ending. There can be no doubt that what French had in mind was to put Ford into the starting blocks for the race to supply pent-up demand for new cars and trucks the moment the war ended. Ford, not GM–H, would have become Australia's first car maker.

But the Federal Government did not respond to his proposal, commissioning a Tariff Board inquiry instead, which shelved any decision on local car manufacture until after the war. As we shall see, French would be there even then, with a counterproposal to that from GM–H.

In late 1941 – astonishingly, as the war in Europe was little more than two years old and Japan had not yet bombed Pearl Harbor – Canberra was talking informally to manufacturing industry about the post-war use of

factories, skills and employment to expand secondary production, including motor vehicles. On June 9, 1942, the Tariff Board formally advised Ford Australia, GM–H and other assemblers that it would be inquiring into the use of labour and plant for the full local manufacture of a car. The following December board members inspected Ford's Geelong site to assess its potential.

Bibliography

J. D. Beruldsen, *Beneath The Bonnet,*
Longman Cheshire, 1989.
Rosemary Broomham, *On The Road,*
Allen & Unwin, 1996.
Norm Darwin, *The History of Ford In Australia,*
Eddie Ford Publications, 1986.
Geoff Easdown, *A History of the Ford
Motor Company in Australia,* Golden Press, 1987.
Geelong Advertiser, 70th anniversary issue, 1995.
Douglas Lockwood, *The Front Door, Darwin 1869–1969,*
Rigby Ltd, 1968.
Bill Tuckey, editor, *Australian Motoring Year No. 3,*
BFT Publishing Group, 1985.

CHAPTER 7

Of Bathtubs And **V8 Engines**

Today, as you blip the remote control for the garage door and insert the transponder-controlled rolling code key into the ignition switch of your engine in a car with perhaps 20 different microprocessors on board, it is extraordinarily difficult to imagine what using a motor vehicle must have been like in the drear dark days of WW2 and its aftermath.

Not only was petrol severely rationed (and rationing did not disappear until February 1950), not only were thousands of cars and trucks summarily snatched by the government for military service, with little or no compensation, but those who could drive were monstered by a bureaucracy with powers inconceivable today.

It was all, however, rendered logical by wartime events. Darwin was bombed with more ferocity than Pearl Harbour. And in 1943 three Japanese midget submarines entered Sydney Harbour, in response to which silvertails from luxury waterside homes snatched up children and possessions and fled inland to the Blue Mountains. Most

Australians were convinced the Japanese were going to invade.

Some people put their cars up on blocks for however long the duration might be, and some went back to the horse and cart. The most desperate resorted to the gas producer. Burning hardwood chips into glowing charcoal produced a gas mixture of carbon monoxide and nitrogen, on which the engine could run – just. It was stored in a balloon on the roof or a tank on the rear bumper and was a cheap solution for taxis and commercial carriers.

In *Wheels Across Australia* historian Pedr Davis says the average car could be driven for 80 kilometres (50 miles) on a 15 cent bag of charcoal, or about one-sixth the cost of petrol, then six cents a litre. Another method was to burn charcoal in a closed bin on a rack on the back of the car; the problem was the filthy black clinker which had to be raked out every day or so. In *On The Road* Rosemary Broomham says there were 13,375 vehicles

OF BATHTUBS AND **V8 ENGINES**

Left: in 1949 cars from any source other than Britain were in short supply, because of foreign exchange restrictions. The Ford Prefect was, at £724, Australia's lowest priced 10 horsepower four-door sedan, claiming fuel consumption of 'up to 40 miles per gallon' – about 7 litres/100 kilometres in today's terms. Below: Holden's 48/215 wasn't the only new car Prime Minister Ben Chifley was photographed with. This is the launch of the 1946 Ford V8, Ford's (and Australia's) first all-new post-war car. It was donated to the Limbless Soldiers' Association of Victoria. Opposite: typical advertising of the time – petrol was still rationed.

IN SYDNEY AND MELBOURNE EVERY SECOND STREET

registered in 1942 as having gas producers.

As the Japanese swarmed over much of Papua New Guinea there was more than a whiff of panic. But it was never Japan's intention to invade Australia, despite the air and submarine raids. In *The Reluctant Admiral*, a superb biography of Japan's highest-ranking wartime naval officer, Admiral Yamamoto, author Hiroyuki Agawa says that in February 1942 the Imperial Navy General Staff's plan was to stop the US deploying its air forces in Australia and isolate it, so it would drop out of the war.

Strongly opposed to invasion, Yamamoto died when his

Most consumables were rationed, including clothing (schoolchildren were actually measured so those classed as 'oversized' would qualify for extra clothing coupons). Men's trousers lost their cuffs to conserve material – there was even a 'Victory Suit', comprising a two-button single-breasted jacket, cuffless trousers, four pockets and no sleeve buttons. School uniforms were banned. Rubber disappeared because of the occupation of (then) Malaya. Bottled beer was virtually unobtainable and black marketing and 'sly grogging' were rampant. In Melbourne, firewood was rationed. Cosmetics

IGHT WAS TURNED OUT

plane was ambushed and shot down by American P38 fighters off Bougainville on April 18, 1943. Japan's high command always intended only to limit the ability of America to establish Australian bases. This strategy was ruined by two naval battles: Coral Sea and Midway.

But in Australia street and railway signs were removed, bomb shelters built in backyards, sandbags stacked against important city buildings, shops and theatres forced to close early and in Sydney and Melbourne every second street light was turned out – which the media dubbed a 'brownout'. In blackouts all vehicle lights were limited to the size of a halfpenny (about 50 mm) by applying black paint inside and outside the reflectors and glass, while bumper bars had to be painted matt white.

A national speed limit of 40 mph (64 km/h) was legislated from February 1, 1943, ostensibly to conserve fuel, tyres and tubes, spare parts and manpower. On April 21 it came down to 30 mph (48 km/h) and on weekends police and volunteers would stop cars to check none was being used for pleasure.

He "Amazing how little these V-8 Utilities cost to run when you think how hard they work."

She "They're as smart as a car and just as comfortable – heaps of room for three grown-ups too."

manufacture was banned. On September 3, 1942 Prime Minister John Curtin appealed via a national radio broadcast to all Australians to live as frugally as they could and to invest in the coming £100 million Austerity Loan.

There would come an end to all this self-sacrifice – which, of course, was not nearly as austere as it was in Britain, the Mother Country. Government was aware of two

things: wartime production was building up enormous manufacturing capacity; and when the war ended there would be tremendous unfulfilled demand for motor vehicles and, because Australia didn't make its own cars (as distinct from assembling them), precious foreign exchange reserves would be drained to pay for imports.

On May 17, 1939 Prime Minister Robert Menzies, reflecting a Federal Government unhappy at the Tariff Board's wimpish 1938 report on local vehicle manufacture (see Chapter Five) said his government had 'definitely decided that motor vehicle engines and chassis are to be manufactured in Australia and that there should be no undue delay in establishing the industry'.

His justification included defence preparedness, conservation of overseas funds, immigration, employment and the use of Australian raw materials. Importantly, the statement said: 'The Commonwealth Government is not able to grant a manufacturing monopoly to any single company', and further: 'The Commonwealth Government desires that any company formed to undertake manufacture should be Australian in character and policy'.

The art of the political back-flip is not a modern invention; astonishingly, not seven months later, on December 8, 1939 Federal Parliament passed the Motor Vehicle Engine Bounty Bill, which in effect gave Australian Consolidated Industries (ACI) exclusive rights to produce motor vehicle engines and chassis in Australia – although it was a glass-making company, with no

FORD

THE NEWEST CAR IN THE WORLD

Opposite: stylist Raymond Loewy's dramatic 1947 Studebaker was the first modern 'three-box' sedan design and was labelled the 'coming-or-going' car – some people seriously suggested it was dangerous because you couldn't tell which end was which. Ford's answer, pictured here, was the 1949 Single Spinner, advertised as having space for 'six big passengers' and as 'a complete break with the past'. It also replaced the ancient transverse springs with independent front suspension. Left: Ford's Geelong plants 1 and 2 in the mid 1950s. In 1946 the company announced an investment of £750,000 to expand the Geelong plant and triple output at Homebush (Sydney) and Eagle Farm (Brisbane). Below: dubbed the 'jail bar' truck for its distinctive grille, this was the 1946 three-quarter tonne utility.

vehicle-building experience. As well, more than 65 per cent of its capital was owned by British subjects living in Australia – and it would benefit from a bounty of £30 on each of 20,000 engines to be produced. This was supplemented by the Motor Vehicle Agreement Act 1940, which reinforced the monopoly.

ACI's managing director, W. J. ('Knockout') Smith, had told the government the company had a licensing agreement with the Willys car company in the US under which Willys would design the car and ACI build it in Sydney. But parliament smelled a rat when the story broke that Smith had bought a racehorse for then Minister for Trade and Customs, John Lawson.

Lawson was able to show that he had only leased the horse from Smith, but he then resigned to become ACI's legal adviser. The Willys deal was off. The government wasn't at all miffed; it had up its sleeve a proposal from the Melbourne-based Pengana Motor Industries Pty Ltd, a plan to raise £2 million to buy the tooling and equipment of the Hupmobile company, which had gone belly-up in the US, and produce a car to sell for £200.

But GM–H was ahead of the game. In 1940 its Woodville (Adelaide) plant had actually started working on Project 2000, a car based on a Chevrolet chassis and Willys engine. This would become the basis for GM–H's proposal.

Nothing happened until November 6, 1942, when the industry body, the Chamber of Automotive Industries, submitted a paper to the Tariff Board outlining the state of readiness among vehicle assemblers and component suppliers for full scale post-war manufacturing. 'If local manufacture should eventuate then no form of monopolistic control, import quotas or prohibitive tariff barrier should be introduced', the report said. It slammed the ACI concept, claiming it would 'disrupt the entire industry'.

This was one hell of a distance from what both GM–H and Ford would be asking for several years down the road. In fact, Ford Australia managing director French wrote to the Tariff Board on December 15, 1942 to the effect that giving just one manufacturer the go-ahead would cost jobs in rival companies, that his concept of building trucks in Australia was still on offer, and that there was room for three vehicle makers.

Nobody had to remind the Federal Government that

... THE FAMOUS V8 E

swift, sturdy... *and* more fun to drive

Opposite: in 1939 there were 820,296 cars and commercial vehicles registered in Australia. There were just 2123 new registrations in 1946 but in 1949 (the arrival year of the Single Spinner), there were 66,471 new cars registered and 36,678 commercial vehicles – the total fleet had exploded to just over 1.1 million.

French and Ford controlled Geelong, which was within the electorate of John Dedman, the Minister for War Organisation and Industry and a main player in the debate about a future Australian car. In *A History of the Ford Motor Company in Australia*, Geoff Easdown says French spent 135 minutes in Dedman's office on December 31, 1943 and Dedman told him there had been serious dispute within Cabinet about who would head a new portfolio of post-war reconstruction.

Dedman said he was setting up a committee under John (later Sir John) Jensen, chairman of the Secondary Industries Commission, to look at the future of local vehicle manufacture. What French didn't know was that 11 days earlier, on December 20, Laurence Hartnett had secretly directed a small group of senior GM–H engineers to start a detailed study on a unique, locally designed car for Australia with a high percentage of local content including BHP steel, and analysing existing component suppliers and estimated post-war taxes, registration and petrol prices. It would be based on Project 2000, now codenamed Project 120. Here began a bizarre poker game in which the future Australian car was decided by accidents of timing – just days, in some cases.

Ford was even further behind the eight ball than it

realised. Minister Dedman had told French that housing
had to be first priority in the government's post-war
reconstruction plans. But Ford had six years earlier
pledged that any employee who enlisted to fight was
guaranteed a job on return. Knowing this, and with little
sign of any government enthusiasm for vehicle
manufacturing, in June 1944 the Geelong plant director of
manufacturing, Slim Westman, put to Ford Canada a
proposal that it should invest about $150,000 (Canadian)
on dies for Geelong's existing Baldwin stamping presses
to allow mass post-war production of bathtubs, kitchen
sinks, wash basins and similar household essentials. On

FORD V·8
PASSENGER CARS

GINE POWERING A SUBSTANTIAL, ROBUST VEHICLE ...

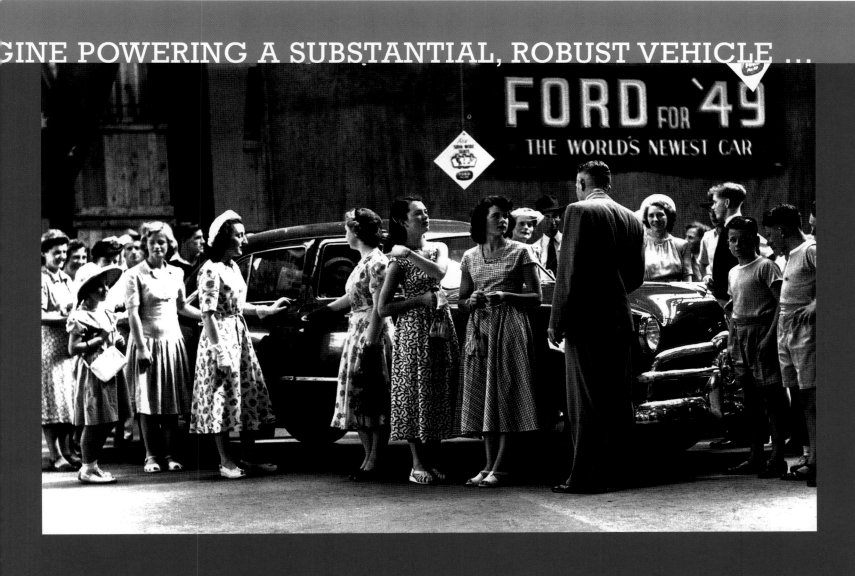

July 14 Canada gave him the thumbs down.

Then, out of the blue, on October 5, 1944 the Controller-General of the Department of Trade and Customs wrote a letter to the managing directors of all those companies who before the war had been assembling vehicles. They included, of course, GM–H and Ford, Britisher Nuffield (Austin and Morris), CDD (Chrysler, Plymouth, Dodge, De Soto) and International Harvester.

The carrot within was a hint that there could be tariff barriers to protect any maker who promised high local materials and parts content. The stick was in this clause: 'If satisfactory proposals are not received as a result of the invitations to interested parties, the government should set up a corporation to manufacture a complete car'. The government would repeal both the engine bounty and motor vehicle agreements Acts to get rid of the ACI monopoly. The bounty ceiling had been set at £600,000 a year – £30 each for 20,000 units of 15 horsepower or more and 90 per cent local content.

Geoff Easdown claims that eight days before the August 31 meeting at which Cabinet approved the October 5 letter, Dedman had secretly rung French and tipped him off that it was all going to happen. And he made it clear that if the motor industry wasn't interested, the government would set up a company with the Australian people holding all the shares and there would be tariff barriers, favourable freight rates and other hurdles put in the way of any commercial rival. Dedman told French he had to act fast.

By October 7 French and two other senior Ford executives had taken ship for Canada to start a feasibility study that would take three months, with senior Ford US people also involved.

But again, timing intervened. On October 10, with French three days at sea, the Secondary Industries Commission's Jensen wrote to the same interested parties outlining the car package the government envisaged. It would be sized between the big pre-war American car and the smaller British models. He broadly detailed specifications, including a six-cylinder engine, and a basic price aimed at being 'within the reach of the ordinary Australian'.

Before the war cars had been a luxury; Jensen knew that Australians had saved extremely well during the war, that bank deposits were high and that wages would go up because of consumer product demand. 'A smaller car with a light petrol consumption and inexpensive operating costs is the type I think many of our people will require', he wrote.

The lingering question here is did anybody in Ford Geelong telegram French in Canada with this information? Given 20:20 hindsight, it seems that Ford Canada and Dearborn were obsessed with running things the way they had before the war: V8 engines, assembling from completely knocked-down components, taking advantage of British Empire tariffs. GM–H's Hartnett had met the chairman and father of GM, Alfred P. Sloan, and the full Executive Committee in Detroit in November 1944, and on January 5, 1945, it delivered to the Australian Government its proposal for what became the Holden 48/215.

French's own correspondence files show that by early March, several weeks before it lodged its counter-proposal, Ford Australia had all the detail of the GM–H plan. Did it come from Dedman, one might ask? Either way, French knew GM–H's submission to the Secondary Industries Commission asked for no subsidies, no increase in protective tariffs apart from duty-free import of about 10 per cent of components that could not be sourced locally, and that it would use existing plant facilities. On March 23, six days before Ford's proposal was filed, a letter over French's signature went to all Ford's dealers detailing the GM–H proposal's main points.

Ford's counterproposal, comprising 13 pages plus appendices, was handed to Jensen on March 29. Where GM–H had gone in head-on, asking for Commonwealth Bank help for an 'Australia first' project, Ford paused for breath. Studies were continuing … cost estimates still going on … it asked for an independent tribunal to review the possible impact of international trade agreements and tariff policies.

At this distance it appears to be the single major mistake Hubert French made during his illustrious career. But Ford president Edsel Ford had died tragically, early in 1943, the company was losing money and some of its sense of direction, due partly to Henry Ford's unwillingness to relinquish control.

Demonstrating a misreading that was repeated later by others in automotive history, Dearborn and French had failed to understand what the politicians meant by a smaller, lighter, more fuel-efficient car than the pre-war models. With war a burdening memory, the Ford advocates mounted instead their strong (but unsuccessful) case for the famous V8 engine powering a substantial, robust vehicle. The submission said: 'One of the outstanding lessons of this war is the vital importance of power in motor-driven vehicles and implements. Further, the light type of vehicle and engine certainly does not give the primary producer or commercial vehicle user the power required for other than light work. After careful analysis we have based our proposals on the production of the Ford V-type eight-cylinder engine with appropriate chassis'.

This analysis exposed Ford's prime weakness, the lack of a viable six-cylinder engine around which to create a new car. In the 1930s it had jumped from four-cylinder engines to V8s, with no sixes in between, and its British cars were all four-cylinder. (Paradoxically, Australia in the 1970s would demonstrate that what the country really wanted was a big, tough car with either a six or a V8, but it wanted the choice.)

Ford set 25,000 – about one-third of the potential 1946–47 new car market – as its target. It asked for duty-free admission of components and increased protection

by way of tariffs and import quotas on competition. Ford Australia would not remit profit back to Ford Canada as imported parts were replaced by local components. One interesting factor – given Ford's traditional (dating from Henry) antipathy towards any external shareholding – was that Ford Canada would offer the public 40–49 per cent of the shares in a new manufacturing company by way of listing on the Sydney Stock Exchange.

The submission put the total cost of the project – over and above the existing investment – at £3,733,552, specified that most machinery, tools and equipment would be locally sourced, that overseas executives would be sparingly used, but said it would take five years to reach full manufacturing flow. A significant omission was that it did not suggest a probable retail price. One can only wonder why not, considering the detail supplied on specification and models.

There would be two cars, one on a wheelbase of 114 inches (2896 mm) and one on 118 inches (2997 mm) – today's Falcon is on 2793 mm and long wheelbase Fairlane on 2922 mm – with matching station wagon and utility versions on both wheelbases plus a van on 114 inches only. Engines would be based on the 100

Opposite: the all-new British Ford Consul reached Australian showrooms in June 1951, with a 1.5 litre overhead-valve engine and styling Ford Australia's advertising described as 'low-wide … years ahead of the industry'. It also modestly described a 'revolutionary system of suspension' delivering 'miracle ride'. Unhappily, the car was dreadfully unreliable. Below: the styling of Ford's proposed post-war car for Australian manufacture wasn't far removed from this 1940 model, except it was a four-door. Some observers have said that Ford US, upset by heir Edsel's tragic early death and the founder's increasing senility, didn't pay enough attention to its bid for the Australian government's go-ahead.

FORD HAD SUBMITTED A TIME FRAME OF FIVE YEARS

horsepower (75 kW) flathead V8 and the styling sketches illustrated something very like the 1939–40 cars.

In the Ford archives in the Ford Discovery Centre in Geelong is a file copy of the formal proposal with pencilled comments (apparently by a high government official) on various clauses. Among those marked as approved were exemption from all import duties and taxes on machinery and equipment imported for the project, plus precious overseas exchange to fund such purchases, duty-free admission of chassis component imports after Ford had reached 'substantially complete manufacture of a chassis', and reservation for Ford of one-third of the 25,000 vehicles bought annually by Federal government departments, plus bounty of £15 per car.

The pencilled notes rejected demands for taxation writeback on all buildings used, increased duty on all rival imports and favourable sales tax for locally made vehicles.

Clause six required the government to discuss with Ford some financial help in raising capital locally. Against this was pencilled 'Cannot recommend'. This seems extraordinary in that GM–H got the nod for the Holden on the basis of a £2.5 million loan from the Commonwealth Bank and a £500,000 loan from the Bank of Adelaide – admittedly guaranteed by GM in Detroit. There was no provision for Australian shareholding; in fact by 1952 GM had bought all remaining equity from the former Holden company.

In 1948, after four years, GM–H produced just one model, a sedan, where Ford had submitted a time-frame

of five years to build a far wider range. Perhaps Hartnett's friends at court were more powerful than those of Hubert French. Whatever the truth, Ford had lost the battle but, ultimately, not the war.

Bibliography

Hiroyuki Agawa, *The Reluctant Admiral,*
Kodansha International, 1979.
J. D. Beruldsen, *Beneath the Bonnet*
Longman Cheshire, 1989.
Rosemary Broomham, *On the Road,*
Allen & Unwin, 1996.
Pedr Davis, *Wheels Across Australia,*
Marque Publishing Company, 1987.
Geoff Easdown, *A History of the Ford Motor Company in Australia,*
Golden Press, 1987.
Michael McKernan, *All In – Australia during the Second World War,*
Thomas Nelson, 1983.
Bill Tuckey, editor, *Australian Motoring Year No.3,*
BFT Publishing Group, 1985.

Left: the Anglia was promoted for its 'security and comfort' for younger passengers. New 1954 Geelong-built Prefects and Anglias went to the three-box styling of the Consul. Opposite: crystal ball gazing, late '40s style.

O BUILD A FAR WIDER RANGE

CHAPTER 8

From Paddock To **Giant Plant**

Edsel Ford was only 49 when he died of cancer on May 26, 1943. His father Henry was re-elected president on June 1, but senior executives, alarmed at the old man's increasing eccentricity, organised for Edsel's son Henry II to be named vice-president on December 15 and executive vice-president 38 days later.

Henry Ford II, it has been claimed by some historians, blamed his grandfather's domineering nature for Edsel's early death and set out to rid the company of the 'yes men' and 'old faithfuls' who had surrounded the founder. In fact he would turn out to be as tough as his grandfather.

He became president on September 21, 1945, almost as a symbol of the end of the war and of an era. He took over a company that was losing several million dollars a month and badly in need of the total reorganisation he would bring to it.

On April 7, 1947, aged 83, Henry Ford – a giant of history despite his flaws – died at Fair Lane, his home in Dearborn, Detroit, Michigan. In late 1999 American *Fortune* magazine worthily embedded Henry Ford's footprints in the sands of time by naming him its 'Man of the Century'.

The Australian Prime Minister, John Curtin, ill and frayed by the enormous pressure of leading a country at war, died in 1945 and was succeeded by the pipe-smoking former Bathurst locomotive driver Ben Chifley, who had been named by Curtin as Minister for Post-war Reconstruction. John Dedman was now behind that desk, and on September 12, 1945, Ford Australia managing director Hubert French flew to Canberra to talk to Dedman and Chifley.

The company had expanded enormously through its wartime production and was faced with the problem of feeding the giant with both imported and assembled vehicles to meet the demand that was sure to explode. In 1945 there were about 854,000 vehicles on register, or one for every 8.7 people; at the end of 1956 this had

'WE MUST SUPPLY AUSTRALIAN

Above: the 1959–61 Ford Zephyr Mark 2. Launched in 1956, the Mark 2 underwent a major facelift in 1959, and was produced in utility and wagon versions out of Geelong, as well as a luxury Zodiac model. Right: the 1950 Single Spinner differed little from the 1949. But it was still much dearer than the Holden, even though local content was high, at 80 per cent. Opposite: to many Ford enthusiasts the 1958 Star Model Customline was the handsomest of the line. It featured a big V8 emblem as the heart of its grille. Page 76, top: overhead-valve V8 engine line, Broadmeadows. Below: Sir Henry Bolte, second from left, and Charles Smith, second from right, discussing plans for the new plant at Broadmeadows in 1958.

Famous "Mid-ship" ride is preserved in Ford for '50. The going's always smooth in Ford's low centre section. "Hydra-coil" front springs, "Para-flex" rear springs, double acting Hydraulic shock-absorbers and new torsional stabiliser smooth out the roughest roads.

The Ford V-8 for 1950

grown to 2,344,998, or one vehicle per 4.1 persons.

Ford had told French that from August to December that year the startup of production in Canada and the US would see about 200,000 new cars turned out, and if Australia wanted an allocation, it had better be quick. As French walked into Chifley's office his aim was to get the government to release Ford Australia from foreign exchange controls so it could buy the cars from its parent with Canadian dollars.

His notes of the meeting say, in part: 'I stated that it was urgently necessary that we should commit ourselves for

the Canadian company's November–December 1945 production and for at least the first quarter of 1946. I very strongly stressed that if this could not be done nothing could prevent our facing a very serious reduction in staff. I also pointed out that we have more than 900 men returning to our service from the armed forces, and that their re-employment was a matter of deep concern'. Chifley refused.

The unions were just starting to become active within Ford Australia. One W. H. ('Tunner') Kenworthy – a former boxer and 24 years a Geelong City councillor with two stints as Mayor, who started with Ford in the mid-1930s and had 21 years on the Ford production line before an 11-year role as personnel officer in the industrial relations department – headed the Vehicle Builders' Union.

In a 1988 interview he recalled some of the problems of the late 1940s and early 1950s – not the least the difficulty of dialogue with the wave of post-war immigrants, refugees from Europe, brought here by a visionary program established by the Labor government's Immigration Minister, Arthur Calwell, that was the basis for Australia's extraordinary multicultural mix today.

'A lot of them in the plant turned out to be general foremen, superintendents ... good men', he said. 'When I started here Ford was just starting to build the V8. Everything was done by hand ... there was no holiday pay on the hourly rate.'

Kenworthy said the role of industrial relations and the unions began to be recognised in the very early 1950s. 'It seemed to bring a bit of air into the plant ... the conditions and social activities such as the children's Christmas treat ... that was started by the Vehicle Builders' Union in the 1940s. It got too big for us to hold in halls so I came to the

WITH THEIR TRUCKS, CARS AND TRACTORS': FRENCH

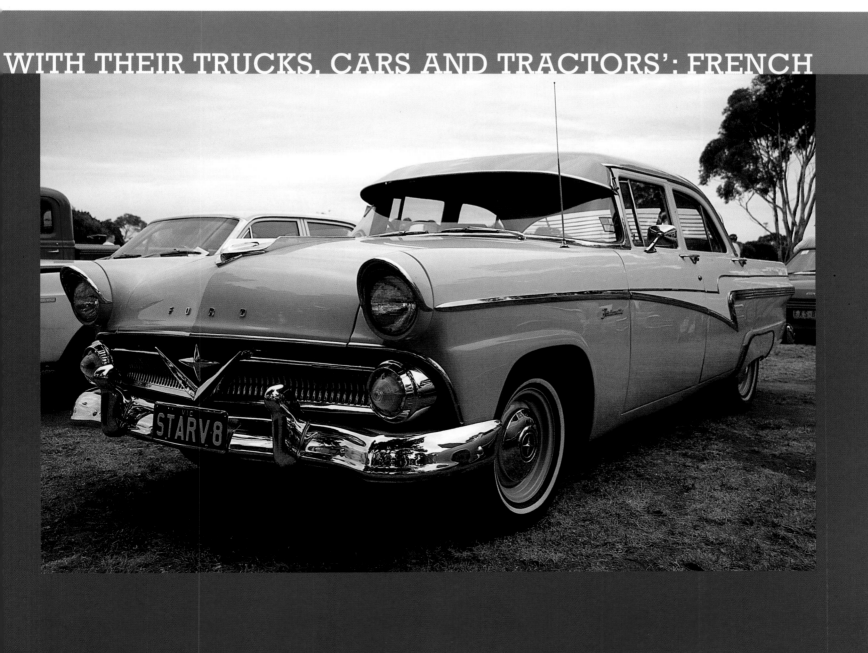

Above: in June 1950 Hubert C. French retired after 25 years. He was succeeded by the balding, dark-eyed Englishman Charles A. Smith, who immediately gained approval for the huge investment needed to install an assembly line to enable local production of the side-valve V8. Right: Ford's 1951 20-model truck range got a new grille and improved (locally built) cab to boost an already considerable reputation for toughness.

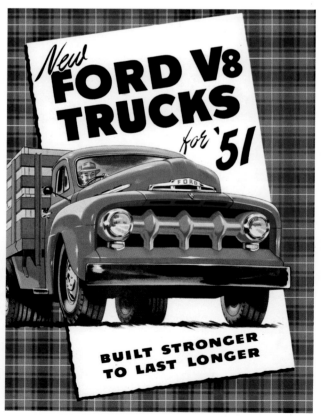

company and asked for its support and the company said yes and went 50:50, pound for pound.

'It got that big we started holding it in the factory, and it's still put on there. We had family days when you could bring your wife and kiddies out, such as the 25th and the 50th anniversaries.'

Kenworthy made a point of personally instructing new migrants in safety procedures and then taking them down to meet the foreman on their job, introducing them on first-name terms and having them shake hands.

Jessie Pitman, the first woman employed in the industrial relations department, recalled some of the migrant workers: 'I remember one fellow who came in. He wrote beautifully, I was standing at the counter watching them, and when he wrote "Polish" I said, Oh, you're Polish, and he said, I can speak seven languages. Here was I, giving out the jobs … I said I knew two – the good and the bad.

'He was a doctor. It was Friday and they'd finished the employment for the week. He said, I badly need a job – I'll take anything at all. I told him there was only one job, as a floor sweeper. He said, Well, that will do nicely.

'It used to break my heart to see him; he would touch his hat, like that, when I'd go past. I was always on to them in the office to get him a vacancy down in the first aid department.' One day it happened and she told him to report on the Monday morning ready to go to work. 'There he was in his doctor's coat and he was so happy. He worked there until he died.'

Union boss Kenworthy had nothing but praise for Ford's attitude to employees. 'If a man wasn't up to standard they'd fall over backwards to help him', he recalled. However, at war's end a lot of women had to be laid off, except in the trim department on the sewing machines. 'Women wanted the jobs and I never had any trouble with them. Their heart and soul was in it. There was a harmony in the place and it continues.'

When he left Ford, Kenworthy started an organisation for retired employees. 'We got wonderful support from the company; we had a big Christmas luncheon on December 13, over 250 attended. There's men in their late 80s in the Town Hall meetings every two months. You never heard one of those men condemn Ford ... the feeling is still that the backbone of Geelong is the Ford Motor Company.'

In the 1960s Ford Geelong allowed its line workers to stay on three years after the company's statutory retiring age of 65. It introduced a life insurance plan with a premium of one shilling and sixpence a week and a payout of £1000.

'I used to say to them, Gawd strike me, it's only one glass of beer a week. We had a battle with it but it turned out to be the greatest thing that happened', said Kenworthy. He remembered one man who wouldn't sign up until he confessed privately to Kenworthy that it was because he couldn't write.

Thames Express Bus — smooth, roomy comfort for eight people — *and an all-purpose usefulness with big and easily accessible load space.*

With a smartness of appearance that matches its many-purpose usefulness, this Express Bus is built on the same 84" wheelbase as the 15 cwt. Van. The load area is immense, from floor to roof, from the front seats right to full-width rear double doors that give instant access. And should you need extra passenger facilities one trip, extra load facilities the next, it's a matter of seconds to install or remove the back seats. Side doors are wide for easy entry and the second kerb-side door has an automatic folding step. Big, slide-opening windows give landscape vision for eight people. Added to the extra ease of forward control is a brilliant, thrifty performance. The 16.9 h.p. O.H.V. 4-cylinder "oversquare" engine has big, "easy" power development and consistent fuel economy.

Above: some vans and utilities were assembled from Canadian-sourced kits, but the big range of British Thames light commercials through the 1950s and into the 1960s included this eight-seater bus that could be seen as a forerunner of today's 'people-movers'. Left: Ford Australia was the leader in employee relations in the industry. It employed thousands of migrants; between 1947 and 1966 Melbourne's population grew faster than Sydney's, mainly through immigration. The Austra-Ford Gazette profiled employees and featured cartoons, cooking and product news.

'WE HAD TO MANUFACTURE A CAR HERE IF WE WER

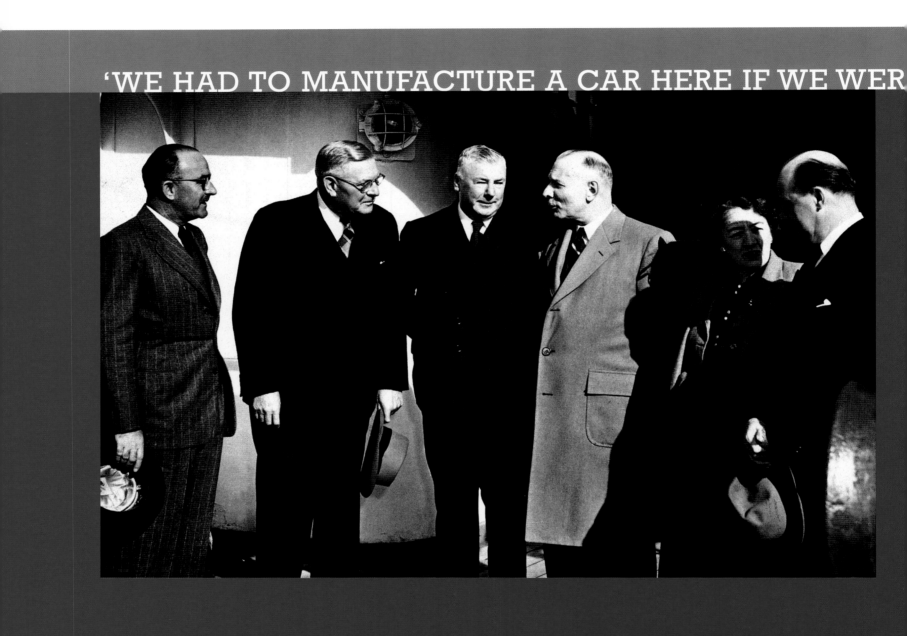

Kenworthy filled out the details for him and helped him sign his name. Three weeks later the man was killed backing a utility out of his driveway, on his way to buy some paint. Kenworthy had to break the news to the widow, but came back three weeks later with a £1000 cheque.

It was mid-1946 before the company could return to normal production, assembling Ford and Mercury V8

sedans and the Aussie ute, a few heavy Canadian trucks and Fordson tractor kits from the UK. Late in the year it would resume assembly of the British Prefect and Anglia sedans and soft-tops.

Chifley had told French the war debt had to be paid, the British Government would not release the Australian sterling reserves it was holding and even importing vehicles from the UK would put a strain on the sterling

'O COMPETE WITH THE HOLDEN': SMITH

balance in London within possibly 12 months. Chifley agreed that imports of commercial vehicles were essential but drew the line at passenger cars. So Ford started recovering thousands of its military vehicles from the services, reconditioning them and converting them to civilian use for sale. Even used cars were being bought for many pounds more than their original pre-war, new car prices.

On July 1, 1946 at a Geelong plant ceremony (attended by Chifley and Dedman) to celebrate Ford Australia's 21st anniversary, Hubert French announced an investment of £750,000 in facilities in Geelong, Homebush and Eagle Farm to build components it was then importing: steel wheels, axles, brake components, clutches, radiators, exhaust systems, fuel tanks and more, adding:

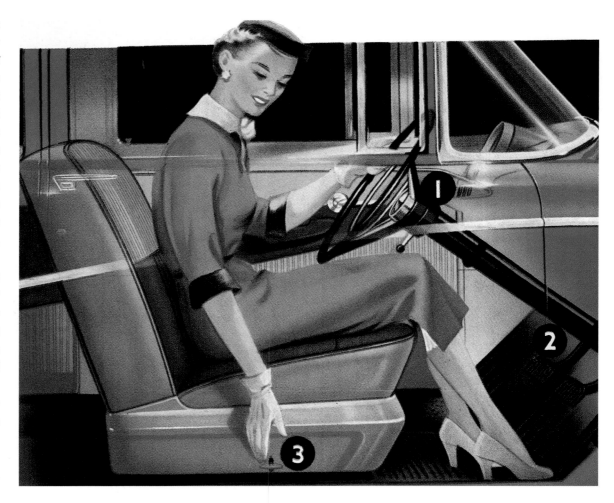

'It is the opinion of our directorate that this will merely form the first step in real chassis and engine manufacture. We are a pretty big team, but we have a big job of work to do. We must supply fellow Australians with their trucks, cars and tractors. They are waiting for us and we mustn't let them down – that is the point I would like to make to you.

'We work for the people of Australia, they are our friends, our neighbours and our fellow citizens ... the men outback and all the others who need and use motor transportation. If we keep them in our thoughts as we work we will have the right vision of the future.'

Rivals had visions too. They were based on the reintroduction of a demon called import licensing. Designed to save on hard currency (notably the US greenback), the government legislated to allow the import of three CKD vehicles to the value of two fully built units.

In 1936 a firm called CDD, distributor of Chrysler and Dodge vehicles, had bought out Adelaide bodybuilder T. J. Richards and Sons in an almost carbon copy of the GM takeover of Holden's Motor Body Builders. On June 6, 1951, Chrysler Corporation bought 85 per cent of CDD's capital and set up Chrysler Australia Limited to assemble US models and the French

Opposite: second from right, Mrs Smith and incoming MD Charles A. Smith are welcomed by treasurer and deputy prime minister Artie (later Sir Arthur) Fadden and Hubert C. French, aboard the Aorangi at Sydney, May 22, 1950. Above: in the 1950s women drivers were appealed to on the basis of space and ease of driving.

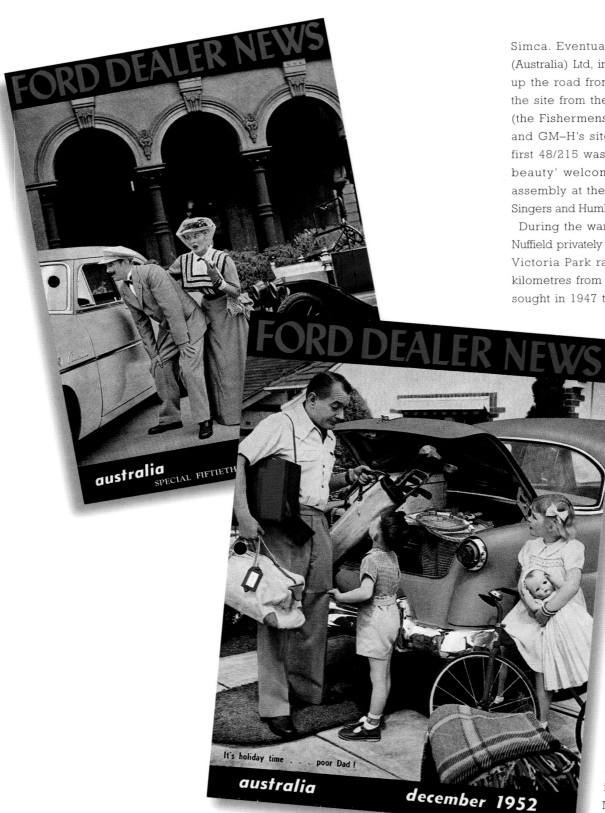

Simca. Eventually it added the factory of Rootes (Australia) Ltd, in Salmon Street, Port Melbourne, just up the road from GM–H. Rootes Ltd in fact bought the site from the Department of Aircraft Production (the Fishermens Bend airstrip backed onto both it and GM–H's site) two-and-a-half years before the first 48/215 was ushered blinking into the 'She's a beauty' welcome of Ben Chifley. Rootes started assembly at the end of 1956, turning out Hillmans, Singers and Humbers.

During the war the British Morris car maker Lord Nuffield privately had bought the 113-acre (46 hectares) Victoria Park racecourse at Zetland, less than six kilometres from the Sydney CBD. However, when he sought in 1947 to use it to build a plant for Nuffield (Australia) Pty Ltd the government allowed him only 57 acres (23 hectares), so he sold the rest to other companies such as Olympic (tyres), Lucas (electrical components) and Leyland (trucks and buses).

In 1948 the Austin Motor Corporation bought (ex-Tarrant) Ruskin Motor Bodies in West Melbourne as the basis of its own assembly operation, and when Austin and Morris merged in 1952 to become the British Motor Corporation it plunged into a new manufacturing plant at Zetland, coming on stream in July 1958. From here would emerge milestone cars like the Mini, Mini-Moke, Morris 1100 and 1500, Austin 1800 and – yes! – the Leyland P76.

Standard Cars Ltd was assembling Vanguards from 1949 in a plant in Port Melbourne – which in the 1960s produced the first locally built Toyotas. In 1952 Australian Motor Industries took it over and by 1960 was assembling Mercedes–Benz, Standard Vanguards,

3 BIG PEOPLE

Triumph Heralds, American Ramblers and Ferguson and Fiat tractors. Volkswagen started assembly in 1954, Rover in 1956. Boosted by the first Holden and these camp followers, Australia's components industry blossomed.

Australia loved the 1948 Ford V8 – particularly after Jack 'Gelignite' Murray drove one to victory in the second Redex Round-Australia Trial in 1954. In 1949 came the less popular first all-new post-war Ford Canada model, the 'Single Spinner' Ford Custom V8 sedan and utility with independent front suspension. The company added some Thames V8 trucks and 10-horsepower small vans from the UK.

And then there was the bizarre Ford Pilot. It was created by Ford's Dagenham plant in England for essentially the same reason that was driving Ford Australia – desperate buyers and a dire shortage of dollar currency. It was built using the old tooling from a 1936 UK Ford called a Model 62, was shorter than the lookalike US Ford and had the lower-powered V8 60 engine.

After it was rehashed in 1947 with the more powerful V8 dating back to 1937, Ford Australia swooped on every one it could get. A Ford Australia senior marketer at the time, Lyn Hamilton, remembered:

Left: production of the Mark 2 Zephyr was shifted from Geelong to Broadmeadows when the big new plant came on stream. There was a lot of bitterness among Geelong employees about the whole affair. Opposite: covers from Ford Dealer News, including a special 50th anniversary edition from May 1953 and the holiday time issue of December 1952, featured photography by the up and coming Helmut Newton.

IN 1952 FORD WAS ASSEMB

'Ford Canada didn't believe we could sell the Pilots – they were unattractive and already obsolete. But the market was prepared to buy anything at that time, and we sold them as fast as we could bring them here. We chartered ships in England ... most Pilots were fully assembled and needed only tyres, but some were semi knocked-down and we sold them to dealers like that and they finished them off.

'As quickly as they put them on their showroom floors buyers would come in and take them.' The car had a die-cast grille which, on rough roads, fell apart. It couldn't be

In the 1950s car radios were still a relative novelty, and never included as standard equipment. The valve radio installation was bulky and often had to be mounted below the dash.
Right: Bill Hayes and co-driver Tom Quill came home class winners and fourth outright in the 1955 round-Australia reliability trial in their Customline. Opposite: it was to be the biggest automotive plant in the Southern Hemisphere at the time, and Victorians were cock-a-hoop about it. This shot from Ford Dealer News of February 1958 shows (from left) president of Ford Canada, Rhys Sale, vice-president overseas Jack Dalton, Ford Australia managing director Charles Smith and his successor John McIntyre.

repaired, so owners got used to buying a new grille at every service.

In June 1951 the company started assembling the first British Consul, its 1.5 litre engine and three-box styling a revelation in British design for those days, despite severe clutch and differential problems, as it turned out. In 1952 came the 'twin-spinner' Fords, and with them the first suspicion that Ford in North America had no idea – or had

forgotten because those pre-war cars gave magnificent service – about building cars for harsh Australian conditions. The damper mounting rubbers would last about 500 kilometres and owners would carry spares.

But before that H. C. French had retired. The man whose 'excellent adventure' had given birth to Ford Australia had aged visibly since the war ended, and decided enough was enough. He was succeeded on June 1, 1950 by

NG 12 DIFFERENT MODELS, AND THE FIRST LOCAL V8

Charles A. Smith. Born in Birmingham, England, in 1894 and educated at Handsworth Grammar School and Tamworth Agricultural College, he left for Canada in 1912 to seek his fortune as a farmer. That didn't last long, and he joined Canadian Pacific Railways as a yard clerk and then went into the Canadian Army for WW1, gaining a field commission. After demobilisation he got a job as a clerk in the Taxation Department and stayed there, probably bored out of his wits, until in 1926 he joined Ford Canada as a sales clerk in Regina, Saskatchewan.

Smith worked his way through the finance and sales departments, and in 1948 became managing director of Ford South Africa.

He recalled later: 'I suppose I had come to be regarded by the company as something of a troubleshooter, and I think that led to my appointment as managing director of Ford Australia.

'Certainly Ford in Australia needed new ideas and new life. The company had lost the initiative to General Motors with its locally manufactured Holden and Ford's market share had slipped. It was time to expand if we were to

regain the initiative.' Sir Brian Inglis (then a senior manufacturing engineering executive) said Ford executives saw Smith's ideas for Ford Australia as 'dynamic and aggressive ... Ford Australia had fallen a little bit asleep'.

One of Smith's first moves was to persuade the parent to spend £4.6 million on the latest overhead assembly line for Geelong to allow the complete assembly of the V8 engine, which became operational in 1952. In 1954 £260,000 went into new, bigger body panel presses, both expansions helped by the government giving Ford special financial allocations. But that was just the start.

'We had to manufacture a car here if we were to be able to compete with the Holden', Smith said later. 'When I took over we were partly manufacturing and assembling the Anglia, Prefect, Thames trucks and Fordson tractors. We introduced Consul and Zephyr on the same basis, but that wasn't good enough; we had to find a product we could manufacture if we were to remain a major force in the Australian motor industry.'

Canada didn't agree. Ford Australia was profitable from its assembly of only 160-odd cars a day and returning healthy dividends. The Zephyr was selling steadily against the Holden, although it was £150 dearer. But as GM–H boosted production of the 48/215 and in 1954 launched the FJ with the first derivatives, Ford's market share slipped below 10 per cent.

In 1955, finally wilting after three years of Smith's nagging, Windsor gave him the go-ahead to build the Zephyr in Australia. Smith instantly fired in an already prepared business plan involving spending an enormous £20 million on a completely new factory and tooling. 'They knew as well as I did that I had built in about 10 per cent of that to cover emergencies, so it wasn't difficult to bring that figure down to £18.5 million', he said; it was the figure he had planned anyway. Although no-one realised it at the time, this was the historic moment that led to the Falcon.

In 1952 the company launched US-designed Customline sedans and Mainline utilities with the flathead V8, even though the US had switched to the new 239 cubic-inch (4 litre) overhead-valve V8 – Australia would get it with the 1955 models. Ford was now assembling 12 different models of passenger and commercial vehicles in Geelong, Homebush, Eagle Farm and Fremantle, as well as building the first local V8, a leisurely thumper producing 82 kilowatts at 3800 rpm.

By 1955–56, with the approval to invest in a new plant to build the Zephyr, Ford had spent £335,000 on new tooling for the Mark 2 Zephyr and Consul and gave chief designer Lew Bandt the green light to design a local station wagon version for the Zephyr, which would be built outside the company's plants and released in 1959. The Zephyr in 1956 had about 56 per cent local content; the Holden's was just over 90 per cent and accounted for around half the new vehicle market.

In February 1957 Ford formally presented to Canberra its plan to manufacture the Zephyr locally, to reach full production by 1961. A basis of the proposal was the allocation by the government of extra sterling quotas, equal to around 20,000 Zephyrs a year. Ford had already been getting extra cash quotas – £3.7 million (equal to 16,819 North American units) in 1953–54, £3.885 million (16,717) in 1954–55 and £3.335 million (14,712) in 1955–56, but these would have stopped had the company not gone into local engine manufacturing.

There were two Tariff Board hearings, in 1954 and 1957,

Above: the Mark 2 Zephyr featured on the October 1959 Dealer News cover, complete with exotic Fijian location. Left: Canadian John McIntyre, who reigned until 1963, replaced Charles Smith, who retired as managing director just before the first Falcon was launched. Opposite: the Mark 2 Consul for 1956 shared the same basic body platform as the Mark 2 Zephyr, but with four-cylinder power instead of the Zephyr's six. Both were assembled in Geelong then.

and the reports made it plain that the government hussy was shamelessly giving component suppliers more than a glimpse of her fiscal petticoats, to get them to commit to local production and supplying the growing number of assemblers and full manufacturers.

However, Ford's immediate problem was finding the right land for the new manufacturing plant – Geelong would expand from the original 40 to 66 hectares (163 acres) by 1977, but at this time there was no space for a

THE GOVERNMENT HUSSY SHAMELESSLY GAVE MORE TH

large plant, much of the equipment was out of date and Ford was building too many models in too many small-volume variations.

Sir Brian Inglis remembers that in about 1956 Charlie Smith had been invited to look through Holden's plant at Fishermens Bend and had invited GM–H's director of purchasing to have a look through Geelong; Inglis was given the job of taking him through.

'I must say he had a very high reputation. He was the man that took the Holden product and established the vendor [parts supplier] body in Australia. He had an enormous impact on the Australian motor industry at that time by insisting on certain quality criteria, and insisting on certain facilities.

Inglis took the executive around the plant – including showing him presses that had been second-hand in 1924. 'The stamping

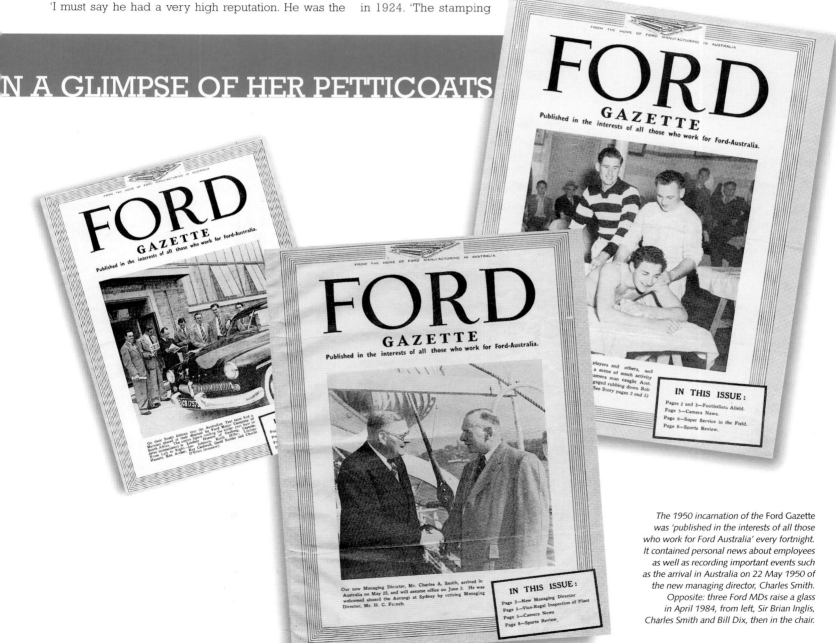

The 1950 incarnation of the Ford Gazette was 'published in the interests of all those who work for Ford Australia' every fortnight. It contained personal news about employees as well as recording important events such as the arrival in Australia on 22 May 1950 of the new managing director, Charles Smith. Opposite: three Ford MDs raise a glass in April 1984, from left, Sir Brian Inglis, Charles Smith and Bill Dix, then in the chair.

stamping plant was really a hodge-podge. It was fairly crude when you look back.' When they had finished the GM–H man asked if he could comment on what he had seen and on Ford's position.

Some may judge it to be a case of GM arrogance, but there was an inescapable element of truth: 'I would have to say that you're 20 years behind us. We have new facilities just installed … our productivity is substantially greater than yours … the tempo of your workforce is hampered by the way you have to organise the work. It's just a very old-fashioned labour-intensive activity compared to what we have.

'I'm the purchasing director and I have volume problems three or four times yours because you've got low volume but you've also got it fragmented, so you've got the worst of all worlds.'

He pointed out that GM–H's volume had allowed it to buy components at substantially lower cost than Ford. 'Our dealers are in prime positions, they are wealthy, they have facilities which you can't match in any way, shape or

form and they're re-investing their wealth in even better facilities.'

According to Inglis, he finished by saying: 'You know, I can't honestly see how you'll ever catch us'. And, of course, he was wrong.

The company examined Geelong, Werribee – about 30 kilometres up the Melbourne Road – and Dandenong, where International Harvester had a big factory and GM–H would later build, for sites. Then in April 1957, Victorian Premier Henry (later Sir Henry) Bolte and his Housing Minister, Horace Petty, offered two State Housing Commission sites at Campbellfield, astride the Hume Highway about 25 kilometres north of Melbourne.

There was 450 acres (182 hectares) on offer on the western side of the highway for £500 an acre and almost opposite, on the eastern side, another 200 acres (81 hectares). Smith recommended to Canada that they buy both parcels, but the president, Rhys Sale, reminded him they were not in the real estate business. 'I have always believed it was a mistake not taking up that extra parcel of land; it is extremely valuable property now and perhaps the company will one day need it for further expansion', Smith said later.

Bolte organised for the site to be rezoned for heavy industry and assured Smith there would be significant residential development around it to provide the nucleus of a workforce, and that migrant labour would continue to flow in to Australia.

But wait – there were several sets of steak knives to go. Ford had to lend the Government £300,000 at bank interest to get a rail spur into the site. Then it had to cough up £500,000 interest-free – free! – to have city water supplied. And there was another £100,000 loaned for sewerage works.

On February 11, 1958 Smith, Bolte and Petty headed a ceremony to announce the shape and size of the newest and largest automotive plant in the southern hemisphere – the main single-level steel-framed building with pre-cast concrete and asbestos cement siding was one of the

Not everyone was happy

The decision to set up the huge new plant at Broadmeadows caused a serious, if short-lived, split within Ford Australia. Many Geelong employees bitterly resented it – to the point of circulating rumours that there had been a secret arrangement between managing director Smith and then Victorian Premier, Henry Bolte, to profit from the real estate deal by buying land around the site.

Toolmaker Dave Block said years later that Smith initiated the practice of advertising staff jobs to the blue collar workers and that helped break down the invisible wall between the two levels. 'But it seemed strange to us that they would move from a position where they've got a railway line and a port at our back door, a main road which later became a four-lane highway past our front door – all services front and back.

'The only thing possibly against Geelong was, we were told on the grapevine, that it was easier to get workers in Melbourne than it was in Geelong, where you would be limited by the smaller numbers of people living here. And it upset a lot of families, having to uproot their homes and move to Melbourne.'

It did disrupt families, while those who commuted the 220 km round trip every day got tired of it. Geelong employees felt that Ford was Geelong and Geelong was Ford, said Block – Melbourne was 'another world'.

92

largest industrial buildings in Australia, designed for 2750 people to build about 200 cars a day.

Campbellfield would swallow £11 million; another £7 million was spent at Geelong expanding the foundry, casting and machining to make a new six-cylinder engine as well as modernising the stamping presses and

expanding the tool room. Remarkably, the new factory came on stream in just 18 months, its first cars the 'Tank' Fairlane range and the British Zephyr/Consul.

And at this stage everyone expected Ford's new Holden challenger to be an upgraded model of the Mark 2 Zephyr of 1956.

Above: ready for the '50s, a Single Spinner Ford Custom chases a Consul. Left: the famous 105E Anglia with the rearward-sloping back window. It was a great little car, the 997 cc engine producing some astounding power outputs when modified for motorsport. Far left: the very latest testing equipment and techniques, circa 1950. Opposite: program for a 1957 dealer dinner for the Geelong district office, held at the Chevron Hotel. Charles Smith proposed the toast to the dealers, and dessert was Crepes Chevron au Creme.

FIRST AUSTRALIAN-BUILT
FORD FALCON - JUNE 28 1960

CHAPTER 9

The Falcon **Takes Wing**

In 1999 Peter Costigan, one of four very successful sons of a Melbourne Irish Catholic family, became Lord Mayor of Melbourne. A brilliant journalist, he had been motoring editor of the *Melbourne Herald* afternoon newspaper before moving to Washington as its political correspondent, then back to the Canberra Press Gallery and later to a seat on the Australian Press Council.

The media launch of the new XK Falcon was scheduled for September 11, 1960 but Costigan was to be married and go on honeymoon during that week. Because the *Herald* was important to Ford, Costigan managed to persuade the then public affairs manager, a trim, balding, moustached, nervous tic of a man called Ralph Hosking, to let him have the super-secret car the weekend before.

This was something that was never done – in fact, the common riposte of car makers and importers was to deny any and all knowledge of a new model before the year 2000, or somesuch. Hosking swore Costigan to embargoed secrecy on the grounds that the car would be driven only under the cover of darkness.

'I had a bridesmaids' party to go to at Mario's in Exhibition Street', Costigan remembers. 'I think it was the original licensed restaurant in Melbourne – it was quite famous. Anyway, it was opposite Her Majesty's Theatre; I got there about 6 pm and Exhibition Street was deserted, so I parked it in the middle area.

'What I didn't know, however, was that Ford had all its Australian dealers in town for their first viewing of this fabulous new car the next morning and had taken them to Her Majesty's for the first night of *My Fair Lady*. They walked out of the theatre and there was the new car they weren't supposed to see until tomorrow.

'I left the party at midnight and didn't know a damn thing. Hosking was on the phone to me at six o'clock the next morning. I think he wanted to kill me.'

In the week leading up to September 11 a group of 37 motoring journalists was flown in from all over Australia to

Right: motoring writers were flown in from all over Australia for the launch of the new Falcon. In this group, complete with hats, pipes, trench coats and narrow ties, are David McKay, Paddy Ulyatt, Steve Simpson, Jules Feldman, Frank Platell, Clyde Hodgins, Lionel Hurst, Pedr Davis, Harold Dvoretsky, Pat Hinton and Keith Lukey. Below: promotional material made the car look lower and wider. Opposite: the journalists got the full showbiz treatment during the XK launch. On the left, the Sydney Sun-Herald's motoring editor, the late Clyde Hodgins, centre, MD Bill Bourke, right, future president David Morgan and far right, Harry Firth enjoy the show.

AS DANCING GIRLS SWIVELLED TO TH

other luminaries such as Harold Dvoretsky, Pedr Davis, Paddy Ulyatt, Frank Platell and Pat Hinton were briefed on the new car for two days without seeing it.

Then on the big night, as dancing girls swivelled to the Falcon song, the journalists in Falcon ties and socks toasted the new car with Falcon-embossed pewter tankards. The next day about 23 kilometres of bitumen and dirt roads in the Broadmeadows–Somerton area were closed to the public for the test drive program, with champagne and chicken served during the four hours (today of course a strict no-booze rule applies to all test drives).

The journalists' stories were embargoed until 9 pm on Sunday, September 11. The then editor of the Melbourne *Age*, Trevor Davis, wrote his major story on the Friday night for Monday morning. He wrote later: 'I left the office about 10:30 that night only to be summoned back close to midnight. My news editor showed me a copy of the *Sun News-Pictorial* (the opposition morning newspaper) printed only minutes before.

'Most of its front page was occupied by photographs of the Falcon and a description of it. He said, To hell with the embargo now it's been broken. This is the biggest

stay for several days in Melbourne's then-finest hotel, the Chevron in St Kilda Road. Heavy hitters such as David McKay from the Sydney *Daily Telegraph*, the editor of *Modern Motor* magazine, Jules Feldman, Sturt Griffith, the much-feared motoring editor of the *Sydney Morning Herald*, the editor of *Wheels* magazine, Ian Fraser, and

motoring story in years – we have to match it.

'I hastily rewrote my piece and soon after the front page of Saturday morning's *Age* was recast to make room for it.'

Ralph Hosking's nightmare was complete. A further irony was that the *Sun*'s motoring editor who broke the embargo, Keith Lukey, became Holden's public affairs manager a few years later.

In *The History of the Ford Falcon, 1960–1994*, John Wright records that the Falcon project was codenamed '19XK

Thunderbird' and introduced in North America in the third quarter of 1959 to rival the Chrysler (Plymouth) Valiant and the ill-fated Chevrolet Corvair (later to be slated by safety crusader Ralph Nader and others). Wright quoted Sir Brian Inglis:

'The Falcon represented the image of a smaller, more economical car, with sculptured stylish lines free of excessive chrome and within the price bracket of the lower income group or second car buyers.

FALCON SONG, JOURNALISTS TOASTED THE NEW CAR

'As originally conceived, the new car was to be similar to most European small cars then being imported into North America in large quantities. Several versions of four-cylinder cars were designed, some with the engine at the rear, others with a definite sports car look, and in all, some 18 full-sized clay models were developed for consideration by the Product Committee.

'During the period of management appraisal of these new and smaller cars, the planners began to see the need to change the original concept of manufacturing a replica of European small cars and instead place more emphasis on offering something closer to a full-sized car as known in North America, at a price and with a performance which would substantially lower the cost of automobile ownership.

'Acceptance of this … led to numerous problems. For example, it was decided to set the interior package dimensions equivalent to the 1949 Ford Custom, but at the same time request substantial reductions to the exterior size. It may come as a surprise to some of you to realise that the Falcon interior is quite comparable to that of the 1949 Ford.'

According to Wright, reducing weight to the target figure of 2400 pounds (1088 kilograms, about 90 kg lighter than the comparable FB Holden) was a major element in the new US Falcon program and worked to the detriment of the car's strength.

Sir Brian Inglis has told many times how the Falcon at the last gasp replaced the British-sourced Mark 2A Zephyr on which the new Broadmeadows plant was already spending tooling money.

Born in Adelaide in 1924, the young Brian finished his education as a boarder at Geelong Grammar after his father Scott had joined Ford. He left school in 1941 to join the RAAF – his father had been a pilot with the Australian Flying Corps (AFC) in WW1 – and while waiting for his call-up was a casual pay clerk in the Ford finance office.

He recalled later: 'My job was to go through the records of the hours that had been recorded on the time tickets by each person and calculate the time, or the awards or whatever … then my boss used to go to the bank and get the money. We would put it into envelopes and distribute it to the workforce and then answer the innumerable questions as to why it was wrong.

'I remember it well. Imagine a callow youth of 17 – I had a whole canister, a tray of money in envelopes, many thousands of pounds, and they said, Be here at six o'clock in the morning to distribute this to the night shift. My boss gave me the trays – two trays – and I staggered out across the Melbourne Road, unescorted, without any fear or trepidation, I suppose it was two or three hundred yards, and paid the men. In those days you could leave your door unlocked and nothing happened.'

That callow youth, still 17, was shipped to England, and flew Spitfires throughout the war. Back in Australia in 1945 he gained admission to Melbourne University for a course in metallurgical sciences as a step towards joining BHP, then Australia's largest company. He was about to graduate after three years' study when the executive

vice-president of Ford Canada, Rhys M. Sale, came out to look at Ford's Australian operations and in a conversation at the Inglis home offered him a place in Ford's new graduate training scheme, to start in February 1949.

This was the first annual intake of a hugely successful program that has trained generations of Australians as international Ford managers. Scratch many a CEO in major Australian companies today and under the sharp suit you will find an ex-Ford Australia graduate. Current Ford Australia president, Geoff Polites, himself an illustrious former graduate trainee, says that one of the big differences between the company now and in the past is that

Opposite: April 1960 and the first Falcon six-cylinder engine comes off the Geelong line. The company spent £7 million upgrading and expanding the engine plant to produce the new 144 cubic inch unit. Left: a young Brian Inglis in his wartime days as a Spitfire pilot.
Below: the new Falcon engine produced 67 kilowatts from 2359 cc capacity – average for a 1.5 litre four today, although with significantly greater torque. It outclassed Holden's old 2261 cc 'grey' motor.

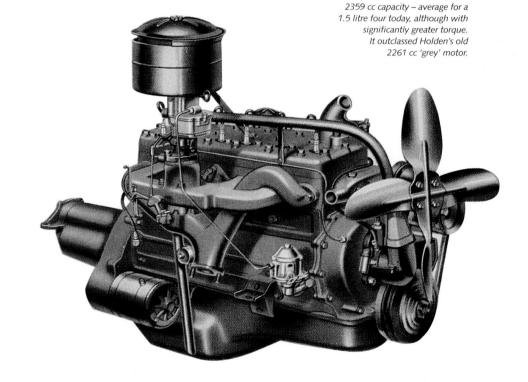

these incoming graduates are given big career challenges almost from day one. It is impossible to conceive a better training system for industry than an honours degree followed immediately by hands-on responsibility under demanding supervision.

After his year in Ford Canada Inglis was assigned to examine the manufacturing processes there and in the US and was asked by the new MD of Ford Australia, Charlie Smith, to return to the job of manager of industrial engineering, as it was then known.

He said later that the Geelong plant then was run much the same way as Ford's Rouge complex in 1925. 'It was

Above: some of the first Falcons were exported to New Zealand. In 1962, Ford Australia became the world source for right-hand drive Falcons. Right: getting the all-new plant up to speed with an all-new car was an awesome achievement. Sir Brian Inglis remembered it as a 'mad scramble'. Opposite: not what is normally meant by the 'flight' of the Falcon, but there is no question the XK got off to a flying start in the sales chart. This was staged as a demonstration of the car's toughness.

pretty much catch as catch can. They used concrete for some of their tools, and used wooden dies. But their natural abilities made unbelievable things.'

Of Slim Westman, who had been director of manufacturing since 1925, Inglis recalled: 'He was very much what I'd call an army type, with the do what I say, don't ask questions type of approach, but he was a great Ford man … hours didn't mean anything'.

All Inglis had was a small group of six to eight people, established by a production engineer called Harry Ruffin, as the nucleus to reach his aims of setting up proper manufacturing cost controls, materials handling, manufacturing processes and work standards unheard of in the Australian company, which was then assembling the full-size Ford Customline, Pilot, Anglia and Prefect, all bolted together – not on an overhead line but on hand-pushed wheeled sleds.

When Charlie Smith got the Broadmeadows investment approved, it was to build the Zephyr they were then assembling, to combat a hugely successful Holden priced significantly lower than the UK-sourced design.

In an interview in 1988 Inglis said the huge new factory was not designed with the Falcon in mind. Retooling for an all-new car, including engine and transmission, in just 21 months, to be built in a brand-new plant with a yet-to-be-trained workforce, was an appalling challenge. Even today it would be dismissed as impossible.

Inglis declared: 'It was saying, we really don't have the ability to design our own car. When I look back now, we had 100 people, I had a new stamping plant, a new chassis plant, a new engine plant, all at Geelong. There was no chance in the world anybody could do it. It was a complete underestimation of the requirements'.

Ford's Dearborn studios were working on restyling the Mark 2 Zephyr into the Mark 2A for Australia when on July 31, 1958 executive vice-president of Ford Canada (Sale had become president) Theodore Emmett cabled Charlie Smith to come over and look at the car. Smith took Inglis (by then manufacturing director), production manager Gene Chorolsky, Alan Tyrer and Lyn Hamilton with him.

Said Smith later: 'When they wheeled out the Zephyr at the design studio I simply didn't like the look of it, and I said so. Then Mr Emmett asked whether I would like to see the mock-up of the Falcon that was being designed for the Canadian and American markets. When I saw that I said without hesitation: That's the car I want for Australia. It

BROADMEADOWS COULDN'T BUILD THEM FAST ENOU

was a new car, it had the advantage of Detroit engineering and design, and I suspected Ford UK already had plans to discontinue the Zephyr range'.

'There was no doubt which was the better-looking car', Inglis recalled. 'But the Falcon was not as robust as our restyled Zephyr and we had certain misgivings. Among the things I believe influenced Mr Smith to decide on the Falcon was that it was a lighter and easier car to build, that it would cost less than the Zephyr to manufacture and therefore be more competitive with the Holden, and also the fact we had in Ford Australia far more experience of building American cars than British'.

In 1988 Sir Brian added: 'Strangely enough, we might have done just as well with the Zephyr – although that's conjecture – because the Falcon wasn't perfect. But when you look at the clay model you don't know those things. At that time it looked heaven-sent'.

Inglis cabled Geelong that day to drop plans for the Zephyr, even though tooling and components worth £137,000 had been bought or ordered, and stayed in Dearborn creating blueprints and engineering designs.

'I've got to say we worked like dogs; it was a mad, mad, mad scramble', said Inglis. 'Everything was new – that's a recipe for disaster, I can tell you; it was even a new location.

It was heroic, although we didn't know it at the time.'

It would suck in an extra £6.5 million in tooling and launching costs – £3.3 million over budget.

Broadmeadows was opened in August 1959, the first car off the line a 'Tank' Fairlane. The first new six-cylinder engine rolled out in April 1960, and XK Falcon Job One at 2:30 pm on June 28. Smith had retired at the end of 1959, his successor the young (38) John George Wallace McIntyre, promoted from assistant general manufacturing manager in Ford Canada. So McIntyre, described as a quiet, thoughtful man with a passion for chess, literature and classical music, presided over the launch of the new car on which the entire future of Ford Australia depended.

On that day Henry Ford II said, among other things: 'It is a beautifully sophisticated new kind of Ford that combines low cost and great economy with beautiful styling, superb comfort, and complete resources of power and safety. In the Falcon we have summed up all this experience in producing an Australian-built economy car, specifically designed for Australian driving conditions'.

The last of course was misleading (and based perhaps on an assumption that what would work in North America would work here). The car had been extensively tested in the US but nowhere else. It did, however, have a number of advantages over the Holden. On a wheelbase of

Opposite: motoring writers inspecting the new engine line. The editor of the then Modern Motor, Jules Feldman, is second from left in the group. Above: on the XK production line. Below: the Squire wagon, featuring an abundance of fake timber.

H – AT FIRST

109.5 inches (2782 millimetres) against 105 (2667) for the FB Holden but about the same length, it was a much more modern car than the Holden, which suffered from a wraparound windscreen with 'dogleg' corners, vacuum-operated non-parallel windscreen wipers, and tailfins that screamed 1950s.

The Falcon had a 144 cubic inch (2359 cc) 67 kilowatt six-cylinder engine against the Holden's old design 138 (2261 cc) unit, with the option of three-speed column-shift manual or two-speed Fordomatic transmissions. The Falcon cost just £30 more and had 90 per cent Australian content.

THE FALCON **TAKES WING**

Above: the target for the new Falcon was Holden's FB range, which dominated the market. However, the new XK looked far more modern, had much better drivetrain and performance and handled better, despite five turns lock-to-lock on the steering. Right: in 1962 came another rival, the Australian-assembled US Chrysler Valiant, with its egg-crate grille and the biggest engine of the three. Opposite: the XL replaced the XK in 1962, with a squared-off rear 'Thunderbird' C-pillar, heavy duty clutch, improved transmission and optional seatbelts. It was launched six weeks ahead of its US sibling, Ford Australia claiming no fewer than 724 new parts.

to me with a durability problem again.'

Max Gransden was NSW regional manager when the XK arrived. He said the car had front suspension and clutch problems 'from day one'. It was under-tyred and the ride was too soft. 'If you drove over a damn piece of paper the bloody thing would bottom', he told Geoff Easdown for *A History of the Ford Motor Company in Australia*.

When he unveiled the car to the NSW dealers they came back from the test drive 'one after the other saying the

Broadmeadows couldn't build them fast enough – at first. In 1959 Ford had 10 per cent of the total Australian market, compared with just on 50 per cent for GM–H. With the new XK Falcon that went to 16.5 per cent in 1960 and 19.4 per cent in 1961, but the car was to prove a disaster.

Sir Brian Inglis recalled: 'The damn thing had a front suspension problem: the ball joints failed in very short order. I think if I'd made that part I would have been fired, because we lost a fortune in replacement parts. I always remember Henry Ford heard of this ball joint problem – I don't know how – and he sent a man out to investigate. The story goes that he went back to see Henry Ford who said, What's the problem?, and he said, Here it is, right in my hand – it's just not robust enough'.

At the time Ford US had a larger joint for the 'Compact' Fairlane, then still under development, and that became the replacement part. On a subsequent visit to Australia Henry Ford asked why it hadn't been tested in Australia; the answer was they had assumed that would all be done in the US. Inglis told him Ford Australia didn't have a test track. 'He said: I will give you a test track, but never – never – come

suspension nearly came up through the bottom. It was dreadful and we quickly realised that a boulevard ride was not for this country'. (Gransden moved to head office in 1971 as general sales manager and in 1975 replaced the much-respected and feared Keith Horner in the all-powerful job of director of sales and marketing.)

Ford added the station wagon two months after the sedan, building it on the same wheelbase because the two US-built wagons imported for evaluation with an extra 200 millimetres of overhang scraped their rear ends on gutters and driveways. In May 1961 came the panel van and utility, with larger-section 6.70 x 13 tyres instead of the 6.00s.

But other criticisms began to emerge: the steering was too light and indirect at five turns lock-to-lock, the spare wheel took up space in the shallow boot, the 144 with the two-speed auto was lamentably short of grunt. Ford took 6 per cent market share from GM–H, but nobody was

THE NEW FALCONS TRIM, TAUT, TERRIFIC!

helped by the Federal government's lifting sales tax from 30 per cent to 40 per cent in the 1961 'credit squeeze'. In the 23 months the XK lasted, 68,465 were built in Broadmeadows and Eagle Farm, compared with the budget target of 70,000 for the first two years.

However, in those first two years the company fell into serious trouble. New Zealand-born David Letford came to Australia in 1956 for the Melbourne Olympic Games, stayed on, and in 1958 joined Ford Australia. He was employed in the finance office, where he would spend his career, eventually becoming controller.

At the time the Broadmeadows site, he said, was 'great flattened heaps of red clay'. The 1960 switch of control from Ford Canada to Ford US saw '40 to 50' American executives moved into the Australian subsidiary and their impact was very severe. Why so many?

Falcon – first to go racing

If you look at a photograph of the start of the 1960 Armstrong 500 – the embryo of what became the Bathurst 1000, Australia's greatest touring car race – you will see two XK Ford Falcons departing the front row, sandwiching the Vauxhall Cresta that eventually won.

The classic enduro was created by Ron Thonemann, who had a small automotive public relations company and was looking for an idea to promote the dampers made by a client, Armstrong York Engineering. He talked managing director Jim Thompson and the Light Car Club into organising a 500 mile (800 kilometre) race for standard production sedans, divided into classes according to engine size. It was run on November 19–20 at Phillip Island, Victoria, where lies the soul of Australian motor racing – the first Australian Grand Prix was held there in 1928 on a huge rectangle of gravelled public roads.

Regulations for the five classes allowed only minimal changes to showroom floor specification: aircraft seatbelts, Perspex covers for the windscreens and removal of hubcaps. Some importers threw in money for 'semi works' teams of cars, but two dealers were bold enough to enter the just-released XK Falcon (Ford at the time had a worldwide ban on motorsport participation).

Bob Jane's Autoland dealership entered Jane and the now-legendary hotel entrepreneur Lou Molina in one and Wangaratta Motors had two great drivers, Ron Phillips and Ernie Seeliger, in another.

On that historic morning 47 cars lined up for the Le Mans start, the large engine class to the front, and 35 were still running after 167 laps and eight-and-a-half hours. A Mercedes–Benz 220 SE entered for John and Gavin Youl, sons of the Tasmanian grazing family who later built the Symmons Plains race circuit on their property, led from the start. When it rolled after popping a tyre, the Vauxhall Cresta of John Roxburgh and Frank Coad took over, with the Jane/Molina Falcon second. But the track started to fall apart and near the end Molina rolled car 30; it ended on its wheels but without a windscreen. He drove it back to the pits; the officials looked at it and waved him away – it finished second in class and fifth outright.

There were only 26 starters in 1961 – probably representing the impact on the motor industry and trade of a particularly vicious recession – but among them was the first Holden to compete. Like Ford, GM then had a global ban on racing, but the EK model was secretly prepared at the Lang Lang proving ground – even to the extent of freezing fuel to try and increase tank capacity, a ploy that was used two decades later at Bathurst. The drivers were Ian Strachan/John Lanyon/David Collins, and there was also a Falcon, driven by Ken Harper/Sid Fisher/John Reaburn, which was widely suspected of being a covert factory entry.

In practice the Falcon lapped in around 2 minutes 53 seconds and the Holden in 2:54, thus setting the stage for their enduring rivalry. But the race went to a Mercedes–Benz 220SE – assembled at the Australian Motor Industries (AMI) plant at Port Melbourne and driven by Bob Jane and Harry Firth. The Holden was leading the Falcon when it lost a wheel.

The next year, 1962, the pairing of Jane/Firth won the last Phillip Island Armstrong 500. In an XL Falcon wearing the number plate HOT 506, rebodied (by the factory) after it flipped in practice, they led the field of 41 cars over a circuit that was destroyed into such rubble that the race had to be moved in 1963 to Mount Panorama.

There were two factory-supported cars, both with the bigger Pursuit engines – Jane/Firth were joined by Harper/Reaburn/Fisher, plus three private entries. There were three Valiants, but all were retired by holed radiators, so badly did the circuit collapse. The Falcon driven by Kevin Lott holed its radiator in the first hours and because under the rules he wasn't allowed any help on the car he regularly stopped alongside a small pool on the back straight to refill it. At Siberia corner there was a hole almost two metres long, a metre wide and over two centimetres deep.

Falcons finished 1–2–3–4 in class and 1–2–4–6 in (unofficial) outright placings. Just one of the new EJ Holdens was entered (privately) and it finished seven laps behind the winning Falcon. As the tumult and the shouting died, left behind was a ruined 4.75 kilometres of road around a muddied dairy farm.

'Well, the company was going bad very quickly', Letford recalled. 'The change from being a small operator to a big one caught the company totally unprepared, from the point of view of a staff structure.' He said that in hindsight the Falcon selection was a bad decision. (Current vice-president, product development, Ian Vaughan politely disagrees, recalling how poor the British cars of that era were.)

'It nearly brought this company totally down … we didn't have a product engineering support function, we just picked up the engineering overseas. So the US poured more and more resources into it.'

There was another problem: the Ford dealer network, such as it was. In the late 1950s Ford dealerships weren't making much money, Ford couldn't attract quality owner candidates, and generally an existing dealer would buy any surrendered or new outlet.

Gransden again: 'In Sydney by the end of the 1950s we had two major organisations controlling nine of our 17 dealerships. Their attitudes were years out of date, their philosophy of marketing our products was the same no matter which dealership or which market it was in.

'We had exactly the same thing in Melbourne. We had 16 or 17 dealerships with one man controlling five of them through a public company. He had very diversified interests and only 10 per cent of his time would be spent on what dealerships were doing. So we were going from bad to worse.'

Gransden said the public companies controlling all those dealerships had managers who were often poorly paid by their absentee landlords. It was this situation that gave birth to Ford Australia's amazing dealer development program during the 1960s, which revolutionised automotive retailing in Australia – but more of that later.

Ford had other things to worry about now. In January 1962 Chrysler Australia introduced the dramatically styled and locally assembled R-Series Valiant, with a 225 cid (3690 cc) engine – bigger than either of its rivals.

In August 1962 came the XL Falcon, marketed under the slogan of 'Trim, Taut, Terrific!' and unveiled just one month after the totally restyled (and smaller) EJ Holden, thus setting the stage for new Ford–Holden model launches leapfrogging each other, as they do even today. It was a facelift, the only major sheetmetal change a squared-off C-pillar dubbed the 'Thunderbird look', and the concave grille became convex.

There was some underbody strengthening as well as suspension changes, and a 170 cubic inch (2275 cc) restroked version of the 144 was added, dubbed Pursuit (as had been an XK option earlier), plus a new manual transmission, clutch and starter motor. It was also the first Falcon to get seatbelt attachment points (the belts would come later).

Two new models were added: the 'bustling' new Futura with full carpeting, padded dash, Thunderbird-type front bucket seats and violent scarlet upholstery, and the Squire wagon, a truly American fake 'Woody' with glass-fibre 'timber' framing and grained plastic veneer panels. The Futura was cheaper than the equivalent Holden Premier, but closer examination showed it didn't have its rival's heater, reversing lights, metallic paint or windscreen washers.

Ford launched the XL to the motoring press in Melbourne, the drive program designed by the company's motorsport manager, a noisy, lovable ruffian called Les Powell. It started, appropriately, at the Melbourne Zoo at 8 o'clock on a wet Monday morning and demanded an average of nearly 80 km/h – 80! – over the first stage of 55 kilometres through the suburbs.

It was a disaster. They lost four cars – the one I saw was a utility teetering atop a bluestone sheep wall. I was in a Squire with the late Paul Higgins. Around the back of Bacchus Marsh we were flat-knacker at around 150 km/h when the road suddenly dropped into an unmapped river ford. We hit the other side with a crash and all four wheel

covers sponged off into the shrubbery. Still, we clean-sheeted the 200-odd kilometre route, and won a rally jacket and a silver tray.

Ford sold 75,705 XLs (only 728 of them Squires) until the model was replaced by the XM in February 1964.

In 1962 the company also introduced the new UK-designed four-cylinder Consul Cortina, an immediate hit, alongside the successful 105E Anglia.

The North American Compact Fairlane was locally

assembled like its 'Tank' predecessor which had itself superseded the last of the Customlines (the famous Star model) in August 1959. The 'Compact' Fairlane – with minor facelifting – would run from late 1962 until 1965. Ford also brought in the US Galaxie with 289 and 390 ('Thunderbird') engines for assembly at Homebush.

The Zephyr Mark 2I was about to be phased out and Ford opened small export markets for right-hand drive

The all-new Cortina – badged initially as the Consul Cortina – started rolling off the lines in October 1962, replacing the Consul and available in both two and four-door forms. Properly re-engineered for Australian conditions, it quickly became very popular.

Opposite: with the 1964 XM – touted as Certified Golden Quality – Ford finally got it right. Styling changes were minor but the two engines got uprated power and a third Super Pursuit unit was added. It also brought in the first two-door hardtop, new interiors and 15 new exterior colours. Left: Falcon prototypes underwent thousands of kilometres of punishing development testing on South Australia's Eyre Peninsula. The new car was a lot tougher, with extensive suspension and chassis modifications. Its successor, the XP, would prove even better.

Falcons in New Zealand, Papua New Guinea, Hong Kong, Fiji, Japan and Malaya (as it was then). But the company was suffering growing pains, and during the year McIntyre announced further investment of £7 million, partly funded by its first profit announcement of £2,932,415. This was to build the new Cortina, expand and modernise Sydney and Brisbane, and erect the black obelisk, the stand-alone building that has, since 1964, been Ford Australia's head office, frowning out at the Hume Highway running away towards Sydney.

The new £1.25 million head office was the final slap in the face for long-time Geelong employees, because this effectively moved the heart and soul of the organisation up to Sydney Road. Built between the assembly and parts and accessories (P&A, in industry vernacular) plants, it had a pleasant rear patio area that would later lead towards a new Design Centre. There was a cafeteria able to seat 270 and a management dining room, plus a men's (not women's) barber shop selling cigarettes, tobacco, pipes, 'toilet requisites' and magazines – doubtless the slightly raunchy *Man* and *Australasian Post* of the time.

One section of the shop sold cosmetics and stockings and there was a dry cleaning agency combined with a shoe repair shop. Office hours were 8:30 am to 4:30 pm with half an hour for lunch, and female employees were allowed up to four hours' shopping time one afternoon per month – a company shuttle service left each day for the city at 1:30 pm.

But Campbellfield was a long way from anywhere then, and the company had applied to the government for a

Above: Barry ('Bo') Seton hustling the battered dealer-entered Cortina GT500 through Murray's Corner on the way to winning the 1965 Armstrong 500 at Bathurst. Opposite: XM wagons were also subjected to dust-laden testing.

anything. And he did the sensible things. He said: Look, I need a world-class salesman – and they sent him Bill Bourke.'

Inglis said Booth saw the fundamental problems of Ford Australia and set out to get the manufacturing systems right, create a product engineering base, set up a new sales operation and dealer body, and discipline the component suppliers.

That was all very well, but Ford's main product was still on the nose in terms of durability and resale value, particularly with the growing fleet market, which had been badly burned by the disastrous XK and XL experiences. So, for the first time, the engineers started using Australia as a proving ground.

GM–H had been doing this since the original 48/215 –

THE ENGINEE

special bus service to and from eastern and north-eastern suburbs. Senior management was more sensitive to such needs than many companies in the climate of the day.

A crew-cut 40-year-old American called Wallace Wray Booth took over as managing director in July 1963. A finance man who sold women's hats and shoes to fund his way to a BA and MBA from the University of Chicago, he served with the US Army Air Force during WW2. He worked for the famous R. J. Miller in the finance office of Ford US before being made director of finance and vice-president of Ford Canada.

One version had it that the mission Miller gave him was to fix the product and make Ford Australia efficient or shut it down – much the same mission as two other CEOs were given decades later. According to Sir Brian Inglis: 'He was a finance man with imagination, and there aren't many of those in my experience. Wally Booth did a tremendous amount in quite a short time. He had what I found later on to be the key to international operations, the complete confidence of the senior executives back in home base.

'With R. J. Miller behind him Wally could do almost

and it showed. The infant Ford product design team discovered South Australia's Eyre Peninsula. They based themselves in Port Lincoln and proceeded to beat the crap out of the first Australian-developed Falcon prototypes. The roads were flinty, white-dusted maulers, and led directly to the spending of more than £1 million on 1500 modifications aimed, mostly, at making the car tougher.

The motoring press launch of the new XM Falcon in February 1964 was run over the SA durability test circuit the development engineers had been using, and Booth was there for it. He hammered the line that this was a tough car – and it was. However, it had a short sales life (one year) and was actually only an interim step towards the model that really made it, the XP.

Marketed under the slogan 'With Certified Golden Quality', the XM kept most of the styling of the American version but with major changes to the grille, bumpers and rear panels and tail lamp assembly. The body gained torsional rigidity with chassis 'torque boxes', Fairlane front upper wishbones, and stronger rear spring hangers and mountings, wider rims and tyres, and a new 200 cubic inch Super Pursuit six-cylinder engine – imported at first.

It produced 90 kilowatts, giving the buyer a choice of three mills, with the 170 Pursuit and the 144 both given power boosts. They persevered with the geeky Squire wagon, but at the other extreme of Falcon style was an elegant two-door hardtop coupe based on the US Falcon Sprint. It had an imported Canadian roof pressing but the vast doors and stretched rear quarter panels were all stamped at Geelong. The Hardtop was in advance of Australian taste (and five years before the Holden Monaro!).

In its short life the XM sold a handsome 47,110 units. However, it was ambushed by GM–H, which in August 1963 released its first answer to the Falcon, the EH range.

In 1964 Ford Australia lost a record £4.87 million. But the combination of Booth and Bourke was about to haul the prematurely born infant out of the humidicrib – the XP was coming.

Bibliography

Collectible Automobiles magazine, June 1998.
Geoff Easdown, *A History of the Ford Motor Company in Australia,* Lothian Publishing, 1989.
Bill Tuckey, *Australia's Greatest Motor Race,* Lansdowne Press, 1981.
Elisabeth Tuckey/Ewan Kennedy, *Chrysler Valiant,* Marque Publishing Company, 1996.
John Wright, *The History of the Ford Falcon, 1960–1994,* Ford Australia, 1994.

STARTED USING AUSTRALIA AS A PROVING GROUND

Lunatics In Charge Of The Asylum

This is undoubtedly the silliest story in the entire history of the Australian motor industry. It would be classed as an act of corporate stupidity except that it was so crazy – and so successful – that it can be regarded as a fluke of genius. However you categorise it, it changed an entire nation's perception of a car and laid the foundation for Ford Australia's eventual recapture of the market leadership it had held way back in the 1930s.

It dates to that moment when Henry Ford II promised Brian Inglis a proving ground (see Chapter Nine). Dearborn would approve £750,000 to buy the dirt and build the complex in the You Yangs, amid the rocky outcrops and windswept straw-grass west of Melbourne. Along with administration buildings and access roads went the first unsealed road circuit and a 2.25 mile (3.6 kilometre) ride and handling track. Narrow, coarse-surfaced, bordered by two-metre granite boulders and ancient gums, with no straight longer than 400 metres, it

swooped up a one-in-four hill and down dale, with off-camber corners, lumpy jumps and a nasty hairpin that pounded the brakes. It was designed as an evil road to demonise a car's dynamics, so Ford Australia would never build another XK Falcon.

Later it was claimed this was not the circuit Bill Bourke had in mind when he announced in April 1965 that the company would run five of the new XP Falcons for a total of 70,000 miles (112,630 kilometres), non-stop over five days, bog standard, at an average of 70 mph (112 km/h).

Ford Australia lore has it that Bourke created the idea as a flamboyant marketing ploy, but thought it would be on the new high-speed oval, which had been approved by Detroit but not yet built. The story goes that by the time Bourke realised he had made a gross error of judgement the challenge had been widely publicised and could not be withdrawn. However, one cannot imagine this street-smart, media-savvy American not knowing exactly what was involved.

Bourke had been pulled by Wally Booth out of the Ford Canada office to take on the thankless task of trying to sell Falcons in Australia. Bourke, then only 37, had the title of assistant managing director. In the US Army during WW2 he made lieutenant at 18, and was the youngest commissioned officer in the US ground forces.

After the war he served almost three years in Europe as a counter-intelligence agent at the start of the Cold War. His work involved tracking Nazi war criminals and recruiting German scientists to move to the US (codename Operation Paper Clip); after that he went to college under the GI Bill to get a degree.

He started his automotive career in 1952, with Studebaker in Indiana as a financial analyst, left there to join the Edsel group at Ford US in 1956 as national distribution manager, and went to Ford Canada as general sales manager from 1960 to 1964, when he was sent to Australia.

BOURKE SPRAYED IDEAS I

Bill Bourke, the bold marketer who engineered the sales turnaround that happened with the XP Falcon. Below: a section of the 'gypsy camp' set up at the start/finish line of the ride and handling circuit at the You Yangs. It was never designed as a high-speed track. Opposite: XM and XP hardtops have attained classic status. This XP has had some loving modifications.

Bill Bourke was a hugely charismatic man who brought with him a quieter sidekick, Bill Hawkins. It was a classic pairing: Bourke could sell refrigerators to Eskimos and would spray out ideas like a broken fire hydrant, while Hawkins, in the background, applied the mop and worked on the detail. There was a third leg to the stool – national sales manager Keith Horner, head-hunted from Australian Motor Industries (AMI), which had variously assembled Triumphs and Standards, Ramblers and Mercedes–Benz.

Horner, whom I once described as a miserable, irascible curmudgeon with a head that looked as though he had been sleeping face down for a year on a chenille bedspread, was a great man who effectively turned the Ford dealer network from a rag-tag assortment of mediocrities and millionaires into the most formidable sellers in Australia.

Like his equally long-serving successor, Max Gransden, he easily affected the cloak of bastardry – particularly

where the motoring press was concerned.

The XP range was launched in March 1965. The main men behind it were Americans: Al Sundberg, Carl Mueller and Jim Martin. Sundberg was a product planner on the first US Falcon, and told me in 1966 that even before the XK was released in Australia it was known that it would have to be re-engineered for our conditions.

Some of the early changes, like the chassis frame 'torque boxes' and self-adjusting brakes, were slipped into the XM without much bragging, because they were part of XP design. So focused was the group on the message that the XP would be tougher and more durable that product planning manager Mueller memoed to the effect that the styling had to be suggestive of massiveness and masculinity.

In *The History of Ford In Australia* Norm Darwin says: 'The front fenders, bumper and engine hood were 1960–63 US Mercury Comet as well as the dash, but used

Page 114: the end of the epic enduro. Wild Bill McLachlan was chaired from the first car to finish. Carrying the right leg is Max Stahl, then editor of Racing Car News. Top: Harry Firth in action.

E A BROKEN FIRE HYDRANT; HAWKINS APPLIED THE MOP

a locally designed grille with single headlamps; the Comet always used dual headlamps'.

XP was the first car out of the new Product Engineering group which, as Sir Brian Inglis pointed out, didn't exist for the first three Falcons. It had to be dominated by Americans – Sundberg as manager, powertrain manager Dave Doman and test and development manager Dan Wertz – because Australia simply didn't have the depth of talent and expertise.

But working with them were some Australian engineers who would become legends – Jock Garwood (chassis design and electrics), Jack Taylor (body design and soft trim) and Don Dunoon (supervisor of laboratory testing). But the man who gets the most credit for the great chassis balance and durability of the XP is slight, middle-aged, sandy-haired Yank Jim Martin, who made a preliminary visit in 1961 and came back in 1962 as chief engineer.

In *Wheels* magazine in January 1966 I wrote: 'He drove his engineers to the fringe of distraction and worked himself even harder in his eagerness to put together the best motor car he could, right down to the last mild steel nut. Martin had a rare gift in an engineer – he could explain techniques, materials and treatments in layman's language to anybody willing to stand still long enough'.

While the XP prototypes were accumulating huge durability mileages on the Eyre Peninsula between June 1964 and March 1965 (eventually the total would be 762,550 kilometres) Martin took his annual holidays and drove one around Australia, via Perth and Darwin, mainly on unsealed roads, in 10 days.

The day after he returned to Melbourne he went to a party and the next day handed in an eight-page trip report and analysis. Two days later he was in another car, heading for the Eyre Peninsula. He liked some of the roads in the difficult country around Port Lincoln so much he had them measured and photographed for reproduction at the still-being-designed You Yangs proving ground.

The new Falcon range added the Borg–Warner Type 35 three-speed automatic transmission to the Fordomatic two-speeder, mainly to lift local content, but it was available only with the 200 cid engine. The Fordomatic was restricted to the 170 and the continued 144 engine

FORD MAKES AUTOMOTIVE HISTORY!

FALCON 70,000 MILE DURABILITY RUN MOBIL

Opposite: Looking decidedly ill-at-ease in his role as flag marshal, managing director Wally Booth poses for the camera – or maybe he had just heard that Henry Ford II was going to helicopter in for a looksee … This page: formation driving by five shiny new cars before the start (one was held in reserve and actually substituted). At the end this XP quintet had all had more hits than Elvis. A slight rearrangement of the cars, some vanishing white lines and, hey presto, the advertising agency had a highly effective publicity shot.

was three-on-the-tree manual only.

Ford kept the Squire wagon in the range for a few months, but built only a handful before dropping it. The XP also marked the start of what became an options race, by offering extras such as electric rear glass in wagons, tinted windscreen, carpets, heater/demister and windscreen washers. Six months after the initial launch came the first Fairmont, replacing the Futura and Squire, complete with the first all-black interior trim.

The You Yangs 70,000 mile madness started at 8:28 am on April 24, 1965. Competition manager Les Powell – who not long after retired to run a hotel in Geelong, probably still suffering from stress – was in charge. There was no electricity or water, and the nights were freezing. The sound of generators throbbed endlessly through the temporary tent and caravan city where drivers would crash onto camp stretchers and where, in a huge marquee, the country's crankiest cook and his cringing staff shovelled out food 24 hours a day – more than 3000 meals was the final estimate.

There was a bank of floodlights across the start/finish line, but the rest of the track and the gloomy countryside were in inky blackness. The worst had happened. The lunatics were in charge of the asylum, handing to maniacal race drivers the car over which so much talent and money had sweated and which was the entire –

Coming towards dusk and complete darkness. The scarred earth and new bitumen give a good idea of the circuit's rawness.

entire! – future of the company in Australia.

There were actually six cars, one in reserve, a mix of two and four-doors, red, white and blue, all bog standard right down to brake linings and Dunlop SP41 cross-ply tyres boosted to 50 psi, either Pursuit 170 engines with manual shifts or Super Pursuit 200s with the Borg–Warner Type 35 automatic. Each car had been run in for 2000 miles (3220 kilometres) and scrutineered by the Confederation of Australian Motor Sport (CAMS).

Powell started with 12 of the best race and rally drivers in the country: Ian 'Pete' Geoghegan, Harry Firth, John Reaburn, Bob Jane, Kevin Bartlett, Allan Moffat, Barry Seton (father of today's Ford V8Supercar driver Glenn), Bruce McPhee (who had won the Bathurst enduro in 1968 in a dealer-entered Holden Monaro), round-Australia veteran Bill 'Wild Bill' McLachlan, Brian 'Brique' Reed, Fred Sutherland and Allan Mottram.

Powell thought they'd be enough. In fact, Firth and Reaburn shared car number 1, a red two-door, for the first 24 hours, refusing to let anyone else in the car until sheer tiredness forced them to hand over to Victoria Police driving instructors Sutherland and Mottram. (This pair was famous for optimistically running ex-police Studebaker Larks in the Armstrong 500, duly taking pole position so they could run out of brakes by lap 15.)

The enduro began with refuelling from four-gallon (18-litre) drums but progressed to gravity hoses. Soon it became obvious there had been a serious underestimation of tyre wear – wet weather had interfered with tyre testing. The test track surface was new and aggressive; at first they were chopping out a tyre in 12 laps, but the wear rate improved as more rubber went down.

In number 1, the fastest of the five, Firth was averaging 1 hour 40 minutes per tyre on a lap average of 1:48 (76 mph/122 km/h). But by the Monday Dunlop was trucking its whole Australian daily production of SP41s out to the You Yangs.

The gun drivers were averaging three hours' sleep and the crashes began, because the circuit would kill you if you blinked, and there wasn't a straight where you could relax. Early in the event Bob Jane said: 'It's the hardest circuit on a car I've ever driven on or even seen … bends

all the way. Ford have really set themselves a task here; my two hours each in cars 1 and 5 I found harder than any Armstrong I've put in. If you make the slightest mistake you're in real trouble'.

Victorian Ern Abbott, whose efforts in a Chrysler Valiant touring car betrayed no lack of *cojones,* said of the place: 'It scared the living pants off me for the first 10 laps. You go up in the air and all you can see is sky and suddenly someone takes the road from underneath you'.

The cars were unheated and a bitter wind often swept across the land. Towards dusk they had to cope with the setting sun in their eyes and in the mornings the rising sun in the east as they topped the hill and plunged down onto the fastest part, which was generally slippery with dew.

Marshals were kept busy sweeping away rubber and gravel and then patching the holes on the fast line. Seton left the road and rolled five times. Car 1 hit a huge rock and reputedly moved it; another broke a stub axle and rolled twice; another had to be pulled straight with power jacks. All but one of the five rolled, and were being held together with wire, straps and race tape.

Max Gransden said later: 'We were out to prove durability, and it looked bloody hopeless after the fourth or fifth day'.

Down to two-hour stints, most of the top drivers decided they'd like to live to see their children grow up. Ford sent out the call for reinforcements. Up on the notice board of the Light Car Club headquarters in Melbourne went a handwritten message on Ford letterhead asking anyone with a competition licence to report to the You Yangs. Motoring writers were called in – Max Stahl and I both did a shift, and I remember it was much scarier than any moment of the three Bathurst enduros I later drove.

Ian Geoghegan had the best story. At around 2 am he was hurtling down from the escarpment through the long, long left-hander, the fastest corner on the circuit, and he flashed past a fire, not a metre off the edge of the road on the exit clipping point.

He was going to report it but kept going for another lap and slowed down to look. It was a family who had somehow force-marched their way through pitch-black wilderness and other people's properties to get over the fence and set up a barbecue on the edge of the

THE CRASHES BEGAN, BECAUSE THE CIRCUIT WOULD

bitumen, the best seat in the house.

On the last Sunday Henry Ford II, in Australia on a special visit, decided he would helicopter out to inspect the troops. Some Ford Australia directors found urgent reasons to visit dealers in Broome, Cairns and New Zealand. As Gransden said later: 'He didn't have to stay too long to come to the conclusion that we were out of our bloody minds. He left no doubt in anybody's mind that he thought we were a bunch of damn fools'.

At 1:42 am the next day, May 3, Les Powell waved the chequered flag at Wild Bill McLachlan in car 3, the only one that hadn't rolled and the one in the best shape. His co-drivers chaired him away.

Ford put car 1, the red two-door, battered like a demolition derby loser, into the foyer of the Southern Cross, then Melbourne's glitziest hotel; the gawping crowds were enormous. Media coverage had been amazing, with radio stations crossing every hour, television running film clips, and more.

Today it is unlikely the public would be able to restrain a yawn at such derring-do, so much is reliability a given in cars that come with a warranty of three years/100,000 kilometres. But at the time, and given the overwhelming sales power of GM–H, it was a stunning tour de force.

Wheels magazine gave the XP its Car of the Year award, a gong I, as editor, had created two years earlier, and restricted until the mid-1970s to locally built cars. In the edition announcing the award I wrote of the Falcon:

'It certainly has its share of Detroit in its make-up, as the outline is still closely related to the original and fondly dis-remembered XK series of 1960, but so much Australian work and knowhow has been packed into it to make it competitive, that it is now only distantly related to its American cousin … One of the first signs of its success was the acceptance of the model by taxi drivers, those most demanding and voluble of car users.

'Then came the You Yangs 70,000-mile epic, which for all its ballyhoo and avalanche of beautifully handled advertising and promotion, was still an outstanding achievement. But brouhaha and epic feats alone seldom sell cars, although they help. What was more significant was that big fleet owners started to switch to Falcons. People like Avis, the NSW Police, Rothmans, James Hardie and dozens of others put in replacement orders for fleets of up to 1000 … So there you have it. The ugly duckling becomes a beautiful swan.'

Suddenly the fleet buyers weren't slamming the door in Ford's face. The company went for it, handing out long-term loan cars. Gransden recalled: 'We said, You drive it for six months. At the end of six months, if you like it, you buy it, or buy more like it. They did'. It laid the foundation of Ford's future fleet sales domination, wherein more than 70 per cent of Falcons would go into government and business fleets.

It was also an enormous boost for Ford dealers and Ford Australia employees. The company was arguably the leader in what was then called industrial relations in the

Opposite: Ford's competition manager, the larrikin Les Powell, flags a signal to car 4 during the night. Powell handled most of the logistics for the mammoth operation. Above: the 1964 Ford Galaxie. Below: pitstop for car 1 during the You Yangs epic. This red two-door, after the triumph, went on display in the Southern Cross hotel.

ILL YOU IF YOU BLINKED

Australian motor industry. Because it had to generate an enormous new colony of immigrant and low-skilled labour for Broadmeadows, in an area far from Geelong and where there was little residential property, it expanded the emphasis it had had since 1925 on looking after its people.

Typical of this approach was a wallet titled *Your Job At Ford*. It contained booklets explaining the company life insurance plan, safety instructions, educational scholarships, bonus plans and employee suggestion rewards. The company also handed out vinyl records on those subjects, in English, Turkish, Greek, Italian and other languages, explaining the company and the job environment. A 16 millimetre film on the assembly lines was dubbed in six languages.

But the model planning treadmill waits for no-one. Even while joy at the success of the XP was unrestrained, Ford Australia's design centre modellers were sculpting clay

King Billy's country

Ford's research into its proving ground site's history has established that the original inhabitants arrived probably 30,000 years ago. Their custodianship ended during the 1850s when white settlers looking for grazing land forced out the Yawangi tribe. They called the mountain range Wurde Youang, meaning 'big mountain in the middle of a plain', but white usage changed that to You Yangs. The last surviving Yawangi, called King Billy by the locals, lived in a mud hut on the present boundary of the proving ground until 1889 or later.

The first European known to survey the area was explorer and navigator Matthew Flinders. Appointed to the rank of Commander, he was given the *Investigator* to sail from Spithead on July 18, 1801, to explore and chart the entire Australian coast (the results were so accurate that the Australian Navy was still using some of Flinders' charts in the early 1960s).

He often ventured ashore and noted the Flinders Ranges and named Mount Lofty near the future site of Adelaide. He entered Port Phillip Bay and on March 1, 1802 climbed the tallest point of the Wurde Youang, naming it Station Peak (later changed to Flinders Peak).

The You Yangs National Park adjoins the proving ground and because of this there are mobs of Western Grey kangaroos inside the Ford property, along with small colonies of koalas, brown falcons, sulphur-crested cockatoos, eastern rosellas, galahs and the occasional wedgetail eagle. The property has been extensively re-forested with new plantation trees helped by the regrowth from the 1985 bushfires. However, rabbits are a constant problem, burrowing into embankments and under roads and causing erosion.

About 60 kilometres of roads thread through the site, the most spectacular being the double-ended high-speed oval. There are several durability circuits, special surfaces tracks, and noise and brake test sections. There are barrier crash, corrosion and fire test facilities, mud, saltwater and dust 'baths', an emissions laboratory and a Noise, Vibration, Harshness (NVH) and hot/cold weather test laboratory. A permanent crew of 10 maintains the roads, looks after the plant nursery and handles fence maintenance, soil conservation and general repair work.

models of the XW, four years into the future. And in March 1960 Ford had laid the platform for a range of cars when the Product Committee (mainly half a dozen top management) decided to attack the large prestige market. Thus the locally assembled Fairlane (Tank) 500 replaced the Customline in 1959, and in April 1965 the Galaxie 500 replaced the Compact on the Homebush line, with the 289 V8 and the option of the Thunderbird 390 cubic inch (6.4 litre) engine, aimed at competing with GM's locally assembled Chevrolet Bel Air and Pontiac Laurentian, the Rambler Ambassador, and Chrysler's locally assembled Dodge Phoenix – each car taking 9–10 per cent of the luxury car market.

However, the XP's successor, the XR, due for launch in September 1966, was well down the development road. In July 1965 the Product Committee approved power steering as an option on XR – wow! There were problems with rear axles being supplied by Borg–Warner and it was decided to start with imported US Fairlane units. By November the committee – advised by the Product Planning Office – was still worrying over the boot size in the XR as well as the feasibility of doing a coupe version further down the track. Even that early there was discussion about importing the 351 cubic inch Windsor engine for the range, although it was probably too late to modify the engine bay.

The V8 question was postponed because of the upcoming local Fairlane – mainly to enable Ford Australia to meet its commitment to local content. And that had now become political.

You see, by the early 1960s, every man and his dog was into Australian vehicle assembly and/or manufacture. It wasn't just GM, Ford and Chrysler; Chrysler was building not only Valiants and Dodges but assembling French Simcas, and had bought the Port Melbourne Rootes Group plant to continue assembling Hillman, Singer and Humber; Volkswagen was building high local content Beetles in the Clayton plant that would eventually be taken over by Nissan; Toyota had started building a local Corona and was planning to add the Corolla; Nissan had Clyde Industries in Sydney assembling Datsun Bluebirds; BMC at Zetland in Sydney was building the Mini and Morris 1100; Renaults, Peugeots, Ramblers, Studebakers,

Mercedes–Benz and Citroens were being assembled from CKD packs. Even a small Adelaide firm called Lightburn, whose main business was supplying glass-fibre-shrouded washing machines to the Australian armed forces, decided to enter the market with the Zeta. Based on the British Frisky Sprint, it had a rear-mounted two-cylinder Fichtel und Sachs engine from Germany and actually had 65 per cent local content.

The Federal government had been fretting about the extent of rorting by assemblers (as distinct from manufacturers in that they used a high proportion of imported packs and components) in the claiming of exceptions from import duty on parts used in the industry. There was also the need to protect the developing component suppliers so they could invest and expand. Component imports had doubled from 1961–62 to 1962–63 and the industry body, the Federation of Automotive Product Manufacturers (FAPM), was hammering on Canberra doors.

Because of the euphoria associated with six car makers involved in full manufacture, there hadn't been a full-on Tariff Board inquiry into the motor industry for years. After talking it through with the key industry bodies, the government announced on May 1, 1964 that from January 1 by-law exemption for components in passenger vehicles would be granted only for those entered into one of three approved plans.

Plan A required local content to reach 95 per cent in prescribed stages within five years – deadline December 31, 1969. Makers signing for Plan A would be able to import components duty-free and, once at 95 per cent,

keep the exemption for the other 5 per cent until the end of 1974. Plan B1 entrants had to start at 40 per cent, hit 50 per cent in 12 months and 55 per cent for another year, while B2 had lower local content targets, but in both plans duty was wiped only on components needed to reach those targets.

Curiously, the government refused to make public which makers had registered for what plan. J. D. Beruldsen in *Beneath The Bonnet*, the definitive history of the Australian

Wheels *magazine gave its coveted Car of the Year award for 1965 to the XP Falcon, in recognition of its engineering excellence. Here author Tuckey, leaner and still dark of hair, hogs the microphone with Bill Bourke on his right and to his left, Ford PR manager Ralph Hosking and Bob Geraghty, then general manager of Murray Publishers.*

component industry, says that 'as far as is known' Plan A entrants were GM–H with Holden and Torana, Ford with Falcon/Fairlane and Cortina, BMC with Austin Kimberley/Tasman, Morris 1500/Marina and Mini, Volkswagen with the Beetle and the 1600 Type B, and Chrysler with Valiant. AMI had started building the Corona in 1963 but plumped for the low volumes of B1/B2,

as did Pressed Metal Corporation in Sydney, contracted to assemble the Datsun P411 (Bluebird), and Renault Australia with Renault and Peugeot.

In 1964 imports of fully built (CBU) passenger cars accounted for 10 per cent of total sales and in 1963 Japanese imports totalled only 4300 units, or 1.4 per cent of passenger registrations. The August 1964 Budget delivered a bonus by reducing motor vehicle sales tax from 40 per cent to 25 per cent.

But there was a fly hidden in the ointment. As usual, the government couldn't resist fiddling at the edges, and started to water down the rules harnessing the low-volume makers. In 1966 it deleted B1 and B2 and substituted the Small Volume (SV) plans. These based the local content percentages not on a time frame but on volumes. This allowed the makers unlimited CBU imports of the same model for almost three years, so they could build the lowest economic number of cars here and import as many as they liked to meet excess demand.

This was jim-dandy for Toyota and Nissan – although

Ford also entered its Galaxie under SV, Leyland the MGB and Volvo its 120 Series. Mazda Motor Corporation got a foothold in the early 1960s through Brisbane-based importer Westco Group, added State distributors, and finally took over via a wholly owned subsidiary, Mazda Australia. But it never had any intention of manufacturing here, while Toyota Motor Corporation quietly bought up 10 per cent of AMI – the first time a Japanese car maker had taken an equity stance in a local car maker.

Imports boomed. Imported Japanese vehicles went from 23,131 in 1964 to 50,827 in 1968, and by 1974 imported passenger cars would account for nearly 32 per cent of annual sales (today the figure is stable at around 65 per cent!).

Of course, passenger cars were only part of the problem. Four-wheel drives and commercial vehicles were exempt from the plans, but local truck assembly – a flow-on from the war years – was big business. In 1965 GM–H had 30 per cent of the truck market, mainly British-sourced Bedford, down from a 35.8 per cent peak in 1962.

International Harvester held 19 per cent, while Ford was on 12 per cent, mainly the US-sourced F-Series and British K-Series trucks. But the government moves on local content made future passenger vehicle product decisions – some of them as much as four years out – even more crucial.

On November 18, 1965 the Product Committee advised that Ford Australia's proposals for the XT – the model to follow the still-unreleased XR and not due until April 1968 – had been approved by Dearborn, as had the final XRA program. XRA was the second codename for the first Australian-designed and built Fairlane, the ZA; the first was XRL, of which more later.

In *Wheels* magazine of January 1967, I wrote:

'November 14, 1963 was a fairly ordinary day. On that day an RAAF Sabre jet made an emergency landing at Richmond with an engine on fire; Sir Robert Menzies had his rowdiest political meeting for years when he said he would not retire as long as he had his health and vigour; a 15-foot white pointer shark was killed after it attacked a shark meshing boat off the Queensland Gold coast.

'On that day an explosion rocked the US Atomic Energy Commission's nuclear weapons plant in Texas; it was announced that Australia would reach a population of 11 million two days hence; flags were flown from Britain's public buildings in honour of Prince Charles' birthday; and the Namoi Regional Library announced that it had banned James Jones' novel The Thin Red Line. *An ordinary day.*

'The NSW Premier called for a report on allegations of thuggery and prostitution at Kings Cross, and a new Valiant series was announced.

'And on that day, eight men around a native mahogany board table in Ford Australia's headquarters in Melbourne decided to build the Falcon XR.'

Bibliography

J. D. Beruldsen, *Beneath The Bonnet,*
Longman Cheshire, 1989.
Geoff Easdown, *The Falcon Story,*
Lothian Publishing, 1989.
Bill Tuckey, *Wheels magazine, January 1966.*
Bill Tuckey, *Wheels magazine, January 1967.*
Walter Uhlenbruch, *Australian Motor Vehicles and Parts,*
Committee For Economic Development, 1986.
John Wright, *The History of the Ford Falcon 1960–1994,*
Ford Australia, 1994.

CHAPTER 11

A **Fairlane** At Fair Lane?

In 1998 one Jac Nasser was widely quoted as saying he would love to see the day when there was 'a Fairlane at Fair Lane'. This, of course, was a reference to the possible sight of an exported Ford Australia luxury car in the driveway of the Ford family home after which it and its predecessors were named. The quote gained considerable currency.

The Australian Fairlane was a masterstroke. As John Wright said in his definitive work on Ford's long-wheelbase luxury cars, *The Lineage Of A Legend*: 'More than any other car in Ford Australia's history, the Fairlane reveals the forethought and sheer creativity that distinguishes great product planning from the more common kind'.

In fact, the first was more an accountant's car than one from the brain of a product planner or designer. As Wright points out, the lineage goes directly back to the Single Spinner Ford Custom of 1949, which within a year had 80 per cent local content and in 1951 segued into the Twin Spinner, using an imported side-valve V8 that was basically a bare engine block. The rest – valves, pistons, timing gear, valve springs, generator, starter motor, carburettor, fuel pump and sump – was made in Australia and the engine 'dressed' at Geelong.

The 1952 Triple Spinner had a completely local V8 (apart from the block and crankshaft); the rival Holden-assembled Chevrolets were sixes. And in July 1953 came the Customline. John Wright declared:

'There can be no doubt that to some conservative observers these big Fords were flashy, immodest even. But what they possessed in abundance was glamour, the allure of the American dream come to Australia, thoughts of ice-cream sodas and Hollywood and beautiful film stars; here, if you like, was 77 Sunset Strip on whitewall tyres, the perfect car for the Toorak Village drive-in theatre on Saturday night.

IT WAS 77 SUNSET ST

Page 128: a rumble of V8s. Clockwise from bottom left, 1961 Tank Fairlane, 1974 LTD, 1985 LTD, 1957 Customline, 1950 Custom Single Spinner, 1966 Galaxie. This portrait depicts the continuity of big Fords through the post World War 2 era. Only the 1985 model lacks a V8 engine. The V8 returned to Ford Australia's lineup in 1991. Above: the American Customline was designed as the right car for the big family. Certainly, as an alternative to the much less expensive Holden, the Customline in Australia quickly became a lifestyle statement for those who could aspire to greater things. Pictured here is the last of the line Star model of 1958–59. Opposite: the Fairlane 500 won a gold medal for styling at the 1959 World Fair in Brussels, Belgium. Ford Australia promoted its new models as 'the world's most beautifully proportioned cars'.

'In the mid-1950s Australia was not the sophisticated and cosmopolitan society it has become over the past 20 or so years. We still called Great Britain the Mother Country, sang God Save The Queen at the start of every school day, had six o'clock closing of pubs and very little popular culture that didn't come straight from either Britain or the USA. We had no television until 1956.'

The first Fairlane badge arrived in Australia late in 1959 when Canadian-sourced models replaced the classic Customline Star Series (8A). There was the Custom 300, Fairlane 500 and the vast Ranch Wagon – the first two with three-on-the-tree manual shift and Fordomatic option, the Fairlane 500 with the two-speed auto as standard.

It had a 332 cubic inch (5.4 litre) V8 which seemed gigantic at the time but which actually delivered only 168 kilowatts – today's designers are getting more than that from normally aspirated 2 litre four-cylinder engines – but a massive 440 Newton metres of torque. It wasn't all that expensive but it was dubbed 'The Tank' and it didn't sell particularly well.

The arrival of the Falcon gave Ford Australia the chance to develop more and better-defined niches in its model range. In 1962 came the Canadian Mercury Comet, badged as Fairlane, soon to be called Compact, fitting

between the Falcon and the Galaxie, which replaced the Tank. Both by 1964 were being assembled in the Homebush (Sydney) plant, but the Compact was dropped in 1965, too expensive for its market segment, so the Fairlane name vanished locally again.

The Galaxie was being imported in kit (CKD, completely knocked down) form, sold with the choice of the 289 and 390 cubic inch V8s, and in 1969 – a year after GM–H had stopped assembling Chevrolets and Pontiacs – there came the LTD option (which stood for Lincoln Type Design), but the biggest Ford was phased out early in 1973 after a lusty career as big cars for government members and Ministers.

However, the LTD badge was switched to an upgraded, further stretched variant of the flagship local Fairlane, although not without some agonising.

On December 22, 1965 the Product Planning Office had asked the Product Committee to suggest a name for the coming new ZA, codenamed XRA. Managing director Wally Booth and Bill Bourke nominated Fairlane, while another member listed Fairlane first, then Monarch and then Pacific. Chief engineer Jack Prendergast wanted Fairlane S-C, standing for Southern Cross, supported by a badge of the Southern Cross 'arranged around a very delicately sculptured boomerang'. Hmm. Prendergast's idea at least found expression in the bonnet emblem, which featured the Southern Cross, if not the boomerang.

GM–H's main offering then was the HR Holden, with the modifications designed to reduce the effect of styling demanded by autocratic GM design chief Bill Mitchell with the HD. The frontal treatment entailed projecting fenders, which Australian motoring writers derided as 'kidney scoops'. There was a station wagon version, but it was on the same 106 inch (2692 mm) wheelbase as the sedan and there were no long wheelbase luxury derivatives.

In that year Ford Australia had yet another stroke of luck, acquiring from Ford's European base in Cologne its first design chief, a brilliant stylist called Jack Telnack (who went on to be Ford's global design head, retiring only in 1998). He was merely 29 years old. Identifying precocious talent, he headhunted 22-year-old London-born, Ballarat-bred John Doughty from GM–H and then 25-year-old Brian Rossi from Ford UK; he arrived on October 1, 1966.

'We were located in Geelong in a tiny shoebox of a place – I mean, it was a pretty frightening-looking place compared with what we had been used to', Rossi recalled

P ON WHITEWALL TYRES, PERFECT FOR THE DRIVE-IN

later. 'But it was regarded as the design office.'

It was Ford Australia's first, and its premier task was the minor XT facelift of the XR – the first truly indigenous Australian design work on a Falcon. But they were about to achieve something unique: the ZA Fairlane.

Integral to this was a V8 engine with local componentry. On February 14, 1968, Australia asked Dearborn to approve what was then the massive sum of $14.9 million to develop and tool for it. The V8 engines were built from imported blocks (excepting 1977 when they were cast locally) which were machined and fitted with Australian parts.

The basis of the business plan was this: in 1964 Ford Australia had committed itself to the Federal government's car plan to

achieve 95 per cent local content in the Falcon/Fairlane by August 1966. In December 1966, said the submission, it had reached 95.8 per cent, but this had since declined marginally because 90 per cent of Fairlanes were being sold with the imported V8. If it were allowed to drop below 95 per cent, duty would be payable on all imported components. 'It is anticipated that if no integration action is taken, the local content will fall to approximately 93 per cent by 1970 and 91.3 per cent by 1974; duty would average $4.9 million per annum from 1970–74', it said. The document also pointed out that GM–H had invested $16.9 million in its engine plant to produce a local version of the imported 307 V8. It was a subtle but legitimate form of corporate blackmail, and the

money was approved.

The creation of the Ford Fairlane represented a fine example of the engineering ingenuity for which the Australian automotive industry is now internationally respected. 'We just took the Falcon wheelbase and stretched it', says Ian Vaughan. All the extra space went into the rear compartment. The Falcon doors were retained and those five extra inches could be seen between the trailing edge of the door and the rear wheel. Impressively this feat was accomplished without compromising the XR's style but, rather, enhancing it. The rear quarter panels and bootlid were taken from a US model. With a longer wheelbase at their disposal, it was logical for the product planners to apply it to the next generation Falcon wagon (the XA), this time devoting the extra space to load carrying. Ford beat GM–H with its long wheelbase concept by more than four years, but in one way the model cycle counted in GM–H's favour. The XR would need to undergo three facelifts before XA time and Holden's next all-new car was due earlier. When the HQ range was launched in July 1971 it wasn't only the belated Statesman (to supersede the Brougham) that got the stretch, but also the wagon, six months ahead of the still unreleased XA Falcon.

The conception of the ZA was nothing short of brilliant. Managing director Bill Bourke was courageous to approve this radical piece of product planning, which created a whole new niche market sector still thriving some 33 years down the road.

However it was conceived, it was a felicitous intercourse which was to be a major contributor to Ford Australia's viability for the ensuing 30 years.

The ZA was launched on February 27, 1967, with 95 per cent local content, costing just $3080 with the 200 cubic inch six-cylinder engine and $3885 with the 289 V8 and three-speed – three-speed! – SelectShift automatic and front bucket seats instead of the bench type in the cheaper version. There was even fake timber trim, described in the press release as 'an attractive walnut

The US brochure used pastel colours and floral phrases to promote the 1959 Galaxie. Note the pillarless bodywork, which was not used in the Australian-built Tank Fairlane range.

finish applique', across the dash. And there was an optional vinyl roof, and whitewall tyres, no less.

GM–H panicked. It had already been traumatised by the Mustang-styled XR Falcon, and now it had been leap-frogged again – the harbinger of a sequence of model-release timing that survives to this day. Ford and Chrysler had V8 engines; Holden did not. GM–H's chief designer, Joe Schemansky, demanded an extra three inches (76 mm) on the 1968 HK Holden's front fenders to match the XR's length and stitched an awkward stretched boot onto the Premier and called the result the Brougham, a name as repellent as the tacky brocade trim. Even Peter Nankervis, who retired in late 1999 as GM–H's longest serving designer, admitted it was a cheap and half-arsed answer that didn't work, because the car was no bigger inside; particularly, it couldn't match the Fairlane's rear seat legroom.

And so it goes, and so it went. The ZB, launched a year later, put the Custom badge on the lower of the two models but delivered a 221 cubic inch (3.6 litre) six-cylinder as standard equipment, along with the 302 cubic inch (5 litre) V8 in the Fairlane 500 instead of the old 289. Put simply, there was no equivalent locally built car that could match the Fairlane for interior room and boot space and engine. And the real breakthrough was being able to offer that much luxury at an affordable

price, only just above a Fairmont's. The new flagship for Ford Australia was somewhat extravagantly advertised as 'Unique In The World Of Luxury Motoring'. The fleet market loved it.

But Ford was still looking for niches. A memo from the Product Planning Office to the all-powerful Product Committee on November 13, 1968, floated the idea of a 'low series' Fairlane, to be sold at the Holden Premier's price of $2860, $370 under the Fairlane Custom's, which would then get automatic as standard and be repriced to $3500. The idea was to delete front and rear armrests, carpet, heater and courtesy lights, but the memo added that it was a 'high risk' proposal which could do little better than break even.

The same memo discussed a performance version of the Fairlane, called the Cobra, to be launched with the coming ZC for 1969. It would have the imported 351 cubic inch (5.8 litre) V8 with four-barrel carburettor, automatic transmission, special non-reclining bucket seats, centre console, disc front brakes, Falcon GT wheel covers, revised suspension and ER70 x 14 'wide oval' tyres, to sell at $4090. It didn't make the grid.

Ford needn't have worried. In sales terms, with the Fairlane Ford Australia was on Murder Road. In August 1969, with GM–H having released its first local V8 in May, a small 253 cubic inch (4.2 litre) for its

Opposite: the 1969 Homebush-built Ford Galaxie brought the LTD badge into the range for the first time. It featured concealed headlamps and was the car of choice for government VIPs. Below: a US brochure for the 1959 Galaxie happily claims some Thunderbird heritage. Incidentally, the US Galaxie was similar to the 1959 Custom 300/Fairlane 500/Ranch Wagon models sold in Australia and popularly dubbed the Tank. Right and further right: two faces of Customline from the 1950s, the farther one being the ultimate 1958 Star model.

HT range, Ford slammed the two-barrel 351 V8 option in its Fairlane. With the ZC came huge Kelsey–Hayes ventilated front disc brakes (but it still had rear drum brakes, like most cars then), vertically stacked quad headlamps and fake leather trim plus – wait for it! – optional factory-fitted air-conditioning.

The next model, the ZD, launched in November 1970, had a minor makeover that included an egg-crate grille, individual front seats with a folding centre armrest that became a bench, six-inch rims with standard radial-ply tyres and most importantly, the six-cylinder engine expanded to 250 cubic inches (4.0 litres), with power up to 115 kW and torque to 325 Nm at a very low 1600 rpm – a real lugger.

It was developed by Ford's Geelong engineers with many new internals and a new exhaust system. It was a great car, this last of the four generations of the clever original design. In May 1972, two months after the launch of the dramatically restyled XA ('Coke bottle') Falcon, came the ZF Fairlane, equally significantly changed and for the first time using all-Australian styling. The XA and ZF were largely penned by the team of Telnack, Rossi and Allan Jackson (albeit in conjunction with the Dearborn studio, mainly because there were no experienced clay modellers in Australia).

Rossi says the Americans suggested adapting their Torino but a quick clay showed it would look too stumpy if reduced in wheelbase. Then Ford president Semon ('Bunkie') Knudsen took a personal interest in the project. Rossi: 'I well remember the dawn patrols, where we would have to roll the clays out into the courtyard, so Knudsen and his entourage could inspect them early in the day. There was never criticism, always encouragement'.

Bill Bourke flew across the Pacific every second week to check out the design stages. Geoff Easdown says that Rossi told him what was done in Dearborn was the big chance for Australia to get design autonomy. 'This was our chance and no-one wanted to blow it', he reported.

Later Knudsen, who believed the boss should visit the design studio every day, told Bourke to create his own in Broadmeadows – Geelong was too far away.

The ZF styling followed the XA theme, with quad headlamps now horizontal and a pronounced rear hip-line, and there was muted criticism that it looked too much like the smaller sibling. The 302 V8 was standard in the Fairlane 500, optional in the Custom, which for the first time had ventilated front discs.

John Wright records that the options list had burgeoned to the point where one could buy the lower Custom and option it up to cost more than the 500 with items like sliding steel sunroof, factory air, electric windows, 351 V8 and stereo sound system. There were even five choices of vinyl roof colour: black, beige, green, brown and blue. The advertising burbled ungrammatically: 'A Completely New World Of Quiet'.

GM–H had released its radically styled HQ lineup in July 1971, with wagons for the first time on a longer, 115 inch (2921 mm) wheelbase that would enable it to add two models of Statesman, the standard drivetrain the 308 (5 litre) V8 and three-speed Tri-Matic auto. But Ford continued to erode GM–H's market share, the Fairlane outselling the Statesman three to one.

Another Ford riposte came in August 1973, when it added the LTD and the Landau above the Fairlane. Codenamed P5, the LTD was designed on a wheelbase stretched to 121 inches (3073 mm), borrowing the concealed four headlamp treatment from the US Mercury Cougar and with full-width slotted rear lamps. The Landau

Proved—and now improved **FORD** V8's BIG, BETTER DIFFERENCE!

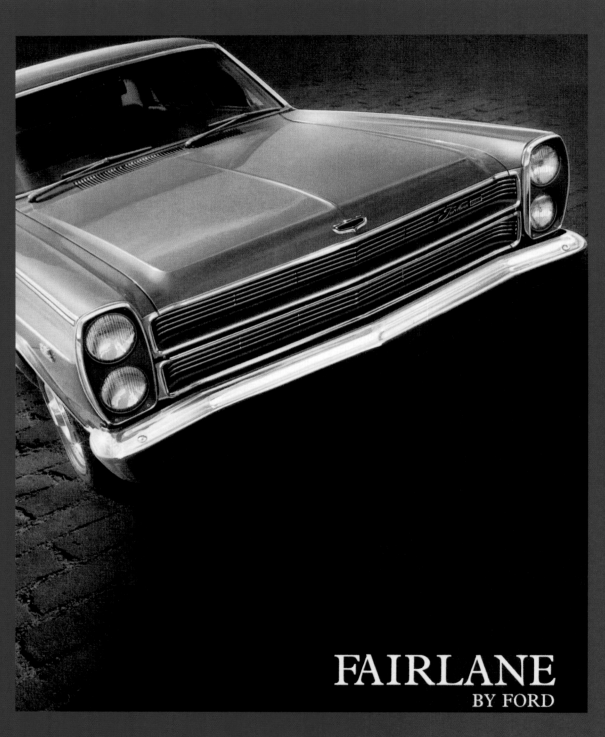

FAIRLANE
BY FORD

IN SALES TERMS, WITH T

was somewhat incongruous, structured as it was on the tail-heavy Falcon Hardtop but with the LTD front and rear sheet metal. Both came with the 351 V8, auto and limited-slip diff, and vinyl roof.

The ZG was released in tandem with the XB Falcon in October 1973. Both were really upgrades, costing $38 million in development and tooling. The ZG banished the three-on-the-tree manual shift, but continued the excellent SelectShift automatic, with which you could engage 2 and the car would start in that ratio – good for avoiding wheelspin in the wet or getting out of a bog.

The 351 V8 delivered all-wheel disc brakes for the first time, and also for the first time a radio became standard

on the Custom. The restyling, while giving the car a more aggressive face, was fairly minor. Ford was playing it safe with its flagship.

The ZH lineup, however, launched on May 12, 1976, received a major going-over. Ford had heeded the call for greater differentiation from the Falcon. This year brought in Australian Design Rule (ADR) 27A, which demanded lower emission standards, but where GM–H chose to hang emission control equipment onto its engines – a poor band-aid solution – Ford gave its 3.3 and 4.1 litre sixes all-new cross-flow cylinder heads with larger valves, new inlet manifolding, revised ignition timing and more power (80 kW and 92 kW respectively). The 4.9 litre (151 kW)

Opposite: the 1969 ZC was the first Fairlane 500 with the option of a 5.8 litre V8 (if 4.9 litres were not quite sufficient). Left: the 1965 Galaxie also offered two V8s – the standard 289 cubic inch unit (4.7 litre) or optional 390 'Thunderbird' (6.4 litre) to make it one of the fastest sedans on the Australian market.

Best year yet to go Ford!

FORD GALAXIE 500

E FAIRLANE FORD AUSTRALIA WAS ON MURDER ROAD

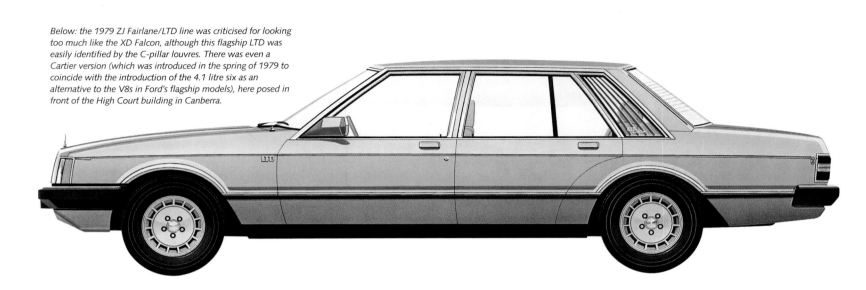

Below: the 1979 ZJ Fairlane/LTD line was criticised for looking too much like the XD Falcon, although this flagship LTD was easily identified by the C-pillar louvres. There was even a Cartier version (which was introduced in the spring of 1979 to coincide with the introduction of the 4.1 litre six as an alternative to the V8s in Ford's flagship models), here posed in front of the High Court building in Canberra.

and 5.8 litre (162 kW) V8s also got more power. GM–H had added a Caprice version to the Statesman in late 1974 to combat the Fairlane 500 (it was not on a longer wheelbase and thus not as roomy as the LTD), and in July 1976 the HX Holden range further upgraded the flagships.

The ZH was B-I-G. Still on the same wheelbase, it added almost 150 mm to overall length and 61 mm to width. In *Lineage of a Legend* John Wright describes the look as 'big, bold, brash and aggressive'. Every external panel was new, the Coke bottle hip-line had been flattened out (although the rear doors were the same as the Falcon's) and the interior completely redesigned.

The Custom model was dropped, leaving the 500 as the base car and adding the Marquis (pronounced 'marquee') to combat the Caprice, leaving the LTD above it in size and price. Equipment levels were lifted through the range, with steel radials, four discs, air-conditioning, T-bar automatic and, for the Marquis, leather trim as standard along with a divided front seat from the US Thunderbird.

Placing the Ford oval in the grille (in 1978) for the first time was a suitable touch for the last – and the best – of this second generation local Fairlane.

In October 1977 came one of those watershed points in the maturing Holden–Ford rivalry. A new managing director for GM–H, Chuck Chapman, brought with him a new chief engineer, Joe Whitesell, accompanied from

Some four months after the arrival of the EA Falcon came a fresh new shape for the
Fairlane (codenamed NA). It shared surprisingly few body panels with the Falcon.

THE AUSTRALIAN MASTERPIECE

NEW FORD FAIRLANE

FORD WAS CO

Top: clay model experimentation for the long wheelbase versions of EA26 (note number plate). Above: the LTD emblem is a familiar part of the luxury car market today. Opposite: the NC Fairlane/LTD arrived in 1991. This model marked the return of the V8, except it was an imported fuel-injected version.

Germany by the brilliant young Peter Hanenberger as chassis development manager (he returned in 1999 as Holden's chairman and managing director). The new team transformed the good looking but clumsy handling HQ–HJ–HX Holden series into an altogether sharper performance package by redesigning the suspension around radial-ply tyres – which the Fairlane had long had as standard. The Radial Tuned Suspension (RTS) treatment flowed through to the HZ Statesman/Caprice in November 1977.

Ford Australia had also undergone a major change in its design fraternity. Bill Bourke and the legendary Lee Iacocca, then still with Ford, talked Detroit-born Frederick W. Bloom out of retiring from his job as chief engineer of Ford Europe to come Down Under and run the $72 million program approved for the development of the next Falcon/Fairlane lines, the XD/ZJ – that figure would blow out to over $100 million by launch time in March–April 1979.

Called Project Blackwood, it began in 1974 when an American with the unlikely name of Thomas W. Shearer Junior II was product planning manager and Keith Horner was still director of marketing. The story of the enormous struggle Ford Australia had with Dearborn to get the Blackwood it wanted is told in a later chapter. Shearer was

replaced in September 1975 by David ('no relation') Ford, born in the Melbourne suburb of Glen Iris on September 1, 1942, graduate of Scotch College and Melbourne University, who joined Ford Australia in 1964.

In the way the superb Ford global scholarship system works, in 1967 he was sent on overseas assignments that saw him work in Dearborn and Cologne, then back to Dearborn and finally to Broadmeadows for Blackwood. Bloom was director of engineering and he tabbed David Ford as a future replacement.

(Current Ford Australia president, Geoff Polites, was another beneficiary of the Ford graduate training scheme. Graduating from Monash University with first-class honours in Economics – having studied 'nothing that was practical because I didn't want to become an accountant; I wanted to learn to *think*' – the 22-year-old Polites moved straight into product planning where he worked alongside Ian Vaughan, Dave Fewchuk [later to become father of the Capri roadster], Peter Gillitzer, and of course David Ford. Polites was sent on an assignment to the US just two years later – evidence that he must have made a pretty reasonable start to a career that would last 18 years and 5 months ... before resuming in 1999 when he took up the presidency.)

The ZJ Fairlane and FC LTD, launched in July 1979, went back to being 'big Falcons' in their styling – although they stood apart with their six-window profile. Still designed on the long wheelbase (shared with the wagon), they were 155 mm shorter overall and 75 mm narrower, but lighter and with far more interior leg and headroom.

Marketed as 'A Car For The Big Country' the 500 and Custom designations vanished, replaced by Fairlane and LTD, with the 4.9 litre V8 standard and 5.8 optional. There were technological advances such as a plastic fuel tank from the new Broadmeadows plastics plant, electronic instruments, alloy wheels for the LTD and a special LTD Cartier model.

However, the world was still engaged with the second Middle East oil crisis and in October 1978 GM–H had taken the bold (later to be seen as premature) step of downsizing the Kingswood to the Commodore. Ford went into mild panic. It stitched the 4.1 litre six-cylinder engine into the Cartier as a short-term measure. But soon would come one of those astonishing events, typical of this crazed business, which are planned three or four years in advance but on release look like a stroke of genius.

In November 1976, David Ford went with Bloom to Japan to look for a supplier of an alloy cylinder head for the six-cylinder. Ford Australia signed an agreement with Honda for the new head in 1977 and the Geelong plant had it

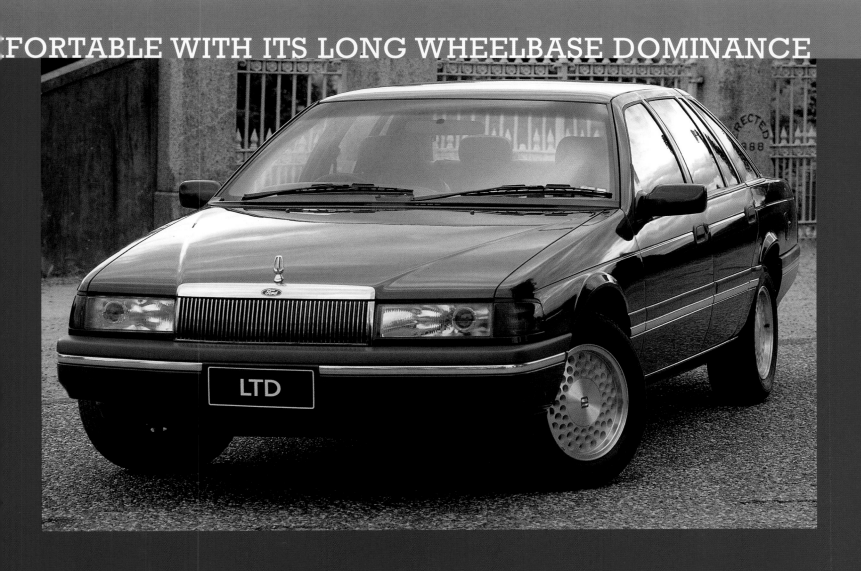

FORTABLE WITH ITS LONG WHEELBASE DOMINANCE

LTD

ready to introduce during the life of XD/ZJ (1980). It gave a higher compression ratio and 10 per cent better fuel consumption and, equally importantly, a point of difference to advertise and promote.

It worked. In 1982 Ford wrenched from GM–H the number 1 sales guernsey it had held since 1950 and reported an after-tax profit of $66 million, compared with GM–H's $126.6 million loss; the Fairlane/LTD contributed in large part to both. The year also saw the unveiling of the ZK Fairlane/LTD, followed by electronic fuel injection on the 4.1, which became standard equipment on the LTD. The ZK took the new Watts link rear suspension from the Falcon.

But there was some bad news. Ford Australia had decided to discontinue its V8 engines, the PR people arguing that the EFI 4.1 was more than a match for the 4.9 V8 – but where was the alternative to the 5.8? The Fairlane/LTD went through to 1987 with little change to the massive, sharp-edged styling but progressive upgrades to freshen things. Unsurprisingly, GM–H dropped its tired WB Statesman/Caprice range – essentially a stretched HZ Kingswood – early in 1985, effectively abandoning the luxury market to Fairlane/LTD until 1990.

Ford was comfortable in that dominance until the VR Commodore-based big cars arrived in 1994.

The NA/NC/NF/NL line of Fairlanes/LTDs ran from 1988 to 1998 with little change and is too fresh in memory to require extensive recall. It has been a memorable life for the second oldest nameplate in Australian automotive history (although 'Fairlane' is older than 'Falcon' it has not run continuously here) – and it's not over yet. About the only trophy not on the mantelpiece is export to the US – and Jac Nasser has still not ruled out that possibility.

Bibliography

Norm Darwin, *The History of Ford in Australia,*
Eddie Ford Publications Pty Ltd, 1986.
Geoff Easdown, *A History of the Ford Motor
Company in Australia,* Golden Press Pty Ltd, 1987.
John Wright, *Lineage of a Legend,*
Ford Australia, 1997.

Opposite: there's always a new Fairlane in the pipeline. Above: one of the many advantages of the Fairlane/LTD luxury models is comparatively inexpensive maintenance.

CHAPTER 12

Years Of **Triumph**

In the 1960s, if you were a bright young Holden dealer employee who could rustle up $20,000 by mortgaging a house, you could walk into a Ford capital city dealership.

It helps to understand the climate of the time. In 1963 GM–H held 45.6 per cent of the total market, Ford 16.9 per cent and Chrysler 5.1 per cent. GM–H was fat, rich and smug. Typically, it would find a rich grazier with several properties and get him to finance one or two sons into running a dealership, with GM–H providing the financial and sales expertise, of course. The slow kid on the block, the one you would take round the back of the dunny in the schoolyard, beat up and steal his Vegemite sandwiches, was Ford Australia.

Not only had it inherited a sales mentality dating back to the original Hubert C. French plan, but it didn't know who owned half its outlets. In any case Ford US, having just assumed the parenting role from Ford Canada, wasn't all that interested in this snotty-nosed kid on the other side of the world in a weird country where kangaroos hopped down the main street.

Managing director Wally Booth had yanked the company into designing and building better quality into its output, and the XR was very much his car. His successor, Bill Bourke, realised the retail network needed open-heart surgery, but it was Maxwell F. Gransden, born in Adelaide on April 5, 1924, who was most involved with the operation.

Gransden passed his Intermediate Certificate at Adelaide High School in 1939, and his Technical (Leaving) Certificate at Thebarton Technical College the next year. His first job was as a 'travelling salesman' (as they were called then), doing sales and service outside Adelaide for the Dunlite Electric Company.

Like Sir Brian Inglis he joined the RAAF, but as an aircraft technician, and after the war he moved to Sydney for a while. He fell into a job buying and selling ex-service disposal vehicles. That led him to selling cars for Ford

Below: the XP Falcon utility benefited hugely from the new image of durability created by the You Yangs endurance epic, returning the icon to the status its unique birth created.
Opposite, top: the XP range also brought the first Fairmont and a new level of luxury to the Falcon range. Narrow-band whitewall tyres were much in vogue.
Below: the double chequered flag badge that denoted the Super Pursuit engine was a broad hint of things to come. Page 144: hints of The Man from Snowy River in this photograph on the theme of 'more – more – Mustang in the new Falcon'.

dealer R. J. Dawson and then another, McArthur and Co. In July 1952 he won the job as a NSW district sales manager – one of several such browbeaten flunkeys – for Ford.

He came in a few months after Charlie Smith had been appointed managing director of Ford Australia. Smith had quickly decided to discontinue the State distributorship system that operated through sub-dealers – Metropolitan Motors in Queensland, Hastings-Deering in NSW, Melford Motors in Melbourne, Dalgety in Adelaide and Lynas Motors in Perth. Smith replaced them with State sales offices, reappointing sub-dealers as full dealers where suitable.

Gransden then was flogging the dated Ford Pilot, British

Prefect and Anglia, and later the weak-kneed Consul and (better) Zephyr, the Customline, and F-Series and British Thames trucks and vans. Recognised as a bright and enthusiastic young man, in 1960 he became NSW car marketing manager and, three years later, assistant manager of the Victorian State branch.

The successive stepping stones as regional manager of first southern, then northern, then eastern regions made him a main player in the dealer development (DD) concept Bourke had picked up from Ford North America and given to Gransden's boss, general sales manager Keith Horner. Horner had been head-hunted from Australian Motor Industries to run Ford Australia sales. He was the kind of man people tell stories about 30 years

'THE DEALERSHIP'S WORTH $900,000; FORD WILL SELL

T TO YOU FOR $450,000'

later. Current Ford president Geoff Polites said in 2000 that when Horner spelt his name out on the telephone: H-O-R-N-E-R 'you knew you were in for an unpleasant conversation'. (Gransden replaced the acerbic but visionary Horner on January 1, 1976, as director [later vice-president] of sales and marketing, retiring in April 1989. Polites says that he learned everything he knew about selling from Gransden, who was absolutely meticulous. 'He wouldn't let a single memo go out to the dealers unless he had personally read it.')

Of the DD program Gransden said in 1988: 'Virtually every dealer in the country had been there for maybe 30 years and was targeted for replacement. Today we have only three major metropolitan dealers who were there when I joined in 1952'.

Gransden said that by the early 1960s dealership owners were making a lot of money, because the post-war population boom meant there was still an excess of demand over supply. Gradually they put in general managers and became absentee landlords, content to reap the profits as long as all went well in that era of Menzies and prosperity euphoria.

Dealer's tale

I personally knew the young sales manager for a big Sydney Holden dealer who in 1970 was able to take over City Ford with a deposit of $20,000. Now one of Australia's richest men, he no longer owns it, but it is now Australia's biggest Ford dealership and for most of the 1990s was run by Geoff Polites, current president of Ford Australia.

'We found it difficult to attract the enterprising young men we wanted. They were sales managers or general managers at GM dealerships because 50 per cent of the cars sold were through their dealerships. To attract one of those people to a Ford dealership – where we were under-capacitised anyhow ... our people were making a pittance compared with them.'

Ford couldn't even sell one of its dealerships when it became available, so an existing dealer would, of course, buy it.

'The result was that in Sydney by the end of the 1950s we had two long-established organisations controlling nine of our 17 dealerships. Their attitudes were years out of date, their philosophy of marketing our products was the same no matter which

dealership or market [they] were in.

'In Melbourne we had exactly the same thing: 16 or 17 dealerships and one man controlling five of them through a public company ... he had many interests and only 10 per cent of his time would be spent in the dealerships.' Three of the owners were public companies. Ford set out to buy the properties and fund the employment of aggressive and ambitious young men into them.

Gransden: 'We decided we would never, ever appoint

Above: Ford promoted the XR as 'Mustang bred', importing more than 200 1965 Mustang hardtops, converted to right-hand drive in Sydney. Opposite: although based on the US 'Coke bottle' style, the XR Falcon was really Ford Australia's first locally designed car. There was a choice of sedan, wagon, utility and panel van, a six-cylinder or V8 engine and three transmissions. Falcon was Wheels' Car of the Year for the second time running.

anybody unless that young person had an absolute commitment to that dealership. The fact he was hocked, if you like, meant he had to work.

'We used to encourage them to put in every penny they could without causing unnecessary hardship … there were many cases where we would do business only if they sold their house and put the equity into their dealership. That was pretty much par for the course. We also insisted that no one person could have more than one dealership in that multiple-market capital city.'

The agreement specified a young dealer could buy Ford's equity in the business after 11 years. Gransden: 'The guy would say, I've got a house worth $25,000. We'd ask, Well, what else have you got? and he would say, I've got $3000 in the bank and we'd say, Well, we want at least $10,000 and we would put in the rest.

'Then we'd say, Now this is going to be tough; you've got 11 years to pay it back … we'll only take it back out of profits. You've got your debenture money, you're earning 6.5 per cent or whatever it was at the time … if you don't make any money you don't make any payments. If in the event you are very successful over the first three years we

The only Falcon convertible

The late Lewis Bandt, the Australian father of the coupe utility that was adopted by North America and later became its most popular type of vehicle, designed the only known production Falcon convertible.

A famous senior designer, in 1964 he was given the job of producing six special cars for the Miss Australia Quest, which Ford Australia long sponsored hand-in-hand with the Spastic Centre, as it was then called. Bandt took the XP Falcon utility and, working with Geelong-based bespoke fabricator Bodycraft, turned it into a convertible with a retractable steel top.

This was the second-last year of the Ford Thunderbird convertible, the top of which folded down under the huge steel lid of a vast boot. But that was a fabric top and Bandt's version had a steel roof that folded in two upon itself and slid back into the utility tray, to be covered by a rear-hinged steel panel. The other main difference was that the Thunderbird fold-and-stow motion was electric – the Falcon process was all done manually, which must have been quite something, given the weight of the steel. As the ute had only a bench front seat, Bandt designed a panel to blank off the rear section and dropped in the rear bench from the sedan.

Six convertibles were built and paraded bearing the State Miss Australia finalists. However, despite the best efforts of Ford Australia researcher Adrian Ryan to track them down, all seem to have vanished. The only existing photographs show that one had the Victorian registration number HRB 333.

There is another story from this time. Ford imported a 1964 Thunderbird convertible and a Lincoln Continental to trundle around the show circuit as Ford brag cars. Ford's Melbourne PR man Max Ward was driving the Thunderbird to the Sydney Royal Easter Show, with his Sydney PR operator Bob Forster following in the Lincoln when, near the corner of Pitt and King streets in the CBD, Ward spotted something of interest in the crowd and slammed on the brakes.

Forster promptly buried the Lincoln's nose into the T-bird's rear, thus rendering impotent the complex electro-hydraulics that raised and lowered the lid.

Both cars were due to be unveiled the next morning on the Ford stand at the show. Somehow Ward and Forster found a Sydney crash repair shop that could fix them and somehow the pair kept the lid on their horror story – until now.

The completely new ZEPHYR SIX

ZEPHYR

Left: the all-new Mark 3 Zephyr was imported as a kit and locally assembled. Selling against the Falcon and priced above it, this good car slowly went downhill in sales and in 1966 was dropped. Below: a Ford Australia message to its dealers emphasised how the XR Falcon had leapfrogged Holden, then some 18 months short of introducing the all-new HK range with its own V8. Opposite: a view of the Ford 'money tree', from a profile of the company in the Summer 1965 edition of US magazine Ward's Quarterly.

FALCON
versus
HOLDEN
You've still got it all over the Holden Dealer — his "new" product is

MUTTON DRESSED UP AS LAMB

CONFIDENTIAL: For Ford Falcon Dealers and Salesmen only

will sell you that property at our cost.

'From 1968 on property escalated like you couldn't believe. All of a sudden those young men had made good money, generated a lot of business, made very good money for the finance company they were dealing with and they would go along and say, what is the valuation of the property? It's $900,000 and the Ford Motor Company is prepared to sell it to you for $450,000.'

Ford's dramatic reconstruction of its entire metro dealer network took 10 years. Not content with cannibalising GM–H's best and brightest, Ford also went for the big guns. Berma S. ('Bib') Stillwell owned a huge Holden dealership in the Melbourne suburb of Kew. Not only was it one of the two or three biggest GM–H outlets in Australia but Stillwell – later president of the Lear Jet Corporation – was famous as one of the country's best race drivers (he died in June 1999).

In January 1966, Horner, Gransden and Bourke secretly met Stillwell three times for lunch in a private room in Melbourne's Southern Cross hotel. Eventually Stillwell agreed to switch franchises; it made national headlines.

Some months later Canberra Holden dealer and top race driver Greg Cusack also agreed to change. Heartened by the success of the XP Falcon, the fleets began to listen. The first to switch from GM–H was also one of the biggest – Rothmans.

What really swayed the fleets was the 1967 XR – the car Ford cheekily marketed as the 'Mustang-bred Falcon'. Bourke even imported a bunch of Mustangs, converted them to right-hand drive locally and flogged them off to help create the image. It must be said here that when the basic design parameters were approved by the Product Committee on November 14, 1963, buyers were still thumbing their noses at the XM 'Golden Quality' Falcon and the legendary XP enduro was a year away, but the program was to launch the new car in August 1966 – an astonishingly short lead time for an all-new car in those days. Product Planning put up five separate and complete variations for the six-seater – this at a time when there was only a mewling infant of product engineering in Geelong and Broadmeadows.

The basic definitions would be that the wheelbase would be stretched by 85 millimetres to 2800 mm, the front track would get a massive three-inch (7.6 cm) widening, the rear 3.2 inches (8.1 cm). It would thus have more interior room than the XP, but could be no longer overall. It had to have a lower centre of gravity, despite going up to 14-inch wheels, a larger fuel tank, and it would for the first time offer the 289 cubic inch V8 engine as an option.

These were all translated into preliminary package drawings in scale, accurate to plus or minus 1.2 mm, showing the placement of all major components and including important factors such as front wheel turn radii, door openings, interior headroom, front and rear screen angles and lamp sizes. This was costed before it went to the Product Committee and on approval went to styling, which started sketching its outlines around the package. Ford Australia by this time had learned to bring the manufacturing department into the process

early, to make sure the car was 'buildable'.

Says current vice-president, product development, Ian Vaughan now: 'That 60-inch track was really where the current car comes from. We used to talk about 60-inch shoulder room and 60-inch track as what an E-class car should be in Australia. It's important because it's the differentiator from the D-class car, which is what we call the Camry and the Magna, which typically have 58 inches of shoulder room. And there is a difference inside: one's comfortable for six people and the other's squeezy'.

The clay model that emerged as a result of the tiny styling department going to Dearborn was approved on November 23, 1963 – remarkably fast work, although it was closely based on the US 'Coke bottle' styling, so short cuts were possible. In the way it was done then, the clay was used to make templates which could be sectioned and broken down into manufacturing demands,

FORD AUSTRA

Above: MD Bill Bourke (right) with Harry Firth, champion racer and Ford Australia's motorsport manager. Opposite: Ian Vaughan drove the most famous of all XT GTs, KAG 002, to third place in the 1968 London–Sydney Marathon (he was second in the anniversary event, 25 years later). The car is now garaged in Ford's Discovery Centre, Geelong.

and fine-line drawings for toolmakers and outside suppliers. They also went to full-sized mahogany 'skin models', as well as a multipiece transparent Royalite plastic model – today Broadmeadows does all this with high-speed computers, both here and linked by satellite to the massive Crays in Dearborn's computer centre.

Early in the program Ford brought in similarly-sized North American Falcons that were converted to right-hand drive, stripped and fitted with local components as prototypes. Much of the early testing, particularly dust-proofing, was done on huge loops from Melbourne to the SA Flinders Ranges through Wilpena Pound and Arkaroola, then back to Mildura and up to Broken Hill.

The first hand-built Australian prototypes didn't appear on the You Yangs proving ground until just 10 months before – uncomfortably close to – the launch date, which had been moved from August to September 1966 to allow dealers to run out about 4500 XPs. Job number 1 rolled off the Broadmeadows line six weeks before release, even though management had decided just five months earlier to widen the front seats by about 2 centimetres, to give the interior a more prestigious feel.

In 1966 a Falcon (this time the XR) won *Wheels* magazine's Car of the Year award for the second consecutive year but, apart from the cloned Telstar sharing the gong with the Mazda 626 for 1983, that's the last time Ford has achieved the blue ribbon.

One of the last decisions made for the XR might seem strange now given so many years of hindsight but was simply pragmatic at the time. Australian Design Rule ADR4 would not require front belts for passenger cars until January 1, 1969 but the matter had been raised by the Product Planning committee.

On December 15, 1965, Ford decided there was 'no marketing advantage in fitting seatbelts as standard equipment'. The company would wait for the Valiant and Holden facelifts expected in March/April 1966 and if they didn't have them fitted, neither should Fords.

On January 1, 1966 the Product Committee was briefed on the new HK Holden due 14 months later. They heard remarkable detail, including the fitment of a Buick V8 engine, which turned out to be a Chevy. They learned, too, that in June 1965 GM–H management had approved a full scale clay model of a two-door fastback Holden. Industrial espionage was alive and well even then.

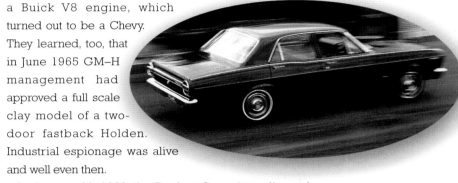

On January 20, 1966, the Product Committee directed that front lap belts should be made standard on all Ford passenger vehicles, including Cortina and Galaxie, with

A WOULD INTRODUCE A GT VERSION OF THE FALCON

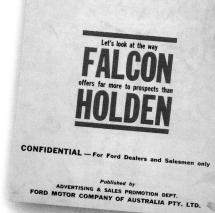

Ford could afford to be boastful in comparing its Falcon with what GM–H was offering. The XT which succeeded the XR continued the climb towards Bill Bourke's bold target of 25 per cent market share. Opposite: from 1963 until the arrival of the Falcon GT, Ford Australia's motorsport flag was carried by the Cortina GT. Here Bob Jane punts the winning car around Mount Panorama in 1963. With co-driver and team manager Harry Firth, car 20 won by more than a lap from an EH Holden.

a 'supplementary sash section' available through dealers as an accessory, in black only, costing an extra £1 over the belt cost of £6/10 shillings, with the full kit costing £8/10 shillings when sold together. The decision was announced in April, to come into effect in July.

Another decision was announced at about the same time: Ford Australia would introduce a GT version of the Falcon, to be built in limited numbers. The company had already recognised the sales potential of the performance market. After its successes with the Falcon at Phillip Island, ebullient competition manager Les Powell had overseen the required production run of 100 disc-braked GT versions of the Cortina small-medium car for the debut of the transferred Armstrong 500 at Mount Panorama, Bathurst, in October 1963.

Ford entered a three-car team plus a Mark 3 Zephyr in a higher class, while GM–H – ostensibly bound by a GM global ban on motorsport – used the rules to build some very special S4 versions of its strongly selling EH Holden

and enter them covertly under David McKay's Scuderia Veloce race team banner. Harry Firth/Bob Jane won again in a works GT, by more than one lap from an S4.

In 1964 four 'works' GT Cortinas fronted, but while GM–H had further modified the S4 to produce a new car code-named S22, with front disc brakes and a top speed of over 200 km/h, the company put it in the too-hard basket. This time the win went to Jane again, but with George Reynolds. That same year, the cunning veteran Harry Firth – by now Ford motorsport manager – won the Ampol round-Australia trial with navigator Graham Hoinville.

For Bathurst 1965 Firth came up with a brilliant purpose-built Cortina. Dubbed the GT500, it had a highly modified engine that could run to 7000 rpm instead of the stock 5000, a Lotus–Cortina close-ratio gearbox, lower suspension, special Koni dampers, alloy brake scoops and a 77 litre fuel tank with twin snap-lid fillers atop the boot lid. GM–H built 110 units of a performance version of its unhappy new HD; badged X2, it had modified suspension and wider rims with fatter tyres and disc front brakes.

Of the 10 GT500s that started two were works team cars, but at the end of the 500 miles it was Barry ('Bo') Seton, with friend Midge Bosworth, who got the chequered flag in a dealer-entered Ford.

The 1966 Bathurst regulations saw the minimum production requirement raised to 250, and not enough of the expensive GT500s had been built to qualify – the race was swamped by Mini–Coopers, the last time it would be won by a four-cylinder car until the Ford Sierra Cosworth RS in 1988.

FORD CORTINA TAKES 1963 ARMSTRONG 500

But the first Falcon GT was just around the corner. Ford's official version is that new MD Bill Bourke drove the prototype of an XR V8 being developed as a police pursuit car at the You Yangs and, being a confirmed petrolhead, decided to put it into production. The GT badge was unusual because at that time it was normally the province of two-door performance coupes. He assigned the development task to Firth and proving ground manager Don Dunoon – a very capable engineer who had driven Hillman Minxes in the 1960 and 1962 Armstrong 500s.

They took the new Australian-built 289 cubic inch (4.7 litre) Canadian-designed Windsor V8 and, by replacing the two-barrel carburettor with a quad, installing higher-compression pistons, new camshaft profile and slicker inlet manifold, kicked the output from 200 bhp (149 kW) to 220 (164). If that sounds limp-wristed by today's standards, understand that it cut the standing quarter-mile (400 metres) in 15.8 seconds and could top 122 mph (195 km/h). Its acceleration was of similar order to that of a current model Falcon XR6 with VCT engine and five-speed manual transmission – in other words, *very* impressive for 1967.

It had a four-speed manual gearbox, special suspension and wider rims with radial ply tyres and cost $3890 retail compared with $2411 for the Deluxe with manual and the Super Pursuit 200 engine. Ford ended up building 583 of them between March 1967 and February 1968, all in lustrous deep golden bronze with black stripes – except for 12 special cars finished in silver with red stripes, to match the premium cigarette package of the new Bathurst race sponsor, Irish tobacco company Gallaher. Gallaher gave the cars to senior company salespeople to fly the flag around its retailers.

Ford entered three factory cars for Bathurst, with Harry Firth/Fred Gibson, Leo Geoghegan/Ian Geoghegan and Bob Jane/Spencer Martin to drive. Four more were dealer-sponsored entries, and not a Holden in sight. As in previous years the regulations called for showroom stock standard cars, but engineers like Firth were expert in getting eight matching pistons from a lineup of 2000, smoothing out rough castings and valve stems without actually polishing, getting exclusive use of the finest

The menu for the January 1964 'Fordorama' dinner for the national dealer body. It included the words for 11 songs to be sung, including (to the tune of 'Oh You Beautiful Doll') the following: 'Oh you beautiful Ford, you great big beautiful Ford; let me put my arms around you, I could never live without you' ... it got worse.

competition brake pads: 'blueprinting' a stock engine exactly back to textbook standard.

More importantly, works team managers could access the best brains in the factory's design, engineering and manu- facturing areas, labs and test rigs.

But the new XR GTs didn't have it all their own way. Back then there was no chance to use the Mount Panorama public road circuit other than on the Saturday and Sunday of practice and racing, so Firth had no data on things like tyre and pad wear and fuel consumption. While the three works cars stormed away from the start, they lost the lead to an Alfa Romeo GTV after 80 minutes when they began making early refuelling stops because of an alarming thirst of eight miles per gallon (38 litres/100 km).

Firth started to realise that brake and tyre wear weren't going to demand extra-long stops as the Fords went back in front and stayed there. The Geoghegan car went through without a pad change, the last 10 laps on bugger- all brakes, and got the flag – but after three hours of argument and lap chart checking, the decision was

handed to Firth/Gibson, which was still a Ford factory 1–2. It would be the last for a while.

The interior of the GT, with its big brass-studded wood- rimmed deep-dished wheel, was partly the work of a junior designer called John Doughty. He was born in London on February 29, 1944; in 1949 his parents migrated to Ballarat before moving to Geelong. Doughty went to Geelong High and then the new industrial design course at the Gordon Institute of Technology. His mother worked for Ford in the parts buying department and he learned to drive in a Mainline V8 ute, so he was doomed.

But he couldn't get into Ford straight away. Two months after graduation he joined GM–H as a trainee designer under design chief Joe Schemansky and did some work on the coming new HK Monaro before Jack Telnack arrived from Detroit and grabbed him for his tiny new studio in Geelong. He moved in just before the XR was released and they were working on its successor, the XT, due out in April 1968.

In its first 12 months the XR sold 62,613 units and lifted Ford's market share to 20.7 per cent in 1967; GM–H had dropped to 37.8 per cent and Chrysler increased to 9.4 per cent. Ford Australia had converted a $9.8 million loss in 1964 to a before-tax profit of $12.1 million in 1967 and $17.0 million in 1968.

But it was not all sweetness and light. In 1968 imports of complete (CBU) vehicles from Japan had gone up by almost 50 per cent to 50,827 a year; in December the Federal government announced yet another change to the vehicle plan that by February 1, 1969 would demand an 85 per cent local content for models being built here at a rate of less than 25,000 a year. This was mixed news for the components makers who, unlike today when there are just four car makers, had a far greater economy of scale and much higher tariffs to protect their interests. The new rules had the effect of bringing Toyota and Nissan into the plans for lower content levels, but they were committing for the long haul.

Volkswagen's Australian subsidiary started assembling Datsuns and Volvos, British Leyland Motor Corporation took over from Pressed Metal Corporation assembly of what were known as BMC cars and Renault decided to begin local assembly of Renaults and Peugeots.

In 1968 Ford Australia sold 45,372 Falcons, 16,128 Cortinas, 8002 Fairlanes and 565 Galaxies – all locally assembled. In March that year the company launched the XT, to be a short-lived (17 months) update of the XR.

Marketed as 'There's More – More – Mustang In Falcon', it was a bit more than a facelift. A Ford badge appeared on the flatter, plainer grille, with a deep chromed strip across the width of the rear with revised rear lamp assemblies. This was the year Ford switched from imperial to decimal measurements for its engines, and increased the capacities as well. Thus the Pursuit 170 (2785 cc) became the 3.1, the Super Pursuit 200 (3277 cc) became 3.6 litres and the 289 cubic inch (4.7 litre) V8 turned into a 302 (4.9 litre) with more power and torque. The sixes had new cylinder heads, inlet manifolds, camshafts, valves and electrics. But the manual transmission on the base car was still a column shift three-speeder, with synchromesh on first gear an option, and the all-synchro three-speeder standard on the better 500 model. The basic price went up only $14 but there was nowhere near the variety of options being offered on the new Holden HK range. However, the utility and panel van versions were doing well. And of course, there was another GT model. But that's another story.

A famous moment in Australian motor industry history: one of Holden's biggest dealers, Bib Stillwell (right), signs up with Ford in the Broadmeadows corner office of sales and marketing chief Keith Horner (left). Standing is Horner's deputy, Max Gransden, who with Horner wrought a tremendous change in the structure of Ford Australia's dealer body.

CHAPTER 13

Snorting, Sweaty Draught Horses

Around the world, 1967 was a year full of drama. Israel blitzed Egypt, Jordan, Syria and Iraq to win the Six-Day War. A flash fire on the Apollo launching pad killed astronauts Virgil Grissom, Edward White and Roger Chaffee. Britain devalued the pound and Lord Clement Attlee, elected Prime Minister in 1946 to replace wartime leader Sir Winston Churchill, died.

Just one horse, Foinavon, survived a mass crash at the 23rd jump to win the British Grand National steeplechase at odds of 100–1. New Zealander Denny Hulme won the World Drivers' Championship in a Brabham–Climax, while his boss, the 1966 champion Jack Brabham, won only the French and Canadian GPs. With just a year left of his meteoric life, Jim Clark won the Tasman Cup, victorious at Christchurch, Teretonga, Lakeside and Sandown Park. Spencer Martin drove a Brabham–Climax to win the Australian Drivers' Championship and Ian Geoghegan piloted a Ford Mustang V8 to the touring car title.

It was also a significant year for an Ian called Vaughan, who had returned to Ford Australia from Europe and was working on the XT Falcon. Today vice-president, product development, Vaughan went to Melbourne Grammar, the school that has produced two Australian Prime Ministers – Lord Bruce and Malcolm Fraser – and humorist Barry Humphries.

'I was a bit too smart and a bit naughty at school', he told me in mid-1987, during an interview for *Wheels* magazine, 'and sometimes too smart for my own good'. He grinned the cheeky grin he still has, a rueful smile that makes him look younger than his years.

Ian Vaughan graduated from Melbourne University in 1964 with honours in mechanical engineering and went straight to Ford. University hadn't taught him much about the practical side of design and manufacturing – he spent his holidays working at the Royal Australian Navy dockyard in Port Melbourne and the Commonwealth Aircraft factory to snatch up assorted morsels of understanding.

Ian Vaughan, Bob Forsyth and Jack Ellis in the XT GT with Big Ben and the Houses of Parliament in the background after the start of the 1968 London–Sydney Marathon, an heroic adventure that ended with KAG 002 in third place and Ford Australia winning the coveted team's prize.

Honours graduates were head-hunted by the big corporations dangling glittering prize careers. Ford was a leader among them, and Vaughan was something of a petrolhead, his first car an Austin Seven which spent most of its days in bits, then a Singer Nine roadster, followed by a Fiat 600 in which he began his rallying career ('It didn't handle', he said, in a masterpiece of understatement).

As for the Singer Nine, it was the roadster for those who couldn't afford an MG but who had enough nous to know how to weld the alloy body that always cracked across the

THE XT GT WAS

rear of the boot opening, repair the wooden frame and tune the overhead-cam engine.

Vaughan was plonked straight into the tiny Product Planning Group, then working on the 1966 XR Falcon, but after 13 months he applied for, and got, leave of absence, sailing on the P&O Line's *Orcades* to Naples, hitch-hiking his way from motor race to motor race across Europe. He worked for Ford UK for nine months, and in January 1966 came back to his old job.

The XT launch was two years and three months away, and GM–H would beat Ford to the punch with its January 1968 unveiling of the all-new HK series, complete with stopgap imported 307 cubic inch (5 litre) V8 engines while it waited for the home-grown versions. (There was also the frightful HK Brougham, an attempt to match the Fairlane, with 10 cm of sheet metal stitched onto the end of the standard wheelbase and interior trim resembling that of an especially tasteless bordello.)

But Ford's spy system reported that GM–H would, mid-year, unleash the industry's first two-door coupe, running six-cylinder engines and a 327 cubic inch (5.3 litre) V8. It was cleverly named Monaro, after the mountain shire near Canberra. The Monaro had Bathurst atop its agenda, and Vaughan found himself working on Ford's answer – the XT GT. This was the real beginning of the Ford–Holden racing rivalry that endures today.

The Telnack-styled XT GT came with the XR's 289 V8

expanded to 302 cubic inch (4.9 litres) and pushing out 230 bhp (171 kW), up from the XR's 225 (168).

Torque was bounced considerably to 420 Newton metres and the compression ratio was up to 10:1. It was also a much more refined, better-handling car, easier to drive on the limit with a ride height dropped by 57 mm and a limited-slip differential as standard. 'The XT', says Vaughan now, 'was probably the best balanced, lightest feeling GT we ever made'. For the first time you could buy one with automatic transmission and there was a choice of five

Left: the boast badge did more than hint at what was underneath; it was probably Bill Bourke's idea. Below: fisheye view of the XT, which Ian Vaughan still believes was the nicest of all the GTs to drive – but he would, wouldn't he? It was certainly much more refined than the first GT, the XR.

HE REAL BEGINNING OF THE FORD–HOLDEN RIVALRY

colours, including the XR's GT Gold, but only the all-black interior from the Fairmont.

Vaughan was able to add a few rally-inspired finishing touches, most notably the driving lights. Then there were those beautiful green-glowing Stewart–Warner gauges, the chromed gear lever, the red GT badges ... Bathurst, here we come again.

Ford, with a team of three GTs, was also planning a major attack on the maniacal first London–Sydney Marathon, to be run in November 1968 over nearly 17,000 km, through 11 countries in 11 days. But first, Bathurst 1967 (see 'How the Grey Fox did it', later in this chapter).

Even today old Ford hands wince when you mention the 1968 Hardie–Ferodo 500 (miles; race distance then was 800 km) at Mount Panorama. Sydney motoring writer David McKay had managed to get secret backdoor funding from GM–H (GM management then still banned motorsport participation worldwide) for his Scuderia Veloce team to prepare three of the new Monaros, and enter as the Holden Dealer Racing Team. There was actually no such animal – at least Ford was up-front about direct factory backing.

Bathurst veteran Harry Firth put together the three GT pairings: Leo Geoghegan/Ian Geoghegan, the 1967 winner Fred Gibson with 1963 winner Bo Seton, and 1967 Gold

Star champion Spencer Martin with talented touring car racer Jim McKeown in an automatic.

There were two dozen bottles of the then fad liquor, Bacardi, as a reward for pole position; it was won by a cunning Wyong (NSW) veteran called Bruce McPhee in a dealer-entered yellow Monaro running part-worn Michelin XAS steel radials (race tyres were not allowed until the next year). The fastest Falcon GT was the Geoghegan car, on fourth spot.

The Holdens stormed away from the flag. After about 90 minutes McKeown stopped the automatic at the top of the mountain with a collapsed rear wheel bearing. He ran, jogged and walked about 3 km down to the pits, collected a new axle and, under the race rules, climbed all the way back again to fit it, but the race was over for one of the three works Fords.

Then the first of the covert 'factory' Holdens came in, needing a second set of brake pads after only 45 minutes; when all the flurry of stops ended the order was Gibson (Falcon), Des West (Holden), Geoghegan (Falcon) and McPhee (Holden). Watching the telecast in a hotel suite in Sydney, Bill Bourke and his senior management cracked the first champagne.

Ford team manager John Gowland reluctantly accepted

The Ford Capri went on sale here in 1969. In profile it bears some resemblance to the classic Mustangs of the swingin' '60s. The 3.0 litre V6 version was very popular for excursions to Mount Panorama for the first weekend in October: it was very f-a-s-t for a 3.0 litre six and the V6 configuration was unusual for the era.

KAG 002 shows why Vaughan found it so good to drive. He ran it in the 1993 reprise of the London–Sydney Marathon, and it now rejoices in a well-earned rest in the Ford Discovery Centre, Geelong. In 1968 GM–H covertly entered three Holden Monaros, complete with 327 cubic inch (5.4 litre) V8s, automatic transmission and air-conditioning, but they finished nowhere.

the Geoghegan brothers' demand not to change their pads, but the Scuderia Holdens were coming in thick and fast with Fried Ferodo. By lap 80 West's Monaro was in front and the Geoghegan car behind the pits getting a new front brake assembly: the calipers had overheated and welded to the backing plates.

Bruce McPhee came in for tyres, fuel and new pads and to give co-driver Barry Mulholland the one lap the regulations demanded. Then at 2:45 pm, running second and reeling in the lead Monaro, the dark green car of Fred Gibson came down Conrod pluming a rooster-tail of smoke: a piston had holed. Suddenly the champagne in the Ford hotel suite in Sydney tasted of bile.

McPhee, remarkably, won the race. Holdens finished 1–2–3–4 and the first Falcon GT home was the previous year's XR model.

Ian Vaughan says today that the XT is still his favourite GT Falcon. That may have something to do with the fact that Ford's Discovery Centre in Geelong houses the car – number plate KAG 002 – in which he finished third in the London–Sydney rally. The Ford Australia team, with Gowland as manager, comprised three GTs that on

Bourke's orders were kept as close to stock as possible. With sponsorship from BP and Dunlop, the crews were the cream of the era's rally drivers and navigators: Firth/Graham Hoinville/Garry Chapman in car number 2, Vaughan/Bob Forsyth/Jack Ellis (24) and an indecently rapid Griffith (NSW) country boy called Bruce Hodgson with Doug Rutherford in 29.

David McKay's Scuderia Veloce entered another covert GM–H team of three Monaros, this time with 350 cubic inch (5.8 litre) V8s, automatic transmissions, air-conditioning and circuit racers as three of the six drivers.

When the cars left Crystal Palace in London on November 24 the big Australian cars were regarded as a bit of a joke. Ladbrokes (the bookmaker) had the brilliant Ford UK works driver Roger Clark favourite at 6–1 in his Lotus–Cortina, with Firth's car closer to 33–1 (Vaughan estimates) and Vaughan an outsider at 100–1.

The cars were ferried from Dover to Calais, then driven through Paris and Turin to Turkey, through Istanbul, Ankara, Sivas and Erzincan, the run to Sivas over gravel mountain tracks with an average speed of 100 km/h. The only official rest point for the London–Bombay sector was Kabul, capital

Images of an icon: from the top, the XR GT, the XT GT, the XW GTHO Phase 1, and the XY Phase 3 GTHO 'shaker'. Opposite: Ford beat the London–Sydney Marathon win drum as hard as it could, totally overwhelming Chrysler Australia's unexpected win with the Hillman Hunter.

of Afghanistan, and the entire field lost points over the Lataban Pass to Sarobi and while climbing the Himalayas into Pakistan via the famous Khyber Pass.

In Pakistan enormous crowds jammed the roads, police beating them back with long, whippy canes. The late Evan Green, driving a factory Austin 1800 with Jack 'Gelignite' Murray, remembered: 'Someone threw a bunch of flowers at our windscreen. The only problem was they had forgotten to take them out of the pot'.

Only 72 of the original 100 cars from 13 countries were left when the cars rolled onto the SS *Chusan* in Bombay, bound for Fremantle. Service mechanics had checked the Falcons and found nothing to fix. 'We changed the spark plugs just for something to do', remembers Vaughan. Clark was leading with 11 points lost, Firth was seventh on 29, Hodgson 10th on 36 and Vaughan 11th with 37. Vaughan would grumble later: 'We babied the cars too much in Europe and Asia. We left Perth with perfect cars, which came into their own in Australia'.

The field had three days with no rest stops to race 5700 km across Australia. Only one car would clean-sheet: the Porsche 911 of the Pole Slobislaw Zasada, who had measured kangaroos in the Berlin Zoo so he could fabricate bars running over his entire car from front to rear bumpers – his roo bars were spaced slightly narrower than the body of the much-feared macropod. Unhappily he had measured wallabies and was decidedly vision-impaired – but he too had lost many points in Europe by saving the car for the expected terrors of Australia.

The terrors were there, all right. Average – average! – speeds of 160 km/h were demanded over tracks that today are graded six-lane highways for the ore trucks or in Aboriginal territory. Through places with wonderful names like Youanmi and Marvel Loch they went, the big Fords booming across the Nullarbor at 180-plus.

At Port Augusta leader Clark hobbled in with two burnt valves; teammates Ken Chambers and Eric Jackson sacrificed their Cortina cylinder head to throw him back into the fight. The field stormed through Quorn into the Flinders Ranges, gibbers chattering away at the skid plates through Brachina and Parachilna Gorges, up to Broken Hill. Then it was east to Menindee and down to Gunbar, where Ford fans (many of them close friends of GT driver Bruce

Hodgson, a Griffith local) had laid out an unexpected feast of caviar, roast chicken and vintage wines for the Ford crews – a change from tinned beef and fruit jubes.

The NSW police backed up diatribes about 'speed kills' by freighting pursuit motorbikes by train across the State, four of them staking out Cooma alone.

The last day threw the weary crews on to the mountain range roads that had been used in rallies and trials for 50 years – Omeo, Bruthen (where early leader Roger Clark blew the differential in his Ford Escort), Ingebyra. On the last competitive stage, lip-lickingly smooth sandy bends from Numeralla to Hindmarsh Station, Lampinen/ Staepelaere were running second when their works Ford Taunus totalled the front suspension on a cattle grid fencepost and the French team of Lucien Bianchi/Jean-Claude Ogier enjoyed a strong lead in their Citroën DS.

Near the end of that special stage, about 160 km from the finish in Sydney, after such a huge distance, two off-duty police officers in a Mini–Cooper went into the special stage against the traffic and into a horrible frontal collision with the French car.

So, the unlikely winners of the Marathon were Andrew Cowan/Colin Malkin/Brian Coyle in a Hillman Hunter. The car had been meticulously prepared in the UK, even using the British Army proving ground for development, but Chrysler Australia – building Hillmans in Australia – hadn't heard of the team. Its lamentable failure to capitalise on such golden publicity left the door wide open for Ford Australia. It won the next best thing, the team and manufacturer prizes – the Vaughan car was third on 62, Hodgson sixth with 70 and Firth eighth with 114. Of the 56 cars that finished, 15 were Fords.

The XT with all its racing and rallying success helped Ford Australia to another record year – total sales of 95,750 were an all-time high and after-tax profit was $8,483,121. And 1969 would be another record, with 112,412 registrations and after-tax profit of $13,470,510, despite the company spending more than $10 million on investment to expand production at Geelong and Homebush, building a new Research Centre at Broadmeadows and (finally) that high-speed loop at the You Yangs proving ground.

It hadn't been helped by the worst strike in the company's history, which began with the Geelong maintenance

98 cars started in the London-Sydney Marathon.
3 were Falcons.
56 cars survived the torture.
3 were Falcons.
Filling three of the first eight outright placings ; winning the coveted Teams Prize ; coming home as 1st, 2nd and 3rd Australian cars.
And in good shape, in every way.
Which means, for you, that you get more strength, reliability, performance and road holding in Falcon than in any other Australian car.
There's one for you at your Ford Dealer's, right now.

FALCON *Ford*

workers striking over pay and conditions. They would be out for a grinding three months, and one month into that were joined by the metalworkers' union on the sensible basis that they couldn't operate unsafe equipment.

The Vehicle Builders' Union didn't come in until the last fortnight, and Dave Block – then a shop steward – would later say the whole thing was started by 'a handful of night shift people led by a militant young shop steward'. A shop steward himself, Block always maintained that both sides should try everything before a union, as a last resort, withdrew its labour. 'They used to say: We'll show 'em, but I knew from bitter experience who shows whom.'

A total of 1480 XT GTs (compared with 583 XRs) were built between February 1968 and June 1969. But Ford

Drivers' tales

Belgian Bianchi, who had driven in 17 Formula One GPs, died seven months later during practice for the Le Mans 24-Hours; Ogier and his wife won the 1970 Ampol Round-Australia trial in a Citroën DS, dead-heating for first with Hans Hermann in a Datsun 1600.

Australia was about to up the ante, big-time.

Bill Bourke had told his product planners and designers he wanted the successor to the XT, the XW, to be a much more macho, aggressive car.

Given the power of 20:20 hindsight, it's curious that while the motoring press was full of praise for the new XW range, launched in July 1969, and despite the fact it was the platform for the GTHO badge that immortalises the

craziness with the HK, but Bourke went at it with relish.)

The range was Falcon, Falcon 500, Futura (back again after 30 months), Fairmont and GT. As John Wright wrote in *The History of Ford Falcon, 1960–1994*: 'Options had become a way of life by 1969. The idea of a standard issue car was almost a contradiction in terms. Buyers could go all the way from adding a few basic extras such as a heater, carpets and a pushbutton radio to a Falcon or Falcon 500, to

THE SUPER-ROO WHI

buying a Grand Sports (GS) Option Package for a Candy Apple Red Fairmont'.

The GS package featured orange rally stripes sweeping the flanks, and a 'deep-dished three-spoke wood-grained steering wheel' that sounded the horn when you squeezed the rim, a concept which, thankfully, vanished as quickly as it arrived. But this was the Falcon that brought us the sensational Super-Roo logo: a fighting kangaroo spinning his hind legs in a blurred circle. Remember, this was before people advertised the products of giant corporations on their T-shirts or caps; back then the young bloods would kill for a Super-Roo decal.

most famous of all Australian performance cars, the XW Falcon isn't cherished in many memories.

The base car was the same old 3.1 litre six pack and three-on-the-tree, and while Ford's spin doctors pushed the '1966 changes' (count 'em?), much of the exterior was unchanged. The stylist pulled the trick of using extensions from the Capri coupe to create a recessed rear window, and what Ford called a 'power mouth' grille was a melange of plastic and chrome jiggery-pokery. But it worked.

Most of the development money had gone into the interior and mechanicals – and into lighting the blue touchpaper under the ill-advised manufacturing ploy of inviting buyers to tailor their cars as they liked through a huge range of options. (Actually, GM–H started the

The Super-Roo whispered in your ear, tinkered with your guilt with bucket seats and sports console, a 4.9 litre 164 kW V8, 11-inch 'turbo-cooled' disc brakes, tinted laminated windscreen, vinyl roof, wide oval tyres. Ford's PR releases described the GS pack as 'the base for an economical, build-it-yourself, everyman's GT'. They even put replica stripes and Super-Roo badges on the Mark 2 Cortina GT, for goodness' sake.

The Super-Roo quickly became the symbol of Ford Australia's grasp on the performance heart of Australia, and Ford created its own hymn: 'Going Ford Is The Going Thing', complete with its own rock group called, of course, The Going Thing!

The XW GT was all brass-buttoned, reefer-jacketed, tough ex-Marine Bill Bourke – brash, chrome-lavished, complete with racing bonnet pins, chromed 351 High Performance flank badges, Super-Roo decals and GS striping. It came with the 351 (5.8 litre) Windsor V8 – Ford Australia actually went back to cubic inches (from litres) for this car! – 11-inch brakes, an enormous 164 litre fuel tank (for Bathurst? surely not!) and a final drive ratio of 3.25:1 (ditto).

Left: by 1967 Ford Australia had become the performance car company, the 'treatment' extending even to the humble Mark 2 Cortina GT. Below: a quaint, from a 2000 perspective, way to promote the XW GT.

ERED IN YOUR EAR AND TINKERED WITH YOUR GUILT

Allan Moffat made his Bathurst
debut for Ford in 1969, finishing
fourth behind Colin Bond's
Monaro.

to run the first proper Holden Dealer Team. It was allegedly funded via a slush fund cheque book in the bottom drawer of the desk of the account director of GM–H's advertising agency, Peter Lewis-Williams.

Bourke's reaction was to import American Al Turner early in the year and put him to work on the GT. But here Bourke's US heritage betrayed him, for Turner's background was the booming hot rod and drag racing scene. Here was an engine man, a power man, who knew nothing about how to set up a car for our unique racetrack.

They put him into what they called the Ford Special Vehicles (FSV) department – some 20 years before the start of Holden Special Vehicles (HSV) – a name Ford lost somewhere along the way. That first GTHO (now, not then, called Phase One) was constrained by cost, because the Bathurst classes were still decided on price.

It acquired a front spoiler, a rear stabiliser bar with stiffer dampers, heavier front stabiliser bar, stronger coils, thicker tailshaft and enough engine modifications – new alloy inlet manifold, bigger Holley 650 carburettor and new camshaft profile – to give it 225 kW. The best standing quarter time published was 14.8 seconds, with a full tank of fuel.

Turner was smart enough to retain Canadian born Allan Moffat to do the pre-race setup testing. Moffat had grabbed some attention with his driving of a year-old Lotus–Cortina against the works Alan Mann cars in US racing and had done some testing with Ford's Kar Kraft development arm in the US.

The Phase One GTHO made a Hollywood-style debut. With co-driver John French (who finally won his deserved first Bathurst enduro in 1981, partnering Dick Johnson), Moffat won the then traditional rehearsal for Bathurst, the September Sandown Park Three-Hour.

There were 86 entries for Bathurst and the Australian Racing Drivers' Club – using a lick-your-thumb process that today would result in legal challenges all the way to the

Martin's roll

Firth's selected test driver, Spencer Martin, had an earnest conversation with his Maker when the new Monaro arrived at the end of the straight with the brake pedal to the floor and Martin spun it, crashing through the Armco and onto the access road in flames. The pistons had popped out of the overheated brake cylinders.

The Canadian Windsor engine thumped out 217 kW and an enormous 521 Nm of torque, with a four-barrel carburettor and 10.7:1 compression ratio, and could crank out a standing quarter mile in around 15.3 seconds. It also had non-reflecting matt black bonnet paint pioneered by the London–Sydney rally cars and stick-on fake timber laminate on the dash.

But was it enough to win Bathurst? Ford knew GM–H would soon unleash a far more user-friendly Monaro coupe with the imported Chevrolet 350 V8, so perhaps it was time to defy that old saying: 'For everything have a simple solution: it is difficult to kill a cockroach with a cannon'.

The standard Falcon GT's list price was $4250, but the set of steak knives was to come. In July 1969, Ford Australia unleashed the GTHO for $4495. HO stood for Handling Option, and it happened because GM–H's sales and marketing director John Bagshaw – a man every bit as flamboyant as Bill Bourke – had seduced Harry Firth across

High Court – weeded them down to 60 plus 10 reserves. Of those 60, 15 were new GTHOs, three of them factory team, and only six Monaros, including me in a dealer-entered car. Moffat made his Bathurst debut, as did an unknown called Peter Brock, plucked by Harry Firth from his violent and vicious Holden-engined Austin A30 race car.

Turner teamed Moffat with Melbourne Porsche dealer Alan Hamilton, a very experienced racer, and again paired the Geoghegan brothers and Gibson/Seton.

It was a disaster. On the first lap Bill Brown in a dealer-entered GTHO tried to pass Mike Savva in another Falcon over Skyline, got two wheels up the bank and flipped. I came over the top in 10th place in a Monaro, saw Brown in the air and dived to the right – he fell left. Behind me much of the rest of the field piled into the wreckage of four cars.

The works Fords and Holdens were ahead of the crash, and the Falcons were clocking 220 km/h down Conrod against 210 for the Monaros, with their paltry brakes.

But Turner had made a dreadful mistake with the special Goodyear tyres he had ordered. The Geoghegan car was on pole and led until at 1 hour 24 minutes it blew a tyre across the mountain; at 1 hour 50 Seton rolled the second GT at McPhillamy when a tyre popped.

Colin Bond and Tony Roberts in the HDT Monaro won by the then closest-ever margin of 44 seconds from – that man again – Bruce McPhee with Mulholland in a GTHO. The Moffat/Hamilton car had been off the pace all day, despite sharing fastest lap of 2 minutes 52.1 seconds with the Gibson/Seton car, and finished fourth, the Geoghegans a lap behind in fifth.

I gained new respect for the lyric skills of race driver and motoring commentator Jim Sullivan, who described the GTHOs as sounding and smelling 'like snorting, sweaty draught horses', when they passed him.

To its credit, Ford Australia ran full-page advertisements in the national print media showing the shredded tyres and

The car that started it all, Bill Brown's GTHO (55), lies upside down just over Skyline on the first lap of the 1969 Bathurst enduro as the rest of the field cannons into each other. Author Tuckey had gone through unscathed in a Monaro but the multiple collision took out four cars and eventually caused the retirement of a quarter of the field.

THE CANADIAN AND THE WYONG MACHINERY AGEN

Phase Three GTHOs boom away from the line, chased by the smaller but more nimble Holden Torana XU-1s. This potent car, its braking problems solved with the new Hardie–Ferodo DP1103 pad, dominated the 1971 Sandown Park 3-Hour and Bathurst. Lead Ford works driver Allan Moffat hurled the car around Mount Panorama in practice an incredible 13.2 seconds under the 1970 lap record, and blitzed the field in the race. Below: the touring car rules were changed for 1972 and for the five races (excluding Bathurst) Moffat's car wore the livery of his new sponsor, Coca-Cola.

using the clever line: 'We Were Deflated'.

The XW Falcon had a market life of only 15 months, with 2287 GTs and 662 Phase One GTHOs built. Peculiarly, the Phase Two was released in August 1970 – obviously in time for Bathurst – while the release of the XY successor to the XW was to be in November. The Phase Two acquired the more modern Cleveland 351 V8, a stronger engine with solid valve lifters and a rev limit of 6150 compared with Windsor's 5500.

The Cleveland also got a gulpier (750 cfm) Holley four-barrel, a 3.5:1 final drive with different gear ratios, massive Kelsey–Hayes front disc brakes and marginally more torque

but no more power. It was dubbed so because it came from Ford's Cleveland (Ohio) plant (the previous engine was from Windsor, Ontario).

It was enough. GM–H came up with a quick, nice-handling six-cylinder bullet called the GTR XU-1 Torana, and Chrysler a four-barrel version of its attractive Charger, but the Fords had a litany of woes in the September Sandown pipe-opener and only Moffat – whose ability to cosset a car became legendary – was there to take the chequer.

The Bathurst entry list featured 23 GTHOs and 20 XU-1s; Turner named McPhee and Moffat as solo drivers (the rules had been changed) and Seton/Gibson in his third car. In those days only Saturday was available for practice, and Moffat nailed down pole position in the first session. After five laps Moffat took over the lead and, while five of the draught horses had engine failure and the Gibson/Seton car lunched its transmission, the two most gentle on their equipment, the Canadian and the Wyong machinery agent, were uncatchable, finishing 1–2.

Managing director Bill Bourke left Ford Australia on July 31, 1970 to become president, Ford Asia–Pacific (FASPAC). Before he left, he addressed a lunch in Adelaide organised by the American Chamber of Commerce. It was a long speech and near the end, referring to Holden, he said: 'Now, my great and glorious competitor, the foremost in our industry here ... every year they announce their profit it's good for two hours in Parliament.

'When I first arrived here five-and-a-half years ago I didn't have that problem, because we were losing 10 million bucks a year. But recently the Good Lord has reached down through the clouds and put His hand on our shoulder and we're starting to make a buck.'

Brian Scott Inglis took over as MD on September 1, 1970. The XY was his first new model launch and as an engineer he was proud that the sixes had been boosted in capacity and output, along with a seven-bearing crankshaft. The 188 cubic inch (3 litre) engine had been kicked up to 200 cubic inches (3.3 litres) and from 118 bhp (88 kW) to 130 (97 kW), and the 221 (3.6 litres) to 250 cubic inches (4.1 litres) and from 140 bhp (104 kW) to 170 (127).

The GT 351 ran a two-barrel carburettor instead of the four-barrel and compression ratio of 9.7:1 against 11:1, but the point was you could option it for every Falcon model, including the utility for heaven's sake. And the GT had this big air cleaner sticking out of the bonnet. The motoring press dubbed it the 'shaker', because when you blipped the throttle the enormous V8 torque rocked the plastic cover. This became the trademark of the

VERE UNCATCHABLE, FINISHING 1–2

The kitchen of the XY GT 351. Blipping the throttle would literally rock the beast on its rubber.

GTHO Phase Three, the most awesome of the trio (putting aside the Phase Four, of which more later).

Enter Howard Marsden. The slim, blonde-haired, mellifluously-spoken product of the English public (meaning private) school system had been running Frank Williams' race program when Frank Matich – along with Peter Brock and Ian Geoghegan one of the three greatest Australian race drivers, in my opinion – arrived in Britain in 1968 to buy a Formula 5000 chassis from Williams.

The next year Matich offered him a job in Australia and Marsden arrived on the eve of the 1969 Bathurst, just in time to see the 'We Were Deflated' debacle. Matich was the Goodyear race tyre distributor and within 10 days he and Marsden were on a Qantas flight to the USA to sort out the

tyre problems. Marsden, as infinitely calm and polite as Matich was volatile, lasted until early 1971 when he joined Ford.

Marsden had talked a lot with Al Turner and believes now that Turner upset a lot of people within Ford with his attitude towards racing.

Enter Allan Moffat. Says Marsden: 'We were racing the works Lotus–Cortinas in the USA and there was this young comedian giving us a hard time with last year's car'. That was Moffat, who recommended Marsden to sales and marketing director Keith Horner as Turner's replacement. Marsden says he walked into Horner's office and was asked only one question: 'Can you strip and build a car completely by yourself?'. He could, and he got the job as head of Ford Special Vehicles. He remembers Horner's slogan: 'I make 10 decisions and I get six of them right, and I work like hell to get the others to be correct'.

He inherited the Phase Three, the car that *Wheels* editor Peter Robinson immortalised by running an over-the-shoulder photograph of the speedometer reading 144 mph (232 km/h) on the Hume Highway.

His predecessor as editor, Rob Luck, in the November 1970 issue had run a mostly inaccurate story claiming, among other things, that Ford had spent $60,000 on an order for 200 sets of glass-fibre panels for the XY GTHO, that the engine would have an Australian-developed fuel injection system and there had been tests with turbocharged 351s. The real 'shaker' car came with an even bigger four-barrel (780 cfm), bigger radiator, larger harmonic balancer, improved valvetrain, baffled sump and a choice of four final drive ratios.

Many of the bits came from the American Mustang Boss 302 engine and Ford was surprisingly coy about the output. Officially it was only 300 bhp (223 kW) but the racetrack reality was 290 kW and 513 Nm of torque. *Wheels* slammed it over the quarter in 14.7 seconds: this was one of the world's fastest production sedans.

It would achieve lasting fame not only by finishing in the first six places in the 1971 Bathurst enduro but also because of the appalling footage of Bill Brown rolling over and over along the steel hawser-topped wooden fence at McPhillamy Park, the roof slicing open like a sardine can just behind his head. The Epping newsagent climbed out with just a cut and swollen eye and asked anyone smoking if they would kindly stop.

Hardie–Ferodo had to develop a new DP11 brake pad compound for the Fords because they had gone to a new type of front disc caliper that left only a tiny gap between pad and disc, so overheating became a real problem.

Marsden had just two works cars, for Moffat and French, but there were 10 dealer entries. Moffat stunned The Mountain with a pole lap of 2 minutes 38.9 seconds and in an incredible solo effort absolutely demoralised the field; he led from flag to flag to win by a lap, despite having part of a beer carton flattened over the centre of his grille from halfway on.

With the rules still specifying a minimum of 200 cars to be built to qualify for Series Production homologation (300 Phase Threes were sold), Marsden's Ford Special Vehicles shop started work on the Phase Four for the 1972 race season. It got retuned suspension, a larger capacity finned sump, revised manifolds, new cylinder heads and developed a reputed extra 30 kW in street trim.

Harry Firth had constructed a 5 litre V8-engined XU-1, 'ghosting' it by running in the sports sedan category early in the year. Heartened by good performances from its six-cylinder E38 Charger at Bathurst, Chrysler put together a 340 cubic inch (5.6 litre) V8 E39. And then the brown stuff hit the air-stirring device.

On June 25, 1972 Australia's largest-selling newspaper, the Sydney *Sun-Herald*, screamed across its front page '160 MPH SUPER CARS SOON!' Motoring editor Evan Green, in a story that would haunt him all his days, wrote: 'Australia's three major car makers are about to produce "super cars" with top speeds up to 160 mph'. Green had taken the Mixmaster to the story, although he must have known there was no way any of the three Bathurst specials could crack almost 270 km/h.

Then Transport Minister of NSW, Milton Morris, a Baptist lay preacher who loved seeing his name in print and was an apostle of savage penalties for offending drivers, said he was 'appalled' at these 'bullets on wheels' being sold to 'ordinary motorists'. There was an Australia-wide media uproar, with every journalist on the 'speed kills' bandwagon.

The Sydney *Sun* editorial of June 29 trumpeted: 'The motor industry has hit a grease spot with fast cars. It had to come. Some people have had an unhealthy obsession with the Bathurst 500 race, an event which emphasises speed for the hell of it'.

On June 30 GM–H said it was dropping the proposed Torana V8 because of government threats. Ford had no

The front page of the Sun-Herald story written by the late Evan Green which had the effect of killing off the Phase Four GTHO and delayed for several years a V8-engined Torana. It was what journalists call a 'beat-up', and it forced major rule changes to touring car racing. Ironically, Green later became GM–H public affairs manager and a board member.

In keeping with its hip image in those exciting times, Ford created an advertising slogan, 'The Going Thing'. There was even a band of young musical hopefuls rejoicing in the same name.

comment at first. The Confederation of Australian Motor Sport (CAMS) announced the Bathurst regulations would be changed for 1973 by dropping the requirement for a minimum 200 cars to be sold. On July 1 Brian Inglis confirmed that Ford would stop the Phase Four. Chrysler said it had suspended development of the E49 and withdrawn from racing, but the car was already on sale.

Marsden's team had built four Phase Fours, three red race cars fully caged and ready to go and a Calypso Green car for a private owner; FSV also built what Howard Marsden calls a 'half car', a two-door with full Phase Four specifications for dealer Bib Stillwell. Nobody knows where it is.

How the Grey Fox did it

I n 1969 Harry Firth supplied *Wheels* magazine with a handwritten manuscript of his memoirs. With the magazine's kind permission we reproduce part of the chapter dealing with how he prepared the race cars for the 1967 Gallaher 500 at Bathurst, which the awesome new GT won first time out. Remember that all cars had to be strictly showroom floor stock standard, but be told that the man they called the 'Grey Fox' wasn't telling all …

'Initial preparation was fairly basic – 3000 miles run-in with the car heavily laden to sag the springs. The car had a few faults picked up in the initial program. Too much weight on the front made the car understeer in standard trim. The gearbox and change mechanism were not good and first gear would pick up on the mainshaft due to not enough clearance and end play, so the gearchange was carefully assembled and adjusted and hand-lapped, run-in with thin oil and then filled with special oil containing Anglamol and Lubrizol additives. Distributor advance curves and carburettors were all over the place and we finished up doing an exchange service with the company on these items, as I had one of the few distributor machines around.

'Suspension location points and geometry were out in some cases. The fuel tank pickup had to be put down on the tank base to allow the use of all fuel. I intended to balance every working part of the car after outstanding results from a similar exercise on the Cortina GT used in the Mobil Economy Run – that is, engine, gears, diff, axles, hubs, brakes, fan, generator, wheels without tyres and wheel nuts.

'I had found engines, as manufactured, and due to high demand, were very "green" in castings and inclined to "walk about" after initial machining, so all would require blueprinting. For instance, crank pins were one per cent out of phase and up to 0.010 inches short on stroke and not well balanced, and this took a lot of fixing. Pistons and pins were very tight. Honing bores to straighten them helped and I hand-filed and emery-taped each thrust face down to the right clearance. New rings were fitted as the bore was now larger and would require some bedding-in again.

'It was not quite as easy with combustion chamber volumes: some of the valve seats had to be recessed further to give a reasonable comparison, and then a bit taken off each head to give the required volume to workshop manual specifications. Valve heads were taken down to minimum size, as this gave the

best gas flow. Valves were carefully ground-in and mirror-finished with Brasso. A picked set of valve springs made up the package and the whole engine was now to the best of specification.

'Quite detailed work was done on the suspension. The hardest rubbers that could be found (in Ford's Parts and Accessories division) were used in bushings. The highest of road springs were put on the driver's side of the car (the outside of the circuit) and front geometry set to give 1.5 per cent positive castor plus 1/16th inch toe-in, and all four wheels put exactly in line.'

Firth ran each car for 30-plus laps on the You Yangs proving ground road circuit to check handling and fuel pickup. The best was timed at 127 mph (205 km/h) on Michelin X tyres, which had a taller profile than normal. Firth noticed some temperature increase and took the heads off, to find slight warping of the valve seats, eventually traced to 'core flash' from the initial casting restricting some of the water passages, which he solved by a tedious cleaning out with a mild steel welding rod. The three works cars would be driven by Firth and a young Fred Gibson, brothers Ian and Leo Geoghegan, and Bob Jane with the young champion Spencer Martin. All three had different fuel sponsors, so to be compatible with them the Firth/Gibson car was dark green (BP), the Geoghegans' maroon (Total) and Jane/Martin's red (Shell).

'Each team had elected to do their own preparation and not be told how. I drove up to Bathurst as usual in the car and gave it a final ignition setting check on a side road out near Blayney and did not alter anything. Scrutineering was no trouble but as practice started we found out immediately there was a problem as the car would cut out on the drift across McPhillamy Park at the top of the mountain section. So we took it easy there and concentrated on braking points and general gearchange and driving lines, and compared notes. It was just as fast and far easier on the brakes to lift off on the last hump and give one hard press on the brake pedal down the other side, then coast to about 280 yards and go on-off the pedal about three times, keeping the front of the car down into the corner and putting the power on early to keep the speed up on pit straight.

'The surge problem was easily fixed by raising the outside half of the float level in the carby to its highest extent (about half an inch) and this made no difference elsewhere. We were happy with our lap times and wanted to keep some in reserve. Of course, we passed on the float level fix to other Fords but they would

The brilliant Bruce Hodgson got one race car for rallying and it was destroyed – he still has the number plates. One is in the hands of David Bowden, a Queensland Ford freak with a collection of possibly 60 cars, including examples of all the GTHO models.

Another enthusiast is said to have built an extra room onto his house for the third car and therein chained it to the floor. The green car is owned by a Sydney dentist who consistently refuses requests for photographs.

And that was really the end of it. Yes, the coming XA and XB Falcons would have GT versions, but they were pale shadows.

In 1992, to mark the 25th anniversary of the GT, Ford built 265 of the EB GT, but it was really a luxury Grand Tourer – as was the EL five years later.

The snorting, sweaty draught horses had gone to the Great Stable in the sky, we were the poorer for their parting, and we grieved.

Bibliography

John Wright, *The History of the Ford Falcon, 1960–1994*, Ford Australia 1994.

Harry Firth explaining a point to former Wheels *editor Peter Robinson.*

have only the last session to check it. They also asked for other info, which I gave, such as ignition settings. Fred had a real go at the start of the last session. We were both on the pace, around 3 minutes 6 seconds, and doing it easy where others appeared to be working very hard. The Geoghegans were faster but we wanted them to believe that.'

The three works GTs took the first three grid positions, their nearest rivals two importer-backed Alfa Romeo 1600 GTVs.

'Race day and the moment of truth had arrived – plus all the Ford hierarchy. It was comical. A new Ford PR gentleman turned out in suit, collar and tie and a Homburg hat tried to interfere, then complained to the managing director [Bourke] that I would not talk to him. The MD said: He doesn't talk to me either when he's busy. Exit one red face.'

Ian Geoghegan won the start and led up the hill from Gibson and Martin. The Alfas started to peg them back as the Ford drivers eased off to preserve brakes and tyres – still an unknown on this circuit – and within two hours Doug Chivas in one of the Alfas was second behind Geoghegan and when Geoghegan made the first of the Fords' three necessary refuelling stops the Alfas slipped into 1–2. But Firth, typically, was eerily calm, while non-works Falcon teams were panicking at the rate their cars were drinking fuel.

'We were faster than the other Fords across the top but not as quick as the Alfas, although we ate them in a straight line. Often you would strike two Mini–Coopers dicing together and go through the middle of them and blow them off the road. We were doing 100 (mph) up the hill and 130 down. All the pre-race work was paying off as the car was very strong and really holding its tune – if anything it was better as the race went on. We lost a bit of time to the others at

the middle stop changing pads, but had made this up by the last stop when we were in front. All except the Geoghegans were backed off with brake problems and they did not seem very happy, having slower pitstops but still going strong and quite quickly.

'I told Fred to stay in the car and do exactly what we signalled and not let the others past if they caught up. After letting the Geoghegans crucify their car to within about 10 seconds I gave Fred a signal to go and he took that back to 12 or so. Imagine my thoughts when they were given the flag and we did 131 laps (one more than the required distance). I demanded and got a recount. It was corrected by 7 pm but should never have happened as we had our own lap scoring team and they knew full well we had won.'

At the trophy giving Harry Firth announced it was his last Bathurst as a driver. He drove the car back to Melbourne and bought it from the company. His brother used it for years and Firth tried hard to find it, but failed. He immersed himself in planning for the next year, a year of both triumph and disaster.

CHAPTER 14

Foreign **Correspondence**

In the decade from 1970 to 1980 Ford Australia must have felt like an AFL football team – not Collingwood or Geelong, for those two have their special monsters – but perhaps Melbourne or Hawthorn or Sydney.

In a period infested, like fleas on an old dog, with problems of two global oil shocks, swarming Japanese imports, increasing demands for improved fuel economy, tougher safety regulations, a small car (the Escort) that was sucking away profits and, on the horizon, an all-new Holden from a company then dominant with the Kingswood, Ford Australia must have felt it was always counterpunching.

History now tells us that during this decade totemic change was wrought, not only to Ford Australia but to the entire Ford world.

Ford Australia owned the hearts and minds of the youth/performance market and the big prestige car segments, but 'Going Ford Is The Going Thing' was losing its ring. However, it had developed export markets in a lot of right-hand drive countries – Argentina had bought the drawings and tooling for the old six-cylinder engines and was still building the old XP models – and by 1972 Ford Australia was exporting 25 per cent of total Falcon volume.

The XA was being assembled in Thailand, New Zealand, South Africa, Malaysia, Singapore and Indonesia. In fact, Ford had laid the basis for a comprehensive insertion of itself into the Asia–Pacific area two decades before any car maker outside Japan and Korea had even thought of it. As we shall see, Ford Australia – well ahead of its parent in Dearborn – in the 1970s gathered the firewood for the bonfire of globalisation that would consume the world's motor industry in the second half of the 1990s.

It had established a sound local basis with Falcon and Fairlane, Cortina and Escort, while importing luxury cars, trucks and other product from North America as well as small and small-medium cars from Ford UK, but circumstances would result in its turning Japanese.

So in February 1968, the product planning office briefed

Below: a landmark in August 1973, from left Don Deveson, Brian Inglis, Don Swan, Keith Horner and John Hayward, with the 100,000th export car from the Broadmeadows assembly plant. Page 178, top: the XA Falcon returned the two-door hardtop to the range, and was the basis for the later Landau – a hardtop with LTD luxury.
Below: assistant managing director Edsel Ford II (left) and his sales and marketing director, Max Gransden, with a trio of 1976 models.

the Product Committee (those senior management concerned with product strategy and content – led by the Product Planning Office and also comprising Engineering, Design, Marketing, Finance, Manufacturing, Purchasing and Public Affairs) on the coming mid-1969 UK Ford Capri two-door hardtop. Holden had one – the Monaro – but Ford US had deleted it from the 1966 Falcon line-up so there was no cheap sheet metal available for the local Falcon. This new car would use the 1.6 litre Kent engine and the more potent 1.6 Cortina GT mill, it would fit into the 50 per cent local content plan and be priced up to $500 above the Cortina range. There was nothing like it on the market.

The British were going to badge theirs Colt (son of Mustang – geddit?) but Mitsubishi already owned the name. By May 1968 Ford Australia product planners had drawn up a list of names that included Monaco, Cheetah,

The Capri 3000 GT, assembled in Australia from imported British kits, with a V6 engine (there was also a 2.0 litre four) failed to sell in the target numbers.

THE XW WAS A BIG TEA[R]

Merino, Scat, Fastford, Davos, Tyrolia, Bayonet, Caribou and Slalom. The decision went to Capri, and the Capri coupe hit the Australian market in May 1969 and sold like there was no tomorrow – it even got Super-Roo stickers.

But Ford Australia was getting worried about engine sizes

for its Falcon. Product development is cyclical, so working up to three and four years ahead it's not hard to get out of step with the opposition, particularly with big-ticket items like engines.

A six-page product planning position paper over Ian Vaughan's signature went to management on May 22, 1968, detailing the comparative engine line-ups (figures have been converted to metric for easier comparison):

Ford 188 cubic inch (3.1 litre) six/85 kW; Holden 2.6 litre six/85 kW; Chrysler n/a.

Ford 221 cubic inch (3.6 litre) six/101 kW; Holden 3.1 litre six/94 kW/108 kW; Chrysler 3.7 litre six/108 kW.

Ford 5.0 litre V8/156 kW; Holden 5.1 litre V8/156 kW; Chrysler 4.5 litre V8/119 kW.

Vaughan said that Holden's next model would lift the 2.6 to 3.2 litres and the 3.1 to 3.7 litres, and that Chrysler was expected to launch a new 4 litre US-sourced six late in 1970. He proposed increasing Ford's six-cylinder engines (with the late 1970 XY model) to 3.3 and 4.1 litres – as happened – and suggested changes to the current valvetrains of the sixes because top-end failures had sent warranty costs skyrocketing.

To add to the company's worries Ford US had advised that it would be dropping the 302 (5 litre) four-barrel V8 from August 1968, although Australia had enough ordered to supply the GT models planned. The local 5 litre two-barrel and 351 (5.8 litre) Clevelands would carry on through XY Falcon and ZF Fairlane, although the marketing department campaigned briefly for (and lost) a 400 (6.5 litre) American V8 in the Fairlane instead of the 351.

The XW was a big tearup, as the engineers call it. All the panels were new except for the doors, giving the car a husky, ballsy look that went well with the booming motorsport image and the pedalling 'roo. The Futura name returned, the interior was done over and the three engines got slight power increases (the 351 would arrive with the facelift but was also available with the GT and ZC Fairlane that arrived a month later).

The XW run was succeeded in October 1970 by the XY, with those bigger capacity engines and the kind of torque that made towing a doddle. Even the three-on-the-tree transmission got synchromesh on first gear. The restyling was mainly front and rear cosmetics, down to the first plastic grille. GM–H released the dramatic new HQ in July 1971, but its American chief engineer, George Roberts, had infuriated his Australian underlings by ordering the retuning of the suspension to turn a great-looking car into something with the soggy ride and handling of a melting soufflé – he was sent to Europe soon after.

By the end of 1971 Ford's share of the total Australian new vehicle market had gone from 15.0 per cent in 1964 to 22.3, while GM–H had tumbled from 42.8 in 1964 to 34.3 per cent. Chrysler had actually fallen from 13 to 12.2 per cent in those seven years, but significantly, the share held by

Hero shot of the XW Futura, which brought that name back into the Falcon range for the first time since the 1965 XP. It was also the first Falcon to sport a plastic grille.

P: ALL THE PANELS WERE NEW (EXCEPT THE DOORS)

Japanese vehicles had jumped from 5 to 18 per cent.

Like the XP, the XA was a milestone for Ford Australia. It was the design that broke from the tradition of adapting North American designs for Australia, and created the unique Australian Falcon that thrives today. It was very much the child of Bill Bourke and Ford Australia's chief of design, Jack Telnack, who by 1975 had moved to head the Ford US design studio and who retired only in 1998, handing the crayons to J. Mays.

We have already seen how in May 1968 Telnack, a young Brian Rossi and Allan Jackson flew to the Ford Design Centre in Dearborn, Detroit, to work on the first clay models. Rossi had already been fiddling with the idea of a two-door version to match The General's Monaro. (Adrian Ryan remembers a conversation with Rossi in which the designer revealed that he had sketched the hardtop on an envelope on his kitchen table in the presence of a group of friends from Ford.)

John Doughty, who became Ford Australia's design chief

in March 1980, went on to a senior job in Ford Europe and then to Dearborn to draw the all-new Ford Taurus for 1996, was involved in the XA styling as well, but mainly the hardtop. David Ford went through engineering at Melbourne University with Ian Vaughan and, like him, joined Ford in 1964, both going into the product planning department. He was tumbled into the XA program.

'I was on assignment in Europe and was due to come home', he recalled, 'but instead I got a call from Malcolm Inglis, who was in Paris. He said, Quick, meet me in London. They want you to go back to the US to look after this [the XA development].

'I was basically the product planner in Detroit for a few months supporting all the clay model styling. Alan Tyrer came across with Kevin Bensted and we ended up actually working on selling the program to US management, which wasn't really our job.'

Here were these crazy Australians working with senior engineers, advanced engineering and all the other

A unique, trail-blazingly versatile Falcon ute

The XY did have a bastard child, even if the idea would turn out to be 25 years ahead of its time. Ford was selling its 250 cid (4.1 litre) six-cylinder engine to the AMC–Willys plant in Brisbane for the CJ5 Jeeps it was assembling. A Brisbane Ford plant parts employee came up with the smart idea of slinging Jeep running gear under a Falcon ute, using the existing transmission adaption. Brief testing showed that surprisingly few unique parts were needed, but the front axle and the base of the A and B pillars on the ute body needed strengthening. Eagle Farm had to build the planned 420 bodies and store them in the yard, because the XY was running out, but it took more than a year to get all the axles from AMC and the utes were being assembled well into the model run of the XA that succeeded the XY. Many of them were built at weekends to avoid disrupting the normal production line, and aftermarket customisers even produced a few wagons, as the ute floorpan was common to the wagon.

The 4WD ute was sold only in NSW and Queensland, as commonsense said not only that they were the main markets but that Ford could better control parts and service. It ran the Falcon all-synchro three-speed transmission with a two-speed Spencer transfer case to one-piece driveshafts front and rear, with power-locking freewheel hubs on the front. One teensy problem was that it had a Titanic turning circle of almost 18 metres, ensuring six-point turns in a normal suburban street.

The ute cost $3680 (the base sedan was $2455 then) but when AMC closed down the Brisbane plant and Ford was faced with the choice of sourcing the transmission parts here or importing them from the US, as well as adapting the new XA ute body with its frameless side glass, the decision was obvious.

Above: XY Falcon 500.
Left: Landau's vinyl roof concealed the fact Ford couldn't do the roof as a single pressing – it had a weld mark down the middle.

specialists, and there was bugger-all paperwork. So, David Ford says, he had to start creating documentation, because the Americans were happy as long as they had a piece of paper in their hands. In effect there was this young, wet-behind-the-ears planner masterminding a complete new car.

The XA used the XY floorpan, but the American stylists under Gene Bordinat kept interfering, and Rossi wasn't happy with their insistence on flared guards to emphasise the 'Coke bottle' look – the style which gave GM's Pontiac the edge on image at the time – which gave the car a skinny-tyred air, particularly as it maintained the Ford obsession with big wheel arch clearances. But from the moment the sedan hit the showrooms in March 1972 – the hardtop came five months later – the XA started a roll that made it the biggest selling Falcon ever at that point.

David Ford recalled: 'The hardtop was partly driven by a sporty image ... we wanted a hardtop to go racing ... we could make it more differentiated at the rear. We could get bigger wheels and tyres which Al Turner (then motorsport manager) was pumping for – that's why it had such monstrous wheel arches, which looked pretty terrible with standard wheels and tyres on them'.

Jack Telnack styled the hardtop; according to Ford he was a great stylist because he was a designer as well as stylist. 'When he got the problems of structure around the rear end and engineering was telling him, You can't do this, you've got to have different dimensions, you can't have the roofline like that, Telnack worked with them – unlike some stylists, who just put their blinkers on and stamp their feet and pout.

'It ended up he got 99 per cent of what he wanted in the styling theme, and the engineers were happy.'

Ford says Ford Australia then was small enough for

'IT MADE EVERYBODY FEEL GOOD AND IT GAVE US A

people to break down the walls that were erected in Ford US (and other manufacturers) between styling, product planning, engineering, manufacturing, marketing and the rest. The traditional US system was sequential: each department signed off its part of the overall development program and handed it on to the next, whereas today most design is happening at the same time.

Says Ford: 'In those days you couldn't keep the manufacturing people out. Ivan Tan Sing, the Geelong stamping engineering manager who had to make the tools, would be in the drawing office stealing drawings before they were even completed.

'A lot of this stuff about simultaneous engineering was going on then, even though it wasn't officially recognised.

Of course people would still stand back at meetings all dignified and throw rocks when anything went wrong.' As a product planner, before he even wrote a program Ford would sit down with the engineers and people like Tan Sing: 'You basically had it 90 per cent there before you put the official program up'.

The Holden Monaro was selling strongly, and it had been David Ford's job to evaluate the coupe market. 'When I'd done the analysis I said, This program doesn't make sense. You'll never sell the volumes of this type of vehicle in the Australian market.

'I had violent arguments with Alan Tyrer (then product planning manager) about what the volumes should be. He was Australian debating champion and he loved his ability to analyse and belittle people, and he and I ended up choosing to differ on it. Subsequently my volumes were proved right.

'But people wanted the hardtop, so numbers were fudged and the program went to the US and it got approved, but really, the hardtop was never a profit-making program and it was subsequently dropped [following a careful analysis by then marketing plans and research manager Geoff Polites]. It didn't make sense but it made everybody feel good and it gave us a better machine to go racing.'

Now retired from Ford, David Ford hasn't changed his view. 'I don't see the sense in GM–H trying to reintroduce a Monaro-type vehicle. I just don't see how the volumes will ever sustain it – in which case how do you justify the investment?'

The direct benefit of running the hardtop in racing would fall to privateers. It was launched in August 1972, and its first racing season was 1973, under the new homologation rules. Allan Moffat won the 1973 Australian Touring Car Championship and then Bathurst, with Ian Geoghegan as partner.

But early in 1974 Ford Australia pulled the pin on its financial support of motorsport. Howard Marsden remembers being present when managing director Brian

awards so if they didn't have a break after eight hours they went onto time-and-a-half. They particularly liked Surfers Paradise because the time allowed them to drive up and back shooting rabbits and goannas on triple time.'

David Ford had a similar shouting match with managing director Bill Bourke over the LTD luxo sedan and Landau coupe iterations of the parallel ZF Fairlane, on a 116-inch wheelbase stretched to 121.

'Bill wanted a more upmarket car. He thought if we got a hardtop maybe we should have a Thunderbird type of vehicle in Australia. Out of that he had the styling people start playing around with refining the hardtop to make it a more formal looking, high-series vehicle.

'I then said, Well, that's fine, Bill, but for Australia ... we're not, as I'd said before, a two-door market. What we want is a luxury four-door version ... what we should do is take the Fairlane upmarket by further extending

Opposite: Ford overestimated the coupe market and was left with 400 Cobra Hardtop body shells, so Edsel Ford II's brainwave was to paint them white with blue stripes, the US international motor racing colours. They sold like crazy from the moment they were released in January 1978. Below: the experienced and erudite Howard Marsden, product planner for the first Tickford Engineering variations.

...ETTER MACHINE TO GO RACING'

Inglis and sales and marketing boss Keith Horner were shouting at each other in the former's office.

'At one stage they stood up on each side of the desk and if the desk hadn't been there they would have punched each other. Inglis shouted, We're selling every damn car we build and we don't need racing. The racing budget was a drop in the bucket compared with the other marketing activities.'

Horner (and Marsden) lost, although Horner's spin to the motoring press was that the decision was made to enable Ford Australia to spend more resources on meeting new emission and safety regulations.

Marsden had 18 people working for him in Ford Special Vehicles. 'They liked motorsport. They were on union

the wheelbase for an LTD.'

The huge Galaxie had been dropped only two years before. Ford wrote two analyses, of an LTD and a Landau, and presented them to Bourke, arguing for just the LTD. Bourke was a good listener and his executives could argue with him without malice or threat to a career path.

'He wouldn't call you an idiot or bash you around the ears. He might override you but you didn't feel like you'd been screwed.' Bourke listened to him, sighed, and said, 'OK. You may be right but I want my Landau so we'll do both'.

Bourke would tell David Ford years later that he (Ford) had been right, but he liked Australians because they had the balls to tell him to his face he was wrong.

The dual program actually became somewhat more

FOREIGN **CORRESPONDENCE**

Celebrations for (second from right) Frank Erdman's 26 years at Ford. From left, Bob Marshall, Bill Dix, W. Carlier, Eric Witts, Keith Horner, Brian Inglis, far right John Sagovac.

financially viable because tooling costs could be amortised across both versions. Ford said the pair marked the first time four-wheel disc brakes (from Australian firm PBR) had been installed in a Ford mass production car. There was also a less commendable note. The plant couldn't stretch the roof sheet metal without an ugly weld join in the middle, so the LTD and Landau were specified with a vinyl top as standard.

By the time these two cars were released Bourke had gone to head Ford Europe, taking Telnack with him, and Brian Inglis (later to be knighted for service to the industry) had become the first Australian-born managing director at Broadmeadows.

Nobody in Ford then realised how pivotal the XA timing

would be. It was originally scheduled for a six-year run, with minor facelifts leading to the XC's succession in the first quarter of 1975, and XD the codename for the last facelift in 1978 before an all-new car due in early 1980.

All this predicting and planning would be ruined by the first oil crisis, which the industry calls the 'Shah's oil shock', in 1972–73. On August 22, 1974 the Product Planning Office advised the Product Committee that the XD (codenamed Blackwood) would in fact be an all-new car (known as a 'reskin') in late 1978 or early 1979 because GM–H and Chrysler were expected to launch all-new bigger versions of the Holden and Valiant in 1977.

The planners' spies were out of whack. The new Holden, the VB Commodore, arrived in October 1978 and the last

186

(and best) of the Valiants, the CM, followed in November.

Planning notes also called for a new six-cylinder engine for 1975 with a single overhead-cam cylinder head, which proved to be pretty good thinking that far out. The decision was to put all-new sheet metal on the XC platform, with a lower belt line and larger glass areas with slim pillars, to reduce the overall length but do a new interior with more room and revise the suspension for better ride and handling.

An earlier (February) memo from the product people said fuel prices were expected to keep rising and there had been a market shift away from the big cars to the Cortina/Torana/Corona packages.

'We believe the greatest direct effect of the energy problem will be continuation of the change in vehicle demand patterns to smaller, more economical vehicles, precipitated by the expectation of increased fuel costs', it read.

Here was GM–H planning a downsized car while Ford had plumped for a big 'un. Who was right? David Ford became overall product planning manager in September 1975. By then he had started advanced planning on the XC and Blackwood.

The planners were being driven nuts by Canberra. Apart from the new Australian Design Rules, which from January 1969 through January 1976 kept raising the bar on safety laws and exhaust emissions, in December 1971 the government had announced a post-1974 local content policy which, in effect, kept the 95 and 85 per cent plans to the end of 1979 but gradually eroded import duty concessions to small volume assemblers, with the aim of driving them out of the industry by 1974.

This prodded AMI (Toyota) and Nissan Australia to lodge their cars in the 85 per cent plan. The Whitlam government came to power in 1972, launching itself with a cyclone of reformist measures, which among other things replaced the all-powerful Tariff Board with the government-friendly Industries Assistance Commission (IAC).

In 1973, to the horror of many, Canberra cut all import duties by 25 per cent. Thus a 45 per cent tariff on an imported passenger car came down to 33.75 and that for light commercials and four-wheel drives to 26.5 per cent.

The importers were dancing in the streets, drinking

Bollinger out of gold chalices. The car makers stormed the Canberra battlements with their lobbyists and the Federal Chamber of Automotive Industries, and in November 1974, the government pulled the handbrake with an indirect 10 per cent levy on passenger car imports (but not light commercials and four-wheel drives) and a change in local content demands to a standard 85 per cent.

And Canberra kept fiddling with a new 10-year car plan almost every year, driving the motor industry (and the economy) up the wall. It reduced vehicle wholesale sales tax by 12.5 per cent for February–April 1975, to increase by 2.5 per cent for each of the following five months. This form of economic brigandry demoralised the industry and its retail sector. On top of that came new demands for low-speed bumper impact standards, front crash and rollover tests, better lighting, more stringent exhaust emissions and inertia-reel belts.

Leyland Australia finally said to hell with it and shut down local manufacture in 1982, while Nissan built a new casting plant and Ford and GM–H threatened massive retrenchments (which actually didn't happen, because the Whitlam government was dismissed in 1975).

When the tumult and shouting died and the smoke cleared, Australia had five car makers – GM–H, Ford, Chrysler, AMI-Toyota and Nissan – but the latter two, while entered at 85 per cent local content, still had some juicy import duty concessions.

Ford Australia had committed itself to getting Cortina to 85 per cent local content by mid-1971, but by 1972 the figure was down to 80 per cent because of increased British billing and freight costs and it was losing about $100 per car. On June 17, 1961 an 'executive summary' over Inglis' signature had directed the Product Planning Committee to approve the investment of $2.6 million to put the Falcon 200 cubic inch and 250 cubic inch six-cylinder engines into the 1972 TC Cortina, above the 1.6 and 2 litre fours. The proposition estimated this would improve local content by 5.4 per cent and produce net profits of $630,000 by offering an alternative to Holden's six-cylinder Toranas. (This segment of the market grew from 19 per cent of total passenger car sales in 1968 to 26 per cent in 1973 and was forecast to hit 35 per cent by 1980.)

Then the light car planning manager, Ian Vaughan says

Lamborghini should have sued

On August 10, 1972, on a huge cattle property near the city of Davao, 800 kilometres south of Manila in the Philippines, Ford launched its '$1000 car' for the teeming masses of Asia. Called the Fiera, it was a doorless, flat-panelled, hose-'em-out vehicle codenamed BC for Basic Concept, but inevitably dubbed Bullock Cart by irreverent Ford Australia employees.

It was a FASPAC project, but Howard Marsden's Broadmeadows-based Ford Special Vehicles team got the contract to design it.

Originally it was intended to run a two-stroke engine, but that segued into the existing Escort 1100 cc or Cortina 1300 cc engine. Marsden remembers his motorsport predecessor Al Turner (who had been moved to FASPAC) approving the prototype and Henry Ford II driving it at the You Yangs proving ground in January 1971.

'But it went to hell in a bucket because Ford's engineers got into the act. They have an engineer for petrol tanks, another for windscreen wipers ...'

Bill Hartigan was then running FASPAC's sales operations throughout Asia, one of his tasks being to get on side with trade association ASEAN. He claims the Fiera concept was his creation, designed by his service manager, Ron Wyman.

Hartigan recalls: 'We were making an Escort engine in Taiwan, an Escort transmission and front suspension in New Zealand, but if you are looking at assembling a conventional vehicle the thing you'd most like to sort out early is the sheet metal; in a conventional vehicle you have to spend millions upon millions of dollars on dies.

'My idea was that the chassis and body panels would all be all straight cut, no complex curves. So all that was done in the Philippines.'

Ford invested $2 million in the project and the Philippines-assembled Fiera ended up with seven variants through pick-up and van to 'jeepney' and a 12-passenger bus with metal seats folding against the sides. The base model cost just $US1195, 17 per cent of its componentry was sourced from Ford Australia, and it ran for most of the decade (some were also built in Thailand and Taiwan) ending only when the Philippines ran out of foreign exchange to pay for imported bits. Al Turner had one made with a 2 litre engine and bigger wheels to use on his Victorian farm and Marsden's FSV built a utility with four-wheel drive.

Fiera in Spanish means 'fierce', and the Bullock Cart was launched with the emblem of a savage fighting bull – which happened also to be Lamborghini's motif.

today that Brian Inglis came to him with the demand to organise the six into the Cortina, but describes it as 'a car driven by government regulation'. The engineering people warned Inglis that the basic car really wasn't designed to take surgery such as this.

They were right. The Cortina six would be an awful engineering task that ran over budget and produced a rather nasty car. The modifications included a new dash, radiator support panels, engine mountings, bigger rear brakes, Falcon rear axles, longer driveshaft, new front cross-member, revised front and rear floorpan pressings, new clutch and brake pedals, new stabiliser bars, fatter tyres, three-speed imported US Borg–Warner automatic, etc. At the time GM–H was selling twice as many four/six Toranas as Ford was four-cylinder Cortinas.

Now retired, Bill Hodgson was 27 in 1956 when he joined Ford from Rheem Australia. He went into manufacturing and in 1960 joined the tiny product engineering office and battled through the traumatic years of the first four Falcon models.

He winces today when remembering the Cortina six. 'Oh, wasn't that a dog, eh? Of course, we were good soldiers – we just did what we were told, but I think the thing was that if they could use the six they'd get it for next to nothing off their own plant and it would save them millions – a bomb – in importing four-cylinder engines.'

What were the particular problems? 'Well, it meant that the split driveshaft had to go – it was as expensive as buggery. So it had to have a one-piece driveshaft. It was a real shoehorn job, the front suspension was marginal for the weight we were putting in there and there wasn't much room underneath for rear axle wind-up, and all that stuff.

'But the NVH [noise, vibration, harshness] was the killer. That was just bloody dreadful, because of the one-piece shaft.' They tried a tube-in-tube driveshaft design – first used in the late 1940s – and rubber doughnuts on the axles but time ran out and Hodgson's boss, Eric Lang, eventually overruled everyone and declared the NVH acceptable. Hodgson says Lang was a Mensa member, but not on that call.

By 1974 Ford was breathing down GM–H's neck, but it was almost entirely due to Falcon. Ford Australia was in danger of becoming the Falcon Car Company, and

Spy shot of the 1973 Landau at Ford Australia's You Yangs proving ground near Geelong. This luxurious two-door hardtop version of the LTD brought the Ford Thunderbird 'personal' car concept to Australia. But it was discontinued in 1976, due to disappointing sales.

management knew it, but they were just a coloured pin on the chart of the Ford global structure and were stuck with expensive British designs of indifferent quality.

In the first six months to June, registrations of the new XB Falcon got to within 700 units of GM–H's innovative but flawed HQ – if you took wagons out of the equation Falcon actually beat Holden by some 2000 sales. In a bid to take the title for 1974 Ford pumped in its first 'limited edition' packages on the Falcon 500. Still a favourite sales weapon today, particularly as an alternative to discounting, which ruins later resale values, the limited edition typically will declare, say, $2000 worth of extra equipment for the same price as a standard unit or at the worst, a few hundred dollars more. This first Falcon example added 14 items from automatic transmission to a glovebox decal, costing Ford $234 but adding $565 to the retail price while advertising an added value of $866.

The XB was launched in October 1973. Ian Vaughan remembers that the stylists 'were casting around for a theme strong enough to top off the XA Falcon. Bill Bourke told them to look at the then-current Mustang. They had a yellow one alongside the clay, and did a fine job of transplanting (again!) "More, More Mustang into Falcon"'. The tail lights, too, were changed and standard equipment now included front disc brakes and inertia reel belts. The XB ran through to July 1976 when the XC arrived. This had been an unusually long model run for Ford Australia but one forced on it by the engineering resources needed to meet new ADR 27A emission regulations that brought 3.3 and 4.1 litre six-cylinder engines and a new cross-flow cylinder head that lifted power outputs by 8.9 kilowatts on both engines.

That took most of the cash; the restyling was cosmetic, although there was a new dash with circular instruments and the GT was replaced by the Fairmont GXL. It was also the first Falcon to get radial ply tyres as standard. The Product Committee had been discussing them seriously since February 1974, while the product planners had

FOREIGN **CORRESPONDENCE**

Ideally, there would be no white post in the middle of this photograph but the clue lies in the date it was shot – October 30, 1975 – which was almost a year before the XC Falcon launch. The venue is the You Yangs proving ground but the photographer had not been invited.

wanted them for years. The ER70H14 radial had been made standard in April on all Falcons and Fairlanes with the 351 V8 but, while all the testing had been done on all models including Escort, Australia's five tyre makers were dragging their feet.

GM–H, of course, launched the HZ Kingswood in October 1977 with a very successful marketing and public relations promotion wrapped around Radial Tuned Suspension, but

Ford had been focusing on the wrong target.

In June 1974 the Product Committee approved a spend of $14.3 million to develop the new TD Cortina for launch in February 1977. The Product Planning Office's analysis said the Cortina had about the same slice of the market segment as the Torana, but that GM–H had introduced an all-new four-door Torana in March 1974 with optional four, six-cylinder and V8 engines and integrated air-conditioning

A MEMO OUTLINED PLANS TO RI

(which the company had consistently refused Cortina on the grounds of cost). As well, a new smaller Holden (which the planners identified as Isuzu Kadette but which would be badged Gemini) was coming in 1975 and Chrysler in the first half of 1975 launched a Chrysler 180 (Centura).

Toyota had just upgraded its Corona sedan and the awful Leyland Marina four and six-cylinder models were to be facelifted – as if that worried anyone. The report went on:

were built at Geelong. The projections were that Cypress would cost Ford Australia $9.1 million and Brenda $3.1 million. Although nobody in the entire Ford world realised it at the time, what happened then was to change significantly the way Ford and (much later) some of its rivals would come to understand the concept of automotive globalisation. This obscure item of forward product planning in a relative backwater of the giant enterprise

...ACE THE ESCORT WITH THE HONDA CIVIC

'The Cortina's market appeal lies in the high acceptance of its package, appearance and performance. However, it is projected that as the market approaches a free demand situation, Cortina penetration will start to decline. Since the TC was introduced in 1971, the vehicle has developed an extremely poor quality and reliability image. While concentrated effort has reduced Cortina warranty from 580 repairs per 100 units at three months in service in 1973 to a current level of 480 repairs per 100 units, compared to Falcon the Cortina remains some 60 per cent higher with equally higher warranty costs. In addition, the (six-cylinder) Cortina has come under increasing criticism and owner complaint for its poor ride, steering and NVH'.

The company embarked on extensive design changes, to include power steering and integrated air-conditioning. Prices for the TD would be increased by only $84 per car.

The Escort (first launched here in 1970) was also losing money, and something had to be done about it. By August 1973 it had just 1.5 per cent of the market (10 per cent of the small four-cylinder segment) against 2.2 per cent for the Torana four and 3.7 per cent for Toyota's Corolla. In the frame was a major facelift for mid-1978, but then there were Bobcat, Brenda, and Cypress.

Bobcat was a three and four-door US small car due in 1980, which never happened. Brenda was the codename for a major reskin of the Escort four-door for 1975, using the same chassis and drivetrain. Cypress was a new concept, a unique Australian three-door hatch on a shortened Cortina wheelbase, using imported doors with the rest of the sheet metal locally pressed – two prototypes

Henry Ford had wrought would provide the spark.

The idea came from American Ed Molina, then vice-president in charge of Ford Asia–Pacific. On Christmas Eve 1973, he sent a memo to the all-powerful Product Committee in Dearborn outlining plans to replace the Escort with the Honda Civic. This information has never been made public until this book.

His astonishing memo pointed out that the Escort in Australia and the Asia–Pacific was suffering continual losses as well as irregular supply and increasing freight costs from

'Get Hodgson's arse over here'

When Ford Australia moved its six-cylinder engines up in capacity from 188 to 200 cubic inches for the 1970 XY model it sold the patterns and tooling to Ford Argentina. Drivetrain engineer Bill Hodgson, 70 years old when interviewed early in 2000, said the South American subsidiary was having 'diabolical' troubles building the engine, running bearings and all the rest of the drama.

'We got called up by the States, and they said: Hey, get Hodgson's arse over here – now – immediately – to Buenos Aires. Jack Hawke, my counterpart in manufacturing who'd done all the work on building the engine, was told to go also.'

It's still a long haul flight to Buenos Aires, but in the early 1970s it was a marathon. They flew to Los Angeles, then Miami, then Caracas and finally Buenos Aires in a Douglas DC6B sitting in what was then the circular 'starlight lounge' in the tail.

'When we got to Buenos Aires I had two big portmanteaus of engineering drawings of the bloody engine and a small bag with clothes in it. The bloody Customs locked me up and said it was a design for a machine gun, and I was in real strife.

'Jack didn't have any drawings so he ran around and got someone from the company to sort it out; it turned out not to be a machine gun after all and they let me go.

'The next day we were taken to the plant and this bloke was waiting for us and he said: We know what's wrong ... nothing to do with the design of it, and you blokes can go. They never even opened the bags. So we flew home.'

Jack Telnack, then executive director of Ford North American Light Truck and Car Design, with an early mockup of the 1979 Mustang. Dick Johnson raced this shape Mustang in Group A in the mid-1980s.
Overleaf: Brian Inglis shared the glory of the occasion with Victorian premier Rupert 'Dick' Hamer, allowing him the driving duties.

the UK, plus a lack of updating and non-compliance with tougher Australian safety and emission standards. Today this would be regarded as sensible straight-from-the-shoulder analysis; then it was close to heresy, because the Escort was the jewel in the crowns of Ford Europe and Ford UK – they didn't have to compete, as did Ford Australia, with the Japanese.

Molina's nine-page memo said, in part: 'It would therefore appear desirable that we explore with Honda the possibility of a joint manufacturing and sales program for the Honda Civic car line'.

The revolutionary idea was for Honda to keep control of design and Ford to manufacture the car; Ford would tool and make the sheet metal and Honda supply the engines and transmissions for 1.2 and 1.5 litre two/three and four/five-door models. They would be marketed as Fords through Ford dealers in the Asia–Pacific markets and allow access to Honda's Japanese dealer network. Ford would also supply the Cortina to Honda, and in return would guarantee Honda access to the Philippine and Taiwanese markets (where it was banned) plus lower duty entry to Australia, New Zealand, Singapore, Malaysia and Indonesia.

Molina said he didn't hold out hope that Cypress would be any kind of answer to Ford Australia's problems.

Which brings us to William Anthony Hartigan. Bill Hartigan infuriated many people within Ford with his management style. Right up to the time he retired at the age of 57 in January 1991 from his job as vice-president, sales and marketing, Ford Australia, this silver-haired, big-eyebrowed economics graduate with vast experience in sales and government affairs ran his bailiwicks on the basis of the big picture and did not suffer fools gladly.

At the time of the Honda negotiations he was with FASPAC and became involved in the supplier timing and pricing arrangements. 'At the end of the day we couldn't come to a satisfactory arrangement on pricing. Honda always premium priced their products. We were desperately looking for a competitive source (to the UK) and it had to be Japan.'

Hartigan will appear later in the narrative, because this first Honda foray led indirectly to Ford Australia getting an aluminium alloy cylinder head for its six-cylinder engine and then, perhaps more importantly, to the very valuable joint venture with Toyo Kogyo, now Mazda.

While all this was going on, Ford Australia's own bigger picture was Project Blackwood. Former sales and marketing director Max Gransden said that while the XA was marketed as The Great Australian Road Car, and the XC as The Going Thing, it was decided that, with the XD, Ford had to be seen more as an Australian company.

So the marketing theme would become: 'Ford Australia – We're Moving With You'. It was time for a change, time for being more caring about the environment, about better fuel consumption, smarter use of resources. But first they had to design a car, a uniquely Australian big car. Like the XP, the XD was destined to be the second pivotal model that galvanised Ford Australia and its dealer network and led directly to regaining in 1982 the market leadership it had lost back in the 1930s.

Bibliography

Norm Darwin, *The History of Ford in Australia,*
Eddie Ford Publications, 1986.
Geoff Easdown *The Falcon Story,*
Lothian Publishing Company, 1989.
John Wright *The History of Ford Falcon 1960-1994,*
Ford Australia, 1994.

The last XC Falcon sedan to be shipped (other than a small number of fleet vehicles) by Ford Australia, to make way for the new XD. Shipments of the XC totalled 171,077.

THE 2,00
PR
By FOR
NOVEMBE

CHAPTER 15

The March To **Leadership**

I have written before that the motor industry is the world's biggest casino. It encourages – demands – that its key people endlessly gamble billions of dollars on projects four and five years ahead of real time.

If you disbelieve this, ask yourself who – if anybody – anticipated the enormous Asian economic melt-down of 1998–99.

The act of intercourse that fertilised the embryo that grew into the XD Falcon lineage that finally ripped overall sales leadership from the GM–H grip can be traced back to May 19, 1972 – 10 years earlier. That was the date of the first memo from Ford Australia's Product Planning Office to the Product Committee. It contained the first advice that what was then seen as the 1977–78 Falcon – but which became Project Blackwood and thus the XD for early 1979 – could be based on an overseas design. Probably written by Product Planning's Peter Gillitzer, it said in part:

'It is not desired to be totally [sic] unique as is the Holden but to derive basic designs for suspension,

instrument panel and front end structure from Ford US or Ford of Europe vehicles'. Closest in size were the US Fairmont/Thunderbird/Lincoln compact, the coming all-new US Taurus and the European Granada.

The memo said firmly there was no 'off-the-shelf' car suitable, declared the US wheelbases and tracks too small because they couldn't be stretched to Fairlane size, lacked a coil-spring rear suspension (which GM–H then had) and in right-hand drive would accept only a Windsor (Canada) sourced V8, not the Australian Cleveland. Scratch three.

The Granada was equally unsuitable: it needed considerable re-engineering for the Australian engines, the independent rear suspension would have to be replaced with the carryover coil/leaf design and the wheelbase couldn't be stretched far enough for Fairlane. Scratch four.

The overriding negatives, however, were Ford Australia's determination to retain rear-wheel drive and the fact that

Right: the XD's square, macho look was an instant hit with Australian buyers. As usual, it was launched with the full range of sedan, wagon, van and utility. Below: in Australia to preview the XD outside the Design Centre at Broadmeadows are (from left) Ian Vaughan, Henry Ford II, Edsel Ford II and then Ford chairman and CEO Don Petersen. Opposite, pressing the flesh: Prime Minister R. J. Hawke visited the new plastics plant at Broadmeadows.

THE COMPANY HA

the package sizes offered didn't provide anything like the required width for three adult rear seat passengers. Taking an overseas design would also demand what the industry calls a 'total tearup', which would be far more expensive. The recommendation (which was consistent all through Blackwood except for the timing of the actual launch) was to reskin the platform of the XC scheduled for September 1976, but make it shorter overall, with more interior room, reduce the weight, put the fuel tank under the rear seat, and upgrade suspension, brakes and engines.

Work had started in 1972 on building a state-of-the-art plastics factory alongside the Broadmeadows head office and main plant. This would be a prime weapon in the intensive program to give the new car the Jenny Craig treatment – plastic fuel tank, dash and bumpers – plus as much aluminium as possible. What Ford Australia didn't know then, however, was that by early 1974 GM–H was studying the first drawings of the German Opel Rekord four-cylinder. The concept of the 'packaging' was to cut and expand it to take the current six-cylinder and V8 engines, making it a smaller car overall than the Kingswood but with more interior length. GM–H's response to the 1973 fuel crisis was thus to 'downsize' even more boldly than Ford eventually would.

The XD Falcon would arrive in a market very different from that facing the first Falcon, the XK, in 1960. Since then average weekly earnings had risen by a cumulative 429 per cent, the consumer price index by 212.7 per cent, and the retail price of a Falcon GL (adjusted to similar model levels) by 139.8 per cent. In 1979 the average employee would work for 30 weeks to buy a new Falcon, compared with 67 weeks 19 years before.

In 1971 about 10 per cent of new Australian cars were specified with a V8 engine and by 1979 that figure was 13 per cent. But sixes had dropped dramatically, from 54 per cent to 30 per cent, while fours had screeched upwards, 36 per cent in 1971 to 57 per cent in 1979. It was all to do with the two 'oil shocks', which skewed every world stock exchange, every economic forecast, every established value to an extent that few people younger than 30 today could comprehend.

Ford Australia had been dismantling – down to literally the last nut and bolt – each model of the Holden as it was released. Ian Vaughan says one of his first jobs was to coordinate a teardown and cost comparison 'to the penny'.

LOCKED ITS RADAR ON TO A SINGLE ANCIENT RIVAL

The fourth and third generations of the Ford automotive family – Edsel II (left) and his father – with the XD on the lawn outside the Broadmeadows Research Centre.
Opposite: With the first of many Australian design awards made to Ford Australia (this was for the XE), sales and marketing director Max Gransden on the right.

'We used to weigh every part, put them on a board, photograph them for the engineers to look at. Under each part would be the number of the part – we showed a washer and said seven of these weigh so and so, so you knew the weight of the car and the cost of the car.'

They also pulled apart Valiants and of course their rivals were doing the same to Fords. The company had locked its radar on to a single ancient rival, a focus that would be both its strength and its undoing right through to 2000.

In June 1973 Vaughan had gone to Ford Asia–Pacific (FASPAC) as product planning manager, aligned to sales and marketing, but in May 1977 he returned to Broadmeadows as product planning manager for Ford Australia, to coordinate Project Blackwood.

In an interview in early 2000 he said: 'This is interesting … their car (VB Commodore) would have been planned more in the panic of OPEC than ours was. Everybody saw America downsizing in 1973 when the Japanese invaded them and they said, Wow, small cars are important aren't they, so we'd better have one. So it was downsize, downsize, downsize'. The general American credo for forward planning in those critical years was 'When in doubt, downsize'.

Vaughan says now that the underlying feeling within Ford Australia was that Australia was a big country with a big car tradition. But then, so was the United States.

He remembers the company had imported for assessment a four-cylinder Opel Rekord (which formed the basis of the VB Commodore) and later the bigger six-cylinder Senator. 'We used to get photos of their prototypes out on the road. I remember having photos and actually scaling them … we used to scale off the length of the wheelbase from a photo of a test car out in Central Australia. We had people out with cameras just like the press did, looking for Holdens driving in the bush. So we used to have a pretty good look at each other.'

When did the panic start? To this day Vaughan – a corporate man to the backbone – is reluctant to give ground to the general belief among motoring writers that Ford panicked over the Commodore, believing it had guessed wrong with the XD. Yet Ford Australia did import five 2.3 litre four-cylinder Pinto engines from the US and install them in XD prototypes before deciding not to go that route. (GM–H, memorably, chopped two cylinders off

its ancient six and produced the Commodore Four as a second iteration of the original. If there were an award for the Dog of the Decade, that car would have walked away with it during the 1980s.)

Said Ian Vaughan in a 1981 interview: 'We did a lot of talking about vehicle size and fuel economy. But what really decided us, I think, was that thing called market spread. Then we saw three natural sizes of car – Escort,

Cortina and Falcon. So we went the route of keeping the weight down in the car and keeping the outside bulk down, as well as planning even the alloy head revisions'. He says the four-cylinder engines were a tentative response to the Commodore Four, but that doesn't seem to fit with the timing.

There was also considerable argument about the styling. Vaughan wanted a big 'greenhouse' (the designers' name for the window area under the roof) with low sills and belt line. The US tradition then was for the line of the fenders to continue straight (or nearly) from front to rear under the window sills. The dropped belt line created another problem – getting the engine profile (the height it stands in the bay) down far enough to create a low 'cowl line' (the top of the dash) to join neatly with the sill line.

Stylist John Doughty was on assignment to Dearborn again in 1978 and in 1981 told me he remembered a major ruckus over the XD styling, which was the child of the then Ford Australia chief designer Andy Jacobson – whom Doughty would replace in March 1980. Doughty

said Jacobson 'fought like hell' for the revolutionary low waistline.

'We even imported Opel Rekord doors to get the thinness in the doors and the glass, because at that time they were outstanding.'

David Ford said there was resistance from some local management and from Dearborn. 'We were being told, You can't change the doors. I said, You've got to change the doors. My view was we needed something more like the compactness of the European Granada, which had narrower doors and a lower belt effect. So we went to a clinic with modified doors on a locally done clay. Fortunately, that bombed, for a couple of reasons. One was the way the clinic questionnaire was, I think, structured a little bit …

'We then said we need an alternative clay, so we got Trevor Creed out from Europe – he subsequently became very high level in styling in Chrysler in the US – bringing with him some of the Granada things. There was a certain amount of antipathy in the styling area at this stage. Creed created a Granada-type clay – much tauter, lower belt, tighter door sections – and we used special square Bosch headlamps. It was just chalk and cheese. I knew which one we wanted but we had to go out to a clinic again. I sat down with market research and they made sure the questions were asked in the correct fashion, so it came through with flying colours. So that was the program I took to the US for approval.'

The clays of the XD Falcon and ZF Fairlane were sent to Dearborn and the fibreglass model went into the Lockheed wind tunnel in Georgia for final testing.

One advantage they had was the hands-on policy of managing director Brian Inglis. He would come into the design office at weekends and sit on a stool, watching the clay modellers at work. The budget was $100 million, but he kept the bean counters at bay as the designers discarded more and more of the XC sheet metal, because much as they tried to carry over pressings like doors and roof rails they could 'see the odd bits sticking out'. Doughty: 'The Blackwood project was really a tribute to Brian's understanding of design and the way he fought for us. He has a remarkably good eye for line on cars'. Inglis told Geoff Easdown, for *The Falcon Story*, that they were 'stuck with a lot of things'. He said the basic platform and front suspension was unchanged from the XB: 'It has been 20 years of carryover'.

While all this was going on Ford Australia had taken its first major step towards getting a real edge on GM–H in the area of engine efficiency. The XC Falcon and ZH Fairlane released in July 1976 contained Ford's answer to the new Australian Design Rule 26A, setting the first-ever benchmarks in measured exhaust emissions. Since becoming chief engineer in September 1976, David Ford had worked on XC/ZH as well as the beginnings of Project Blackwood. GM–H took the easier route of fitting additional plumbing to its existing engines, making them less tractable and smooth-running. The Ford Australia decision for a more expensive solution involving a cross-flow head was a significant factor in the growing success of Falcon.

'We'd always felt that if you could improve the engine's sophistication it would help us step over Holden. Peter Gillitzer and I – he worked for me then – believed you could do something with the Falcon engine. So we pushed

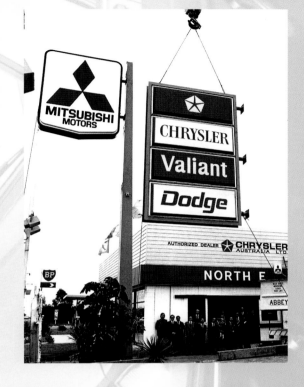

Opposite: August 1981 clay model of Project Capricorn, based on a stretched Telstar floorpan, which Ford Australia evaluated for more than a year. This was a hatchback; there was also a sedan (notchback) version. Above: an historic moment as the Chrysler signage comes down and Mitsubishi goes up on an Adelaide dealership. Mitsubishi Motors bought the two factories and the infrastructure for $80 million – a piddling sum today. In 2000 Mitsubishi itself was subsumed by DaimlerChrysler. Left: the VB Commodore (here the SL/E) had a rapturous welcome from the media and shocked Ford. But in 1982 Ford snatched the number 1 spot from GM–H.

very strongly and used the emissions … as an excuse to say we had to change the engine. Some of the initial outlines and concepts of the engine were drawn by Gillitzer on his kitchen table (yes, a second domestic kitchen used for Ford Australia design!). That was a major plus because I don't think the XC styling was anything to write home about.' (Gillitzer, coming from Mercedes–Benz and GM–H, was an engine engineer before going into product planning.)

Meanwhile, the company was struggling with its Escort

and Cortina lines, and the imported British Capri coupe was hardly setting the salerooms alight. Ford Australia was losing serious money on every Escort it sold, reflecting its British source quality problems, despite a formidable reputation built on international rally successes. It was also being badly battered by GM–H's Isuzu-sourced but locally assembled Gemini, Toyota's locally built Corolla and the Datsun 120Y – which sold well on price and quality long before it became The Great Australian Used Car Joke.

'WE'VE GOT YOUR NEW CAR ON ICE' … IN OTHER W

Ford tried everything with the Escort, including a 'Little Ripper' version of the capable panel van, and in 1977 fixed the ADR 27A problem by dropping the 1.3 litre engine and adding the 2 litre four from the Cortina – a move that hadn't been tried in the UK. But by 1980 it would be gone from the market.

In December 1974 came the TD Cortina upgrade over the TC, which fixed a lot of the minor hassles and added extra models, but the six-cylinder version was still an understeering nasty. A further update came in July 1977 in

DS, 'HANG ON'

the form of the TE model range, and Ford was confident this would be the final fix. It wasn't. The styling was more pleasant and equipment levels higher, plus there were significant changes to suspension, brakes and steering, but it carried the baggage of a reputation for poor quality. However, it added enough 'plus business' to the well received alloy-headed revision of the XD Falcon to tip Ford over the line ahead of GM–H in total passenger car sales. Its final iteration was the TF in October 1980, but the writing was on the wall for both the Escort and the Cortina to be replaced by Japanese-sourced models, Ford Australia's first dramatic dive into badge engineering.

In November 1976 Ford Australia's director of engineering, American Fred Bloom, took David Ford and Dave Cox to Japan to look for a supplier of the alloy cylinder head which was scheduled for Project Blackwood to cope with the flagged next ADR emissions reductions.

The original list was Fiat, Nissan and Mazda; they settled on either Mazda (the parent then named Toyo Kogyo) or Honda, added at David Ford's urging because of his admiration of its technology. Ford: 'Mazda was the most painful, teeth-pulling exercise you've ever been through, because it was early on in the Ford–Mazda relationship. They were a very old-style insular company … in formal meetings we were over this side of the room, they were a long way away over that side of the room, everything painfully done through interpreters, with breaks in the

The very popular Fred Bloom flanked by colleagues in May 1979, including Andy Jacobson (beard and waistcoat) and Ian Vaughan (tallest). Left: Sir Brian Inglis became the first Australian-born managing director of Ford Australia. His father was an original employee and his brother Malcolm, who died late in 1999, was also a senior executive. Opposite: the robust, tough Falcon ute has played a major part in Ford's sales success in Australia.

meetings. Fred Bloom was getting ready to run across the room and clock some of them. He was a very go-go American style of person and just could not handle that Japanese process. I would have to restrain him, saying Fred, just relax, it'll happen.

'With Honda, within 10 minutes of starting to talk to them we had our drawings on the walls and then they threw

The XE got a very positive review from Wheels. Editor Peter Robinson was delighted that the Falcon had acquired a Watts Link rear suspension. That year Ford would outsell Holden for the first time. Opposite: why are these people cheering? Managing director Bill Dix (at left) leads the hoorays as the last V8 Falcon rolls off the line at the end of 1982, with the XE model. It proved a marketing mistake, as Ford started to lose its performance/youth image, but the consequences would not be felt for some years.

their interpreter out of the room and all spoke directly in English. They were great. They were pointing and saying, Oh look, to manufacture this more easily you need to modify the design here and here; even if we don't get the business we're just making these suggestions here ... it was great working with them, fantastic.'

At the time Bill Hodgson, whose background was engine and transmission, was executive engineer, vehicle engineering. Now retired, he said Ford Geelong took a year to design the new alloy head, and agrees Honda was very good to work with. 'They locked us up in a bomb shelter for a week and the president [engineering-trained Takeo Fujisawa, who succeeded founder Soichiro Honda in 1973] came down and he went through every dimension on the head. I don't know if you've ever seen a head drawing but it's about a mile of bloody paper and he just sat down and went through every dimension with his people.

'We sat there for about a week ... there wasn't much they didn't understand and there wasn't much they didn't bloody change. The thing changed every week, it just went on and on and on. We'd get out there at 7 o'clock in the morning and wouldn't finish until around 7:30 at night. They'd drive us home in peak traffic and

we'd get back too late to get anything to eat other than go to the bar and get drinks and sandwiches. But that president was the most remarkable man I've ever met.'

The arrangement was that Australia shipped the aluminium alloy to Japan where it was placed in bond and thence to Honda's high pressure die-casting machines and the machining line; after two years Honda would ship the equipment to Ford Australia.

An interesting variation on Blackwood comes from John Marshall, who in March 1975 returned from FASPAC to Ford Australia as general operations manager for assembly, and retired in 1989 when vice-president in charge of manufacturing. He says now that as early as 1973 there was planning for a downsized Falcon to meet the first oil crisis, but it eventually was canned.

'It didn't get very far, but a lot of people worked on it, and they wanted to put the six-cylinder engine into it.' He was a member of the product committee that guided and approved Blackwood. Did he recall any doubt at the time about the way Blackwood was going? 'Oh, yeah. They came out looking like champions at reading the turn of the oil crisis downwards, when the fact was actually that they were too bloody slow in moving to where they thought they had to go. That's a different version from what

you'll get from Ford, but in fact they were still undecided when the oil prices came down.'

It doesn't matter to whom you talk, the fact remains that Ford Australia – including Edsel Ford II, who at the time of the XD launch was still Ford Australia's assistant managing director and head of marketing – was worried whether it had read the chicken entrails correctly with the Blackwood. GM–H laid on the most expensive dealer and media launches in its history to reveal the new VB Commodore in October 1978 and Ford's advertising agency countered with posters and TV

commercials of an XD hidden within a huge block of ice that gradually melted as the months went by to the unveiling the following March. 'We've Got Your New Car On Ice', was the slogan. In other words, 'hang on'.

The media response to the Holden Commodore was lyrical in its praise, particularly for the European styling and the quality of ride, handling and brakes. The common theme was: 'It's hard to believe it's a Holden'. *Wheels* called it 'far and away the best Australian family car ever'. But as those months rolled on, the negatives started to appear – poor body panel fit, dust leakage,

side rubbing strips that sprang the plastic clips, exhaust lines that jumped their rubber O-ring hangers. *Motor Manual* in its January 1979 issue said the motoring press had been 'nicely conned'. And more problems arose – ashtrays jumping out of the rear armrests, steering rack rattles, water pump failures and an air-conditioning overflow pipe that would pop out of its socket and void itself under the front passenger carpet.

This was bad for consumers, who were progressively demanding from Australian car makers the sort of quality the Japanese were offering. But the new Commodores

IT WAS XD WITH WHICH FORD CARVED THE G

Opposite: rally ace Greg Carr expressing a very positive attitude in his Escort during the 1980 championship. Right: John Marshall, director of manufacturing during the dramatic times leading up to the unveiling of the EA range.

finished 1–2–3 in the 1979 Repco Round-Australia trial in which Ford's over-complex Cortina sixes demolished themselves, and the public flocked to buy the Holden. Worse was to come. Sales of the traditional Kingswood would decline through 1979 and late in the year the OPEC oil exporters started the second oil shock by increasing crude oil prices by 140 per cent. Before the Kingswood was dropped in 1980, GM–H knew it had made a grievous mistake by electing to keep the old Kingswood engines in the new Commodore. People began asking why they should pay relatively more for a car that was smaller and offered less performance and worse fuel economy than a big Falcon.

All car makers in their history can point to milestone models, and there is no doubt that the XD was the car with which Ford carved in stone the gospel that stands today of a big, tough, roomy car for Australia. Eventually costing $130 million – the original appropriation from Ford US was $72 million – it was built on the XC floorpan, was 136 mm shorter and 40 mm narrower overall, with a 13 mm wider front track; it had the same interior space within a huge glassed area.

The styling looked big, aggressive, butch. Engines and transmissions were carried over with a few upgrades, the suspension was largely unchanged although the steering was quickened – but would you believe power steering still wasn't standard? The XD also introduced the GL badge for the bottom line, replacing the Falcon 500, with Fairmont and Fairmont Ghia the other two models. A bench seat with three-speed column gearshift stayed in the mix – one feels mainly for the taxi trade, which then, as now, was dominated by Falcon.

Despite being dearer across the range the Commodore outsold Falcon through 1979 and 1980. Ford's product people fiddled with those four-cylinder engines for the XD and for almost a year toyed with stretched clay models (codenamed Capricorn) of the new Telstar, the Australianised version of Mazda's 626, before reaching the

turning point – the introduction of the Honda-sourced alloy cylinder head after a year. But it would be the facelift model, the XE, that finally blasted the GM–H colossus from its pedestal in 1982.

Bibliography

Norm Darwin, *The History of Ford in Australia,*
Eddie Ford Publications, 1986.

Geoff Easdown, *The Ford Falcon Story,*
Lothian Publishing, 1989.

John Marshall, *The Automotive Industry,*
IMC lecture, September, 1979.

Bill Tuckey, *Commodore Lion King,*
Quill Visual Communications, 1999.

Wheels magazine, October, 1981.

John Wright, *The History of Ford Falcon 1960–1994,*
Ford Australia 1994.

PEL OF A BIG, TOUGH, ROOMY CAR FOR AUSTRALIA

CHAPTER 16

Turning Japanese

If Ford Australia were into revisionism it might start with the year 1979. It opened the New Year's Eve champagne with mouth pursed over the rapturous press reception for the new VB Commodore released three months before, then tried to trump GM–H's ace in March with the new XD, and soon after that made the crazy decision to contest the Repco Round-Australia trial not with the new car, but with six-cylinder Cortinas.

The Repco – the first round-Australia since the 1970 Ampol – was to start in Melbourne on August 5. Rally Director Stewart McLeod – later killed by a bomb in his Melbourne apartment – deliberately set the highest possible speeds over the worst available roads, demanding average speeds of more than 100 km/h on some of the special stages.

After his preliminary route survey in January he told me: 'When this is over the crews are going to think I'm the biggest bastard who ever lived. They'll never forget this'. The longest rest break he allowed during the entire 20,000-odd kilometres was 14 hours. The 2250 km Adelaide–Perth segment gave only three hours' rest in 62 hours at the wheel.

GM–H boldly entered three of its just-released six-cylinder VB Commodores, formidably bankrolled by its main race sponsors, Marlboro, Castrol and TAA (now Qantas).

The crews were top-drawer and media-attractive. Their eventual triumphant 1–2–3 finishing order was Peter Brock/Matthew Philip/Noel Richards, Shekhar Mehta/Rauno Aaltonen/Barry Lake and Barry Ferguson/Wayne Bell/Dave Boddy – all except Brock very experienced rally drivers or navigators. Team manager was George Shepheard, whose father Reg had conceived the idea of the first round-Australia trials as a publicity vehicle for his employer, Redex – the first in 1953, won by Maitland chemist Ken Tubman in a humble Peugeot 203.

Street-smart, wily and tough, Shepheard began with a small advantage. GM–H had lent McLeod a couple of

Commodores to use in his route surveys. Early in the piece Shepheard got Holden to build him a 'mule' Commodore (later christened 'Old Silver'), and gave it to Bell, Ferguson and Aaltonen to test and then to Brock and Philip. Their task was to hammer it from Melbourne out into Victoria's Western Desert, break it, bring it back, get it fixed, and go out again. While Shepheard was using the basic Commodore as a platform and keeping it simple, modifying only things like front suspension, engine mountings and engines, Ford had given Colin Bond the task of preparing three highly modified Cortinas. Ironically, Bond and Shepheard had grown up together in Gladesville

Bond was starting to slip back. By Kingoonya Carr's Cortina had a cracked rear axle housing and Ford PR Richard Power was frantically trying to get through a message demanding three Borg–Warner heavy-duty rear axles in Perth. The front suspension started working loose, but by Perth the three Cortinas were running first (Bond), fourth (Carr) and fifth (Fury).

Then it all went horribly wrong. During the first stage out of Perth Bond became lost and dropped 17 minutes getting to the special stage at the Wanneroo race circuit (now Barbagello Raceway). The unflappable Bond, the cheerful chuckler and legendary master of car control, fretted while

CARR'S CORTINA, COM

(Sydney) and paired to win the under-21 novice section of the 1964 Ampol Round-Australia impressively in a Volkswagen 1200 Beetle.

Shepheard had the full backing of the (covert) Holden racing team organisation and the GM–H engineering department, which would design and build anything he wanted, as well as a big service backup comprising an 11-seat Piper Navajo Chieftain aircraft and five vehicles, compared with Bond's two bog-slow Transit vans, two F100 pickups and a small plane. Ford's motorsport group had been disbanded and many in the company didn't want to know about this adventure.

Bond began with a Cortina six that was a fairly nasty car dynamically; in hindsight he tried to make a silk purse out of a sow's ear, with an exotic mix of a much-stiffened body, four Bilstein gas-filled dampers in the front suspension, a Falcon disc-braked live axle rear end and a single central rear seat that could be slid forward and aft for weight distribution. The crews – arguably the absolute cream of Australian rallying – were Bond/Bob Riley/John Dawson-Damer, Greg Carr/Bob Morrow/Fred Gocentas, and George Fury/Roger Bonhomme/Monty Suffern.

The cars were quick out of the box and very competitive, but within the first three days all three had a broken nearside front shock absorber and, from fourth in Adelaide,

the service crew replaced the brake pads. In a bid to make up lost time, he charged out of the circuit into a crest at a T-junction. The brakes refused to work and the Cortina slid off the soft shoulder and rolled down a grass bank. Pulled out by a tractor, they had to drive 300 kilometres through drizzling rain north to Geraldton with the windscreen partly caved in and Bob Riley – one eye black and swollen – jamming it with his feet. The Geraldton Ford dealer then tried to make him pay for the replacement windscreen, and from that moment the Repco was lost to Ford.

It got worse. Near Newman Fury's Cortina smashed its steering and cracked the new rear axle housing. He pulled up to wait for a service crew, but those in the Transits had stopped by the side of the road, exhausted. Bond's engine had sagged so much the crankshaft minced the sump baffles and destroyed the oil pressure – in the asbestos town of Wittenoom (now deserted) he spent $150 on 50 litres of oil and petrol, stopping every 30 km to pour in more oil. By Port Hedland in northern Western Australia the best-placed Cortina was Carr's, seventh. Coming in to Wittenoom he broke a rear spring centre bolt and jury-rigged it in place with the winch cable looped over the car and locked to the front roo bar. Then the Ford plane got lost trying to find Port Hedland.

By the time the field left Darwin after 12 hours' rest

Carr/Morrow/Gocentas were up to fifth, but the two other Cortinas, while still running, were gone for all money – Carr had lost upwards of three hours' more time than Brock, Bond was 32nd and Fury 35th. In Darwin they all got major rebuilds of engines, mounts and suspensions, but their luck continued to be atrocious; between Darwin and Goodparla all three Fords hit the same big rock in the middle of the track and ruined their engine mounts, sump and radiator. Bond smashed his sump and had to be towed in to Borroloola; he retired the hapless car, telling journalists: 'We broke the toy'.

At Townsville the three red-and-white Commodores were still 1–2–3, Ferguson from Brock and Mehta, and the Carr Cortina was eighth, but had lost more than 10 hours compared with just over two for the two leading Commodores. The route down the coast was a lot easier than the first half of the event had been, but the Fords now had too much lost time to make up. It was a shame, because Carr's Cortina, now rebuilt completely, was flying as though it were day one. By Brisbane he was fifth and Fury seventh, but the official scoring system was a shambles. Greg Carr had been fastest of the field from Townsville to Brisbane, dropping only 4 minutes 40 seconds. Down the NSW coast McLeod put them through

ETELY REBUILT, WAS FLYING AS IF IT WERE DAY ONE

many of the blindingly fast special stages of the famous Southern Cross championship rallies and again, between Brisbane and Port Macquarie, Carr was fastest and running fifth, although Brock still led Ferguson, if only by 1 minute 37 seconds.

From Sydney the battered, weary field was flung into the

Snowy Mountains. Again fastest on practically every stage (mind you, the crews were babying the three Commodores because Shepheard had threatened death to anyone trying to race a teammate) the Carr Cortina was still clawing back time, but time was running out. He actually caught Brock, the leader on the road, around Buchan in eastern Victoria and Brock waved him past. But after Beechworth and the Kelly country in heavy rain, the trial would virtually end at Albury, as the last day was a 309-kilometre 'transport stage' down the Hume Highway to Melbourne. The three Commodores swept onto the white shell-grit trotting track of the Melbourne showgrounds in triumphant formation, 1–2–3 and, predictably, monstered the publicity.

Of 167 starters, 92 finished. Carr/Morrow/Gocentas were fifth and Fury/Bonhomme/Suffern 25th. The Jaffa Mafia had given the new Commodore a stupendous baptism.

But back to January. With the XD launch coming up, Ford still had 400 XC hardtop body shells to move. Edsel Ford II came up with the idea of painting them white with blue stripes, and they quickly sold. Edsel would grab the limelight in the XD motoring media launch, staged in March

out of Wilpena Pound in the Flinders Ranges (the family resort owners were long-time Fairlane customers and appeared in Ford's TV advertising). Although he denies it now, Edsel started trying to play the saxophone in the band after a long and liquid dinner, and around 1 am we threw him in the motel pool as a payback, and his room keys with him. When he climbed out the manager hurried off to find the master key but Ford PR Richard Power decided to be the hero and climb in by removing the glass louvres in Edsel's toilet window. So when the famous name got into his room and went into the bathroom he found one of his Ford Australia PR operatives stuck halfway through his dunny window (Power did survive this career move).

That afternoon he was with another writer, Phil Christensen, when Christensen lost control of the car on ball-bearing gravel and spun through a bridge, without hitting anything. Later, early into Port Lincoln for the charter flight out, we took Edsel into a typical Aussie pub, tiled high up the wall so they could hose out the mud and blood and beer, and bought him a large Southwark; it was the first time he had been in such a place, and he was delighted. Back in Melbourne that night at a Ford Australia cocktail reception I was telling a group of suits about these adventures when a PR man tugged at my coat sleeve. 'Would you please shut up', he hissed. 'Two of those blokes are our insurance people and they'll be shitting themselves about what we've allowed you to do to the son and heir.'

The XD got a good reception from the motoring writers, although some saw it as less Euro-modern than the Commodore. Ford copped another indirect back-hander when its brilliant new plastic fuel tank technology didn't get the recognition it deserved. It had had to go to enormous lengths to prove the safety of the design to the relevant authorities, to the point of dropping it from great heights, and trying to set fire to it but, as John Wright said in his *History of the Ford Falcon*: 'It was a sad irony that the brilliance of the new fuel tank design was not properly acknowledged at the time because fuel gauge malfunctions plagued the XD for the first few months of production until a fix was found'. (The same 'all for the want of a horseshoe nail' syndrome would be repeated years later with the equally adventurous EA model.)

However, many within Ford were still jittery about whether the company had put the chips on the wrong slot in the roulette wheel of this gigantic gamble. David Ford came back from North America as chief engineer in mid-1979 and told me 20 years later: 'The panic was starting. Everyone was running round ... fuel crisis, and compact, and this Commodore over at Holden ... I didn't understand it. Edsel was saying Oh, we've got fuel economy and all that and I said, But Edsel, the Falcon is a bigger car, has more performance and actually can have better fuel economy than the Commodore – why can't you sell that to people for about the same money?

'I said, You guys don't understand your own product. I was flabbergasted. They were so down that they hadn't really stood back and looked at it. They overreacted in many ways but the momentum built up and we rolled over GM at last.'

Ian Vaughan has a more reserved corporate view about the company's crisis of confidence over the XD: 'I don't recall there was much panic – we were pretty confident about what we had. We contemplated selling a four-cylinder Falcon and just thought it wasn't credible, because in a smaller body it was credible but in a larger body it wasn't'.

His contemporaries claim Vaughan was a major proponent of the idea of taking the rear-drive Mazda 626 and stretching it – Project Capricorn – as an addition to Falcon. That obviously came directly from his stint with Ford Asia–Pacific.

But as John Wright pointed out, Ford countered the new Holden by focusing on its new car's towing ability, fuel economy from a larger engine and the fact you could sit three adults comfortably across the rear seat. These three factors would prove the killers, although it took more than three years. Dedicated Holden buyers, confronted with the proposal of paying about the same money for a car that was smaller, thirstier and slower than the Falcon, switched – as did, importantly, many large fleets.

The arrival of the alloy cylinder head upgrade in June 1980 – the first aluminium cylinder head used in a Ford six worldwide – was a body blow for GM–H, which by then was realising it had made two major mistakes in (a) keeping its old inefficient six-cylinder engines and

Brilliant and outspoken chief engineer David Ford (right) with Ford president Don Petersen, admiring the alloy cross-flow head, which would do so much to help the XD Falcon's fortunes.

(b) developing a four-cylinder version of the Commodore.

Ian Vaughan had a stint as small car planning manager in the early 1970s and today describes the six-cylinder Cortina then in his bailiwick as 'a car driven by government regulation'. The late 1973 energy crisis forced a massive refocus onto more fuel-efficient engines while the car makers were struggling to meet tougher local content regulations. To cut through all this and get out of the expensive and poor quality Escort and Cortina, Ford went hunting for alternatives. FASPAC had been set up – it would include such international luminaries as Frank Erdman and a future president, Alex Trotman – but Vaughan says the American who pioneered the Mazda connection was Ralph Peters, in the mid-1970s.

'It grew out of the joint arrangement with the Courier (Mazda B1600 light commercial) for North America. FASPAC under Ralph Peters went to Mazda and said, Gee, we think a Ford version of the Familia (323) would be a good idea for FASPAC, and can we talk about it.'

Established in 1971, FASPAC was run from St Kilda, Melbourne, and because many of its people came from Ford Australia it had a loud voice. Inflation in the UK was

FORD FALCON *Ford*

February 2000: 'We were desperately looking for an alternative source and Japan was clearly where the competition was. So what do you do? You get a Japanese player if you can'.

But Hartigan revealed a story that so far has been kept secret. Mazda was into its lead bank, Sumitomo, for billions of dollars after its rotary engine ploy had had a head-on collision with the energy crisis in the North American market because of lousy fuel economy. Hartigan says Sumitomo was so concerned about Mazda it suggested to Ford it might contemplate making an approach to invest in Mazda. 'We tried MITI (the Japanese bureaucracy that controlled manufacturing industry and trade) but they told us to piss off – they would much rather amalgamation take place within Japan as opposed to with a foreign company.'

Ford US since the pre-war days had owned an old plant on 36 hectares in Yokohama, which had been taken over by the Japanese Government during WW2.

'We revived the plant (in Yokohama) because to be able to sell our products from whatever source into Japan ... there were a thousand fiddling little things we had to do to the cars ... every light bulb had to be identified ... we were actually putting all our imported cars through this process of refinement. The Japanese were unimpressed with

JAPAN WAS PROCEEDING IN LEAPS AND BOUNDS IN T

running at over 12 per cent a year, the local Escorts and Cortinas were costing too much in imported components, were of poor quality and Ford and its dealers were losing money on virtually every sale. Finally, the Japanese rivals were ambushing market share through higher equipment levels, lower prices, far better quality and better reliability.

Ford's discussions with Honda about the possibilities of badge-engineering the Civic for the region, plus Ford Australia's successful negotiations on the alloy head, had redrawn the culture boundaries. The now-retired Bill Hartigan, who went to Ford Japan in 1980 under Bill Dix as president, had 10 years with FASPAC and was at the heart of Ford's trip into a Japanese joint venture, told me in

quality... and that went on for a while, but it became fairly clear that we didn't have the right sort of cars for the Japanese market and Japan was proceeding in leaps and bounds in terms of quality and cost control.

'So in effect we traded our 90 acres of land for 25 per cent of Mazda. Had we sold it and repatriated the money we would have been up for extremely substantial capital gains tax, knowing that we bought the land in 1934.' This commonsense ploy actually laid the foundation for Ford taking control of Mazda in the mid-1990s.

It gave FASPAC the opening for the replacement for the next European Escort, which was planned to switch to front-wheel drive, just as Mazda was planning to make its next

323 the same way. Bill Dix, then vice-president of finance for Ford Europe, soon to head Ford Japan and then become managing director of Ford Australia, was pushing for the Escort.

'In Europe the price of bloody cars had gone out of sight and we were looking for an alternative to the Escort', says Hartigan. Europe couldn't meet the Japanese quality and price. 'That was where we made the decision to drop the Escort and go with Mazda. Having made the decision my next job was to negotiate the operating contract between Ford worldwide and Mazda.' Based in the Mazda home city of Hiroshima, negotiating all the terms and conditions, covering patents, copyright, royalties and the rest, took Hartigan a painful two years. The Sumitomo Bank people sat in on all the meetings, day by day.

Hartigan recalls: 'We used to meet pretty much every day. I wrote detailed notes. We might only do a clause in a week. The primary difference was the Western view of contract and the Japanese view. The Western view of contract is that it is black and white – there is no grey. The contract covers everything and if for some reason there is something you didn't think about or predict and the contract doesn't cover it, then stiff. Fortunately Ford, being the sort of family company it is, understood the deal had to be beneficial to

of the facility. To the best of my knowledge there's never been an argument about the agreement.'

The most difficult point was the level of agreement about how much differentiation there should be between the Japanese 323 and the Australian Ford Laser. Bear in mind that from 1975 GM–H had been assembling the local Gemini version of a Japanese Isuzu small car, closely related to the Opel Kadett, but Ford was going much further, with different styling and selling the same platform with different cosmetics and specifications in the same market as its parent.

Polish-born migrant Tadeusz ('Tad') Zyppel, who started with Ford in 1951 and became fluent in German and Japanese, was a specialist in engineering and manufacturing program timing – itself a very sensitive operation. In 1979 he was appointed as timing manager of FASPAC, controlling the dynamics of product development and assembly in Australia, Japan, Taiwan, New Zealand, Thailand, Singapore, Malaysia, Indonesia and the Philippines.

RMS OF QUALITY

both parties ... if we were going to make a dollar out of it they were going to make a dollar out of it. We had to deal with matters of pride – they were very proud of their design and so on.

'The point I was trying to make was that we would make our best effort along these lines. We are buying vehicles which you will manufacture to our specifications. We're asking you to do a couple of things for us. We're asking you to carry out the engineering – we'll do the design. We're asking you to reserve very substantial capacity, we're asking you to invest in bricks and mortar, etc, on the grounds that we will buy it from you and if we don't buy it from you, you lose the sale of the goods and the utilisation

Opposite: the XE Falcon was the car that turned the corner for Ford Australia and, allied to the Laser, won it market leadership in 1982. Left: Bill Hartigan, ebullient, confident of his ability and someone who called a spade a spade, was a major figure in the interface of Ford and Mazda.

Right: Ford Australia managing director Bill Dix poses for a publicity shot of a Model A and an XF on the lawn outside the company's Broadmeadows head office. Opposite: Wheels gave the new Laser a big tick, but didn't hand over its prestigious Car of the Year award.

Of Toyo Kogyo (Mazda's parent), he says now: 'Initially they had a very narrow focus ... very hesitant and suspicious, but later better and better. I put it down to the way Australians go about doing business with other cultures. I think Australians are very adaptable and very low key, and I think that served to keep good the relationship'.

He agrees the Ford Australia people were on a steep learning curve as well. 'We learned that to be effective with them you had to keep the bullshit down to an absolute minimum, to refrain from snowing them with too much paper, to discuss principles and get agreement on principles.' Dix and Hartigan were his superiors in the negotiations but Zyppel says most of the time he had to detail the specifics on his own.

Zyppel, a precise, neat man who retired in Geelong and plays golf every Wednesday, is meticulous in his comments about the unique Ford–Toyo Kogyo relationship. He is careful to emphasise the interplay of the difficult melding of Australian and Japanese cultures, and hesitates when asked about how Ford's American executives handled this frail relationship. 'There were certain issues which became apparent from time to time, and underlying them was this constant Ford–TK competitive position we were placed in. Right from the start Mazda had a very interesting cycle plan which they were reluctant to let us in on – the total Japan motor industry cycle plan and how Mazda fitted into it – the

intelligence on competitors in Japan was damn good. Eventually we became a participant and got to know what Mazda thought would happen within 10 years, in terms of engines, platforms, bodies and so on.'

What was at stake here was the world's first experiment in designing a model to be shared between two big makers in different cultures but sold as rivals in the same markets – as distinct from the 'badge engineering' invented by the giant British Motor Corporation in the 1950s with Austin, Morris, Riley, Wolseley, MG and later Triumph and Rover. Today common platforms are the norm, but the FASPAC–TK concept was truly revolutionary – and few industry commentators at the time understood its enormous significance.

Zyppel explains that Mazda people started the design process while Ford people were allocated an area in the same building but divorced from Mazda. The principle was that Mazda would in its separate design area 'freeze' the styling of the clay model of its coming Familia, so Ford could work on achieving the maximum differentiation in styling for the Laser. Because the platform, suspension, drivetrain and sheet metal were common, differentiation was confined to grille, headlamps, rear treatment and such.

Zyppel: 'Our people claimed that at night, when everybody was asleep, the host would sometimes have a good look at our things and – lo and behold – next thing our guys would start to recognise some of their goodies on the Mazda clay. Quite often a brushfire would ensue and sometimes the bigger guns would have to have a discussion on what would happen'.

The problem was that Mazda had to lock in its styling to allow the Australians to make the Laser different enough so that in the local market it would be seen to be a different car. But Mazda kept moving the goalposts. 'Our people claimed their freeze used to thaw, but they claimed they were merely going through a refinement or feasibility refinement ... I mean, they held the aces ...', said Zyppel. Management in both companies were working through the details but the engineers and designers had to keep it all moving. Zyppel's main task, as far as Dearborn was concerned, was to guard jealously the corporation's timing interests for the models. He made probably 25 trips to Hiroshima, difficult at that time, involving flying into Tokyo or Fukuoka or Yokohama and then taking bullet or regional trains.

Ford Australia wanted to introduce its Laser through its dealer network at the same time Mazda Australia, a subsidiary of the parent, introduced the new front-drive 323. What really got in the way of all this was the Japanese system which gave the component supplier the patent and intellectual rights over various systems and parts in the car, so that with Ford trying to boost its Australian content on a car that was to be built in the Homebush (Sydney) plant – with a $13 million refurbish for the Laser – it had to raise local content on other models to meet government rules, and all this took time. Tad Zyppel recalls: 'Many of the vehicle features on a Mazda are owned by the vendor, he is called in at the conceptual stages, he is told what to develop, what to design, he owns the design ... and the intellectual property ... therefore his target is far more efficient than ours would be. So local content became a huge issue.

'The way we overcame it [to meet government legislation] was to raise local content temporarily on other vehicles, such as Falcon and Fairlane, and as we increased local content on Laser so we reduced it on the others.' Much of this was eased over time as Ford Australia managed to introduce Australian component suppliers directly to Mazda and/or its domestic vendors – Henderson Seats was

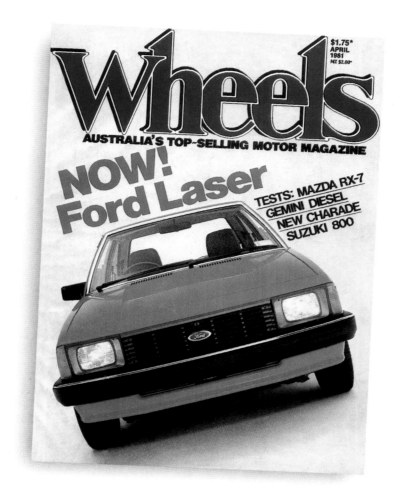

probably the first example of the two-way flow of intellectual property.

The aim of the joint venture was to have the first Lasers on the same ship to Australia as the first 323s. It never quite happened. Zyppel said in February 2000: 'Somehow as the last 323 was loaded on the first ship, whoops – there was no more space and our Laser had to follow on the next ship'. There was considerable strain between the two top managements during the release of both cars. Mazda launched its first front-drive 323 in Australia in October 1980; it had a four-door sedan, three hatchback versions and both a 1.3 litre and a 1.5 litre engine plus a twin-carburettor 1.5, while Ford launched Laser six months later, minus a sedan and the twin-carburettor engine. There were other hiccups.

Ford's decades-old system was that as you put a new model on-stream you would order huge numbers of

The Falcon–Commodore comparisons which obsess motoring magazines today had their genesis in the Commodore versus XD Falcon confrontation. On Wheels' cover of June 1982 are the XE Falcon GL and XE Fairmont Ghia, matched against the VH Commodore in 'base and best' form.

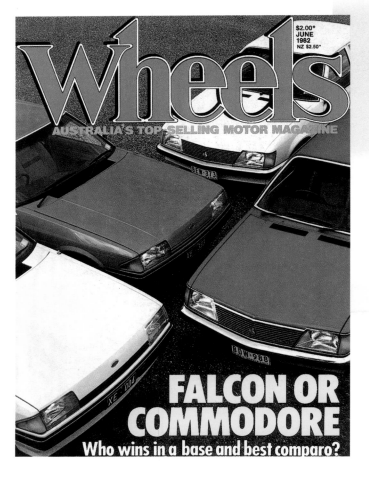

'production parts' – not replacement parts – as a backup to things that went wrong on the assembly line.

Hartigan remembered: 'So the Japanese said, What is this? And we said, This is our pre-production parts order, and they said, Why are you doing that? And we said, Our experience has been that when we start a new model, both because of the import source and because our own people are not familiar with it we lose a lot of parts, dropping on the ground, they don't come in the packs, and so on. They said, How do you know which parts you need? And we said, From our experience. And they said, If you know which parts you need, why don't you do something to fix it? And they were absolutely right.'

That, in a nutshell, was the main benefit of Ford Australia's association with Mazda. It wasn't so much the quality of the product as the remarkable difference in manufacturing systems. Zyppel says the company's purchasing people, after the initial order for 'production parts', based on their experience with British kits, didn't place another order for

'a bloody long time'. Putting aside orders for body panels and headlamp and tail-lamp assemblies and other 'supermarket damage' parts the need for mechanical bits was astonishingly different because the car went together at Homebush like a Lego set, to use Tom Pettigrew's (of whom more in Chapter 18) vernacular of the time.

'Our assembly engineers were absolutely thrilled', said Zyppel. 'But in terms of assembly tooling our people thought they taught Mazda a lesson. They thought Mazda's tooling was lightweight.' Zyppel was coordinating timing for assembly of both 323 and Laser on the same line in places as different as Indonesia and New Zealand, so the tooling had to be strong and compatible.

Ford US started to become interested in how this unique new relationship was working and in February 1985, Zyppel was asked to go to Dearborn to brief the heavier end of the company. 'When Ford US entered the scene, because of its huge size and its very narrow specialisation, they started to overwhelm. Our approach of a handful of people dealing with a handful of people, in the Ford US context became a busload of people. Mazda felt obliged to field a busload of theirs on the other side, so the conferences became larger and larger, and there came a time when Mazda started to charge Ford US an absence fee.

'Ford US baulked and said, What's this, and Mazda said, Well, we're charging you for the absence of large numbers of our people, for the time they're away from their jobs. Of course, FASPAC had never charged them any such thing as an absence fee. And despite this we found they [Ford US] didn't learn from our experience, much as we hoped they would.'

Despite that, FASPAC – being Australian-dominated – allowed Ford Australia its autonomy in the relationship with Mazda. Before long the odd marriage became very harmonious and segued quite naturally into the Mazda 626 and its Ford Telstar clone to replace the Cortina. The differentiation between the two brands became more marked, and Ford was able to get unique Laser versions like the TX3. From the moment the Laser hit the showrooms at a very competitive price, and with markedly better quality than the Escort, sales skyrocketed. It was a major factor in Ford's snatching market leadership from GM–H at the end of 1982, but before that there had been other boosts.

As we have seen, Ford then utterly owned the hearts and minds of Australian youth. Falcons won Bathurst in 1970, 1971, 1973 and 1974 and in 1977 two hardtops produced the unforgettable image of a staged 1–2 finish half a car's length apart, Allan Moffat nursing a dying Falcon with co-driver Colin Bond ordered to stay aft of him. Brock came back at them in 1978 and 1979 and in 1980, with both GM–H and Ford officially out of racing, Brock in a brand new Commodore – albeit with covert factory support and the same Marlboro Holden Dealer Team sponsors as before – massacred the Bathurst opposition, Commodores filling the first nine places and not one privately entered Falcon finishing.

One of them was car 17, the Tru-Blu Falcon of a little-known Queensland driver called Dick Johnson (who started his racing in an EH Holden and then an XU-1 Torana). Johnson had been running an XC version for Brisbane's Bryan Byrt Ford, and late in 1979 went to the dealership principal, John Harris, who was about to auction off all the racing equipment.

'I'd had a few sherbets and was feeling a bit brave', he later recalled.

Johnson put in front of Harris a deal in which he would buy the XC and all the parts plus a new or second-hand XD Falcon. 'I said: Look, I've got $32,000 in my private bank account. That's all the money I've got without putting myself into hock. I'll give you that, and you give me the car and the XD and all the bits, engines and what-have-you, and I'll build a car and run the Bryan Byrt name on it for 12 months from the day the car hits the track. I had no idea how I was going to finance the actual running of the car.'

Harris had his staff buy a very used 43,000-kilometre highway police XD from Maryborough at the State government auctions, which became car 17. Johnson got extra backing from an old school friend, Ross Palmer, who was expanding the family steel tubing business, and was thus able to get the right wheels and tyres for Bathurst in October, plus two engines, one cranking out a massive

(then) 411 horsepower. He shattered the establishment by being second fastest in practice, just 0.14 seconds behind Kevin Bartlett in the quick but brakeless Chevrolet Camaro.

'My little trick was to unnerve the guy next to me on the grid by just moving the car a fraction. You have to really concentrate on it. I just went bump with the clutch, like that, and saw it catch KB ... he had to look at me, back at the starter, then back at the tacho and then dial himself in again, but by that time I had gone. I got to the top around Reid Park and there was nothing in the mirror. Mate, I couldn't hear the engine. This is true. All I could hear

Hotted up turbocharged Lasers were a consequence of the more relaxed relationship between Ford Australia and partner Mazda.

was the crowd. This was the best feeling of my life. There were Ford flags everywhere and they were going ape.' As Johnson pulled top gear on Conrod he looked in the mirror and Bartlett, Allan Grice and Brock were just coming out of Forrest's Elbow.

On lap 18 he was nearly 40 seconds ahead of Grice – Brock had pitted with minor damage from shunting a slow Gemini – and going up the hill and into The Cutting he saw a white flag, meaning vehicle ahead. Through The Cutting in second gear he sighted a lift truck, hard over to the left, and an instant later saw a big rock sitting on the track halfway between the truck and the near-vertical grass bank. The truck had stopped to pick up the rock.

'I flicked the car right and went to do a wall of death up the bank but I got the rock with the left front wheel. That broke the wheel and flattened the tyre, and the load change then blew the back tyre as well. The car went straight across the road at 45° and rode up the fence like that. I thought, We could be going over here. It ran along the top of the fence and the next minute we crashed down and stopped dead.'

It was an appalling moment. Within half an hour Johnson was on national television, and he broke down in tears. An hour later the Seven Network announced a nationwide

Doug Jacobi, who headed the parts and accessories division of Ford Australia, was a big fan of Dick Johnson, and diverted a substantial chunk of his Motorcraft advertising/ sponsorship budget to the Queenslander when Ford pulled out of racing. He also worked hard, without success, to push through a Johnson turbocharged Falcon to challenge Peter Brock's HDT Commodores.

appeal for funds to build him a new car, and Edsel Ford announced Ford Australia would match every donation dollar for dollar. The floodgates opened. Cardboard cartons jammed with letters and telegrams started arriving at the Johnsons' Daisy Hill home. Eventually the total came to $74,324. Dick Johnson flew to Melbourne for a formal lunch with Edsel Ford, Max Gransden, Peter Gillitzer and Doug Jacobi, head of the Motorcraft parts and service division of Ford. Jacobi took him quietly aside and offered him some sponsorship, and other sponsors then started knocking on the door.

It was a seminal moment in Johnson's life. The next year he won his first Australian Touring Car Championship, and then at Bathurst, he and his 1980 partner, veteran Queenslander John French, won the Big One when the race was red-flagged and declared after Bob Morris and Christine Gibson in Falcons collided at McPhillamy on lap

WITHIN HALF AN HOUR

121, starting a multiple crash that blocked the track.

In June 1980, Ford had introduced the Honda-sourced alloy cylinder head on its six-cylinder engines. The Mazda-sourced Courier light commercial had been released in 1978, followed by the Econovan and Trader in 1979. April 1982 brought the Meteor four-door sedan version of the Laser. So the 'turning Japanese' process was advancing apace. The Fremantle plant's capacity was doubled to underpin Ford's new role as top tractor seller. Then came the killer punch. In March 1982, the company unveiled the XE – not a facelift of the three-year-old XD, as expected, but a major makeover. The most important was the all-new six-link Watts Link coil-sprung rear suspension, replacing the multiple leaf springs that had been on the car since the 1960 XK. The old system had behaved very well, but in one bound Ford had been able to leapfrog the Commodore's hitherto more sophisticated five-link Panhard setup – it even introduced the first plastic-coated progressive-rate coils to reduce noise and harshness and some very clever synthetic bushings, the heart of any suspension. The six-cylinder engines gained dual-throat Weber carburettors for

The end of exclusivity

Two of the several major reforms introduced by the Whitlam Labor government between 1972 and 1975 had significant impacts on the motor industry. The new Prices Justification Tribunal ended the long-standing practice between Australia's (then) five tyre manufacturers of colluding to fix all prices exactly the same, to the cent, for every one of hundreds of tyre sizes – they would actually all change on the same day. The other was to set up the Trade Practices Commission, aimed at ending perceived monopolies by way of exclusive dealing and restraint of trade.

It soon targeted the motor retail trade, declaring that car makers and importers could no longer insist on only one franchise per dealer. Most moved quickly to multi-franchising, as we know it today, but Ford Australia, which had built up a formidable network of high profile dealers, resisted to the end.

Before the Act came into effect on February 1, 1975, Ford in late November 1974 lodged with the commission what were called 'clearance applications'. In effect, these were aimed at exempting from the provisions of the Act the company's sales agreement with its dealers. Ford was adamant that to end single franchising would be extremely detrimental to both the dealer and the consumer. In a letter to the TPC on May 29, 1975, it set out 16 reasons, arguing that multi-franchising would reduce the number of outlets, thus harming the public's ability to negotiate terms, would ruin small dealerships, force a dealer to carry smaller stocks and thus reduce customer choice, and erode after-sales service, because parts prices would rise and mechanics would not be as highly trained over a variety of makes.

At the time Ford had 414 dealers, GM–H 540, Chrysler 341, Leyland 480, Toyota 332, Datsun (Nissan) 290 and Mazda 197. In short, Australia was vastly over-endowed with dealers. The commission rejected Ford's pleadings.

better breathing and response, which justified the Alloy Head II badge on the flanks, a long bow though it was. But astonishingly, power steering was still an option on most models, rather than standard: fleets and plebs had to tolerate a gargantuan 5.2 turns lock-to-lock.

But it was not all gaiety and laughter. On November 25, 1982, the last V8-engined Falcon rolled off the Broadmeadows assembly line. Although V8 Fairlanes and LTDs would still be produced at the funny old Eagle Farm plant for a couple of months, this was the end of an era that started 50 years and three months earlier with the imported V8, supplemented by the first locally built bent-eight in 1966.

With hindsight, it was a silly decision, just as misguided as the decision to abandon motorsport. Those two moves effectively handed to GM–H Ford's ownership of the hot car market. In a similar way, GM–H had abandoned a different market to Ford when in dropping the Kingswood it also lost the long wheelbase luxury car business and the priceless one tonne cab-chassis utility buyer.

But early in January 1983, none of that really mattered. The note presented at the office door of sales and marketing director Max Gransden on a silver platter confirmed that Ford had sold more vehicles in Australia than all its rivals, by a slim margin of 137 registrations. It was the first time in half a century that Ford had been number 1 in Australia.

Bibliography

Bill Tuckey and Thomas B. Floyd, *Old Dog for a Hard Road,* Lone Tree Hill Press, 1979.
Bill Tuckey, *The Unforgiving Minute,* BFT Publishing Group, 1984.
John Wright, *The History of Ford Falcon, 1960–1994,* Ford Australia, 1994.

The famous 1–2 finish at Bathurst in 1977, when lead driver Allan Moffat, even though his Falcon hardtop was dying, got the flag after Colin Bond was ordered from the pits to stay behind him.

OHNSON WAS ON NATIONAL TELEVISION

Coming Soon
DEALERS
TRU-BLU
STEEL TUBING
1000
17
CRC
Valvoline

Main pic: Dick Johnson in the famous Tru-Blu. Inset, co-driver French.

CHAPTER 17

Speed Humps Ahead

Even as late as March 1981 – two years after the XD's introduction – Ford Australia was still showing signs of paranoia about size and fuel economy. In that month it kick-started Project Capricorn, the stretched version of the Mazda 626 on which the Ford Asia–Pacific (FASPAC) team were then working. The normal version, the Telstar, was to replace the Cortina, scheduled to run out in April 1983.

Toyo Kogyo's first domestic Capella (the 626) would come off-line in September 1982 and Australia's first Telstars were shipped fully built in November 1982 – the kits for assembly were not despatched until April 15, 1983 – and it was launched on the Australian market in May, three months after the Mazda.

Product Planning saw Capricorn as a hedge against energy crisis downsizing, as a 'significant Commodore fighter', according to the early notes. Marketing didn't like it, and the product committee looked at putting a V6 into it. There was also the complication of having to ensure 85 per cent local content. But it was in the planning and design stage for almost two years, stretched from the centre floor to the rear. It was 135 millimetres longer in the wheelbase than the Telstar and 229 mm longer overall, making a long, skinny car that, thankfully, was consigned to the dustbin of history.

But indirectly, as we shall see, it led straight to the considerable problems the company would face with its next all-new Falcon, the EA.

The background to this kind of belt-and-braces dithering was to be found in the evolution of the Federal government's 'car plans' for the future of the local car manufacturers and the component industry. From 1974 to the early 1980s there were endless Industries Assistance Commission (IAC) inquiries, to which all parties had input. For most, the important message to the commission was that whatever the government decided had to be carved in stone for a decent period of time to allow for the certainty of long-term planning so vital to the industry. So when, in

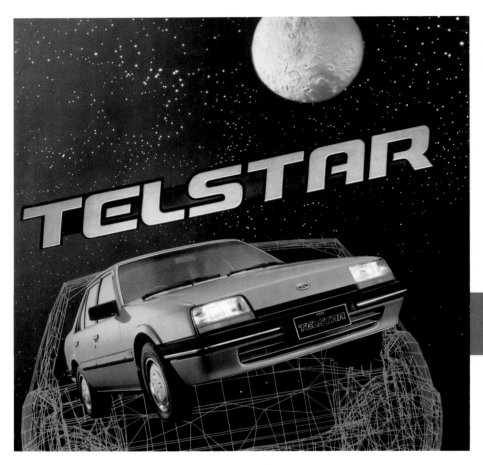

TELSTAR

Like the Laser, the Mazda-derived locally assembled Telstar was a big winner for Ford Australia. It was an infinitely better car than the Cortina it replaced. Opposite, bottom: Bill Dix, left, and Max Gransden, right, congratulate Neville Schryver on the opening of Neville Ford in March 1988. Page 226: Ford president Don Petersen (left) and David Ford at the You Yangs proving ground during evaluation of the EA Falcon late in 1987. Sales began early the following year.

fiddling with the plan from January 1976, which allowed Toyota and Nissan to come in as full producers. This new plan was supposed to run for eight years. But in February 1979, Canberra announced a major change that shocked everyone. It invented 'export accreditation', which in broad terms rewarded exports of cars and components with duty-free imports (and in part drove Ford to undertake the Capri program). And it seemed the changes were for the benefit of just one company: GM–H.

GM–H, that January, had put to Canberra a proposal to spend $330 million on a four-cylinder engine plant in Melbourne, conditional on generous treatment for components it would import, to allow it to be integrated into GM's so-called 'world car' project (only one such would

ever happen: the J-car, or Camira in Australia). GM–H briefed the FAPM on these pre-conditions, and the FAPM, while not directly opposed to the concept, was startled by the urgency GM–H was demanding. In its newsletter it said: 'The federation is alarmed that the government is revealing such ready willingness to consider the dismantling of existing motor vehicle policies to meet the specific demands of one part only of the industry. It is our view that the implications are so complex, so far-reaching and potentially damaging to the Australian components industry that no decision should be made to respond to the GMH [sic] proposition within the time-frame being dictated by this company'.

The federation was brushed aside, but GM–H was still not happy, and greedily dangled another carrot in front of Canberra: it would invest another $750 million over the next five years if export facilitation were made more generous in terms of maximum number of credit points allowed. That didn't happen, and in July 1980, GM–H announced it would close its Pagewood (Sydney) plant, with the loss of 1200 jobs. At the same time the IAC announced quotas of 94,000 imported cars for 1981, 110,000 for 1982, 130,000 for 1983 and 150,000 for post-1984.

October 1974, the Whitlam government's economic and trade committee outlined a plan to run for 10 years, there were broad smiles all round. The plan would require a local content of 85 per cent for cars built here and import duties of 35 per cent when imports accounted for 20 per cent of total registrations, going up by 10 per cent when imports went over that market share. It also recommended light commercials and four-wheel drives should get the same tariff treatment (which hasn't happened to this day) and that the tariff on imported components be set at 25 per cent instead of the 35 requested by the Federation of Automotive Product Manufacturers (FAPM). The plan began in 1975, and opened the floodgates for light commercials and four-wheel drives, but the industry felt it at least had a long-running policy.

Wrong. The new conservative government under Malcolm Fraser felt it knew better, and announced its first

This infuriated the FAPM, which could see its parts-supplier members going down like ninepins as they lost local business. In a press release it said: 'The word "catastrophic" is no exaggeration. If the IAC is allowed to proceed in the way it has indicated, and if government policy for the motor vehicle industry continues to drown in its own complexity, then the future for the components manufacturers is just going to be a series of Pagewoods'. But the plan didn't seem to faze Mitsubishi Motor Corporation, which in 1980 paid the miserly sum of $80 million for Chrysler Australia's two South Australian factories and infrastructure. However, Renault in 1981 shut down its assembly plant on the site of the 1956 Olympic village at West Heidelberg in Melbourne and

E EARLY 1980S THERE WERE ENDLESS IAC INQUIRIES

FASPAC's patchwork quilt

Pestered by all the argy-bargy, Ford Australia's planners daily were juggling and balancing and shifting the complexities of costing, model and parts sourcing and design trends up to five years ahead. At the same time, its developing involvement in the swamps of the Asia–Pacific market made crystal balls essential.

Many of its best people were seconded to FASPAC, the arm of the first auto maker in the western world to challenge the mysteries of the Asia–Pacific region. Paul Duhig was born in Kent (UK) in 1949, migrated to Australia in 1973 and joined Ford Australia in the communications section at Broadmeadows. After just nine months he was transferred to FASPAC, where he stayed until 1986, so he had a bird's eye view of the difficulties of dealing with Japan and other Asia–Pacific countries while trying simultaneously to second-guess Canberra bureaucrats and politicians.

FASPAC was responsible for a patchwork quilt of Ford production facilities in Australia, New Zealand, Singapore, the Philippines, Taiwan, Indonesia, Malaysia and some smaller countries – Guam, Fiji and Thailand. Duhig said the differences in industrial relations, work practices and government regulations in all these countries made FASPAC's task very complicated. Ian Vaughan, seconded from Ford Australia to FASPAC in 1971 as a planner, eventually becoming product planning manager until recalled in 1985, grimaces when remembering the awesome task of balancing the demands of the different facilities for three doors, five doors, sedans, hatchbacks, differently sized engines, different emissions and design rules and the rest. For instance, the Ford Laser Meteor sedan launched here in 1982 was developed earlier as a Taiwan taxi.

By the early 1980s FASPAC had grown to more than 100 staff; through its life its managing directors included the original, Frank Erdman, two Ford Australia CEOs – Bill Bourke and Sir Brian Inglis – and a future president of Ford, Alex Trotman. Duhig said that during that time the Singapore government told Ford it was to stop assembling vehicles in Singapore, and Ford abandoned the Philippines because of unstable governments, lack of foreign exchange and underuse of facilities – at one stage it was making coffins to keep people employed. Ford Thailand was sold off in the mid-1980s and although two major study teams looked at China in 1974 and again in 1986, with optimistic reports, nothing came of it. By contrast, Ford Lio Ho in Taiwan had been a busy and profitable manufacturing operation since the early 1970s, and still is.

One example of the headaches of a multinational operating in this jigsaw puzzle came from Max Lowe – first a finance man, then a manufacturing executive, who would finally put in 44 years with Ford Australia, three of them as managing director of Ford Malaysia.

'Ford had an operation from about 1925 onwards in Singapore. It stayed there except for the war period, when the Japanese occupied the plant (in Bukit Tima Road where, incidentally, in the Ford boardroom, the British forces signed the surrender of Singapore) until the late 1970s, when the government of Singapore didn't have a motor industry as part of its plan to industrialise the country. The industry itself had to look around for something else. Now, it so happened that Ford Malaysia had been established in 1974 purely as a distribution outlet and a parts depot. In 1979 it became very obvious that we had to do something more about it.'

Ford had a contractor assembling cars there and in August 1981 set up a joint venture with a local firm to buy out his business. Lowe said Ford retained 51 per cent of the business, on condition that, as a foreign company, Ford had to reduce its equity by January 1986 to 30 per cent and that the employees had to be set on quotas reflecting the national mix – 56 per cent bumiputras (Malay nationals), 20 per cent Chinese and 12 per cent Indian. The company eventually assembled Laser, Telstar, Land Rover and Mercedes–Benz (including the S-Class), finally producing around 65 units a day, so it was a busy, healthy plant. Ford got up to third place in the Malaysian market, behind Nissan and Toyota who were also assembling there; in the early 1980s there were a staggering 13 assembly plants in Malaysia for a total annual market of only around 130,000 vehicles. Then the government signed a joint venture agreement with Mitsubishi Motor Corporation to build the first local car, the Proton Saga, with guaranteed fixed pricing, selling every Saga at a loss, and high tariff walls against imports. (One strange by-product of this rush to become a government car maker was that the seats in those first Sagas were stuffed with either horsehair or coconut fibre; in Malaysia's high humidity the latter would start sprouting weeds and the former, maggots.)

One by one the rival makers closed down. Reduced to building only light commercials, Ford finally sold 21 per cent to its joint venture partner, getting back all its original capital investment plus a net US$1 million – Lowe says the negotiations were handled by the then Malaysian Trade Minister, Dr Mohammad Mahathir, the current Prime Minister. Faced increasingly with what would later be dubbed 'recalcitrance', Ford eventually sold the rest.

Leyland Australia would vanish in 1984.

The government did listen to the federation this time, and the 1981 quota was set at 88,000, with provision for yearly reviews. But there would be another shock with the 1979 IAC draft report on the post-1984 plan. This recommended that from January 1985 (or earlier) the current plan be scrapped, the 80:20 local:import ratio be dropped, and that passenger cars and original equipment parts be slugged with 60 per cent import duty, reducing to 35 per cent by January 1990. State governments, unions, car makers and parts suppliers blasted the plan, but the draft was amended only by setting the 1990 duty rate at 50 per cent.

Predictably, much of the media and public was outraged by what it claimed was government increasing the prices of quality imported cars while protecting local makers whose cars were already too expensive. Finally, Canberra decided to retain export facilitation, with expanded benefits to local car producers, to retain import duties as they were, and increase annual car import quotas by 4000 a year, with the local makers entitled to import 7000, and bring in a system of quota licences that could be bartered. This didn't stop the arguments and the Federal Labor opposition flagged a different policy that would make substantial changes – thus producing more uncertainty.

Bill Dix had watched all this happen, at his post as president of Ford Japan from 1979 until he was named president and CEO of Ford Australia in July 1981. Dix was born in Western Australia, finished his schooling in Geelong College, and joined Ford in 1941 partly because his father was sales manager of the local Ford dealership and partly because it gave him a chance to continue some form of postgraduate training; the family couldn't afford to send him on to Melbourne University. He did evening courses in accounting and cost accounting. A deep-voiced, precisely intonated, reserved, chisel-faced man with a wry, chuckling sense of humour – one could wrongly judge him as a motor industry finance man straight from central casting – he started as a mail boy. Spotting his talent early, Ford sent him to Windsor in 1953 for six months to work in the export finance operations department of Ford Canada, then Australia's guardian.

Dix said later: 'The next real opportunities in terms of development both corporately and individually came with the transition from Canadian control to US control in the beginning of the 1960s'. Two future Ford Australia managing directors had been sent from Dearborn to Ford Canada – Wally Booth as vice-president, finance and Bill Bourke as general sales manager – to provide a better link between the two. Booth made a tour of the overseas affiliates.

'I was nominated at that time to go overseas for a two-year training and development program, which involved spending some time in the US operation and some time in Ford Canada, 1960–1961', Dix recalled. He came back to find the head office had moved from Geelong to Melbourne and that Booth was MD. 'I guess that was no disadvantage to me in terms of an opportunity', he said dryly. 'It comes back again in the final analysis in any company ... you've got to make your own waves and you've got to prove that you can do the job'.

In 1965 Dix became finance director of Ford Australia, replacing an American who had recommended him – the first Australian to hold the post. In 1970 he moved to FASPAC as staff director, finance – an Asia–Pacific version of the same job – and that segued into being operational director for the affiliates in the region. In the mid-1970s he became involved in the first talks with Mazda as a possible source of vehicles for Australia; at the same time the corporation was looking into buying its initial 25 per cent of Toyo Kogyo. However, he was then shifted to the job of vice-president of export operations for Ford of Europe, a soul-destroying task at the time when the Japanese were making the British and European cars look utterly stupid in terms of cost and quality. 'I've got to say I wasn't all that successful in achieving the objective of turning Ford of Europe around as an export activity', he said. In 1979 came promotion to the presidency of Ford of Japan, to help in the transition of the new relationship between Ford and Mazda.

Dix came back to the top job in Ford Australia in August 1981, armed with the knowledge that the association with Mazda would very likely punt Ford to market leadership in his first full year as president, energised by Max Gransden as director of sales and marketing. 'We might have made it eventually because of the erosion of the strength of General Motors here in Australia, but it would have been a harder job to achieve [without the Japanese products]', he said.

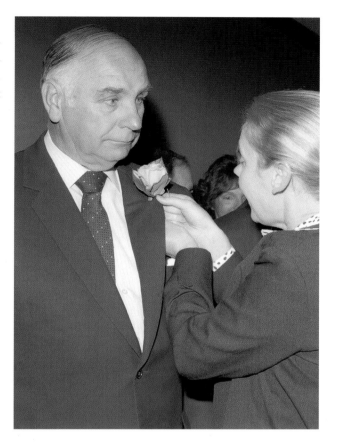

Left: Brian Inglis, the first Australian-born MD of Ford Australia, was knighted for his services to the local automotive industry. Below: Bill Dix, left, returned to Australia in the top job in 1981, succeeding Sir Brian.

The company was only marginally in profit. 'The progressive formulation and the decision to take the equity in Mazda and clearing the way to get full access to Mazda product in the area where we were weak gave us the last segment of what we wanted ... and with a good dealer body to sell it and with improved quality ... all those things were in place fundamentally when I got back into the organisation'.

Four weeks after his arrival back in Australia the Broadmeadows assembly plant went out on strike for six weeks, at a time when the company was coming so close to matching GM–H in market share. 'Probably the most important problem we had to deal with was the relationship between the company and the unions, and the employees they represented. I guess I spent a disproportionate amount of my time early on analysing those issues and problems, working with the people to find a better way.

'What we wanted to do was to get some of the Japanese philosophy of appreciation of the workers and workers' loyalty to the company ingrained into our people.'

In 1988, not long before he retired, Dix said he wasn't

Wheels ran scoop shots of the coming Ford Capri, and fuelled expectations that the sports car would be both a domestic and export success. Opposite: Telstar/Laser dealer meeting in September 1987: from left, Geoff Polites (now president of Ford Australia, then national sales manager), Jim Ireland, New Oakleigh Motors, Melbourne, Ric Collins, Jarvis Ford, Adelaide, Max Gransden, vice president sales and marketing and Bill Tilbury, Tilford Hobart.

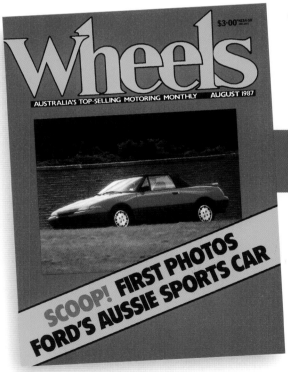

satisfied he had achieved more than a grudging acceptance of the company by its employees, instead of expressed loyalty.

But he did achieve some significant profits. Bill Dix was the first Ford Australia CEO to drive hard for cost reductions, greater productivity and higher efficiency (he once told me he ordered his executives to start recycling paper clips). By 1988 Ford Australia was able to report $126 million in net after-tax profits, a number it wouldn't beat until 1996. Dix was also

partly responsible for bringing product engineers and manufacturing engineers closer together, removing the traditional 'walls' to the point where the manufacturing people knew they could build a car before they started. The old US Ford way was that you practically had to be a director to get a look at advanced drawings.

He also started making each department responsible for its own budget – before then they were told each year by the finance office what their budget would be. Dix was also able to push the manufacturing people to a better understanding of what sales and marketing wanted them to build, in terms of numbers, options, model mix and so on – reflected in today's understanding that the prime objective is to build a car with the buyer's name already on it.

While all this was going on, Ford Australia was in the early stages of planning the EA Falcon for early 1988, and the ill-fated Capri roadster. At least it had market leadership, thanks largely to the formidable XE that replaced the XD in March 1982. The XF that followed in October 1984 had another facelift: a new dash, a state-of-the-art ECU (electronic control unit) for the injection system and more power and torque from the 4.1 litre injected and carbureted engines (but none for the 3.3). Magazine tests saw the XF crank off the standing 400 metres in an impressive 16.8

BILL DIX DID ACHI

seconds. But in one of the great ergonomic dead-ends of the period, Ford followed Toyota, Fuji Heavy Industries (Subaru) and others into digital readouts on the gauges (they failed, mainly because they were unreliable). In 1985, to match the greatly improved VL Commodore and anticipating the arrival of the first full-sized wide-bodied Holden Commodore, the VN, the XFII got all-wheel disc brakes and power steering as standard across the range, plus an optional five-speed manual transmission and sports suspension. However, Capricorn had built speed humps.

David Ford, chief engineer at the time, says FASPAC and product planning had become so obsessed with Capricorn that they failed to plan past the XE model. 'I kept saying, You

E SOME SIGNIFICANT PROFITS FOR FORD AUSTRALIA

can't possibly do this ... they spent huge amounts of time doing clays and we had to supply precious engineering resources ... it was only when Bill Dix replaced Sir Brian Inglis as MD that Bill suddenly said, Hey, hold on, do we really know what the hell we're doing here? But they'd spent a fortune on it (Capricorn).' Then came the decision to drop the V8 and re-equip the Geelong engine plant to produce four-cylinder engines.

'It felt like the ship had lost its rudder, or something', said David Ford in 2000. 'Those decisions caused a lot of the downstream problems, because you had no follow-on Falcon – proper Falcons – in the system. After the decision had been made to can Capricorn, there was no XF, so all of

a sudden we ran around to pull together the EA program. It was then decided we needed an interim facelift to help keep it alive until then, and we started to handle all that. So the XFII was just a hodge-podge program ... there again, some more advanced emission controls were coming in. But the EA was done in much more of a rush and with less thought than if we'd had this intermediate thing.'

Bibliography

J. D. Beruldsen, *Beneath The Bonnet,* Longman Cheshire, 1989.
FAPM Newsletter No. 2, 1979.
Walter J. Uhlenbruch, *Australian Motor Vehicles and Parts,* 1986.
John Wright, *The History of the Ford Falcon, 1960–1994,*
Ford Australia, 1994.

CHAPTER 18

Big Profits, Tough Times

The four years of design and development of the EA, the first all-new Falcon since the XD, were dogged by the Federal government's new post-1984 car plan. Prime Minister Bob Hawke had first trailed his coat in October 1983 when he said that if a government were to start with a clean sheet of paper there would be fewer car makers in Australia. In December of that year came the news that GM–H would be rebadging Nissan Pulsar five-door hatchbacks as Holden Astras.

In 1984 GM–H closed down its big assembly plant at Acacia Ridge in Brisbane and the smaller Woodville operation in Adelaide. In May came the unveiling of what has since become famous as the Button Plan, its undoubted father being the visionary and respected Minister for Industry and Commerce, Senator John Button. The plan's declared goals were to cut the number of models from 13 to six (or fewer), keep car price rises to the minimum and gradually reduce import restrictions to make the industry more efficient. The ultimate aim was to have, by 1992, no more than three manufacturers (or joint ventures) producing between them no more than six models.

By the start of 1986 there were five makers producing 13 models, although in its annual report the Automotive Industry Authority said two would be dropped in 1987. Ford had been in profit since 1981, GM–H in loss for the previous six years, while Mitsubishi had seesawed, Toyota was holding its own and Nissan was losing more and more money every year and threatening to fold its tents. In fact, in 1986 the five makers by aggregate actually lost $192 million, after a profit of $56 million the year before. (The market had collapsed from the 1985 record year, mainly because of uncertainty about the new Fringe Benefits Tax and the arrival on January 1, 1986, of unleaded petrol.) However, locally built cars still held just over 80 per cent of the Australian passenger car market.

Ford's local content across its range was then averaging 82.23 per cent, GM–H's 92.74, Mitsubishi's 85.25 and Toyota's and Nissan's each 85 per cent – the latter two were

Ford president Bill Dix (left) with managing director of Nissan Australia (and later Lord Mayor of Melbourne) Ivan Deveson at a 1989 press conference to announce a new product-sharing joint venture to fit with the Button Plan. Ford would take the Nissan Patrol badged as Maverick, the Nissan Pintara badged as Corsair (to replace Telstar), and Nissan – incongruously – would get the Falcon ute (opposite). Somewhere in Australia there is a buyer who bought one of these sincerely believing it to be a Japanese product.

FORD WAS LOOKING PR

taking advantage of the export facilitation scheme by sending aluminium castings to their Japanese parents. (Mitsubishi was even getting credits by having alloy wheels from ROH and tyres from Bridgestone shipped to Japan without crossing Mitsubishi's Adelaide threshold.) GM–H was the leader by far in exports, thanks to substantial shipments of its four-cylinder engines to Germany, Brazil and (at first in secret) South Africa – after all, it was for GM that the scheme was essentially structured in the first place. Thus it was the export credits carrot that partly pushed Ford Australia into the Capri.

The loophole in the plan – as far as the local components industry was concerned – was that the export credits allowed the local car makers to apply them to reduce duties, where before they could be applied only to components. However, Button was speaking softly but carrying a big stick. In December 1986, the government announced that car makers would lose some or all of their duty concessions if they failed to meet certain targets by either ending production of some cars or increasing production on others. In other words, 'we're serious'. Ford was looking pretty good, with the Laser heading for big volumes and the Telstar hard on its heels (eventually it would be replaced by a shared product with Nissan, the Nissan Pintara/Ford Corsair). But essentially, Ford wasn't quite ready for its new Falcon.

In 1975 John Marshall had returned from FASPAC to Australia to become national assembly general operations manager reporting to the director of manufacturing. This took him over the 'E-roll' (sic) threshold, an extremely high rating in the Ford hierarchy, and indeed in 1983 Marshall would succeed his boss, American Ted Gardner, as vice-president of manufacturing, with a seat on the board. To him would fall the main burden of building the troubled EA, and he was a member of the all-important product committee that made the vital forward planning decisions. He took early retirement in 1989 after the tragic death of his wife, and in 2000 was critical of the company's uncertainty in the early 1980s about future models, including a 'downsized' six-cylinder Falcon. 'They came out looking like champions in reading the turn of the oil price downwards, when it was actually the fact they were too bloody slow in moving where they thought they had to go. It was luck more than anything', he said. It was the Laser that saved them.

As the Laser was in the final stages of replacing the Escort in the Sydney factory in 1981, Homebush plant manager Bill Maher suddenly died and Marshall had to make weekly trips up to Homebush to push it through.

'The Japanese had sent us down the typical process sheets, which in Ford terms used to be detailed stuff – almost down to which hand you picked up which nut with. In the case of the Mazdas, sheets came down and they were more like crude assembly drawings. And I thought they were having us on, they were really making it hard for us to assemble these cars, because virtually all of it came in a box at that stage, almost like a Meccano set. Even so, to put it together was very tricky, and it took a while for the penny to drop. The penny did eventually drop and it said: Gee, in Japan they train their people better, so you don't have to tell them which hand to use, you tell them what results you've got to have, so the guy putting in the side door windows was told this was the way to do it, the torque on the handle had to be this, it was to be flush there and this and that and that was it.

'So we were in the Homebush plant using employee involvement – little ''e'', little ''i'' – well before the corporation picked it up as big ''E'', big ''I'', pocket-savers, seminars and all that ... we cheated the finance office. I used to put in a week's induction training before they went onto the floor and it got counted as part of the foreman's productivity efficiency measure. That really was the starting point for the cultural revolution at Ford. It was primarily Ken McDonald, who was then head of employee relations. We went right to the top of the ACTU and then down the line to the shop steward in each plant and we got ownership from the very top down.'

TY GOOD, WITH LASER HEADING FOR BIG VOLUMES

Tom Pettigrew was in charge of quality at this stage and many Ford engineering and manufacturing people give him the greatest credit for the quantum leap in quality that began with the Japanese example – although later he received less for his failure to control quality with the EA and Capri.

Says Ian Vaughan: 'The Falcon people looked over the shoulders of the Sydney people and said Gee, what are you learning about how cars go together ... like Lego? This was Tom Pettigrew's quality assurance philosophy. It was like night and day compared with assembling cars the previous way'. Vaughan returned to Australia in 1985 as manager, product quality assurance, and in 1987 took over as Broadmeadows plant manufacturing manager under John Crew and John Marshall. He was heavily involved in the EA26, as it was codenamed.

'For EA we raised our standards a whole lot in terms of what we expected of the car, and we delivered a whole lot better motor car', he recalls.

But Vaughan's then president, Bill Dix, interviewed six months after the EA was launched in February 1988, admitted: 'We stubbed our toe a bit on quality at the launch of this car ... because we did it all ourselves without all the [corporation's] depth of experience and expertise. We're getting the quality right now, but it's still got a long way to go before we get it where we want it to be'. Given the priceless attribute of 20:20 hindsight, most of those involved with the development of the EA26 agree that the company tried to do too much too quickly – and it had the gestation of the Capri sports car and its export program looming over it at the same time.

David Ford says now the company 'bit off more than it could chew. We had to remake the plant to do both Capri and EA and this required an enormous amount of manufacturing and engineering resources. John Marshall kept asking for more engineering resources and was denied them'.

David Ford's assistant chief engineer from 1983 was Bill Hodgson. He confirms the revolution that came in with EA. The engineers were required to give design direction from the outset, so that 'we should stop doing it twice', meaning

design a car once and then re-design bits of it so it could actually be built, which was the old way. 'We ran structures meetings once a week which really everyone who had any say in feasibility came to.'

Could he see trouble coming on EA? 'Well, no-one in Ford had ever put weather strips on doors and I guess I was one of the people who pushed very hard not to do it. But the assembly people and Tom Pettigrew won the day.' The chief body engineer, Klaus Glagow, a clever, dynamic man, was apparently very persuasive about such major changes in technology and attitudes.

This was the first car for which Ford Australia had used CAD (computer aided design). Then in its infancy, it in effect replaced much of the manual draftsmanship with three-dimensional computer images from which dimensions could be measured. Said Bill Hodgson: 'We were so full up in drafting that we had to get another 150

Opposite top: the Australian Design Council's 1988 award for excellence to the EA Falcon was some clawback from early negative publicity. Ford Australia president, Bill Dix, receives the plaque while head of design, Brian Rossi, smiles for the camera. Opposite, bottom: the EA Falcon wagon (shown here with 'Sno-Flake' alloy wheels) had a significant size advantage over its rivals. Left: an early clay model of the EA had the completely 'blind' frontal treatment that would appear six and a half years after the EA's launch – on the EF.

DAVID FORD WROTE A MEMO TO PUBLIC AFFAIRS PLI

fellows from England working on CAD over there. We were
on-line with them, basically; we did front and rear bumpers
on CAD, which was the first time [Ford Australia] had done
a major plastic component using CAD'. There was also an
entirely new system which took the surface openings off the

CAD image and used them to get exactly the right gaps
around the doors.

John Marshall: 'We had been doing the doors the English
way, which was cheap ... putting the primary seal around
the door openings ... and I said, For heaven's sake do it the

other way, the way the Germans do it'. But there was a totally new door stamping as well, involving a near one-piece side. Marshall said they also automated the door assembly with a lot of new robotics: 'It was adventurous and it was successful eventually, but it had a lot of problems'. (The system was designed by a small Australian automations company and Ian Vaughan agreed there were huge early problems with it.) Broadmeadows also had to change the model on the run, without the luxury Ford US enjoyed of shutting down a plant for several months.

And there was a remodelled paint shop – always the most difficult quality area of any auto plant. It was supposed to come on stream six to 12 months ahead of the car to allow workup time but it was held up for six months by an industrial dispute and didn't happen until about a month before launch. Ian Vaughan recalled: 'You were trying to solve problems that you weren't sure were new car problems or paint shop problems. I mean, is the automation playing up because of the automation or is the automation playing up because it's trying to paint a new shape motor car? We had two problems to manage, one on top of the other'.

The entire culture had changed. For the first time in its history Ford Australia actually showed its component suppliers the prototypes of the new car. 'We had barbecues in vendors' shops', said Marshall. He was also one of the people the company lined up to brief the motoring press weeks in advance – under embargo – about the revolutionary design and manufacturing systems behind this new model.

David Ford remembers writing a memo to the public affairs department pleading with them to stop hyping the

Bill Hartigan, then managing director of Ford New Zealand, which was battling to get its own CKD assembly plant running with the new car, said in 2000: 'It would have been a goddamn miracle if it arrived perfectly'. In fact, as John Wright says in his book on Falcon's history, in mid-

Peter Brock with one of the EA Falcons he modified. Opposite: Victorian Premier John Cain (second from right) admires a Capri ready for export to the US. On his right-hand side is Ian Vaughan and on his left is then Ford Australia president Jac Nasser.

1987 a group of key motoring writers was invited to a special conference in Broadmeadows, where former World Formula One Champion Jackie Stewart – a paid consultant to Ford and Goodyear – eulogised the dynamics of the coming new car, although supplier BTR wouldn't have the new electronic four-speed automatic ready for its launch to replace the old three-speeder. He also damped down rumours that the new car would have independent rear

DING WITH THEM TO STOP HYPING THE CAR

car so much, not to raise expectations too high among Australia's expert and critical motoring press, and to delay the launch by three months to work through the glitches. But by this time it was resembling nothing so much as a runaway train.

suspension to replace the Watts linkage, saying that IRS wasn't necessarily better! As Wright says, Ford was obviously fertilising the soil for the *Wheels* Car of the Year award it missed with the XD, when in 1979 the magazine awarded the Lemon of the Year to the industry generally;

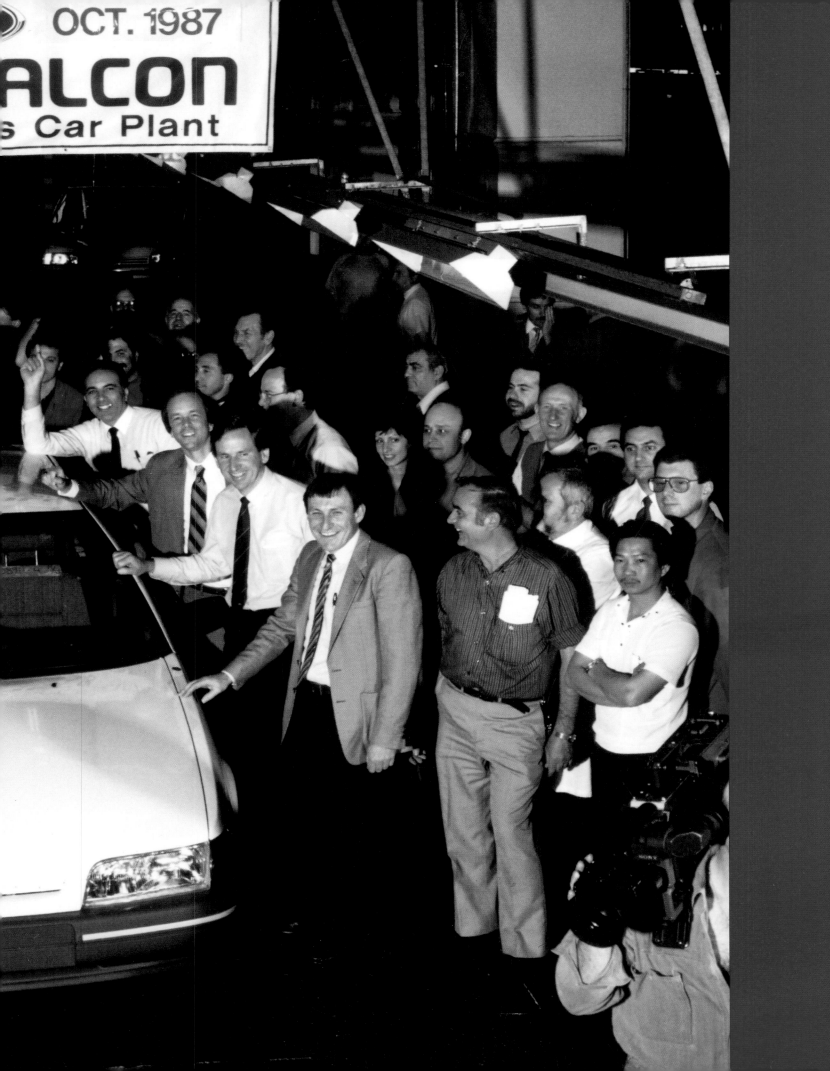

after all. Ford hadn't won the gong since sharing the award for the 626/Telstar with Mazda.

The EA was a good – almost great – car. It was good on aerodynamics, the new overhead-cam engines (3.9 litre with multipoint and throttle-body EFI choice and a 3.2 –

Right: today CAD (computer-aided design) and CAE (computer-aided engineering) have virtually made full-sized clay models unnecessary, particularly when it comes to measuring them accurately for tooling. But the designers and management still like to be able to stand back and look at the clays before making decisions involving millions of dollars. Below: the EA takes shape early in the process. Opposite: many motoring magazines compared the Capri with the Mazda, and the MX-5 won out more often than not because of its overtly sporting nature. Of course, the Ford–Mazda relationship is even closer now.

aimed at the fleet market but short-lived) were very responsive, there was a clever new front suspension with Bishop power-assisted rack-and-pinion steering that cut the huge turning circle down to size, and finally a decent seating position with adjustable steering wheel. But early in its life there were front suspension problems, plus a few overheating dramas; the bootlid fit was awful (on a car I was presenting on television it took four slams to close) and for the first few months the paint was poor.

'It was all the little things', said Marshall in 2000. 'A combination of little things rather than one big thing', said Vaughan, 'it was a huge program. It could partly have been that we had Capri right on top of it. I think that certainly affected our response timing – we didn't respond quickly enough to the EA issues because we were launching Capri ... so they took 18 months to fix rather than six months'.

President Bill Dix, in his pedantic way, expressed some *mea culpa*: 'There was a knowledge in the organisation, obviously, that there were a number of late changes, a

number of areas where some of the facilities were not totally proven, before the car was launched, but the evaluation, a review with the management of the company ... people in charge of the various areas were confident that while there were some causes for concern none of them was sufficiently important to warrant not proceeding.

'So once you've got the thing rolling and you start the production process the only way you can really refine that is to get more experience with it. Stopping production wasn't going to help us at all. We had to keep working with the people to improve every area of concern as we kept operating. The evaluation of quality incidents by the independent people who were supposed to evaluate quality I guess was a little ... they must have been looking through rose-coloured glasses, in retrospect'.

And then there was the Capri.

The Mazda 323-based front-drive sports car was launched in Australia in October 1989. On May 18, 1989, Dave Fewchuk, the Ford Australia executive in charge of planning, reporting to an American called Dick van House, presented the car to a national dealer conference. He summoned for them heroic memories of the Thunderbird and Mustang, of the European Capri coupe, the Ford AC–Cobra, GT40 and RS2000. Ford, with Capri, was to pioneer the rebirth of the affordable convertible sports car, Fewchuk told his audience. The new car was inspired by Bob Lutz, head of Ford of Europe, a man with Swiss-American-German origins, who encouraged the famous Ghia styling studio in Turin (Italy) – which had a close association with Ford worldwide – to produce for the 1983 Frankfurt Motor Show a concept Ford-based roadster. It was called Barchetta (Little Boat), because it actually looked a bit like an upturned rowboat.

However, Lutz couldn't get it through the system, and was moved to head Ford International Operations, which simultaneously appointed Alex Trotman to head FASPAC, the largest client subsidiary of which was Ford Australia, with Dix then president. Between them, Trotman and Dix got the project rolling, appointing Fewchuk to head up what was dubbed SA30. From the start the idea was that Ford Australia, then – as now – a small-volume exporter, would build the car in left-hand drive for the North American market and subsequently as RHD for Australia. Lutz shifted

back to lead Ford Europe, with Trotman as his deputy, and the new president of FASPAC, one Merv Manning, kept SA30 moving forward.

Ghia and rival ItalDesign were put into a competitive styling exercise, the result shown at a research clinic in Los Angeles. The main difference was that ItalDesign went for a four-wheel drive 323 (Laser) platform. Ghia was asked to respond with a similar base, and two new cars went to a San Diego clinic. Both won – the Ghia with a slight edge.

Under the pressure of the export-rewarding Button

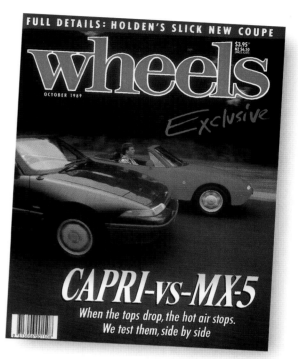

Plan, the well received successor to all previous government plans, Ford Australia had been researching export markets and had actually tried to sell the EA Falcon to Dearborn. It was rejected as being too close to the Taurus – then the top selling passenger car in North America. In February 1986, with the backing of Edsel Ford, who had spent time working in Ford Australia, the Capri project was approved – Edsel wanted it for the Lincoln–Mercury division he was running. Fewchuk told the dealers production would be set at 40,000 a year, with 30,000 LHD cars going to the US. But at the same time Mazda had given the green light to its California-styled MX-5 and Lotus to its Elan.

The Capri got formal approval in September 1985, with the first prototype slated for January 1987. In a weird mix, Ghia got the exterior styling, ItalDesign the interior and roof shaping as well as the detailed engineering; 55 prototypes would be built in the end. It had all the potential to drive sane men to drink. Here was a car that had to meet North American and Australian design rules, be designed and engineered in Italy, and built in Australia from mainly Japanese components, in left and right-hand drive.

The first prototypes would be given to Jackie Stewart for evaluation; body stress and torsional stiffness testing would

be done at the MIRA (Motor Industry Research Association) proving ground in Britain. Emissions development was the responsibility of Australia's You Yangs proving ground laboratory; corrosion protection for snow and salt evaluated at Ford's Arizona proving ground; wind tunnel testing would be done in the Fiat facility in Turin and at Lockheed in the US; air-conditioning developed near Houston (Texas); crash testing in Detroit and high altitude testing at Pike's Peak in Colorado. It was a global logistical nightmare, given the compressed gestation period.

Much of the early weight fell on Tad Zyppel, Ford Australia's program timing manager, and program manager Fewchuk. Zyppel's first trip to ItalDesign in Turin was in early May 1986, and he spent all January 1987 there. Zyppel said the task was originally handed to him as 'a little sideline', but he had some problems 'dogging their timing'. The soft top design was handed to the Scharwechter company, which makes BMW's convertible roofs.

'Our people came back with a story of super-sophisticated fixturing and so forth, and very, very expensive facilities to put the framework onto the car and at the end of that line were two big guys with two rubber mallets to make sure that if anything had gone wrong upstream the mallet could fix it up', Zyppel said. There was great concern about the roof because even the best overseas soft tops weren't perfect and Ford Australia was expected to become expert overnight. 'Here was an area entirely new to us and we had to learn fast. We had to make commitments to a fabric that would sustain production volumes', said Zyppel.

John Marshall recalled: 'We knew the roof was going to be a problem. But the Americans, when we went to them they said, Oh, don't worry about ragtops, you can assume you'll get two or three repairs per 100, that's our experience. Don't worry about making it absolutely leakproof. We had a few problems with the design. It was very delicate'.

Ford US kept pushing for the car to have front airbags, but Australia kept saying they weren't legally required. Finally it was forced on Broadmeadows at the last moment, even though the production engineering task was handed to them far too late. David Ford had to fly to Dearborn just before Christmas 1988 and pore over the data showing

Below: there were some teething troubles with the Capri (and a national current affairs television program did a fairly harsh program on it) but the car actually did quite well. In the US it outsold the Mazda MX-5 in one year. Opposite: Ford rang the changes on the Australian Capri, producing variations called Barchetta (its original name), Clubsprint and XR2, as well as turbocharged versions. The line ended in July 1994.

FEWCHUK AND H

how the car had failed to meet the US passive safety requirements in crash testing. He found the Americans had changed the seat mounting system without telling Australia, so he rewrote the specifications and immediately got the right results.

'I rang Australia two days before Christmas and told them they could meet the requirements but my advice was, don't tell anyone – use it as an excuse to get out of the US program – but it was too late for that. I remember a meeting chaired by Dick van House when he said: Nobody defers Job One. Ford Australia simply wasn't structured to do the job and a lot of people put their heads in the sand'.

Fewchuk would eventually – and grossly unfairly – bear most of the opprobrium. Fewchuk and his faithful Aussies actually worked miracles getting the Capri as far as they did in the face of ridiculous expectations.

FAITHFUL AUSSIES WORKED MIRACLES ON THE CAPRI

The first pilot Capri came off the Broadmeadows line in May 1988 and another 270 were built before full production started; eventually 121 Australian supplier companies took it to 70 per cent local content.

Fewchuk ended his presentation to the dealers with the words: 'It may be the world's highest volume convertible'. Of course, it wasn't. Because Ford Division had the Mustang, the Capri was diverted to the Lincoln–Mercury Division, who weren't used to selling cars to young people, let alone a small sporty number, and perhaps couldn't really be bothered with this funny little low-volume car from Austria or somewhere. The first to hit the local market had problems with leaking roofs and weak door check-straps and paint, but also came in for some blatantly unfair treatment from the sensation-making television current affairs programs. It went through several iterations –

Barchetta, Clubsprint, Turbo and XR2 – before euthanasia in July 1994.

The official VFACTS registration figures indicate only modest success: in the first full year, 1990, Ford dealers sold 4413; in 1991 it was 1643; 1992, 1034; 1993, 1321 and in the first half of 1994, 810.

We'll let David Ford have the last word. Across his final Capri product program papers he had scrawled the comment: 'This duck will never fly'.

And then, to Australia, came a man called Jac Nasser...

Bibliography

Report on the State of the Automotive Industry 1986
Automotive Industry Authority, 1987.
John Wright, *The History of the Ford Falcon, 1960–1994,*
Ford Motor Company of Australia, 1994.

CHAPTER 19

Ahead, The **Broad Sunlit** Uplands

In 1983 John Marshall gave a speech to Ford's employee relations staff in which he said that the company had embarked on 'a massive cultural change'. He was referring to the process of joint ownership between employees and management of the missions, values and guiding principles of their endeavours, plus the philosophies behind them. He said most of Ford Australia's salaried manufacturing people had not understood the economics of the business and the company had become too compartmentalised, with narrow specialists. He described their attitude as 'looking through the narrow slits of the fortress'.

Right or wrong, his approach was sorely tested during the battle to fix the problems that blighted the EA Falcon, and the struggle to get Capri up to speed. But it won out. By late 1988 Falcon quality was enormously improved; in the process this created the concept of constant evolutionary improvement, rather than waiting for the next model, which has lasted right up to the rapid revising of the all-new AU

model into AUII early in 2000. 'And so it was that an EA Falcon built in, say, February 1989 was a better car than its equivalent of February 1988, while the Series II built in October 1990 was demonstrably superior in several key areas, including transmission, suspension, security and finish', wrote John Wright.

That model brought in the new Australian BTR electronic four-speed automatic transmission (GM–H was still using an older, hydraulically controlled US unit), much improved suspension and the dramatically successful Tibbe locking system. This was well ahead of the local rivals, because it made it impossible to lock your key in the car and had the lock buttons flush with the window trim. It came in as standard, as did alloy wheels on the Fairmont and Pirelli tyres on the S, with price increases measured in a few dozen dollars. For instance, the new automatic cost just $10 more than the five-speed manual – traditionally it had been a $1000 option.

Bill Hartigan, retired in 1991 when vice-president,

249

Quiet revolution: Ford chief John Ogden is continuing to improve the image of the Falcon range which was tarnished by quality glitches in the late 1980s.

Sun 2/5

Ford gears up for financial recovery

By James Stack

SMILES, rather than broad grins, are likely to be the order of the day at Ford Australia's corporate headquarters on Thursday when the company announces its financial results for the 1992 calendar year.

Ford is expected to report that it is still running in the red after two horrific years (1990 and 1991) when it racked up pretax deficits that totalled $320 million.

But the figures are likely to show that the company has begun to get its spiralling losses from the past couple of years under control and to confirm that it has taken some important steps down the road to financial recovery.

The new man at the helm at Broadmeadows, John Ogden, inherited an organisation that had undergone a major revamp under his predecessor Jac Nasser, now playing on a bigger stage and running Ford's European operations.

Part of the price of that restructuring was a blowout on the company's bottom line, particularly from soaring redundancy costs.

Ford has slashed its workforce by more than 5000 over the past couple of years, and handing out pink slips always has a short-term cost.

But the company has had its paybacks.

It has worked hard on improving its productivity and efficiency levels and has improved its product quality dramatically in recent years. The current Falcon models, for example, are way ahead of the original EA Falcon model introduced with such fanfare in February 1988.

It has also clawed back some of the ground it lost in the marketplace in the past two years as its main rival, Toyota, continued its relentless march to market leadership.

Last year, Toyota held on to the number one spot by less than 1400 units after Ford mounted a huge sales attack in the last month of the year.

Its December Falcon registrations were 7591 units, almost 3000 more than the company's monthly average. Critics claimed the massive marketing initiative had cost the company millions of dollars in discounts and incentive payments, but Ford chiefs say that was not the case.

As Mr Ogden, who took over last

October, puts it: "We are a lot more aggressive company nowadays. I got accused of all sorts of things late last year. We had a demonstrator program going on, but we didn't do a lot of the things people think we did."

One of the things the company did manage to do in the second half of last year was trade in the black. Mr Ogden says that is one of the reasons why Ford results this year will be significantly better than last year's figures.

Under Mr Nasser, Ford was affected in all areas by restructuring. Production line workers were cut, but the upper echelon of management was also revamped as he sought to bring about a big change in the way the company did and thought about its business.

Under Mr Ogden the revolution is continuing, but in a quieter way.

He points out that many of the productivity changes needed most urgently have been put in place, with hourly paid and salaried staff.

Important work has been done to restore the image of the Falcon range, tarnished because of quality glitches after the launch in the late 1980s. This has helped improve sales, which feeds into the bottom line.

Now Mr Ogden has established an internal taskforce, headed at vice-presidential level by Ian Vaughan, to conduct detailed examinations of all aspects of Ford's activities and come up with strategies which determine which way it will operate through the 1990s and beyond.

Matters the company has to tackle include the future of its Homebush plant in NSW, where the Laser, based on the Mazda 323, is assembled. Most industry observers believe the facility's days are numbered, and that Ford will eventually use an import from its Japanese affiliate, Mazda, or from elsewhere in its global garage to replace the Laser.

Ford will also have to determine the future sourcing base for its next-generation Falcon, due in the late 1990s, and decide on the kind of products it will import to bolster its domestically produced range as tariffs fall, giving carmakers wider scope for showroom diversification.

Mr Ogden says there is nothing sinister in the establishment of the business development group.

"We didn't have a formal business planning group when I got here and we needed one," he says.

John Ogden arrived from the US early in 1993 to succeed Jac Nasser as president of Ford Australia. He is credited with the decision to keep the Falcon an indigenous car. His seat here is the Anniversary Falcon GT, created by Ford Australia's new special vehicles partner, Tickford Engineering, under David Flint. Opposite, top: the EB Falcon was launched in July 1991. Below: during the spring of 1992 Ford Australia introduced the XR6 Falcon and promoted it – via Tickford product planner and former Bathurst mastermind team manager Howard Marsden – as a 'family sports' sedan. Note the backdrop to this Cobalt Blue example. The XR6 subsequently enjoyed success in production car racing.

marketing and sales, and a board member, puts much of this at the door of president Bill Dix. 'He wasn't really a charismatic character, but he was intemperate of idiots. I always think a classic case is when the finance people say: You need to reduce the cost of that vehicle – pull all those components out. And you put your hand up and say: You haven't reduced the cost, you've just reduced the quality. A good car guy would sit down and say: I want a lower cost car but I want to keep all the features. Bill's problem was that many of the product people weren't obeying that dictum.

'Every time they wanted to put in features it cost more and the weight went up and they'd over-engineer the bloody thing and so on. What he was trying to say to them was Fellas, we want to get all these features including better design, better quality ... at lower cost, and they'd say: Oh, no, boss, it's either one or the other. And as we all know, the

Japanese said If you get the quality right you actually save money, in the manufacturing process and that sort of thing.'

Dix was succeeded in February 1990 by Jacques A. Nasser. Lebanese born, he and his family migrated to Australia when Nasser was six years old. With a degree in business studies from the Royal Melbourne Institute of Technology (RMIT), he joined Ford Australia in 1968 at 21 as a financial analyst. In 1973, in tune with the company's remarkable perspicacity in picking and nurturing real talent, Nasser was transferred to North America, returning nine months later as, first, manager of profit analysis and then of product programming and timing. In 1975 he moved to Ford International Automotive Operations

JAC WAS THE FIRST I

and went through a number of international assignments, including vice-president of finance and administration for the Autolatina joint venture with Volkswagen in Brazil and Argentina. The man who speaks fluent Arabic, Spanish and Portuguese was tapped as chairman of Ford of Europe in 1993 and stepped up to the hot seat on January 1, 1999, to succeed Alex Trotman as president and chief executive officer of the Ford Motor Company.

Ford's ace fixer arrived in 1990 back at a Ford Australia deep in debt. It would plummet from an after-tax profit of $124.1 million in 1989 to a net loss of $82.7 million in 1990, with the concurrent market share dropping from 27.0 per cent to 24.9 per cent. Nasser's main task was to cut costs, as it would later be in Europe, where he first got the nickname of 'Jac the Knife'.

He targeted manufacturing costs particularly. Ian Vaughan would say 10 years later that the company wasn't properly structured for the new government car plan, reviewed in 1993 for the post-1984 arrangements. 'We closed Sydney ... stopped building Lasers ... we got out of Capri, Telstar ... we closed the four-cylinder engine plant in Geelong. We decided we were spread too thinly across too many car lines, and that a major focus on Falcon would be the best business strategy for Ford Australia.'

But Nasser was also the first 'petrolhead' to run

Broadmeadows since Bill Bourke, and it soon showed. The EB Falcon of 1991 was the first evidence. Little changed externally, it had a V8 option for the first time since 1983: the fuel-injected 5 litre 165-kilowatt unit built in Windsor, Ontario, and used in the Mustang. The engineers gave it uprated springs, gas dampers, new front end geometry and a stiffer rear end, which sharpened steering and roadholding significantly. The Fairmont model was loaded with extra equipment for a recommended retail price lift of just $763, and the first XR8 was brought in to combat the Commodore SS V8.

In April 1992 came the EB Evolution, which delivered the first ABS (anti-lock) brakes on a mainstream Australian-built

TROLHEAD TO RUN BROADMEADOWS SINCE BOURKE

Edsel Ford II poses outside the Research Centre at Broadmeadows in front of a mocked-up Cobra version of the EB Falcon – note the Edsel B. Ford initials on the number plate. It was this fourth generation member of the family dynasty who conceived the original Cobra, with its memorable colour scheme.

David Morgan took over from John Ogden in late 1995, moving up from vice-president, sales and marketing.

sedan, priced at just $990, plus a new edition of the multipoint six-cylinder, enlarged to 4 litres and 148 kW. And then there was 'Smartlock', a locally developed system that was arguably the world leader. It used a remote keypad and ECU with a transponder that rotated a set of security codes every time the engine was started. This defeated the thieves with scanners, because without the right code the engine's ignition and fuel systems were immobilised and the engine couldn't be hot-wired. To test the system the South Australian police whistled up several experienced car thieves – they gave up the attempt after four days.

All this time Ford Australia and the Falcon were absent from touring car racing. A decision by the Australian motorsport controlling body (CAMS) in the mid-1980s to adopt the international Group A formula had produced cars to which the Australian buyer couldn't relate. Then, when CAMS went from Group A to a local bastard formula the races were fought out mainly between the UK Ford Sierra turbos and the all-wheel drive Nissan GTR 'Godzillas'. The fans strongly disliked it, and wouldn't return in big numbers until the Ford versus Holden V8 formula was restored.

However, Nasser recognised and understood the grip Holden Special Vehicles – developed from the much-publicised 1987 divorce between Peter Brock, his HDT racing/customised Commodore operation and GM–H – had on young buyers. With his global connections, Nasser empowered a trio of executives to search the world for an organisation that could go into joint venture with Ford Australia in much the way Holden Special Vehicles had with Holden. They gave the tick to Tickford Engineering. This British firm could trace its history back to 1820 when it started as Salmon & Sons, building bodies for luxury horse-drawn coaches near its 1990s headquarters in the grounds of Tickford Abbey at Newport Pagnell, home of Aston Martin. Tickford's engineering facilities were at Milton Keynes, heartland of the world's Formula One industry and the firm had put its stamp on cars such as the Group A RS500 Sierra Cosworth, the RS200 rally champion and others.

A new joint venture was initiated between Tickford and Ford Australia and announced on August 13, 1991 with Tickford the major shareholder, and a factory was built close to Broadmeadows. The managing director was David Flint, former manufacturing director of Tickford UK.

Tickford hit the ground running. It developed a Clubsprint version of the doomed Capri, the first XR6 and an anniversary EB Falcon GT. Unlike the HSV cars, which were sold through selected dealers, the Tickford versions would be available throughout the network. In June 1992 the new company got a boost with the arrival of Howard Marsden as product planner. Marsden had been away from Australia for six years, at one stage running the Nissan race and rally program in Europe. Jac Nasser, the man he had first known as a young finance controller, asked him to lunch and offered him the job. 'It was a bit of a shock', Marsden told me late in 1999. 'It had been 18 years since I first walked into the reception area at Broadmeadows, and I have to say it looked exactly the same'. Marsden in 2000 headed the new Ford Tickford Racing operation, back where he had been in the 1970s.

By early 1993, when Nasser left for Europe and was replaced in the chair by American John Ogden, Australia was committed to 'economic rationalism' and the concomitant 'level playing field', which in reality was (and

Vice-president product development, Ian Vaughan, is a dedicated motorsport enthusiast who is particularly proud of how well the latest Falcons steer and handle. The return of the old Ford versus Holden rivalry in the V8Supercar category has been welcomed by other enthusiasts, for whom the local car industry has provided numerous icons.

Howard Marsden, centre, at Winton during season 1999, almost three decades after he first worked for Ford Australia – very successfully as team manager for the works GTHOs at Bathurst and other venues. His current role is motorsport manager within marketing, sales and service. Opposite (top): Team members surround an EL Falcon, among them 'Mr Falcon', Lindsay Dawson, on the left of 'Tom'. Opposite (bottom): the uniquely styled 2.5 litre V6 Probe coupe.

is) distinctly sloped when you consider some of the real world trade policies of the US and some Asian neighbours. With both the Labor Party and the Coalition arguing for a progressive lowering of import duties in the post-1994 plan, the writing was on the wall. The Keating Labor government was re-elected, partly because the conservatives under John Hewson were pushing a consumption tax, and the local car makers benefited from Labor's still tough, but gentler program – tariffs falling by 2.5 per cent per year to 15 per cent by 2000.

(The days when 80 per cent of the market was reserved for local passenger cars were long gone. In 1990 imports took 31.1 per cent; in 1994 38.9 per cent and by 1997, for the first time since the 1950s, imported cars eclipsed the locals, taking 53.1 per cent of the market. By 2000 the percentage of imports was in the region of 65.)

However, what also immediately faced Ogden was a major struggle with the parent corporation to keep a locally designed Falcon. Folklore has it that Dearborn sent him here to shut down local manufacturing. To the contrary, Ian Vaughan describes a huge and complex operation called Project Eagle, put in place in April 1993 by Ogden and under Vaughan, to compare product and evaluate the economics, investment, research and other business equations of a unique local car versus an import, or at least an imported platform.

'I said to John: I need one highly qualified person from each division of the company. So I had one person from purchasing, one from manufacturing, one from finance, sales, product development. We started to map out all the variables, what were the factors we had to take into account, how we were going to go about studying each of these areas.'

The process took about 18 months. 'We continually cross-referenced back into the rest of the company. I had regular review meetings with all the departmental vice-presidents to make sure they were plugged in, every step of the way. If we made an assumption about an investment in the assembly plant I wanted to make sure manufacturing was

'I NEED ONE HIGHLY QUALIFIED PERSON F

behind that assumption. What I said to my team members was, You've got to deliver your vice-president to me. Every element of the analysis has to have the support of your VP.

This in itself reveals one of the simultaneous strengths and weaknesses of Ford. Vertically integrated in the line-and-staff principle that dates back to the Roman legions but also owing much to reverence for the way Henry Ford I ran things, it emphasises obedience to the immediate superior.

Vaughan says Project Eagle got an early look at Ford's new international 'Edge' design thinking – as now expressed in the Ka and Focus. It was reflected in the coming new Taurus – styled by Australian expatriate John

M EACH DIVISION OF THE COMPANY'

Top: sourced from Kia in Korea, the first Ford Festiva arrived here in 1991 and immediately gave Ford a boost in the small car market. Right: more a luxury Grand Tourer than a true GT (in the GTHO sense), the EB Anniversary GT marked Ford Australia's move back towards the performance image it had made its own back in the 1960s.

Doughty – and by the end of 1994 that became the final alternative candidate for an all-new Falcon slated for introduction in late 1998. But the decision was not made yet.

In August 1993 came the ED, a facelift with a total of 5714 new or revised components from the EB Evolution. The 'letterbox' mouth that had begun with the XD was replaced by a slightly ovalised corporate grille, the XR6 and XR8 got the four small quad-headlamp treatment, the Futura name returned and the rear centre lap/sash belt – a world first – arrived.

The EF that arrived almost exactly one year later amounted to a major revamp with a well executed new dashboard and a driver's airbag as standard equipment. But its clean frontal styling – *sans* the customary radiator grille – disappointed some traditional buyers who preferred their cars to have a 'face'. Thus the EL minor facelift of September 1996 featured a quite prominent grille.

The EF's platform was the same as EA/EB/ED, but it gained new front and rear sheet metal (retaining the old doors). The Fairmont versions for the first time got a different frontal treatment from the GLi base model and the nose was made considerably more elegant, with wide, slightly sloped shallow lamp inserts. Somehow the drivetrain engineers got another 9 kW from the 4 litre six, as well as ridding it of much of the coarseness road testers had consistently bagged. In the XR6 it would deliver 164 kW, just 6 kW fewer than the 5 litre V8 in the XR8, and in fact it accelerated faster. A driver's airbag became standard across the range and the awkward and loathed under-dash handbrake was finally moved to the centre console after only – only! – 34 years.

For 1993, the Shell Australian Touring Car Championship (and, importantly, the Tooheys 1000 enduro at Bathurst) would be run under a formula that made V8 Falcons and Holdens virtually the *de rigueur* kit. The first V8 Falcons to race since 1985 had made a late debut in 1992, but now the new race cars were there in force, teams with big-money sponsors like Peter Jackson and Shell. John Bowe in the second Dick Johnson Shell Falcon won the opening round at Amaroo Park, Glenn Seton the third at Phillip

Former open-wheeler champion racer, John Bowe, drove the number 18 Shell car for many years as a key driver for Dick Johnson Racing. He now drives for Caterpillar and was quick from his first outing in this all-new car.

Island in the Peter Jackson car, and finally the title.

The second Peter Jackson Falcon, in the hands of Geoff Brabham and David Parsons, won the Sandown 500 in September. At Bathurst, however, Commodores took the first four places on the grid, Larry Perkins/Gregg Hansford on pole, with Johnson fifth and Seton sixth, and at the end of 161 laps of The Mountain the Holdens had the first five places, with Brabham/Parsons the highest-placed EB, seven laps off the pace. The Glenn Seton/Alan Jones Falcon broke a driveshaft when fifth on lap 147, Dick Johnson was T-boned by another car when he and Bowe were sixth on lap 97 and Charlie O'Brien/Andrew Miedecke broke the gearbox on lap 41. Well, maybe next year ...

The resumption of the old Ford versus Holden formula – albeit in very dramatically modified machines – has been resoundingly successful, bringing large attendances at meetings, huge television audiences and racing as close as you will ever see it.

Meanwhile, for 1994 the company was able to report its second best profit ever at $145.5 million. This was the sign of results Detroit was looking for and provided the springboard for Ogden's announcement on July 14, 1995, that Ford Australia would spend about $1 billion over the next five years.

It was the company's 70th anniversary year: Ford had led the passenger car market for the 13th consecutive year, introduced the new Korean Kia-sourced Festiva car, the UK Transit van and the US-built Probe coupe. Ahead lay the broad sunlit uplands.

Bibliography

Key Automotive Statistics Australia,
Department of Industry, Science and Resources, 1999.
John Wright, *The History of Ford Falcon, 1960–1994,*
Ford Australia, 1994.

CHAPTER 20

Heading For The 75th Anniversary

In 1994 Ford Australia changed its entire passenger car range, including dropping the Capri but adding the US-sourced Probe coupe. The euphoria continued in 1995. The small Festiva, sourced from Kia in Korea, was very popular and Ford Australia would sell a total of 137,800 vehicles for a 21.5 per cent market share, number two overall but top in passenger sales. President John Ogden on July 14 was able to announce a decision to invest about $1 billion in development, mainly on an all-new Falcon due in 1998, but including $85 million on a state-of-the-art waterborne paint facility. The company won the 'Employer Of The Year' award, Falcon production went up to 440 a day, it added the Belgian-built Ford Mondeo to its line-up to counter GM–H's Vectra, and John Bowe won the Shell Australia Touring Car Championship in the Dick Johnson Shell Helix team's Falcon.

But in the second half of 1995 Ogden was unexpectedly replaced by David Morgan, moving up from vice-president, sales and marketing. There had been persistent rumours that we had seen the last indigenous Falcon. Sections of the motoring press wrote that Ogden had been sent to Australia to shut down the Falcon manufacturing operation, but actually he had fought long and hard to dissuade Dearborn from this course; his legacy was even better 1995 and 1996 after-tax profits. Morgan, a quiet, self-effacing man with long experience in sales, had little experience in design and manufacturing, but would be responsible for overseeing decisions relating to the new Falcon, the AU.

The company was also investing massively in an explosion of computer power. It gained the ability to tap into Dearborn's Cray C90 super-computers, which Ford Australia vice-president for product development, Ian Vaughan, estimated would enable it to complete the income tax returns of every Australian in about five minutes. The serious advantage was in cutting down the gestation time for a new model. In 1985 a frontal crash

Right: one of Steve Park's bold sketches during the AU development program. Below, from left: Ken Kohrs, vice-president, large car vehicle centre, designer Steve Park and Ian Vaughan.

ONE STRONG PROPOS

take a full import or some sort of hybrid. Against this background Ford Australia began analysing the parameters for the 1998 Falcon, with the understanding that it had a problem. Close to 70 per cent of Falcon sales were to government and business fleets, large and small, compared with around 60 per cent for Commodore and less than 50 for both Toyota and Mitsubishi. Fleet buyers and finance lenders had got into the habit of screwing every dollar they could out of the car makers, playing one against the other, doing deals for as little as 50 bucks a car, grubbing the greatest possible discounts while knowing their residuals (resale values) would hold up well in three years' time, when private buyers would want their used cars. And it had become a full cream cash cow for Federal, State and local governments, who bought their cars free of wholesale sales tax and, after six months or 4000 kilometres, sold them at a profit. It was a licence to print money, but for the car makers it was profitless volume.

simulation on computer cost around $80,000; by 1997 this was down to around $300 and by the end of 2000 the figure will be under $20. Creating a clay model used to take a dozen people a dozen weeks; today one designer can go from an idea on a screen to a fully animated 3D video of a vehicle in three weeks.

Even so, until just before Ogden departed no firm decision had been made on whether Ford Australia would be allowed to design and build its own car, or be made to

In 1993 Ford launched a dual fuel (LPG/petrol) factory-warranted fitment, again aimed mainly at the fleet market (with the AUII in 2000 Ford introduced a dedicated LPG Falcon). But in 1993, with the recession, total new vehicle sales had sagged to 555,306, well below the record years of 1985–86 (although they hadn't got back to the 'trough' year of 1977). The private buyer was virtually out of the market – the whole structure was founded on fleet sales. Ford's traditional dominance of, and reliance on, fleet sales had started to worry its product planners, because research was also revealing that private buyers of Falcons were mainly 40-plus males and that the car was weak in its appeal to younger men and most women. Thus, thinking about the AU started to drift towards refining the brand's appeal.

Ian Vaughan's Project Eagle group was deep into crystal-balling throughout 1994. 'We were spread too thinly across too many car lines and decided that a major focus on Falcon would be the best business strategy.

'The political writing on the wall, too, was much less

Left: from left, Ian Vaughan, Jac Nasser, and Labor heavyweights Paul Keating and Martin Ferguson. Below: an early clay model of the proposed AU Falcon (photographed in May 1994).

WAS FOR THE 1996 US TAURUS, CODENAMED DN101

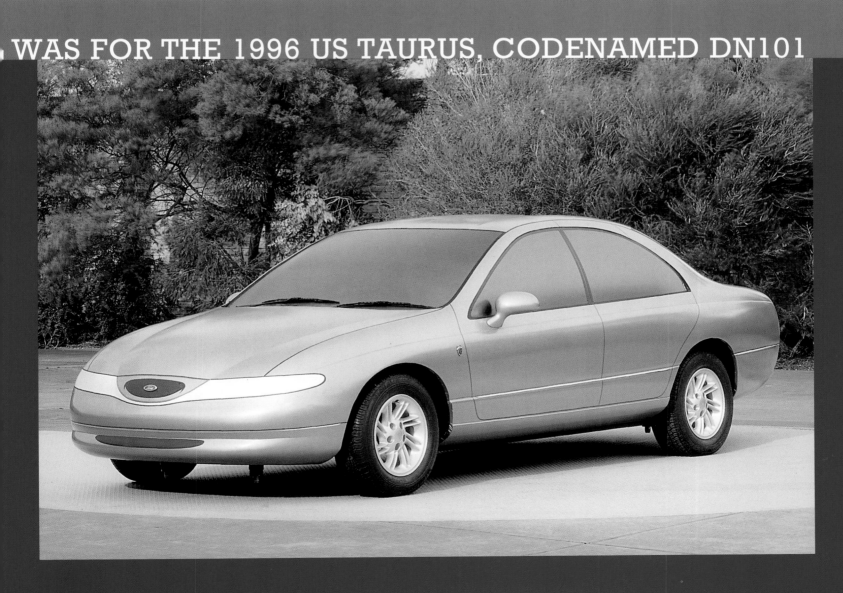

Launched in mid-1999, the AU ute was immediately successful. The XR8 version combined the performance car wizardry of Tickford with immense practicality – a powerful utility of powerful utility. In this era of crash-testing and airbags, the bull-bar requires careful design.

protection for the motor industry.' Late in 1994 the world got to hear about Ford 2000, which in broad terms was a long term plan to rationalise the corporation's product platforms and drivetrain families across all markets, so you would have, for instance, the coming new Jaguar S-Type sharing its platform and engines with the Lincoln LS.

Eagle was a succession of 'what ifs'. Vaughan recalled: 'You could start with a warmed-over Falcon, or a completely new Falcon from the ground up, or some halfway house. You could look at a corporate engine – say, bring in a V6'. One strong proposal was for the 1996 US Taurus, codenamed DN101. What was the feeling about that suggestion?

'We analysed the hell out of it ... we spent a lot of time debating front-wheel drive against rear-wheel drive.' Research told them 69 per cent of Falcon owners had towbars fitted – the proportion with Toyota Camrys was about 20 per cent – and there was a perception that rear-drive cars towed better.

They also looked at engine size and source. The biggest engine in Taurus was a 3 litre V6; a V8 wouldn't fit, so there went the towing market. 'The engine cost analysis was interesting, because the basic Taurus overhead valve engine was nice and cheap but it didn't have enough output. There was a much dearer Duratec DOHC V6 [which is the basis for the Jaguar S-Type V6], which did have sufficient power.' Vaughan now says the Duratec engine proved too expensive, but mainly because Australia would have had to invest in new plant and equipment to produce it, whereas with the Falcon engine – albeit a much-refined 'Grandpa's Axe' – much less investment would return still more improvements in fuel economy, noise and smoothness.

Front-drive means a transaxle transmission, and Australia doesn't produce one, so Ford would have had to go to BTR in Albury and ask it to make a massive investment in new plant, maybe of the order of $1 billion. Or it could import the transaxle, or the combined engine and transmission, which is what Toyota does with its V6. 'If you went in at 85 per cent local content (with Taurus) you'd have the same employment you've got today. That would mean setting up to make the whole V6 engine, having BTR make a transaxle. However, you'd be tempted to reduce that; you'd be tempted to import the transaxle, which is bad news for employment in Albury. We might have only half-made the engine, which is bad news for employment in Geelong, bad news for employment in automotive components. The sourcing subject is very important for employment and of course if you've got less employment in some areas you have to write some redundancy costs into the equation', said Vaughan.

He tried to keep an open mind, because there were some pluses for Taurus, and at times he'd sway from one to the other. 'At the same time you are looking at Falcon you're looking at the derivatives that come with it. There's a sedan, a wagon, the Fairlane/LTD and the ute. You look at Taurus and you get a sedan and a wagon. There was a Crown Victoria, but it was a rear-drive body-on-frame design, which meant two platforms instead of one and no ute. We couldn't stretch the Taurus because it was narrower than the Falcon and you would get a long skinny car.'

The planners also looked at the European Ford Scorpio

and Mazda's rear-drive 929 V6. But the Scorpio was coming to its end and Australia would have had to reinvent it, while the Mazda was too narrow. 'Our market analysis had Falcon and Commodore in one boat and Camry and Magna in another. A narrower car would have put us in the Camry/Magna class.'

Part of the 'what if?' process is what Vaughan calls 'investment versus risk tradeoff'. 'You test the analyses for their sensitivities to variables – like what if the Koreans came in with a 4 litre Falcon-sized car?' Ford knew what the local opposition had in the pipeline. It knew the coming Camry would be bland but had the quality reputation. It

The first AU clay model parked alongside the then current EL Falcon. There would be numerous iterations before the production car went on sale in October 1998. Below: an AU Falcon undergoes aerodynamic testing.

margin on the car would be lower, which would mean we couldn't price it so aggressively to fleets. The government fleets would have bought Holdens and our market share would have dropped instantly if we got out of local manufacture. The fleets have a shopping list and tell employees they can have a Falcon, Commodore, Magna or Camry. That's it'. He says there was a huge internal debate about independent rear suspension (IRS), most of it again concerning fleet sales because of a possible perception that IRS wouldn't tow as well as Falcon's proven live rear axle. So the belt-and-braces decision was made to keep both in the range. 'Cost was also a major factor. A well executed beam axle will outperform a badly executed IRS every time.' This was even though Vaughan and his planners knew GM–H was going to make IRS standard across its range.

They used the BMW 5-Series as a sort of 'stretch-goal', representing something they could strive for but might not achieve. 'It is a way of futuring yourself. In other words, you know that Holden, Camry and Magna are going to get better, so what do you do – you look at one of the superior cars as where they might head for, and you try to head for it too.' Vaughan also drove the Jaguar S-Type, Lincoln LS and Mustang platforms in early testing, with the IRS – 'ours

recognised the Magna as a very good product and knew it had a 3.5 litre V6 coming. As soon as Opel in Germany released its new Omega Vaughan flew to Europe to drive

FORD AUSTRALIA DECIDED TO GO

one, assuming it would be the basis for the next (VT) Commodore. Then they imported one and pulled it apart, leading directly to the conclusion that the Opel–Holden independent rear suspension would not be further developed specifically to suit the forthcoming Commodore and Ford Australia should go to the new and very efficient multi-link design it had in the works.

Here the fleet sales Medusa reared its ugly head again. Vaughan: 'If we had a fully built-up Taurus coming in, our

THE NEW AND VERY EFFICIENT MULTI-LINK SYSTEM

comes from the same bookshelf, if you like'. Eventually the Taurus was dropped from the plan because of lack of torque from the V6, the lack of derivatives, the front-drive factor, and its higher cost level. 'The thing that really swung it was the fact that Falcon was an Australian product designed to be right for the market, with a full range of derivatives and tailored to the consumers' requirements – and the fact that the financial efficiencies were demonstrated, that we could provide a return on

investment to our shareholders.'

At the same time the clay models were coming together, heading for the first customer clinics in late 1994 and early 1995, matching them with unbadged rivals such as the Commodore. Ford's vaunted 'Edge' design, as in the Ka and Focus, were just being seen in the system, running a parallel course in terms of timing. And this was where began the most controversial aspect of the AU: its styling. Any car must last eight to 10 years in its model cycle and

while the ends can change the centre sheet metal must basically stay the same. Vaughan: 'We would have seen some polarisation close to launch in the marketing clinics. We rate respondents as conservatives and progressives – we wanted a higher reading from the progressives because we wanted the styling to live for three years. We got better from the progressives than any other Falcon and we knew it would take time to grow'.

Ford's marketers were searching for a way to make the car look a little – but not too much – smaller, a little softer, less butch, to appeal more to women buyers, but lithe enough to attract the younger males, who could relate it to the lean, agile look of the Tickford XR6 and XR8 cars that had been so successful.

'We consciously made a brave move because we wanted

to reach into the future', was how Vaughan put it, late in 1999.

In parallel with this, engineering was building prototypes of two kinds of IRS, the semi-trailing arm and the multi-link. Vaughan: 'Marketing was worried about cost but the engineers were saying: We can't just do what was invented 20 years ago – let's move into the next generation of IRS and do it right'.

In 1995 Ford Australia, with 21.5 per cent of the market, reclaimed the number 1 sales spot from Toyota for the first time since 1990. In April 1996, David Morgan was able to announce a record after-tax profit of $201.7 million. It was even better news a year later, with another record net profit of $217.3 million for calendar 1996 and passenger car market leadership for the 15th year. It was enough to persuade Dearborn finally that its Australian subsidiary could, on its own, fund a unique car, one that was outside Ford 2000 and had limited potential for export. But the massive investment in the new car chopped the profit to $178.5 million for 1997 and then just $57 million for calendar 1998.

In September 1998 the AU was finally launched, but Ford had ambushed itself in the previous 12 months. Faced with a formidable new rival in the VT Commodore, which immediately started hacking into Ford's fleet sales lead, Ford began discounting the outgoing ELII. The campaign – car makers prefer to describe it as 'incentives', or 'bonusing' – took many forms, but at its nadir Sydney dealers were selling new GLis with 1997 compliance plates for around $24,000, $7000 off the RRP. This immediately started eroding Falcon resale values, and as the months went on fleet owners, fleet management companies and finance houses were looking aghast at disposal figures that in many cases didn't reach the residual on the lease. After the first four months of 1998 Ford's market share had crashed from the 20.3 per cent which had won it the top slot again in 1997 to 15.5 per cent. To April 30, with five months to run before AU launch, 29,907 Commodores had been registered against 18,918 Falcons – the biggest gap in a decade.

There was more than a whiff of panic in Broadmeadows. Ford's marketers came up with the 'two-for-one' deal, repeating a promotion they had run with the Fairlane/LTD about five years before. The 1998 version was that all

The US clay model for the AU Falcon looked lighter and less substantial than the production car or, for that matter, the Australian clay models of 1994–95. Opposite: Ford Consultant Jackie Stewart (third from right) offers his opinion on the AU Falcon – note the clever use of camouflage on the burgundy AU (closest to camera). Opposite, below: Toll Racing's AU in its V8Supercar livery.

buyers, including business fleets but excluding governments, could lease a new EL Falcon immediately and in 12 months' time replace it with the all-new AU at no extra cost. It didn't do all that much. Total new vehicle sales for 1998 hit an all-time record of 807,669, and Toyota took back market leadership with 19.6 per cent, ahead of GM–H's 19.0 and Ford's unhappy 15.9, even given the new AU. The Commodore comfortably outsold Falcon.

It became almost holy writ that the AU had a difficult first year because of the styling. There was saloon bar chat, supported by the media, about the Forte 'waterfall' grille, the feeling that it had a sad face and a droopy rear end and

that the wheels and tyres didn't fill out the wheel arches enough. It also looked smaller than the Commodore, and the swoopily-curved roof line, so much part of Ford's Edge styling, hinted at a bumped head climbing in and out. However, the main problem was marketing. There were the ailing resale values, the innovative but off-centre television commercials, and a few panicked dealers who started discounting after a few months.

There was nothing wrong with the car – in fact, aside from the styling, it got mostly excellent reviews from the motoring press. The AU was a stronger, quieter car with all-new interiors, including the seats, a brilliant new double-

THE AUII RACKED UP A NUMBER OF FIRSTS FOR AN A

FAIRLANE

Live it.

wishbone front and multi-link rear suspension, improved fuel economy, new Intech six-cylinder engines including a new VCT (Variable Camshaft Timing) performance version and a Tickford-developed LPG version that delivered torque equal to that of the petrol engine, with the ability to adapt ignition tuning to fuel quality and operating

AUSTRALIAN CAR

conditions, and trip computer and diagnostic systems that for the first time could be used with LPG.

Then there was the pricing. The sales and marketing people persuaded management to play the value-for-money card, by having the base Forte price of $29,990 – $2700 less than the equivalent Commodore's – include air-conditioning and automatic transmission as standard. What should have happened was that the base price should have been, if anything, a bit higher than the Holden's, which would have had the effect of dragging up resale values. At the same time the company boldly set out to change the decades-old culture of the fleet business. It reduced the discounts it had been giving to the three levels of government, in the belief that they had been buying too cheaply, and making excessive windfall profits on resale; after six months GM–H followed suit. Through to the end of 1999 Commodore was still outselling Falcon but, significantly, if you took government fleet sales out of the equation the two were neck-and-neck. And it seems that Australia's taxi owners still prefer Falcon by a small margin – like about 95 per cent.

The all-new Fairlane and LTD models followed the AU in February 1999. For the first time in years they were both significantly different from the shorter wheelbase models in looks. In keeping with the fact that these are, with the long-wheelbase Holdens, among the largest rear-drive cars now built in the world, Ford Australia went for a massive, solid look and feel. There was also a generous use of chrome, along with top-of-class towing capacity of 2300 kilograms (this varies according to State/Territory), and lavish equipment like traction control, steering wheel-mounted cruise control and sound system switchery, leather, wood

Opposite and left: front and rear views of the AU Fairlane (launched in February 1999). It was the first ever Fairlane to carry the same model code as the Falcon from which it was derived. Below: the AU ute was the last derivative of the series and was a sales success from its debut.

grain trim, six-stacker CD player in the boot and inbuilt phone wiring.

On March 19, 1999 David Morgan, 60 years old and president of Ford Australia since November 1995, announced his retirement. His successor on May 3 was Geoff Polites, who started his career with the company as a

Geoff Polites took up the presidency of Ford Australia in May 1999. His career began as a product planner and he was subsequently a very successful Ford dealer. His determination is to listen clearly to the voice of the customer. He is also a passionate sports fan and has increased the company's commitment to motorsports. Right: Craig Baird close to the limit during the 2000 season.

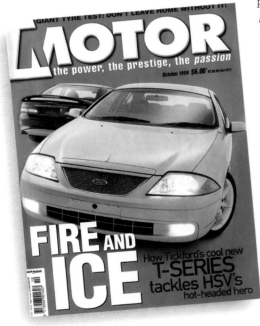

product planner on January 29, 1970 and rose to the position of general sales manager by 1984. He was then head-hunted to run Sydney's City Ford, the country's leading Ford dealership. Why did he leave Ford? Because he was told that his next job and possibly his next two jobs would be overseas and he did not wish to relocate his family.

The loose-strung Polites, a former Australian Rules umpire and subsequently team manager of the Sydney Swans AFL team, was talked into returning by Jac Nasser who had taken over as president and CEO of the Ford empire on January 1, 1999. Polites tells the story that back in 1990 when Nasser assumed the presidency of Ford Australia he rang his former colleague Polites and invited him to dinner. During the meal Nasser asked Polites why he had left Ford. 'They never should have let you go', he said – and asked what it would take to get him back. Polites answered that only the top job would satisfy him. Nasser remembered the conversation and more than eight years later rang Polites to enquire whether he would still be interested in heading

Ford Australia and could he fly to Detroit next week to discuss it.

Geoff Polites' open, down-to-earth approach, his 'a fast game's a good game' play-on style, combined with his high economic intellect, and his intensive sales and customer experience, is already steering the Ford ship in a new direction. We can expect to see big changes from his time at the helm, beginning with a far more intense focus on the customer, reflected in the changes made to the AU Falcon to create the AUII in an impressively tight time frame.

Nasser could see that Polites would bring renewed energy and his distinctive. hard-earned City Ford entrepreneurial experience to Broadmeadows. Very early in his tenure, during his frank monthly, on-the-record analysis for motoring journalists of the previous month's VFACTS registration figures, Polites said Ford had to stop thinking like a car maker and start thinking like a customer.

Two possible faces for the AU clay, May 1994. From left: design manager G Wadsworth, Lionel McWilliam, Mick D'Sylva, Steve Hudson and lead modeller Tom Rossell.

When the writers were speculating about the rumoured pull-forward of the AU's upgrade to lift its fortunes, he challenged them to put in writing their ideas as to how that could be done without spending on changing the sheet metal.

The answer came on April 5, 2000. The AUII racked up a number of firsts for an Australian-built family car: the first to have dual front airbags as standard on all models; the first to make a CD player standard across the range; the first single-fuel LPG option; the first with 16-inch wheels as standard; the first laminated firewall to quieten the interior; the first with a standard overhead driver's console with sunglasses holder. The company also lifted servicing intervals from 10,000 to 15,000 km, with scheduled servicing free to 60,000 km. It put new grilles on all models, using the Fairmont bonnet, installed a squarer and deeper rear bumper in a bid to lift the tail and filled the wheel arches better, with the 16-inch wheels plus 60-series tyres. The interior gained new trim fabrics and different colour schemes. Prices went up by an average $2000 – which they had to do to boost used values – but they were still mostly cheaper than equivalent Commodores. Two weeks later Geoff Polites announced a net after-tax profit for calendar 1999 of $82.3 million, compared with $58 million the year before. It had lost market leadership to Holden in 1999 but, hearteningly, 5900 more Falcons were sold than in 1998.

Thus Ford Australia entered its 75th anniversary year – the 40th birthday for Falcon – by leap-frogging its main rival, as the two have consistently done over the years. Most motoring writers felt the AUII had overtaken the Commodore in a number of areas. It was typical of Ford that it added a number of other small but significant improvements to the range: an overspeed alert chime and display, upgraded audio systems, pyrotechnic front seatbelt pre-tensioners, bigger brakes, traction control standard on Fairmont, a new four-function security system keypad and satellite navigation standard on LTD (optional on Fairlane, Fairmont Ghia and Fairmont).

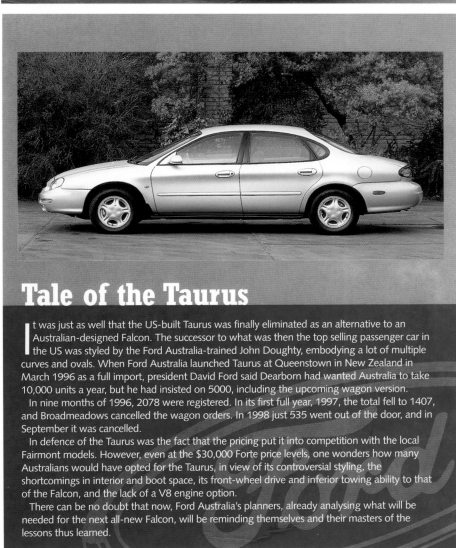

Tale of the Taurus

It was just as well that the US-built Taurus was finally eliminated as an alternative to an Australian-designed Falcon. The successor to what was then the top selling passenger car in the US was styled by the Ford Australia-trained John Doughty, embodying a lot of multiple curves and ovals. When Ford Australia launched Taurus at Queenstown in New Zealand in March 1996 as a full import, president David Ford said Dearborn had wanted Australia to take 10,000 units a year, but he had insisted on 5000, including the upcoming wagon version.

In nine months of 1996, 2078 were registered. In its first full year, 1997, the total fell to 1407, and Broadmeadows cancelled the wagon orders. In 1998 just 535 went out of the door, and in September it was cancelled.

In defence of the Taurus was the fact that the pricing put it into competition with the local Fairmont models. However, even at the $30,000 Forte price levels, one wonders how many Australians would have opted for the Taurus, in view of its controversial styling, the shortcomings in interior and boot space, its front-wheel drive and inferior towing ability to that of the Falcon, and the lack of a V8 engine option.

There can be no doubt that now, Ford Australia's planners, already analysing what will be needed for the next all-new Falcon, will be reminding themselves and their masters of the lessons thus learned.

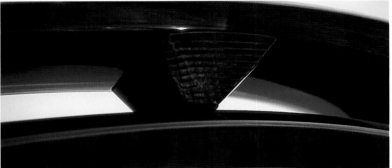

Left: an enthusiastic bundle of Ford's 'Edge' styling came in the form of the Ka, which boldly challenges the Australian buyer to understand how well a micro car fits into our essentially urban environment – in Melbourne or Sydney's crowded streets, for instance. This photo was taken during the cover shoot for True Blue: 75 Years of Ford in Australia. *Bottom: the AUII XR8 is indeed all about performance.*

...RESPECT FOR WHAT THE BLUE OVAL STANDS FOR

This is typical of Ford Australia. Unlike its rivals, it has never been content to step from an all-new model through the stages of minor and major facelifts to the next major change without ongoing improvement in between. For virtually all those 40 years of Falcon Ford has kept returning to the car to refine it, often without trumpeting the fact. Ford Australia has never stopped working at its mainstream car.

That is just one of the things that distinguishes this remarkable company. In my months of research for this book, what continually came home to me was the respect everyone had for the Ford traditions, for what the blue oval stands for, and how the company so often leads the industry – and sometimes the country – in human relations and caring for the people in its charge. There is its decades-old system of graduate training that has produced so much top executive talent – many CEOs of Australian industry are Ford-trained. It has pride in the city of Geelong and its history, and the Australian Rules football team Ford has sponsored for so long.

Ford Australia has the fierce determination to demonstrate that Down Under it can do better, that it can design and build its own unique car and make it one of the world's best. And there is this overwhelming awareness of belonging – belonging to a company whose founder's name is over the door and whom long-term employees still refer to as 'Mister Ford'.

Left: having ushered 3500 entrants through the Falcon Assembly line on Friday The Ford Rally was officially flagged off on Saturday 1 April 2000. Despite inclement weather, the memorable cavalcade departed behind Allan Moffat in his Bathurst winning 1970 GT Falcon blocking the Hume highway for an hour as a convoy 25 kilometres long made its way to Geelong via the Ford Proving Ground where more than 85,000 spectators were waiting. Below: one of the highlights of the 75th Anniversary of the Ford Motor Company in Australia was the arrival of the Ford Mustang just in time for summer. With modifications by Tickford Vehicle Engineering and a fantastic conversion from left-hand drive to right-hand, the Mustang is a genuine legend, combining high performance with an unmatched portfolio of memories.

Ford in Australia – **The Highlights**

1904   The first Ford car, a Model A, imported by Davies & Fehon in Sydney, just one year after Ford Motor Company was founded in Detroit.

1909   Gordon McGregor, MD of Ford of Canada visits Australia, sets up an office in Melbourne and appoints R. J. Durance as manager.

1924   Hubert C. French visits Australia and chooses Geelong as the site for a factory.

1925   Ford Motor Company of Australia Limited incorporated in Victoria on March 31. Ford takes over distribution from State agents and begins manufacture of Model T cars, Model TT trucks and Fordson tractors in temporary premises in Geelong.

1926   Major manufacturing/assembly plants built in Geelong, Brisbane and Adelaide. Temporary factories set up in Sydney and Hobart.

1928   Model A introduced. Manufacture of Model T ceases.

1929   Fremantle Assembly Plant opened.

1932   Ford V8 models introduced.

1933   Small English Ford, the Model Y, launched.

1934 Lewis Bandt designs the world's first coupe utility and it is released as a regular production model.

1935 Ford introduces the all-steel body on the Model 48. Ford 10hp Prefect launched.

1936 Homebush Assembly Plant opened in Sydney.

1937 Model 78 introduced with Australia's first all-steel turret top on sedans.

1938 Popular English-sourced 10/10 panel van released.

1939 Lincoln Zephyr luxury car introduced. Ford plants change over to war production.

1940–1944 All Ford plants concentrate on wartime production. Geelong builds trucks, utilities, trailers, Ships, aircraft fuel tanks, marine mines, gas producers for civilian use and machine tools. Brisbane Plants (Eagle Farm and Rocklea) recondition aeroplane engines, build landing barges, assemble jeeps and heavy duty trucks, tractors and auxiliary fuel tanks for aircraft. Sydney Plant produces Bren Gun Carriers and assembles jeeps.

1945 Production of civilian vehicles resumes. Prime Minister Ben Chifley unveils the new Ford V8 sedan. Fordson E27N tractor launched. Ford buys ex-army vehicles for reconditioning and resale to ease the shortage of new ones.

1946 Ford introduces the famous Ford Freighter pick-up, the forerunner of the F-Series.

1949 All-new Ford V8 sedan with independent front suspension released. Australian utility version also launched. English V8 Pilot sedan and a range of Thames trucks introduced.

1951 Consul 4-cylinder sedan with all-new styling.

1952 First Customline sedan and Australian-designed Mainline utilities. Zephyr 6-cylinder sedan and Australian-designed utility. Fordson Major tractor released..

1954 $540,000 expansion program announced for Geelong including new stamping presses.

1955 Overhead valve V8 engines introduced for Customline sedans and Mainline utilities.

1956   162 hectares of land purchased at Broadmeadows for future expansion.

1958 $37 million expansion announced. Broadmeadows Assembly Plant construction commenced. Engine plant modernised in Geelong.

1959   Broadmeadows Assembly Plant opened (August).

1960   All-Australian XK Falcon range released.

1961 $31 million expansion program. Manufacturing capacity raised from 50,000 to 90,000 units per year. Utility and panel van added to Falcon range.

1962   Falcon production tops 100,000. Fremantle assembly operations cease and the plant converted to do rectification work on cars shipped across from Broadmeadows. Tractor assembly continues at Fremantle. $3 million National Parts Distribution Centre opens at Broadmeadows. Tractor & Implement Division formed. XL Falcon range launched.

1963   Ford Sales Company of Australia incorporated. $27 million expansion program announced. Agricultural implement range launched.

1964 $2 million Head Office opens at Broadmeadows. $160,000 Apprentice Training Centre opens in Geelong. Expansion of Broadmeadows Assembly Plant. XM Falcon launched with two-door Hardtop added to range.

1965   Henry Ford II visits Australia. $1.5 million Proving Ground established in You Yangs. 70,000 mile Falcon-Mobil Durability Run proves reliability of the newly released XP Falcon range.

1966   XR Falcon range with complete new body styling and optional V8 engine introduced. Brisbane Plant gets $2 million extension. Industrial tractors added to agricultural range. Two-door Hardtop dropped from Falcon range.

1967   Falcon GT and long-wheelbase Fairlane models derived from XR series. Export of Falcons to Japan. Ford wins Export Award. One millionth Australian Ford built. XR Falcon GT wins Bathurst 500 mile race.

1968 XT Falcon released. Falcon GTs take Teams Prize and 3rd, 5th and 8th in the inaugural London–Sydney Marathon car trial.

1969 XW Falcon range launched. HO (Handling Option) version of the Falcon XW GT released.

1970 Exports of CKD (Completely Knocked Down) vehicles reach 30,000. XW Falcon Phase 2 launched. XY Falcon released with Phase 3 GTHO. $45 million expansion announced. Ford Credit Australia Limited formed.

1971 Truck Assembly Plant opens in Broadmeadows. Falcon GTHO models take 1–2–3 clean sweep of Bathurst race.

1972 The XA Falcon, third major body change for Falcon and first completely Australian design launched. Two-door Hardtop model re-introduced. Crash Barrier Test and Emissions laboratory established at the Proving Ground. Ford Fiera (Asian vehicle) announced. $4 million Plastics Plant announced for Broadmeadows site.

1973 Falcon wins Bathurst. XB Falcon introduced.

1974 Ford Australia takes passenger car sales leadership for first six months but extended industrial action and strikes disrupt production in latter half of the year. Ford Asia–Pacific Regional Office opens in Melbourne. Falcon wins Bathurst.

1975 Louisville heavy duty truck range assembled in Australia – first right–hand drive version in the world.

1976 $72 million investment in new product and facilities announced. XC Falcon range goes on sale. Last XB GT Falcon produced.

1977 Plastics Plant expanded. Falcons take 1–2 win at Bathurst. Ford Blue Oval badge re-introduced – Falcon is first to have it.

1978 Mazda-sourced Courier light trucks imported. Transit van and D-Series trucks imported from UK. Famous Cobra Hardtop released with only 400 built.

1979 Henry Ford II visits Australia to launch XD Falcon – 4th major body style change. Plastic fuel tank technology introduced – first for a mass-produced vehicle in the world.

1980 $300 million investment program. Alloy head technology added to Falcon. $13 million upgrade for Homebush Assembly Plant in preparation for new Laser production.

1981 Locally-built Laser based on Mazda 323 launched. Ford tractors take sales leadership. Tractor assembly doubled in Fremantle Plant. Falcon wins Bathurst and Australian Touring Car Championship.

1982 'Ford Australia, we're moving with you' slogan launched. Ford takes overall market leadership from Holden. Meteor sedan based on Laser is released. Ford engineers win Shell Mileage Marathon with small vehicle that uses 0.108 litres fuel/100 km (2599.5 miles per gallon). XE Falcon with Watts Link rear suspension. Australian Army buys 550 Ford Cargo trucks and 170 F-Series vehicles. $70 million 4-cylinder Engine Plant to be built in Geelong.

1983 Ford wins Australian design Award for Falcon/Fairlane/LTD range – first time for a motor vehicle. Electronic fuel injection introduced. New mid-sized Telstar and TX5 models released. Employee Involvement (EI) Program instigated at Homebush Plant. Ford engineers lift world economy record to 0.095 litres/100 km (2948 miles per gallon). Ford is No 1 in total vehicles & No 1 in passenger sales.

1984 New Falcon XF model gets electronic engine management system (EEC IV). $69.1 million CAD/CAM computer system for Geelong. World economy record broken again by Ford – 0.090 litres/100 km (3133 miles per gallon). No 1 in total vehicles and No 1 in passenger car sales.

1985 Record vehicle sales at 170,811 units. 2000 Falcon 25th anniversary models built. No. 1 in total vehicles and No. 1 in passenger car sales. Turbo Laser model introduced. Ford engineers again break world fuel economy record at 0.055 litres/100 km (5107 miles per gallon). New Paint facility at Broadmeadows.

1986 Power steering and four-wheel disc brakes fitted as standard to all Falcons. Ford is market leader for 5th consecutive year. TX5 Turbo model for Telstar.

1987 New paint facility begins at Broadmeadows. Ford retains market leadership for 6th year. Production of new EA Falcon starts – fifth major body change. $62 million Paint Facility opens. $2.4 million Training Centre opens at Broadmeadows. Ford New Holland operations formed and moved to Cranbourne. Fremantle Rectification Plant closes. KE Laser. Market leader for 7th consecutive year.

1988 New EA Falcon range released. Production of Capri convertible begins. Ford Australia has major exhibit at Expo 88 in Brisbane. Market leader for 8th consecutive year.

1989 SA30 Capri launched in right-hand drive version for Australia. EA Falcon/Fairlane & LTD Series II fitted with new Australian-built 4-speed automatic transmission. Joint venture with Nissan announced and Ford-produced Nissan utilities built while Ford takes Nissan-built Corsair medium car and Maverick 4WD. Market leader – 9th year in succession.

1990 Left-hand drive Capri convertibles exported to USA as Mercury Capris. Falcon celebrates 30th anniversary. New Louisville heavy truck range announced. Ford retains passenger car leadership.

1991 V8 engines return to Falcon range with the new EB model. 30,000th Capri shipped to the USA in first full year. Korean-sourced Festiva launched. Passenger car leadership again.

1992 EB Series II Falcon with ABS braking system added. Tickford Vehicle Engineering established in joint venture. Capri Clubsprint and Falcon XR6 first models to come from this operation, followed by 25th anniversary EB GT Falcon. Passenger car sales leader.

1993 Ford Australia wins Australian Quality Award. Falcon is most popular car and Ford is passenger car sales leader. Longreach ute launched with one-tonne version available.

1994 EF Falcon launched and wins Australian Design Award. US-sourced Probe sports car released. Production of Capri convertible ceases. Homebush Assembly Plant closed and Laser becomes full import model. No.1 in passenger car sales.

1995 No1 in total market, No 1 in passenger sales and Falcon is No 1 in sales. David Morgan replaces John Ogden as President. Ford Dealer Standards Program launched. 70th anniversary of Ford Australia. Ford wins 'Employer of the Year' award. Falcon engine production raised to 440 per day. $1 billion investment announced. Falcon (John Bowe) wins Australian Touring Car Championship.

1996 Vehicle sales 132,200 – 20.3 per cent market share. No 1 in total market, No 1 in passenger car sales. 21st anniversary of Louisville trucks in Australia. Falcon exports resume to South Africa.

1997 EL Falcon 30th anniversary GT launched. Ford Aeromax heavy truck range introduced. Vehicle sales 130,200 – 18 per cent market share. Market leadership in total vehicles as well as passenger vehicles. Ford Australia achieves ISO 9001 standard in all plants. 3 year/100,000 km warranty announced – 1st Australian manufacturer to offer this. Ford Discovery Centre announced for Geelong. Falcon (Glenn Seton) wins Australian Touring Car Championship.

1998 Completely new AU Falcon – sixth major body change. Brisbane Assembly Plant closes. Vehicle sales 128,800 – 15.9 per cent market share. New Paint facility opened at Broadmeadows Assembly Plant. Fordstar communications system launched to Ford Dealer network. $1.4 million Steering, Ride & Handling Circuit built at Proving Ground. Ford wins Australian Design Award for AU Falcon. Ford website www.ford.com.au launched. Former Ford Australia President Jac Nasser appointed President and CEO of Ford Motor Company. Falcon (Jason Bright/Steven Richards) wins Bathurst 1000 and all three Indy Car Grand Prix support races (Mark Larkham)

1999 New product introductions: AU Fairlane, AU LTD and AU utility, Cougar sports coupe and Ka small car launched. TE Series sedans launched as Ford Tickford Experience (FTE) is set up to market specialist vehicles. Ford Discovery Centre dedicated by Henry Ford III and opened in Geelong by Victorian Premier Jeff Kennett (April). Geoff Polites replaces David Morgan as President of Ford Australia. Ford race driver Dick Johnson retires.

2000 Ford Australia celebrates 75 years of service to the people of Australia. AU Series II Falcon range facelift. V6 Mondeo introduced. Mustang re-introduced to Australia.

Facts and Figures – **The Falcon**

Model	Years	Number	Facts
XK	1960–62	68,413	Original US design 4-door sedan and wagon. Australian-designed ute in 1962. 144 cubic inch, 6-cylinder OHV engine.
XL	1962–63	75,765	Facelift – convex grille/tail lights. Pursuit 170 engine added.
XM	1964–65	47,132	Facelift – grille, droop nose, 'Thunderbird' roof and C pillar, tail lights. Two-door Hardtop and Futura models added. Super Pursuit 200 cubic inch engine.
XP	1965–66	70,954	Facelift – squared off bonnet, horizontal bar grille. Fairmont added.
XR	1966–68	90,810	New body – 'Mustang-bred' look with long bonnet and short boot and 'Coke bottle' side styling. 289 cubic inch V8 introduced. 144 engine and Hardtop body deleted. XR GT introduced in 1967 plus longer wheelbase version – Fairlane.
XT	1968–69	79,290	Facelift – grille/tail lights 302 cubic inch V8 replaces 289. 6-cylinder engines upgraded to 3.1 and 3.6 litres.
XW	1969–70	105,785	Facelift (Falcon model discontinued in USA). Grille, tail lights. 351 cubic inch (5.8 litre) V8 added. GTHO models added – Phase I and II.
XY	1970–72	118,666	Facelift – centre divider in grille. 6-cylinder engines upgraded to 3.3 and 4.1 litres. GTHO Phase III added.
XA	1972–73	152,609	First totally Australian design. Two-door, horizontal bar W-style grille. Hardtop re-introduced.
XB	1973–76	220,765	Facelift – forward cant grille, honeycomb grille with central divider. New tail lights. 121 inch wheelbase LTD produced off modified floor pan.
XC	1976–79	171,082	Facelift – 'Egg-crate' grille, 'Coke bottle' hip line deleted. Crossflow head for 6-cylinder engines. GT deleted. First Ford to use Ford oval badge since pre World War 2.
XD	1979–82	206,974	New square 'European-style' body. Hardtop deleted from range. Ghia and ESP models introduced. Alloy head for 6-cylinder engines (1980). Plastic fuel tank and bumpers.
XE	1982–84	193,890	Facelift – 'waterfall' front styling, fluted tail lights. Watts Link coil rear suspension. V8 engine deleted (1982). EFI 6-cylinder engines introduced.
XF	1984–88	278,101	Facelift – 'soft' front end styling. Unleaded petrol engines.
EA	1988–91	223,612	New aerodynamic body style. New front suspension. Overhead camshaft, redesigned 3.9 litre, 6-cylinder engines. Rack and pinion variable-ratio steering. Two millionth Falcon built.
EB and EB II	1991–93	121,221	Facelift followed by EB II with 4 litre 6-cylinder and 5 litre V8 engines. XR6 and Anniversary GT models added. Smartlock security system introduced.
ED	1993–94	72,571	Facelift – grille, tail lights. Futura added. XR8 added; 'S' and Fairmont wagon deleted.
EF and EF II	1994–97	192,100	Major facelift – more distinction between low and high series models (eg, from Futura to Fairmont). Bonnet slopes to bumper, tail lights flow into boot lid. EF II – airbags introduced. 30th Anniversary GT (1997)
EL	1997–98		Minor facelift – ellipsoid grille, tail lights.
AU	1998–2000		Completely new model, 'Edge' body styling. Multi-link double-wishbone IRS standard on high series models, optional on low series models.
AU II	2000		Facelift – restyling front and rear. Upgraded interiors and equipment.

INDEX

Page references in *italic* refer to captions.

INDEX

INDEX

 TRUE **BLUE**

ACKNOWLEDGEMENTS

Special thanks to Ian Vaughan and Adrian Ryan for expert consultation and to Ford Australia company secretary Sue Allen for scrupulous legal advice. Special thanks also to Rosalind Wright and Neville Wilkinson for their knowledge, professionalism, and endurance.

Archival material from

The Ford Discovery Centre

Bill Tuckey

John M. Wright

Photographs supplied by

The Ford Discovery Centre

MOTOR magazine

Wheels magazine

Ian Vaughan

Bill Tuckey

v8x.com.au

Australian Auto Action magazine

Australian Rallysport News

Additional photography for this book by

Split Image

John M. Wright

Dick Saleh

GALLERY OF **EXCELLENCE**

The Ford Company of Australia gives special thanks to the following companies and organisations, without whom *True Blue: 75 Years of Ford in Australia* would be a lesser publication. As Ford Australia's preferred suppliers, each of these organisations has played a unique role in helping Ford Australia achieve its 75th anniversary.

ROLL OF **HONOUR**

The Ford Company of Australia gives special thanks to the following companies and organisations, without whom *True Blue: 75 Years of Ford in Australia* would be a lesser publication. As Ford Australia's preferred suppliers, each of these organisations has played a unique role in helping Ford Australia achieve its 75th anniversary.

Gold Participants

Automotive Division – Toll Logistics

Denso International Australia Pty Ltd

Finemores Pty Ltd

Flexiglass Challenge Industries

J Walter Thompson Australia Pty Ltd

"K" Line (Australia) Pty Limited

Pacific Dunlop Limited

Plexicor Australia

Tenneco Automotive

Wallenius Wilhelmsen

Silver Participants

Air International Group

Arrowcrest Group Pty Ltd

Astor Base Metals Pty Ltd

Autoliv Australia Pty Ltd

BHP Coated Steel – Australia

Bridgestone TG Australia Pty Ltd

Britax Rainsfords Pty Ltd

BTR Automotive Drivetrain Systems

Hook Plastics

Mobil Oil Australia Pty Ltd

Orbseal Australia

Qantas Airways Limited

RJ Pound Services Pty Ltd

Robert Bosch (Australia) Pty Ltd

Silcraft Pty Ltd

Sumitomo Australia Limited/
Sumitomo Wiring Systems Ltd

Tokyo Boeki (Australia) Pty Ltd

Venture Industries Australia Pty Ltd

Bronze Participants

Australian Arrow Pty Ltd

Automotive Components Limited

Bostik (Australia) Pty Ltd

Castrol Australia Pty Limited

CHEP Australia/Cleanaway

CMI Limited

Coughlin Logistics

Delphi Automotive Systems Australia Ltd

Dowsett Engineering & Materials Handling Pty Ltd

EGR

FMS Audio Sdn Bhd

Hella Australia Pty Ltd

Johnson Controls Australia Pty Ltd

Kirwan Group Services

Mark IV Automotive Pty Limited

Menzies Group of Companies

Meritor LVS Australia Pty Ltd

Mett Diecasting Pty Ltd

Milne Dunkley Customs & Forwarding

NYK Line (Australia) Pty Ltd

Parker Hannifin (Australia) Pty Limited

PBR International Ltd

PricewaterhouseCoopers

Sodexho

Textron Fastening Systems Pty Ltd

TI Group Automotive Systems

Tripac International Pty Ltd

Wayne Richardson Sales/Gaska Tape Australia

*The **XK Falcon**, with Thunderbird memories in its plumage, swooped into Australia in spring 1960, its modernity symbolised by optional automatic transmission (not available on Holden). The 'compact' Falcon was crucial to Ford's future both here and in North America.*

LOGISTICS

Automotive Division –
Toll Logistics
ACN 006 592 089
9 Somerton Park Drive
Campbellfield VIC 3061
Phone: 03 9308 0833
Fax: 03 9308 0811
Email: automotive@toll.com.au

Mr Paul Little
Managing Director
Toll Holdings Limited
Mr Wayne Hunt
General Manager
Automotive Division
Toll Logistics

"Integrated Total Logistics Solutions"

The Toll Group of Companies congratulates Ford Australia on its 75th anniversary. We look forward to continuing the Toll–Ford partnership through ongoing innovation and teamwork.

The Automotive Division of Toll Logistics is the Lead Logistics Provider for Ford Australia. Toll Logistics manages the movement of OE components into Ford's plants at Geelong and Broadmeadows, as well as the outbound delivery of VOR and stock transfer parts and accessories to Ford's major dealers throughout Australia.

The Toll Group's association with Ford dates back to 1995. Our OE synchronous material flow control is provided through an integrated multi-frequency collection service across a multitude of suppliers, located within metropolitan Melbourne, Sydney, Adelaide, Brisbane and country Victoria/New South Wales, picking up and delivering to pre-scheduled time windows.

Additional services include:
- supply chain re-engineering
- multi-modal distribution
- warehousing
- sub-assembly and sequence in line supply
- packaging design, fabrication and contract packing
- computerised route modelling
- stillage control
- wharf cartage and container handling
- international forwarding
- car carrying.

www.toll.com.au

Ken Edgell of Toll Packaging Logistics, packing Ford Falcon hubcaps prior to dealer distribution.

Toll Logistics' on-site supervisor Gus Murrone with Toll driver Jenny Riley, who delivers product just in time for the assembly line at Ford.

Greg Boxer, Ford Material Planning Logistics Manager, presenting an "Awards of Excellence" to Toll's on-site supervisor, Gus Murrone, in recognition of Toll's success in inventory management and control of inbound freight movements from across Australia into the Ford plants.

GALLERY OF EXCELLENCE

DENSO

Denso International
Australia Pty Ltd
ACN 081 951 402
255 Melrose Drive
Tullamarine VIC 3043
Locked Mail Bag 20
Tullamarine VIC 3043
Phone: 03 9279 2900
Fax: 03 9279 2903

Mr Glen Goto
Managing Director
Mr Rodney Wilson
General Manager
Sales & Marketing

Denso is proud to have been invited by the Ford Motor Company to participate in this special anniversary book, *True Blue: 75 years of Ford in Australia*. Denso is one of the world's leading suppliers of state-of-the-art quality automotive components.

The Denso Product range covers thermal transfer systems, electronic body and engine electronics and vehicle power train products. These products are supplied to Ford by three Denso subsidiary companies, namely:
• Australian Automotive Air, Croydon, Victoria
• Denso Manufacturing, Altona, Victoria
• Flexdrive Industries, Gisborne, Victoria.

Denso pays meticulous attention to quality, supply and cost-effectiveness at every turn in meeting Ford's strict performance requirements. It gives us great pleasure to be able to congratulate Ford on 75 years of continuous operation in Australia and we at Denso are sure this will continue well into the 21st century.

From all associates at Denso in Australia and around the world we say well done to Ford and look forward to continuing our close business relationship in the future.

Air-conditioning systems
Engine cooling systems
Fuel/air management systems
Instrumentation systems
Washers and cables

www.denso.com.au

*In February 1964 Ford claimed **'Certified Golden Quality'** for the XM Falcon. There was also, for the first time, a gorgeously proportioned two-door Hardtop variant, nowadays highly collectible, but ahead of its time in the Australia of 1964.*

FINEMORES

Finemores Pty Ltd
ACN 000 697 861
33-47 Doherty's Road
Laverton Nth VIC 3026
PO Box 410
Altona Nth VIC 3025
Phone: 03 9284 2888
Fax: 03 9284 2788

Mr Ron Finemore AO
Executive Chairman
Mr Tom O'Bryan
Managing Director

Finemores' current Executive Chairman Ron Finemore AO established Finemores in 1966 in the small New South Wales country town of Mangoplah near Wagga Wagga as a livestock cartage business.

Today, the parent company of the group, Finemore Holdings Limited, is listed on the Australian Stock Exchange, has annual sales in excess of AUD $360 million, employs over 2000 people and engages over 650 prime movers, 1000 trailers and 40 rigid vehicles.

The alliance between the Ford Motor Company and Finemores began in 1984 when Finemores Vehicle Transport started distributing Ford vehicles to regional areas of Australia. This small operation was the beginning of a dedicated alliance, which now sees Finemores providing 100 per cent of the transportation services required by the Ford Motor Company for finished product distribution throughout Australia. The company provides compound management at Ford's manufacturing plant in Broadmeadows, Victoria, and storage of imported product inventory at Finemores' facilities, purpose built for Ford throughout Australia.

As a part of our mutually successful alliance, the Ford Louisville Prime Mover was introduced into Finemores' fleet, and at the time of writing Finemores is the largest user of this vehicle in Australia.

The Ford Vision Statement reflects the calibre of the company, with its commitment to 'run its business operations ethically, legally and profitably and seek to enhance the well-being of the communities in which it operates by supporting education, community services and improving the environment'.

We take pride in our relationship with the Ford Motor Company, and the contribution that Finemores has made to the success of this industry icon.

Australian Design Award 1990

Established **50** Years

Flexiglass Challenge Industries
ABN 16 008 780 685
26 Cooper Road
Jandakot WA 6164
PO Box 3375
Success WA 6964
Phone: 08 9417 6888
Fax: 08 9414 1142
Email: FCI@iinet.net.au

Mr Robert Klein
Managing Director
Mr Craig Robins
Finance Director

Flexiglass Challenge Industries (FCI) would like to congratulate Ford Australia on 75 years of excellence in the automobile industry. As a manufacturer of utility canopies and various ute accessories, FCI has always had a close association with the Ford dealer network. We are honoured that Ford has chosen us to supply alloy trays direct to the production line for their new Falcon ute.

In 2000, FCI is also celebrating its own milestone: 50 years of devotion to utes. FCI is a third-generation family business that has become Australia's market leader in the canopy industry. Our product is also recognised on an international scale as we export to New Zealand, South Africa, New Guinea, South-East Asia and Europe. Furthermore, FCI produces other accessories for the ute owner including ute liners, mats and lids. We certainly have come a long way since our founder, HH Robins, produced the first fibreglass canopy in the 1950s.

Our success can be attributed to our commitment to quality. We manufacture, assemble, fit and distribute our products under a quality management system based on ISO9002 international standards. On-going staff training is a significant part of maintaining the quality of our customer service. Our research and development department ensures that we are leading innovators in the canopy market. This innovation has twice been recognised by the achievement of the prestigious Australian Design Award.

FCI will continue to provide superior products to ute lovers, in Australia and around the world, well into the 21st century.

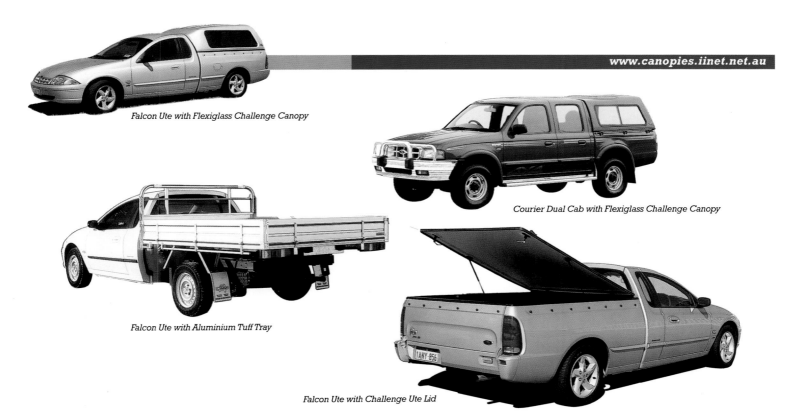

www.canopies.iinet.net.au

Falcon Ute with Flexiglass Challenge Canopy

Courier Dual Cab with Flexiglass Challenge Canopy

Falcon Ute with Aluminium Tuff Tray

Falcon Ute with Challenge Ute Lid

*Perhaps the single boldest public relations exercise in the history of the Australian automotive industry took place in the **You Yangs in 1965**. Five brand new XP Falcons were tortured for a total of 112,000 kilometres. The car's toughness proven, sales improved dramatically.*

J Walter Thompson

J Walter Thompson Australia
Pty Ltd
484 St Kilda Road
Melbourne VIC 3004
Phone: 03 9868 9111
Fax: 03 9867 7568

We live it too.

J Walter Thompson congratulates Ford Australia as it celebrates its first 75 years. JWT shares the vision and is dedicated to helping Ford Australia achieve its goals.

THE V8 FALCON UTE IS BACK.

KAWASAKI KISEN KAISHA, LTD.

"K" Line (Australia) Pty Limited
ACN 007 103 568
11th Floor, 222 Kingsway
South Melbourne VIC 3205
PO Box 1307
South Melbourne VIC 3205
Phone: 03 9696 1599
Fax: 03 9696 0460
Email:
melcarb@klineaus.com.au

Mr Yuzuru Miyachi
Managing Director
Mr Ross White
General Manager

"**K**" Line is proud of its record of service with Ford Australia, and has been Ford's nominated ocean carrier for over 20 years. "K" Line introduced multipurpose automobile and bulk carriers in 1968, and built Japan's first specialised car carrier in 1970. In 1973, "K" Line built *European Highway*, the world's first Pure Car Carrier (PCC) vessel, capable of carrying up to 4,200 mid-size vehicles. "K" Line's fleet of PCCs, complete with state-of-the-art technology, has set the benchmark in the efficient transport of motor vehicles and in the concept of zero damage. As well as improving loading and discharging operations, "K" Line has introduced decks with adjustable height and ramps in order to meet the customer's need for the safe and economical transportation of any type and size of vehicle.

In the fiscal year of 1998, "K" Line, with a fleet of about 60 vessels and approximately 750,000 DWT, carried 1.6 million vehicles. In 1999, "K" Line ordered five additional PCC vessels, each capable of carrying 5,000 vehicles, to update the existing fleet.

It is predicted that worldwide the volume of cars transported and the routes used will continue to increase in line with car makers' globalisation policies. In order to accommodate such change, "K" Line will further develop the combination of available origins and destinations (Thailand–Australia, Australia–Middle East, for example).

"K" Line, in conjunction with its business partners in Australia (including Finemore and Prixcar), is further looking forward to offering a new concept of total logistic service from overseas ports of origin to the final destination – the dealers in Australia.

www.kline.co.jp

*The dramatic **XR of 1966** was proudly 'Mustang-bred' with its long bonnet and short boot. Bigger and more imposing than its predecessors, XR introduced V8 engines, the GT and a whole new rush of Australian motoring history with 'Bathurst' written on every page...*

PACIFIC·DUNLOP

Pacific Dunlop Limited
Level 41, 101 Collins Street
Melbourne VIC 3000

Burton Cables
421 Victoria Street
Brunswick VIC 3056

GNB Technologies
Level 1, 293 Camberwell Road
Camberwell VIC 3124

Holding Rubber
50–56 Redwood Drive
Dingley VIC 3172

South Pacific Tyres
Hume Highway
Somerton VIC 3062

Mr John Ralph AC
Chairman
Mr Rod Chadwick
Managing Director

Seventy-five years of automobile manufacture is a significant milestone anywhere, but in a new country like Australia it is a major achievement. The Pacific Dunlop group is proud to have been a partner with Ford Australia during this time. Having celebrated our own centenary of manufacturing in Australia in 1993, we can understand the pride with which Ford celebrates this milestone. Pacific Dunlop Limited first entered the Australian automotive components industry as a manufacturer of tyres. This business remains today, and is joined by three other businesses, all of which are significant suppliers to Ford Australia.

Burton Cables: For nearly half a century, Burtons has produced cable assemblies for Australian and export OE and retail markets. Burtons has formed a strong business relationship and is an important niche supplier to Ford Australia.

GNB Technologies: Originally known as Dunlop Batteries, this business has now expanded to encompass a strong global presence and is the supplier of batteries for the current Ford range.

Holding Rubber: Specialising in the manufacture of moulded rubber components, Holding Rubber's automotive business started operating in 1951.

South Pacific Tyres: An equal partnership between Pacific Dunlop Ltd and Goodyear Tire & Rubber Co., USA, this company is the market leader in Australia.

The Pacific Dunlop automotive businesses all enjoy majority supply status with Ford as a result of their partnerships, which have developed during Ford's 75 years in Australia. All group members and Pacific Dunlop Limited congratulate Ford Australia on the achievements during the past 75 years. Just as our businesses have evolved with Ford to meet the changing world, we will continue to meet the challenges during the next century in conjunction with our partner, Ford Australia.

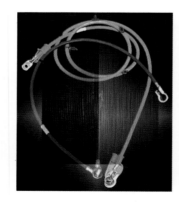

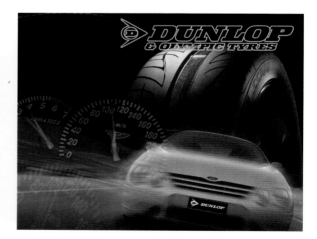

PLEXICOR AUSTRALIA

Plexicor Australia
ACN 004 290 298
235 Barry Road
Campbellfield VIC 3061
Phone: 03 9357 9077
Fax: 03 9357 8457
Email:
true_blue@plexicor.com.au

Mr Steve Clarke
Chief Executive Officer

Plexicor is proud to be the sole supplier to Ford Australia of twin-sheet moulded deck lid spoilers, press formed and polyurethane backed floor carpet systems, integrated boot and wagon load area systems, and complete vehicle NVH systems.

Plexicor is a major supplier of quality products and services to the automotive industry, a diverse range of manufacturing and service industries and the global communications networks.

As industry leaders with QS9000 and ISO9001 and ISO14001 quality standards certification, Plexicor has developed a clear vision for the future, which is driven by customer needs and community responsibility. Focusing on innovative design and methods of production, Plexicor's full service engineering resources develop intelligent solutions to meet the demanding constraints of design, manufacture, usability, cost and environmental impacts.

Plexicor takes its environmental responsibilities to the global community very seriously. We have developed a zero waste policy and have full accreditation to ISO14001. Our support of local community projects is helping build a better future for all community members.

www.plexicor.com.au

Solution:Plexicor

*The locally developed **Fairlane 500** brought a redefinition of luxury by combining easy V8 power with sprawling room for five adults. It would be half a decade before General Motors could even begin to answer its challenge.*

TENNECO
Automotive

Tenneco Automotive
1326–1378 South Road
Clovelly Park SA 5042
PO Box 61
Melrose Park SA 5039
Phone: 08 8374 5222
Fax: 08 8276 1653

Mr Alex Drysdale
Managing Director
Mr Trevor King
Finance Director

Tenneco Automotive has a long and multifaceted association with the Ford Motor Company. The origins of this relationship can be traced back to Michigan, USA in 1917, when Monroe was formed to produce tyre pumps for the Model T Ford. Strong links remain between Tenneco and Ford around the world to this day.

Tenneco currently supplies a range of product to Ford Australia including shock absorbers, struts, coil springs and exhaust systems, built at manufacturing facilities in South Australia and New Zealand.

Tenneco's high profile aftermarket brands, Monroe Shock Absorbers and Walker Exhaust Systems, are also major players in their respective product markets.

As an exporter of note, Tenneco manufactures products for markets in the USA, Europe, Asia, New Zealand and South America.

A commitment to quality and innovation is reflected in the numerous manufacturing accolades and awards presented to Tenneco over the years and our attainment of the Ford Q1 and Lloyds Register Quality Assurance ISO9001 certification.

Tenneco Automotive congratulates Ford Motor Company on 75 years in Australia and looks forward to a continued partnership over the next 75 years and beyond.

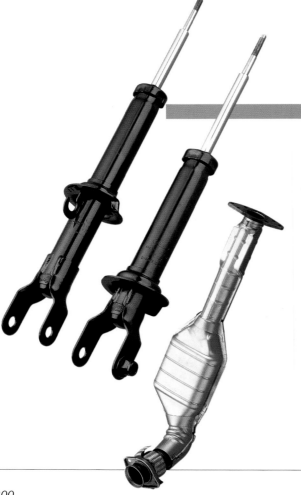

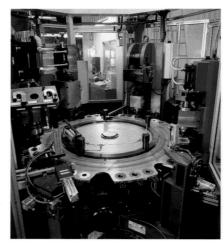

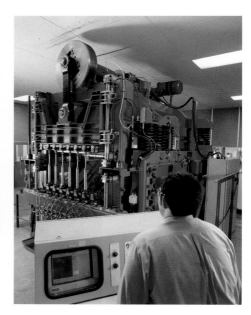

WALLENIUS WILHELMSEN

Wallenius Wilhelmsen
ABN 68 088 185 219
Level 11, 189 Kent Street
Sydney NSW 2000
GPO Box 4787
Sydney NSW 2001
Phone: 02 9255 0800
Fax: 02 9247 9577
Email: info@2wglobal.com

Mr Peter Dexter
Regional Director
Mr Soren Jensen
General Manager
Commercial

On 1 July 1999, Wilhelmsen Lines AS (Norway) and Wallenius Lines AB (Sweden) merged their international shipping and logistics management operations to form Wallenius Wilhelmsen Lines AS, the world's largest car and roll-on roll-off (RoRo) transportation company. The new company's trade routes cover all continents and form an international network of ocean-going transportation services. Wallenius Wilhelmsen is very proud of the long and close business relationship it holds with the Ford Motor Company. The international roll-on roll-off shipping activities for Ford with Wilhelmsen Lines and Wallenius Lines reach as far back as three decades.

Wallenius Wilhelmsen presently transports in excess of 100,000 Ford vehicles and 150,000 Volvo and Jaguar vehicles per annum globally. Since 1995, we have been closely involved with the shipment of vehicles from Europe to Australia and New Zealand. In 1998 we were chosen to provide shipping services for Ford Australia to New Zealand.

Wallenius Wilhelmsen, as part of our on-going commitment to the business activities of Ford Australia, achieved worldwide Ford Q1 certification in 1999. We are actively working in conjunction with our Ford business partners in Australia and around the world to ensure all the benefits of this process are fully realised. In 2000, Wallenius Wilhelmsen was honoured to have our successful involvement with Ford Australia recognised by being the only transportation company to be shortlisted for Ford Australia's 'Supplier Excellence Award'.

Wallenius Wilhelmsen congratulates Ford Australia on its 75th anniversary and looks forward with great enthusiasm to continuing our successful partnership.

www.2wglobal.com

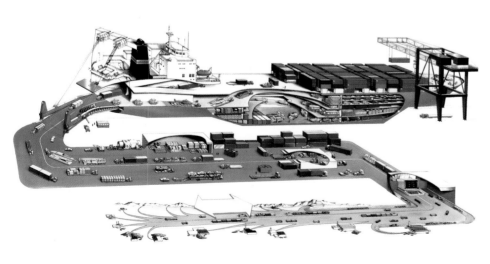

*The horsepower race was gathering speed. The **1968 XT GT** offered 230 horsepower and evocative colours including Candy Apple Red and Zircon Green. More importantly, it was now a regular model in the Falcon range.*

Air International

A DIVISION OF FUTURIS CORPORATION LIMITED

Air International Group
ACN 005 981 984
80 Turner Street
Port Melbourne VIC 3207
Phone: 03 9644 4222
Fax: 03 9645 3292
Email: info@airinter.com.au

Mr Bruce Griffiths
Managing Director
Mr Steve Falconer
General Manager – Business
Development

Air International's origins date back 30 years to when it was a small factory on the outskirts of Melbourne. Today, its manufacturing and engineering base has expanded across the globe.

Air International designs, manufactures and supplies products and systems to the world's automotive industry, specialising in heating ventilation and air-conditioning (HVAC), seating systems, seat hardware, metal pressings and fabrication, steering systems, control modules, and aftermarket air-conditioning components.

Air International's steering systems division, Steering Systems Australia, received an annual (Silver) Ford Australia Supplier Excellence Award in 1999. Investment in advanced engineering technology and a focus on customer satisfaction are our driving forces.

www.airinter.com.au

ARROWCREST GROUP

Arrowcrest Group Pty Ltd
ACN 007 521 280
34 Burleigh Avenue
Woodville North SA 5012
PO Box 5
Regency Park SA 5942
Phone: 08 8468 4000
Fax: 08 8468 4010
Email: rohlm@camtech.net.au

Mr Andrew Gwinnett
Chairman
Mr Cheng Hong
Managing Director

The Arrowcrest Group is a proud 'international' Australian. First established in 1946, it is one of an elite group of Australian companies that has taken quality products and innovative ideas offshore, gaining a reputation as a world-class manufacturer.

Group members of ROH Automotive and Unicast are original equipment suppliers to the Australian domestic market and overseas customers. ROH Automotive supplies steel wheels and rims, alloy wheels and suspension crossmembers to original equipment manufacturers in Australia and overseas. Unicast is a world leader in the technology of die-casting, specialising in high pressure aluminium and zinc for original equipment.

The Arrowcrest Group is proud of its long association with Ford and extends congratulations on the 75 years of Ford in Australia.

www.roh.com.au

"Serving The Industry"

Astor Base Metals Pty Ltd
ACN 000 332 650
512 Punchbowl Road
Lakemba NSW 2195
PO Box 6164
Lakemba NSW 2195
Phone: 02 9750 0111
Fax: 02 9759 0085
Email: sales@astorbasemetals.com.au

Mr Con Gavrilis
Managing Director
Mr Peter Gavrilis
General Manager/Director

As a supplier to the Ford Motor Company for over 30 years, our input, innovative products and finishes for Australian designed vehicles are world class. We have been a Q1 supplier for some years, and were the first in the world to change the appearance of the Ford oval with a polymer coating, which is now a standard finish for most of Ford's products worldwide.

At Astor Base Metals, we maintain a design and development team to ensure that our products are world class. We are a participant of quality driven requirements and accredited with Quality Certifications, such as QS9000, to bring us as a supplier well into the year 2000.

As Chief Executive Officer of Astor Base Metals for over 40 years, I would like to take this opportunity to congratulate Ford Australia on their 75th anniversary.

Autoliv
AUTOLIV AUSTRALIA PTY LTD

Autoliv Australia Pty Ltd
ACN 000 636 626
1521 Hume Highway
Campbellfield VIC 3061
Private Bag 41
Campbellfield VIC 3061
Phone: 03 9359 9822
Fax: 03 9359 6984

Mr Robert Franklin
Managing Director
Ms Patricia DeMasson
General Manager –
Klippan Safety Products

Autoliv is the world leader in occupant safety systems with 60 manufacturing plants in 26 countries. Our Australian operations supply local vehicle manufacturers with a full range of occupant restraint systems and components. Currently, Ford's Falcon, Fairmont, Fairlane and LTD models are equipped with Autoliv's driver airbags, passenger airbags and seat belts.

Klippan, our after-market division, supplies a full range of seat belts for P & A and after-market applications as well as child restraints, pet restraints and car racing harnesses.

Our Australian operation is a key research and development centre for the group in SE Asia and is home to our Barrier Crash and Airbag Testing facilities. Autoliv Australia is accredited to QS9000 and ISO14001. Your safety is our concern.

www.autoliv.com

Utes, invented by Ford Australia *in 1933–34, have always been key members of the Falcon family. Four decades later, the 1972 XA model combined traditional load-carrying can-do with a sleek new line.*

BHP Coated Steel – Australia
ACN 000 011 058
Old Port Road, Port Kembla NSW 2505
PO Box 1854, Wollongong NSW 2500
Phone: 02 4275 7522
Fax: 02 4275 6198
Email: mcdermott.terry.t@bhp.com.au

Mr Col Weatherstone
President
Mr Terry McDermott
National Sales & Marketing
Manager

BHP's long term partnership with the Ford Motor Company of Australia is typified by breakthrough research between the two companies that contributed to making the current AU Falcon a lighter and more fuel efficient car without any compromise to its strength.

Ford Australia and BHP collaborated intensively for more than three years on the advancement of new steel products for the Australian vehicle industry. The technological developments enabled BHP to make new steel grades available for the first time to local vehicle manufacturers as part of a wider BHP product development programme.

BHP congratulates Ford Australia on its 75th anniversary.

www.bhp.com.au

Bridgestone TG Australia Pty Ltd
ACN 075 422 445
1028 South Road
Edwardstown SA 5039
PO Box 800
Melrose Park Business Centre SA 5039
Phone: 08 8372 0200
Fax: 08 8372 0595
Email: bstg@bsal.com.au

Mr Seiichiro Hirose
Chief Executive Officer
Mr Darrel Richardson
General Manager

Bridgestone TG Australia Pty Ltd (BSTG) has enjoyed a proud association with Ford Australia for more than 40 years in the manufacture and supply of rubber, plastics and urethane automotive components dating back to the 1960 XK model Falcon. BSTG was established in 1939 as South Australian Rubber Mills Pty Ltd and is today a world-class designer, manufacturer and supplier of automotive components. In 1997 a joint venture was finalised between Bridgestone Australia Ltd and Toyoda Gosei Co. Ltd, the largest manufacturer of rubber and plastics components to the Japanese automotive industry.

BSTG congratulates the Ford Motor Company on 75 years in Australia and looks forward to the continuation of this partnership throughout the new millennium.

www.bstg.com.au

Britax

Britax Rainsfords Pty Ltd
ACN 007 550 094
Sherriffs Road Lonsdale SA 5160
PO Box 37 Lonsdale SA 5160
Phone: 08 8301 7777
Fax: 08 8384 7634

Mr Brian Freeborn
Managing Director of Britax
Rainsfords Pty Ltd
Mr Grant Anderson
Asian Regional Managing Director
of Britax Automotive Systems –
Rear Vision Systems

Britax congratulates Ford on its 75th anniversary. Britax Rainsfords' mission is to design and manufacture innovative automotive vision systems. Britax is a major exporter with 75 per cent of all products being shipped to overseas customers. We have been associated with Ford Australia since 1976 and have been exporting to Ford North America since 1986.

Recent awards include South Australian Manufacturer of the Year – Automotive, 1994; South Australian Manufacturer of the Year, 1998; and Business Excellence Award, 1999.

Britax Asia Pacific Lighting & Electrical Pty Ltd is a proud supplier of lighting and switches for both domestic and overseas markets. It is an integral supplier to Britax's mirror divisions worldwide.

www.britax.com

BTR Automotive

BTR Automotive Drivetrain Systems
ACN 000 019 536
3rd Floor, 390 St Kilda Road
Melbourne VIC 3004
Phone: 03 9222 5782
Fax: 03 9820 2435
Email: gbulmer@btr.com.au

Mr Graeme Bulmer
Chief Executive Officer
Mr Bryan Potts
General Manager

BTR Automotive has been a supplier of Drivetrain Products to Ford Australia for more than 40 years, and in this time has been successful in the design and manufacture of a wide range of state-of-the-art automatic and manual transmissions. We were one of the first companies worldwide to introduce full electronic control of an automatic transmission. Our company has a focus on partnership which encompasses the full range of business dealings with Ford as our valued customer. The support we provide includes a total field service system which complements Ford's own service organisation.

We are proudly accredited to Q1, ISO9000 and QS9000 status. BTR congratulates Ford Australia on the achievement of its 75th anniversary.

*The **XD Falcon** won acclaim throughout the Ford world for its distinctive contemporary styling. This was the first sedan in the world to use a plastic fuel tank and its plastic bumpers were also the height of modernity in 1979.*

Hook Plastics
ACN 004 331 882
30 McArthurs Road
Altona North VIC 3025
PO Box 155
Altona North VIC 3025
Phone: 03 9391 3011
Fax: 03 9391 7866
Email: Peter@hookplastics.com.au

Mr Frank Hook
Chairman, Chief Executive Officer
Mr Peter Sullivan
Company Secretary

Frank Hook began producing dashboard components in 1950 for the Ford Custom assembled in Geelong. F Hook Pty Ltd, as it was then known, continued to produce various plastic components for Ford. The advent of the Falcon in 1960 saw zinc and aluminium diecast assemblies also being supplied. As Frank Hook Products, we gained the Supplier of the Year award to the Australian Automotive Industry in 1990. In 1991, Frank Hook Products was the first supplier of plastic mouldings in Australia to gain the Q1 rating and was one of the pioneers in black box design. As Hook Plastics, we are recognised as a supplier of precision engineering plastic components and assemblies with in-house design, tooling, moulding, assembly, painting and decorative facilities.

www.hookplastics.com.au

Mobil

Mobil Oil Australia Pty Ltd
ACN 004 052 984
417 St Kilda Road, Melbourne VIC 3004
GPO Box 4507, Melbourne VIC 3001
Phone: 03 9252 3111
Fax: 03 9866 9076
Email:
corporateaffairs_moa@email.mobil.com

Mr Robert Olsen
Chairman
Mr Tony Turchi
Director Fuels

Mobil is proudly and passionately committed to its partnership with Ford. Using the racetrack as their proving ground, the two companies work together to drive the development of world-leading lubricant solutions. Under the bonnet of each Ford Tickford Racing Team car is the technology of Mobil 1 fully synthetic engine oil, ensuring peak engine performance.

Every locally built Ford passenger vehicle is factory-filled with Mobil engine oil, compatible with Ford's latest technology, and commitment to the greenhouse challenge. And the partners' latest initiative – an on-site lubrication management service – is destined to meet the needs of the next generation of Ford drivers.

www.mobil.com.au

Orbseal Australia
ARBN 070 667 391
5 Jesica Road
Campbellfield VIC 3061
Phone: 03 9357 9221
Fax: 03 9357 9223

Mr Robert Orscheln
Chief Executive Officer
Mr Ian Brown
General Manager

Orbseal Australia is extremely proud to be a supplier to Ford Australia. Orbseal is based at Richmond, Missouri, USA, with operations in Melbourne and Adelaide, Australia; Birmingham, UK; and Detroit, USA. Orbseal's leadership in the automotive sealant industry is due in large part to its diverse product line, zero-defect quality program, design capability, engineering expertise and manufacturing excellence. This, combined with a world-class focus on customer service, has led to a strong relationship with the Ford Motor Company. From receiving the President's Customer Satisfaction Imperatives Award in 1995 to being recognised as the only Full Service Supplier of sealant suppliers in 1997, Orbseal today is privileged with the responsibility of Total Sealant Manager (TSM^{SM}) to Ford Australia.

www.orbseal.com.au

Qantas Airways Limited
ACN 009 661 901
Level 9, Building A
203 Coward Street
Mascot NSW 2020
Phone: 02 9691 3636
Fax: 02 9691 3339

Mr James Strong
Chief Executive & Managing Director
Mr Geoff Dixon
Deputy Chief Executive Officer

Qantas is delighted to continue its association with Ford Australia in its 75th year. Qantas is the preferred airline for more than 5000 Ford employees nationally. Qantas provides a wide variety of package deals to Ford, as a valued business client, to destinations such as Detroit, USA and across Asia and New Zealand.

Like Ford, Qantas has played a key role in the development of transport services in Australia since the early 1900s, as Australia's leading domestic airline. Today, Qantas operates to more than 120 destinations worldwide carrying more than 19 million passengers every year.

www.qantas.com.au

*The **1979 LTD** was more compact and luxurious than its predecessors. Vertical grille bars and a formal 'L' emblem remain motifs for Ford Australia's flagship. For the first time a six-cylinder engine was offered as an alternative to the 5.8 litre V8.*

RJ Pound Services Pty Ltd
ACN 005 568 301
76 Lower Heidelberg Road
Ivanhoe VIC 3079
PO Box 90
Ivanhoe VIC 3079
Phone: 03 9490 2299
Fax: 03 9490 2290
Email: admin@rjpound.com.au

Mr Bob Pound
Managing Director
Mr John Pound
Operations Manager

We have been a supplier of Marketing Services to the Ford Motor Company of Australia since 1968. We offer a comprehensive range of services which include:
- *warehousing and distribution services*
- *project management*
- *marketing and internet services*
- *database management*
- *reporting systems*
- *direct mail services*
- *graphic design*
- *copyshop and plan printing facilities*
- *systems maintenance*
- *network installations.*

BOSCH

Robert Bosch (Australia) Pty Ltd
ACN 004 315 628
Cnr Centre Road & McNaughton Road
Clayton VIC 3168
Locked Bag 66,
Clayton South VIC 3169
Phone: 03 9541 5555
Fax: 03 9541 7790
Email: info@au.bosch.com

Mr Kurt W Liedtke
Chairman and Managing Director
Mr Barry M Comben
Director Automotive Sales

For more than 45 years, Robert Bosch Australia has been manufacturing and supplying high-quality automotive products to the local automotive industry. More recently, Bosch Australia has expanded its export business through various multinational vehicle manufacturers around the globe.

Since the mid-1960s, Bosch Australia has been a proud supplier to Ford Australia. Indicative of the strong relationship Bosch enjoys with Ford is the broad range of products supplied, including Anti-lock Braking Systems (ABS), Body Electronics Modules, Remote Keys, Fuel Rails, Injectors, Ignition Coils and Starter Motors.

In 1997, Bosch Australia received Ford Australia's Q1 quality award and the QS9000 certificate. The company also won the 1999 Australian Export Award in the category of Large Advanced Manufacturer.

www.bosch.com

SILCRAFT PTY. LTD.

MANUFACTURING EXCELLENCE

Silcraft Pty Ltd
ACN 004 703 119
163 Forster Road
Mt Waverley VIC 3149
PO Box 21
Mt Waverley VIC 3149
Phone: 03 9544 0222
Fax: 03 9565 9223
Email: sales@silcraft.com.au

Mr James W Sledge
Business Development &
Export Manager

Silcraft is a major high-quality supplier of automotive components to Ford Australia. We commenced operations in 1960, at the invitation of Ford, which at that time was seeking to establish a local content component industry in Australia.

Silcraft proudly supports Ford vehicles with a range of decorative and structural components including radiator grilles, rear ornaments, hood mouldings, wheelcovers, glass and weatherstrip channels. In addition, we supply a similar range of product to the Australian automotive industry and export to Japan, Taiwan and New Zealand.

Silcraft is a quality endorsed company achieving Ford Q1 and other esteemed international quality standards including QS9000, ISO9002, AS9002 and NZ9002.

www.silcraft.com.au

 ## Sumitomo Wiring Systems, Ltd.

Sumitomo
Corporation

Sumitomo Australia Limited
Level 47, Nauru House
80 Collins Street, Melbourne VIC 3000
Phone: 03 9653 1000
Sumitomo Wiring Systems Australia Pty Ltd
832 Cooper Street, Somerton VIC 3062
Phone: 03 9308 9177

Mr Kenji Miyahara
President & Chief Executive Officer,
Sumitomo Corporation
Mr Michio Moriya
President,
Sumitomo Wiring Systems Ltd

Sumitomo has been Ford Australia's supplier of electrical distribution systems since 1994. We pride ourselves on our reputation for providing technically innovative, cost competitive solutions that maximise customer benefit. We believe this is why we have been awarded the major electronic and electrical contracts for the current and next model Falcon.

Sumitomo is committed to quality and continuous improvement, which is evident in our achievement of QS9000 for all of our facilities supplying Ford. Many Sumitomo group offices and plants are already certified to ISO14000 accreditation. Sumitomo is committed to developing a long-term environmentally sustainable business.

In 1999, Sumitomo won the Supplier Excellence Gold Award from Ford Australia and World Excellence Gold Award from Ford Dearborn.

www.sumitomocorp.co.jp or **www.sws.co.jp**

In 1983 the Falcon six got electronic fuel-injection for a big gain in efficiency. It was another first in the local industry, where Ford was the pacesetter and Falcon the top-selling car. But the beloved **V8s looked like vanishing forever.**

TOKYO BOEKI LTD.

Tokyo Boeki (Australia) Pty Ltd
ACN 004 900 994
Level 2, 401 Collins Street
Melbourne VIC 3000
Phone: 03 9283 7878
Fax: 03 9629 8699
Email: itoh@tokyoboeki.com.au

Mr Hiroshi Machida
President – Tokyo Boeki Ltd Japan
Mr Takuji Hiramatsu
President – Tokyo Boeki Australia

Tokyo Boeki Ltd, founded in 1947, is an independent trading firm with a reputation for being the first to explore and take advantage of new business opportunities in the international market within the fields of steel, resources, machinery and materials.

As a pioneer of exporting automotive steel, we are proud to have been supplying Ford Australia with advanced quality automotive steel from leading Japanese steel mills for more than 37 years.

We will continue to satisfy our customers' global requirements, providing valuable advice and guidance to ensure that their goals and expectations are fulfilled.

www.tokyo-boeki.co.jp

Venture Industries Australia Pty Ltd
ACN 068 232 253
1741 Sydney Road
Campbellfield VIC 3061
PO Box 101
Somerton VIC 3062
Phone: 03 9230 0200
Fax: 03 9230 0288
Email: chook@ventureindustries.com

Mr Larry Winget
Chief Executive Officer
Mr Joe Baldarotta
Director

Venture Industries Australia is a key QS9000 accredited supplier of interior and exterior systems. Venture currently supplies Ford Australia with fully assembled instrument panels, heater/air conditioning modules, door trims, consoles, painted bumpers, plastic fuel tanks, body side mouldings, underbody mouldings and interior trim. Venture is currently the only supplier to in-line sequence deliver the majority of these components directly to Ford Australia's lines.

Venture has global experience as a Full Service Supplier of automotive trim, including styling support, design activity, research and development, tooling and manufacturing. This, together with strong programme management, ensures our customer's programme expectations are fully met.

www.ventureglobal.com

*The **1988 EA Falcon** brought aerodynamic efficiency to the local industry. It was the first model to use an overhead camshaft version of the tough and lusty six-cylinder engine. Even 10 years on, its styling remained elegant and contemporary.*

AUSTRALIAN ARROW PTY. LTD.
(A Yazaki Group Member)

Australian Arrow Pty Ltd
ACN 071 956 057
65 Lathams Road
Carrum Downs VIC 3201
Phone: 03 9775 1566
Fax: 03 9775 0477

Mr Ted Tsuda
Managing Director
Mr Charles Spanti
Marketing Manager

Yazaki Corporation established a liaison office in Australia in 1965 at the request of Ford Australia in anticipation of increased local content requirements. The company primarily cares for the Australasian automotive markets with facilities in Victoria, South Australia, New Zealand and Samoa. Products and services include electrical wiring harnesses, electrical distribution systems and electronic products such as anti-theft systems, body computers and instrumentation.

www.australianarrow.com.au

Automotive Components
Limited
ACN 006 542 785
Level 8, 390 St Kilda Road
Melbourne VIC 3004
Phone: 03 9285 4000
Fax: 03 9866 4300

Mr Ivan James
Chairman and
Managing Director
Mr Nigel Tait
Chief Engineer

ACL is Australia's largest manufacturer of engine parts, and supplies pistons, piston rings, gaskets, engine bearings and powder metallurgy components to the Ford Motor Company of Australia and to the other engine manufacturers, Holden (GM), Mitsubishi and Toyota. International competitiveness and optimum product performance are ensured through the use of ACL's modern research, development, design and product testing facilities and state-of-the-art manufacturing techniques.

www.acl.com.au

Bostik

Bostik (Australia) Pty Ltd
ACN 003 893 838
51–71 High Street
Thomastown VIC 3074
PO Box 50
Thomastown VIC 3074
Phone: 03 9279 3333
Fax: 03 9279 9270
Email: dhobson@bostik.com.au

Mr David Hobson
General Manager
Automotive and Direct
Business

Bostik began its Australian operations in 1915 and is very proud of its 75-year association with Ford; two global companies who share the same basic values and ideals – cost, quality accreditation and environmental pursuits. For 75 years, Bostik has supplied Ford with sealants and adhesives, along with numerous noise reduction and trim products. Today, the two organisations work together to develop and manufacture noise attenuating and vibration dampening components. Bostik congratulates Ford Australia on 75 successful years and looks forward to an exciting future together.

Castrol Australia Pty Limited
ACN 008 459 407
132 McCredie Road
Guildford NSW 2161
PO Box 727
Guildford NSW 2161
Phone: 02 9795 4800
Fax: 02 9795 4846

Mr John Owens
Industrial Area Director,
Australasia
Mr Martin Dando
Consumer Area Director,
Australasia

Over the past 100 years Castrol has developed an enviable worldwide reputation as the leader in the field of high performance lubrication. Castrol's 'race-bred' technology has meant that the Castrol brand is synonymous with benchmark achievements in motorsport and industry. Castrol's relationship with Ford has developed to a full spectrum of joint activity, including motorsport, dealerships, workshops and Ford manufacturing plants.

www.castrol.com.au

Cleanaway Industrial
ACN 000 164 938
PO Box R351
Royal Exchange NSW 1225
Phone: 02 9241 1031
CHEP Australia
PO Box 968
Crows Nest NSW 1585
Phone: 02 9200 2437

Mr John White
General Manager
Cleanaway Industries
Mr John Judd
General Manager
Automotive Services
Chep Australia

CHEP and Cleanaway have a long-term commitment to delivering a highly customised product range and service package to Ford Australia. CHEP provides a cost-effective, returnable packaging system for the automotive industry. Cleanaway provides Ford with on-site waste and facilities management, managing their waste stream and ensuring environmental compliance.

CMI Limited
ACN 050 542 553
Suite 3, Level 8
T & G Building
141 Queen Street
Brisbane QLD 4001
GPO Box 1170
Brisbane QLD 4001
Phone: 07 3229 0716
Fax: 07 3229 0711
Email: corporate@cmil.com.au

Mr Max Hofmeister
Executive Chairman
Mr Dan Gallagher
Executive General Manager

CMI Limited is an Australian-owned manufacturer of specialty components to the automotive industry, and is a supplier to Ford in Australia and the USA.
   Its major products include precision engineered components, electrical components and specialist 4WD components.
   CMI is listed on the ASX, employs over 800 people and exports product to 20 countries.

www.brambles.com.au

www.cmil.com.au

A Business of F.X. Coughlin Co.

DELPHI
Automotive Systems

Coughlin Logistics
ABN 26 076 448 514
9 Somerton Park Drive
Campbellfield VIC 3061
PO Box 455
Somerton VIC 3062
Phone: 03 9308 0803
Fax: 03 9308 0563

Mr Joseph T Coughlin
President and CEO
FX Coughlin Co
Ms Susan M Pavlak
COO Coughlin Logistics
Ms Denise D Richardson
Regional Director
Asia Pacific

Coughlin Logistics is a global, customer-focused logistics provider committed to market-value growth by providing program-based solutions through process excellence to the automotive industry.
   Our world headquarters are located in Detroit, Michigan, USA contactable on 734 9462500. We also have regional headquarters in the UK for Europe/Africa, and in Brazil for South America.
   We are proud to be a preferred supplier to Ford Australia. We congratulate them on their 75-year anniversary and look forward to future years of continuing involvement and success.

Delphi Automotive Systems
Australia Ltd
ACN 065 439 885
86 Fairbank Road
Clayton South VIC 3169
Phone: 03 9551 8700
Fax: 03 9551 8764
Email:
petrina.adams@delphiauto.com

Mr Linsey Siede
Managing Director
Mr John Connolly
Operations Manager

Delphi Automotive Systems Australia is proud to be a long standing supplier of exhaust and fuel products to Ford Australia, and a partner for the future. Delphi Australia has twice won the FCAI supplier of the year award, is QS9000 certified and a Ford Q1 supplier.

www.coughlinlogistics.com

www.delphiauto.com

*Ford Australia's partner in high performance is **Tickford Vehicle Engineering**, a company that developed out of Aston Martin. This beautiful emblem is reserved for only those models that have been reworked by Tickford's engineers.*

DOWSETT ENGINEERING & MATERIALS HANDLING PTY. LTD

Dowsett Engineering & Materials Handling Pty Ltd
ACN 006 249 976
80–84 Capital Link Drive
Campbellfield VIC 3061
Phone: 03 9357 8181
Fax: 03 9357 8688
Email: dowsett@netcore.com.au

Mr Ian Dowsett
Managing Director

Founded in 1972, Dowsett has developed a reputation throughout the automotive manufacturing industry for quality and reliability. Dowsett has an annual turnover of $10m, with activities concentrated in the areas of design, manufacture and installation of mechanical handling systems, robotic installations, turn key facilities, and plant and facility relocation. We are proud to be a preferred contractor to the Ford Motor Company in the above capacities.

EGR

EGR
ACN 056 159 570
84 Evans Road, Salisbury
Brisbane QLD 4107
PO Box 171
Salisbury QLD 4107
Phone: 07 3277 7999
Fax: 07 3274 2958
Email: cdm@egr.com.au

Mr Rod Horwill
Joint Managing Director
Mr Greg Horwill
Joint Managing Director

EGR is the major supplier of Ford Australia's range of thermoformed plastic accessories. Over many years of association we have developed a long and mutually successful relationship. EGR congratulates Ford Australia on reaching its 75th anniversary and we look forward to further strengthening our partnership in the years ahead.

www.egr.com.au

FMS audio

FMS Audio Sdn Bhd
Plot 10 Phase 4
Kawasan Perindustrain Prai
1300 Prai Penang Malaysia
Phone: + 60 4 507 8988
Fax: + 60 4 507 8814

Mr Takeshi Harada
Managing Director

FMS Audio has a seven year association with Ford Australia. Radios, CD changers and amplifiers in Falcon, Fairlane and LTD are engineered by FMS Audio in conjunction with Ford Australia. These radios and CD changers are produced in FMS Audio's Penang plant, together with units for Ford Festiva, Laser, Transit and Courier models.

Congratulations Ford Australia on 75 great years!

Hella Australia Pty Ltd
ACN 006 256 524
54–76 Southern Road
Mentone VIC 3194
PO Box 89
Mentone VIC 3194
Phone: 03 9581 9333
Fax: 03 9584 1741
Email: hella@hella.com.au

Dr WWJ Uhlenbruch
AM OLJ
Chairman
Mr Peter F Doyle
Managing Director

Hella Australia is a member of the Hella Group of Companies and was established in 1961 to provide innovative automotive lighting products and engineering design, development and project management services to the Australian automotive industry.

Hella Australia first supplied components to Ford in 1963. Hella today is a QS9000, Q1 and ISO9000 certified company that now supplies Ford with all of its major lighting requirements. We are proud to be a member of the Ford supplier family and look forward to working with Ford in the next 75 years.

www.hella.com.au

*Johnson Controls
Australia Pty Ltd
ACN 002 968 103
196 Settlement Road
Thomastown VIC 3074
Phone: 03 9205 8900
Fax: 03 9465 4224*

**Mr Roger Hawes
General Manager
Mr Ellison Mouncey
Plant Manager**

Johnson Controls is proud of its relationship with Ford Australia. As a global automotive supplier, we supply automotive interior systems to over 22 million vehicles annually. We are recognised as a leader in innovation and solutions for interior trim. Our mission is to continually exceed our customers' increasing expectations.

*Kirwan Group Services
ARBN 096 1041 X
252 Hyde Street
Yarraville VIC 3013
Locked Bag 99
Yarraville VIC 3013
Phone: 03 9689 9999
Fax: 03 9689 9811
Email:
info@kirwangroup.com.au*

**Mr Ron Kirwan
Chairman
Mr Angus Collins
Managing Director**

The Kirwan Group is a privately owned group of companies that provides specialised cleaning and related services to the automotive and general manufacturing industries. With offices in Melbourne, Adelaide, Sydney and the Eastern Seaboard of Thailand, the Group is well placed to service the needs of the automotive industry and is proud to be a supplier to Ford Australia.

www.kirwangroup.com.au

*Mark IV Automotive
Pty Limited
ACN 080 115 966
11 Dansu Court
Hallam VIC 3803
PO Box 1395
Dandenong VIC 3175
Phone: 03 9796 4044
Fax: 03 9796 4944*

**Mr Tom Young
Managing Director
Mr Dave Duncan
Director of Finance**

Mark IV Automotive is a leading manufacturer of engineering systems and components primarily for power transmission, fluid management and air intake systems. Our products are manufactured and sold competitively throughout the world, maintaining the highest quality product and services.

Quality standards include ISO9001, ISO14001, QS9000 and QI.

MENZIES
GROUP OF COMPANIES

*Menzies Group of Companies
ACN 004 967 757
139–141 Franklin Street
Melbourne VIC 3000
Phone: 03 9329 1744
Fax: 03 9329 5641*

**Mr Rodney William Menzies
Managing Director
Mr Merv Cox
Chief Executive Officer**

Our partnership with Ford Australia commenced in 1986 and continues to grow stronger each year, providing quality service to both the Broadmeadows and the Geelong Plants. Menzies business activities cover contract cleaning and maintenance of property facilities.

- Established 1969 and fully Australian owned.
- Quality endorsed.
- Prime Minister's – Employer of the Year 1999.
- Golden Service Award for cleaning excellence – ANZ World Headquarters 1999.

www.menzies.com.au

*There was nothing conservative or compromised about the audaciously modern styling of the **1998 AU**, especially the XR variants with their quad headlights and lowered ride height. Colours did not include Shrinking Violet.*

A Heritage of Rockwell Technology

Meritor Light Vehicle
Systems Australia Pty Ltd
ACN 004 314 372
62 Albert Street
Preston VIC 3072
PO Box 96
Preston VIC 3072
Phone: 03 9484 5082
Fax: 03 9484 5283

Mr William R Byass
Managing Director
Mr Freddie Khanan
Financial Controller /
Company Secretary

Meritor is proud to be the sole supplier of window regulators and door latches to Ford Australia. We congratulate Ford Australia on their 75th anniversary. At Meritor, we have a real passion and tradition for serving our customers. We anticipate customer needs, deliver value and keep our promises. We are focused on developing advanced engineering concepts, new technologies and groundbreaking innovations.

www.meritorauto.com

 **Mett Diecasting Pty Ltd**

Mett Diecasting Pty Ltd
ACN 006 085 927
28–38 Overseas Drive
Noble Park VIC 3174
Phone: 03 9795 9088
Fax: 03 9701 1841
Email:
info@mettdiecasting.com.au

Mr Werner Westphal
Managing Director
Mr Erwin Schulter
Executive Manager

Mett Diecasting has set a mission to provide best value to its customers in terms of quality, service, competitive pricing, use of state-of-the-art technology and innovation. We are proud to be a supplier of quality aluminium pressure diecastings, including CNC machining, to Ford Australia. We congratulate Ford Australia on their 75th anniversary.

www.mettdiecasting.com.au

MILNE DUNKLEY
CUSTOMS & FORWARDING

Milne Dunkley Customs &
Forwarding
ACN 006 789 680
Level 3, 493 St Kilda Road
Melbourne VIC 3004
Phone: 03 9820 3122
Fax: 03 9820 3665

Level 8, Barrack House
16-20 Barrack Street
Sydney NSW 2000
Phone: 02 9262 5822
Fax : 02 9262 5833

Mr John Dunkley
Managing Director

Milne Dunkley is proud to be suppliers to Ford Australia. Milne Dunkley Customs and Forwarding offers its clients all customs brokerage and forwarding services, with something more ... personalised service. Currently employing six experienced and licensed brokers, Milne Dunkley takes pride in having established and maintained excellent government relations.
Milne Dunkley is a member of the Customs Brokers Council of Australia.

NIPPON YUSEN KAISHA

NYK Line (Australia) Pty Ltd
ACN 009 721 751
5th Floor, 45 Clarence Street
Sydney NSW 2000
PO Box N45
Grosvenor Place
Sydney NSW 1220
Phone: 02 9248 1000
Fax: 02 9299 7774
Email: @sg.nykline.com

Mr Hisato Iguchi
Chairman and Managing
Director
Mr Garry Farnsworth
Director Agency

NYK Line (Australia) congratulates the Ford Motor Company on this historic achievement and we look forward to further strengthening our relationship.
We are proud of our partnership, which has spanned 10 years and has become an integral part of NYK Line's sea transport of Ford's vehicles, steel and containerised parts and accessories.

www.nykline.com

*Parker Hannifin (Australia)
Pty Limited
ACN 008 446 893
9 Carrington Road
Castle Hill NSW 2154
Phone: 02 9634 7777
Fax: 02 9899 6184
Email:
marketing@parker.com.au*

**Mr Myles Reilly
Managing Director – Fluid
Connectors Division
Mr Michael Zahra
National Sales & Marketing
Manager – Fluid
Connectors Division**

Parker Hannifin – making parts and providing premier customer service the world over. Parker Hannifin is proud to be associated with Ford. As the world's leading supplier of fluid connectors, Parker Hannifin supplies Ford with the hose and fittings for their LPG gas tanks. Parker's continued support of Ford has led to the formation of a strong relationship. Parker Hannifin wishes to congratulate Ford on their 75th Anniversary.

www.parker.com

*PBR International Ltd
ACN 006 527 340
264 East Boundary Road
East Bentleigh VIC 3165
PO Box 176
East Bentleigh VIC 3165
Phone: 03 9575 2200
Fax: 03 9575 2555
Email:
pbr_enquiries@pbr.com.au*

**Mr John MacKenzie
President
Mr Gordon Bennett
Vice President**

Since the first Falcon, PBR and Ford have worked together to set new benchmarks for customer safety, comfort and driver confidence. Together we introduced disc brakes, aluminium master cylinders and calipers, and the revolutionary Banksia park brake. PBR now supplies high performance calipers for the legendary Ford Mustang and Cobra in the USA and, thanks to our beginnings with Ford Australia, enjoys an international reputation for excellence and innovation in lightweight braking technology. PBR also has offices in the United States, Malaysia, Thailand, Korea and New Zealand.

www.pbr.com.au

PRICEWATERHOUSECOOPERS 🔲

Join us. Together we can change the world

*PricewaterhouseCoopers
ACN 082 982 554
333 Collins Street
Melbourne VIC 3000
GPO Box 1331L
Melbourne VIC 3001
Phone: 03 8603 1000
Fax: 03 8603 1999*

**Mr John F Harvey
Country Senior Partner
Mr Paul Brasher
Managing Partner
Melbourne**

PricewaterhouseCoopers congratulates Ford Australia on their 75th anniversary. Our relationship with Ford goes back many years, a global association of which we are extremely proud.

PricewaterhouseCoopers looks forward to continuing this relationship in assisting Ford achieve its growth potential in one of the world's most rapidly changing markets.

www.pwcglobal.com

*Sodexho
ACN 006 072 975
Level 7, Prince Centre,
8 Quay Street
Sydney NSW 2000
Phone: 02 9213 6100
Fax: 02 9213 6111*

**Mr Jonathan Knight
Chief Executive Officer
Mr Cedric Malivel
Director Finance**

Sodexho Australia has been involved with Ford Australia for the past nine years in providing food and management services at their Broadmeadows and Geelong sites. We offer an extensive range of menu items across eleven cafeterias operating seven days per week. Sodexho assisted with the provision of catering for Ford's 75th Anniversary Rally and Supplier Award Dinner.

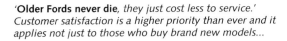
*'**Older Fords never die**, they just cost less to service.'*
Customer satisfaction is a higher priority than ever and it
applies not just to those who buy brand new models...

TEXTRON Fastening Systems

The Global Leader in Fastening Solutions

*Textron Fastening
Systems Pty Ltd
ABN 98 000 482 986
891 Wellington Road
Rowville VIC 3178
Phone: 03 9764 3877
Fax: 03 9755 7352*

**Mr Peter Van
Managing Director
Mr Leigh Sonnberger
National Sales Manager**

Textron Fastening Systems is a multi-national group of engineering, manufacturing and marketing companies, which solves fastening problems and delivers high quality engineered solutions to industrial companies around the world.

As the world's largest manufacturer of engineered fasteners, Textron provides its clients with solutions to all of their fastening requirements including design, manufacturing, engineering, inventory management, service, quality and systems.

www.textron.com

TRIPAC INTERNATIONAL Pty Ltd

*Tripac International Pty Ltd
ACN 006 546 201
16 St Albans Road
Kingsgrove NSW 2208
Private Bag 4090
Kingsgrove NSW 1480
Phone: 02 9502 2077
Fax: 02 9502 4166
Email:
general@tripacint.com.au*

**Mr Stephen O'Brien
Chairman
Mr Gilman E Wong
Managing Director**

Tripac manufactures the latest technology condensers and evaporators for air conditioning systems, power steering and transmission oil coolers, electric cooling fans and motors. Tripac is proud of its association with the Ford Motor Company and as a global supplier to motor vehicle manufacturers and system suppliers is committed to excellence. Tripac's quality certifications include QS 9000, ISO 9001 and QI.

www.tripacfans.com

*TI Group Automotive Systems
ACN 007 541 442
492 Churchill Road
Kilburn SA 5084
Phone: 08 8260 8888
Fax: 08 8260 8858
Factory 2, 13A Monterey Road
Dandenong VIC 3175
Phone: 03 9793 2254
Fax: 03 9793 2423
Email: tiautoaust@tiauto.com.au*

**Mr Peter Gardner
General Manager
Mr Gavin Coffey
Business Unit Manager –
Victoria**

TI Group Automotive Systems has been supplying Ford Australia since the first Falcon was produced in 1960 and is the leading global supplier of brake and fuel assemblies, fuel storage and delivery systems and powertrain lines.

Production and support for Ford Australia is from a Q1, QS9000 and ISO14001 accredited facility.

www.tiautomotive.com

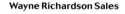

Wayne Richardson Sales

*Wayne Richardson Sales
ACN 005 373 311
1960 Hume Highway
Campbellfield VIC 3061
PO Box 194
Campbellfield VIC 3061
Phone: 03 9357 0100
Fax: 03 9357 0070
Email:
sales@wayrichsales.com.au*

**Mr Wayne Richardson
Managing Director
Mr Russell Ohlsen
General Manager**

Wayne Richardson Sales congratulates Ford Australia on its 75th anniversary. For over 25 years, Wayne Richardson Sales has been a major supplier of specialised tapes, abrasives, protection and paint shop supplies to Ford Australia as well as to many other OE Tier 1 and Tier 2 manufacturers. Gaska Tape Australia, a division of Wayne Richardson Sales, manufacturers PVC foam, nitrile, EPDM die cut and laminated materials. Wayne Richardson Sales/Gaska Tape has facilities in all states and has achieved QS9000, Q1 and ISO9002 quality accreditation.

www.wayrichsales.com.au